An Illustrated Guide to

Virginia's Confederate Monuments

With a New Preface

Timothy S. Sedore

Southern Illinois University Press
Carbondale

Southern Illinois University Press
www.siupress.com

Copyright © 2011, 2018 by the Board of Trustees,
Southern Illinois University
All rights reserved. Cloth edition 2011.
Paperback edition 2018
Printed in the United States of America

21 20 19 18   4 3 2 1

ISBN 978-0-8093-3674-6 (alk. paper)

Cover illustration: Monument to the Unknown Confederate Dead, dedicated June 6, 1879, at Stonewall Cemetery, Winchester. The marble column and soldier are said to be the first monument in the world erected to honor unknown war dead as well as the first sculpture of a Southern soldier.

An Illustrated Guide to Virginia's Confederate Monuments

For my wife and fellow traveler, Patricia,
For my parents, Michael and Annie M. Sedore,
And in memory of the service of Michael Sedore,
U.S. Army Air Force, 1941–1945

Contents

Preface to the Paperback Edition

I am no prophet. I could not foresee the turbulence that would focus on many of the subjects of this book in the years following its publication. There was nothing prescient in my choosing to travel to every county or independent city in Virginia to research the commonwealth's Civil War monumentation. Confederate monuments in Virginia intrigued me for years, for decades really, but especially when a weekly interstate commute by car took me across the Potomac River and up and down the Shenandoah Valley on a regular basis. I did this for several years—spending weekdays in the Bronx teaching English, and weekends and summers in Virginia with family. The battlefield and courthouse detours during my commute became a journey unto itself; the journey became a quest; the quest became a research project: over the Blue Ridge and onto the Piedmont, into northern Virginia and the suburbs of Washington D.C., then to the Tidewater, the Eastern Shore, the South Side, and southwest Virginia.

I wanted a text. I wanted to read the collected Civil War monument landscape of Virginia. I especially wanted to bridge the divide between the "we" of postwar generations and the monument makers who remembered the war or knew the generation who did. Eventually the interest took me to Tennessee and Mississippi for the same purpose. Over the course of several years, I researched and identified some four hundred Confederate monuments in Virginia; some four hundred Union and Confederate monuments in Tennessee, and, most recently, some eight hundred Union and Confederate monuments in Mississippi.

This I learned in Virginia: each monument is different—sui generis. The idea of the standard or typical Confederate monument is a myth. There are no types. None is typical. They may look the same, even banal, but they're not. They are all interesting. They can be variously cryptic, descriptive, mysterious, and provocative. They can be funereal or sentimental, or defiant or restrained or effusive. They can be vernacular and obscure—practically unknown—as well as majestic, artistically notable and prominent.

The ease with which one can generalize or render judgment on this text derives, in some measure, from a lack of awareness of it as a literary text. In fact, it can be read *sensus literalis*, as a distinct genre.

The monument text is a vast, fragmented, complex text, most of it left to us by generations long passed away. Phrases like "Our Confederate Soldiers," or "Our Confederate Heroes" seem clear, but the plain meaning of the text sometimes masks profound understatement. "Our Confederate Dead," the women of the United Daughters of the Confederacy (UDC) declare on the grim granite cemetery obelisk at Marshall, Virginia. The monument was dedicated in 1928, and the women claim the dead for their own even sixty-three years after the war's end.

The complexity of this text should not be underestimated. For example, the monument text—the verbal narratives, tributes, or descriptions—brings to bear rhetorician Richard Weaver's assertion that "language is sermonic"—that language has an ethical import in addition to its communicative value. Twenty-first-century Americans use the term *Confederate monument* or *Confederate soldier*, but many monument inscriptions deliberately avoid the use of the word *Confederate*. At Stonewall Cemetery in Winchester, for example, the Virginia Obelisk remembers "398 Virginia Soldiers . . . Who Fell In Defence Of / Constitutional Liberty And / The Sovereignty Of Their State." Similarly, contemporary Americans speak of the American Civil War, but the monument makers do not. We use the term *American Civil War* to describe the events of 1861–65, but the Virginia monument makers define the conflict as the "War Between the States." In fact, the phrase *Civil War* is rarely used on Virginia monuments, and the official term for the conflict is the "War of the Rebellion." Furthermore, we speak of the Lost Cause, but the monument makers do not. I found only two mentions of that phrase among the four hundred monuments I studied in Virginia; I found none in Tennessee and only one in Mississippi. I did find the phrase "Glory to the defeated" on several monuments. Art historians who are acquainted with nineteenth-century American sculpture need not be reminded that the age of monumentation in post–Civil War America was influenced by French sculptural trends. Nineteenth-century France had its own losses to mourn and soldiers to commemorate. After its defeat in the Franco-Prussian War of 1870–71 and the turmoil of the commune, France erected numerous statues of common soldiers, doing honor to them despite the fact their country had been broken and defeated by the war in which they served. French commemorations of the Franco-Prussian War glorified the dead, as historian Burke Wilkinson observes, "with broken swords, with lions at bay," with "splendidly defiant Mariannes shielding their wounded."[1]

American sculptors of Southern monuments took up these themes. Much admired, for example, was Marius-Jean-Antonin Merci's statue that he titled *Gloria Victis*—"Glory to the Defeated"—which is inscribed on the monuments at Martinsville (1901), Blandford Cemetery in Petersburg (1890), and the Charlotte County Courthouse Common Soldier (1901).

There is no question of an implicit racial hierarchy in this genre, as art historian Kirk Savage argues in his book *Standing Soldiers, Kneeling Slaves: Race, War, and Monument in Nineteenth-Century America*. The archetypal monuments represented an ideal of aesthetic perfection that was decidedly ethnocentric, as history would have it, and thus were subject to a distinct bias to Greco-white-Caucasian forms such as the Apollo Belvedere, in evident contradistinction to other racial groups.[2] The monument makers felt no obligation to conform to the twenty-first century's conception of inclusivist rhetoric. They had their own conceptions of the common man, as it were. It is this quality of sameness that gives the war its fratricidal quality. Historian James Robertson averred that a civil war is possible in America in any generation, "simply because we live in a democracy."[3] The monument to the common soldier appears to validate Robertson's claim.

The statue of the common soldier has a long history, on both sides of the North/South divide. The figure is depicted as being common in the best sense: unexceptional, unbowed, vigilant, and thoughtful. Emphasis is on the individual taking initiative, and carrying on in the ways of the citizen/soldier defending the home country in the tradition of his presumed Revolutionary War forebears. The weapon he bears, as historian John Keegan notes, is consonant with the "emancipated youth of Europe who leveled their rifles, symbols of their status as free citizens, in defence of the values of liberty, equality, fraternity."[4] Daniel Chester French's *The Minute Man* (1871–75), as art historian Thayer Tolles observes, "depicts a farmer becoming a soldier, relinquishing his plow, raising his rifle, and stepping forward resolutely toward battle."[5] French's figure in turn is regarded as being naturalistic in style but classic in pose, inspired by the Apollo Belvedere, a cast of which French studied at the Boston Athenaeum. More broadly, some see parallels between the weapon held by the soldier and the staff held by Moses as a symbol of the authority vested in him as well as the democratic responsibility residing with private citizens.

The common man orientation intimates a broader indictment. "In 1861 America went to war with itself" is the way Eleanor Jones Harvey begins her book, *The Civil War and American Art*.[6] Fratricide took hold of the country in the 1860s. It was a common man's war, with women's active participation on or near the front lines, in industry, and on the home front. It was their war, too. The war had the consent of the governed and the soldiers who served were, in large measure, volunteers. It was and remains, as historian John Keegan avers, the "only large-scale war fought between citizens of the same democratic state." Furthermore, the participants maneuvering in "close ranks were subjected to firepower of an intensity not previously encountered in war."[7] The ferocity of the conflict was rendered all the more sanguinary by the technology of the time such as the repeating rifle and the rifled bullet. Even so, no truly decisive battles were fought. Even after the Confederate defeats at Vicksburg and Gettysburg, the war continued for nearly two years. Instead, both sides struck successive hammer blows until one side finally yielded. Thus as Keegan notes, to "an extraordinary degree, the Civil War was a war of battles—frequent, bloody, but yet not decisive. Both sides at the start expected and sought a great battle that would determine the outcome and end the fighting. No such battles were fought, even as the end approached. The cycle of battles kept on unfolding even within sight of Appomattox, where the war was terminated by surrender."

By and large the participants walked away: the war as an armed conflict on a national scale was over. The Confederate army evaporated. The Union army, apart from a cadre of Regulars, disappeared by 1866. This the monumentation commemorates. Unpredictable in its length and ferocity, the war ended suddenly, and the ferocity and scale have never been repeated. Ulysses Grant, who as general of the armies had a pivotal role in ending the war, described the events of the surrender of Lee's army at Appomattox in this fashion: "The war is over. The rebels are our countrymen again." Certainly peace was wanted, and the monumentation, in some measure, reflects this desire.

When the A. P. Hill Camp of the Sons of Confederate Veterans (SCV) erected a series of granite tablets at various Petersburg-area sites in 1914, they completed their work fifty years after the siege of Petersburg ended. They did so in a new century, at a time that offered no assurance that the world would know or remember what happened. Somewhere along the line during my research and travel and reading about these monuments and the Petersburg Campaign, in particular, I realized that there is a pattern here, that the monuments are prophetic. They carry the message that the war is over, but the fundamental conflict that led to the war is not over. Over fifty miles of fortifications remain extant in Petersburg and Dinwiddie County. Much of it is on National

Park Service grounds or those of the Pamplin Museum of the Civil War Soldier but not all, perhaps not even the majority. The modest but numerous SCV tablets mark key points of the defense lines of the Confederate army on the Petersburg battlefield and in Dinwiddie County during the 1864–65 siege of that city. They are numerous but not prominent. There are no statues at these sites, and there is nothing nostalgic or sentimental about the inscriptions: the words are terse. The monuments are made of solid granite, but they have a low silhouette and are small. Their understated stature means that some can be found only with difficulty.

The grammatical tense they present, however, is significant. In 1914, fifty years after it was erected, Fort Gregg is here. Not was—is. The inscriptions, plain as they are, define the landscape in terms of the war. The Fort Gregg Tablet, now south of I-85/US 460 on the Petersburg National Battlefield at Boydton Plank Road and Seventh Avenue, is clear.

> FORT GREGG / CONFEDERATE DEFENSE LINE
> APR. 2, 1865. / ERECTED APR. 2, 1914.

The tablet at Battery 45, also known as Fort Lee, is at Boydton Plank (Simpson) and Fort Lee roads, and has the same status.

> BATTERY 45 / SALIENT OF CONFEDERATE LINE
> SIEGE OF PETERSBURG. /
> ERECTED APR. 2, 1914.
> BY A. P. HILL CAMP S. C. V.

Trees and undergrowth dominate the landscape of this site, but extensive works remain in a surprisingly evocative state. Battery 45 faces south toward Federal lines. Meanwhile, the Rohoic Creek Dam—part of the defense lines, "Erected By Genl. R. E. Lee / Aug. 1864"—is here and is duly marked, like a cornerstone. The earthen dam can be found in a wooded site northwest of the corner of Dupuy and Boydton Plank roads. Likewise, the Fort Stedman Tablet, on the north side of Blandford Church in Blandford Cemetery, still commemorates the "Fort Steadman [sic] / Heroes."

Most notable perhaps is that Gracie's Salient still stands, albeit on National Park Service grounds, along the Poor Creek Trail, opposite Fort Stedman, south of Colquitt's Salient.

> GRACIE'S SALIENT. /
> THIS SALIENT, NAMED FOR /
> BRIG.-GENL. ARCHIBALD /
> GRACIE OF ALABAMA, /
> FACED THE FEDERAL FORTS /
> STEDMAN AND HASKELL /
> AND WAS SUCCESSFULLY /
> HELD BY THE CONFEDERATES /
> DURING THE ENTIRE SIEGE / OF PETERSBURG.

There is a subtle distinction in this claim. Gracie's Salient did not fall during the siege; it retains much of its physical integrity to this day. The salient was indeed held: it was abandoned when Union troops flanked it on April 2, 1865, but it did not fall. Stolidity and success, even victory, are themes of the memorial. The events of history took their course, but the fort, the monument, and the monument makers are still present.

The cliché about "bringing history alive" is a myth. It *is* alive. We are it; we are part of history; we are part of the past; and the past is part of us. Ken Burns, the popular filmmaker behind the 1990 documentary miniseries *The Civil War*, describes his work as a kind of "emotional archaeology."[8] Maybe that is too sentimental, but it has a truth in it. We sometimes sentimentalize the wartime generation, and they could be sentimental also. Sentimentalization may help us to bring the war down to a moral mortal conflict between citizen soldiers who also got along, who might have been friends, who *were* friends or relatives, who fraternized between the lines and traded tobacco for newspapers. They liked the same music; they often shared the same religious faith. Lincoln in his Second Inaugural Address declared, "Both [sides] read the same Bible and pray to the same God, and each invokes His aid against the other." At some level it is comforting to think of the war in terms of Felix DeWeldon's 1964 bronze sculpture depicting Confederate soldier Sgt. Richard Kirkland rising to come to the aid of wounded Union soldiers on the battlefield at Fredericksburg. The monument is "Dedicated / To / National Unity / And the / Brotherhood of Man"—a direct reference to theologian Adolf von Harnack's definition of the essence of the Christian faith as the universal fatherhood of God and the universal brotherhood of man. It may be in this spirit that the New York Peace monument on Lookout Mountain of Chickamauga-Chattanooga Military Park (1898) is surmounted by the figures of a Union and a Confederate soldier, shaking hands.

That dimension of history is true. Sometimes soldiers of opposing sides did meet and shake hands, and it is tempting to close here, on a positive note. But that would not do justice to the dead.

Historian Daniel Aaron writes that the Civil War is a "vivid but ungraspable story [that] still confounds interpreters."[9] This is a mercy. Some Union soldier shot Sgt. Kirkland at the battle of Chickamauga, and surely Kirkland aimed and fired his weapon as well—as his countrymen did, as his country asked him to.

Walt Whitman was a witness to the war and a great writer, but even he wrote that "the real war will never get in the books."[10] That is a mercy too. Whitman and his contemporaries knew how ugly it was. They knew it better than we do: The monuments continue to preclude the assurance of a satisfying closure to the war. Confederate monuments preside over numerous cemeteries interring thousands of dead from the war. There are sixteen thousand dead at Oakwood Cemetery, Richmond. At Hollywood Cemetery, Richmond, and Blandford Cemetery in Petersburg, thousands of unmarked graves form a valley of the dead that are ranged along the respective slopes—eighteen thousand at Hollywood, thirty thousand at Blandford. The dead form an enormous, affecting absent presence—present but unmarked as individuals. By comparison, "only" three thousand men are buried at Stonewall Cemetery in Winchester, Virginia. There are "only" fifteen hundred dead are buried at Thornrose Cemetery in Staunton. The Hebrew Cemetery Stele displays the names of thirty Jewish Confederate soldiers in three columns, with this tribute: "To the Glory of God / and / in Memory of / the Hebrew Confederate Soldiers / Resting in this Hallowed Spot."

It is merciful that the landscape covers the dead, but they are just below the surface.

The monument movement began in 1861 on the battlefield at First Manassas. It peaked in 1911–15, fifty years after the war, with the aging and passing of the wartime generation. The movement continues to this day, with monuments erected on the Shiloh battlefield in Tennessee in 2015, for example, and at a courthouse site in Mississippi in 2016. The present-day controversy is without precedent.

My goal in writing this book was to present the Confederate monumentation in Virginia as a complex literary text in public space. It was my ambition to let the text speak for itself. It was not my desire to intrude on their message beyond the context I provided. Readers may discern that I recognize the tragedy that caught up the wartime generation, but I avoided final judgments. If slavery was a principal cause of the war, it is also true that many men and women, North and South, were simply overtaken by events over which they had limited control, and that there were as many motivations to fight on one side or another as there are monuments in Virginia—ranging from the personal to the altruistic and from the noblest to the basest.

I cannot claim to know how readers whose ancestors were slaves read monuments, nor can I claim to speak for those whose ancestors fought for the Confederacy or put up monuments and statuary. However, I can testify that indifference to the Virginia Confederate monument seemed to prevail when I did this research. In the years that were required to personally visit these sites, I cannot say that I ever attracted any particular notice or curiosity from local residents, no matter how long it took to photograph a monument, transcribe the inscription, and study it on site. I say this only to point out that I was as much unnoticed as the monuments themselves were. They attracted no more attention than the landscaping, the architecture of adjacent buildings, or the other war memorials at the sites I studied. I never saw any UDC or SCV members at any cemeteries I researched, nor did I see more than perhaps a score of visitors. The world

passed by, it seemed to me. The work of daily life had sway.

Something ignited something that led to the controversy of today. Was it the madness of a twenty-one-year-old man committing multiple homicides at a prayer meeting in South Carolina in 2015, or a thunder-struck impulse to take offense at a statue of Robert E. Lee in Charlottesville, Virginia, in 2017? Was there a sudden burst of administrative insight, discernment, or wisdom that led to the removal of busts of Robert E. Lee and Thomas J. "Stonewall" Jackson from the Hall of Fame of Great Americans in the Bronx, New York? Surely tensions were present leading up to the zeitgeist of today, in the same way that war broke out in 1861, predictable only in the sense that humanity follows unexpected patterns.

The movement may have been unexpected, but there is at least a consensus about the sequence of events. Calls to drop Confederate emblems from public space were raised in the summer of 2015. Proposals have been made to honor Rev. Dr. Martin Luther King with a monument at Stone Mountain State Park, Georgia, on the site of the enormous granite bas-relief sculpture commemorating the military leaders of the Confederacy. Responding to protests, the University of Mississippi lowered the state flag that flies on the campus. Contention over the state flag of Mississippi, with its emblem of the Confederate battle flag, continues at this writing.

The controversy was renewed in Charlottesville, Virginia, in 2017, and drew more attention and opprobrium to this genre. In February 2017, the city council of Charlottesville voted to remove the statue of Robert E. Lee from Lee Park. Opponents of the move sued one month later, contending that under state law the council did not have the authority to remove the statue. (That court case continues at this writing, and the statue is still in place.) In June, the council took further action, voting to give Lee Park a new name—Emancipation Park. The events in Charlottesville led to violence in August 2017. White nationalists in Charlottesville protested the city's plan to remove the statue; counterdemonstrators opposed them. The event descended into violence, resulting in the deaths of a bystander and two state troopers.

Among other events, four Confederate statues were removed from public sites in New Orleans in May 2017. Four Confederate statues were removed from public sites in Baltimore in August. Also in August, administrators at Bronx Community College, CUNY, arranged the removal of busts of Lee and Jackson from the college's hall of fame.

Local communities erected local monuments, and local communities can tear them down as well.

In practical terms, dismantling a public monument is relatively simple, but the larger issues have a dynamism and volatility that makes the task more complex. For better or worse, monuments and the war are still an integral part of the fabric of the American landscape. An examination of the collected Civil War monument text shows that their diversity is confounding. Monuments commemorating both sides—Confederate and Union soldiers—stand at Berkley Springs, West Virginia, and at Crossville, Tennessee. The Marshall County monument in Moundsville, West Virginia, makes no distinction between Union or Confederate soldiers from the county. It commends both sides: "To The Memory of the Soldiers of Marshall Co. W.Va. 1861–1865."

Federal ground has its own conundrums. Do we take down half the Missouri monument at Vicksburg National Military Park, with its tributes to both sides, Union and Confederate? What about the state of Kentucky's monument at Vicksburg, with its tributes to both sides, Union and Confederate, and its statues of Jefferson Davis and Abraham Lincoln? Do we remove Davis and leave Lincoln? Even the Iowa state monument at Vicksburg displays a relief of Confederate soldiers in action, in valiant combat against Iowa Union soldiers. Is this an issue? Who can fault Mississippi's African American monument at Vicksburg, which encompasses the men on both sides of the siege line by dint of its tribute to "All Mississippians of / African Descent / Who Participated in / the Vicksburg / Campaign."

Even if it were possible to reconcile these matters, a thorough purging would not stop with the monumentation. In a sense, the landscape itself is the true testimony and witness, and the monuments are only a liturgical commentary. The war continues to cast doubt on the assurances that God has "shed His grace" on the United States, in the words of "America the Beautiful" (1910); whether "God blessed America," as Irving Berlin would have it (1938); or whether the "land is our land," as Woodie Guthrie averred (1940).

Did God shed his grace on the American South? Historian Stephan Cushman brings this to bear in his analysis of William Faulkner's "The Bear" in *Go Down, Moses*. Cushman observes that Faulkner has his main character, Ike McCaslin, list a series of events from the war "in order to question the proposition, advanced by another character, that God has turned his face toward the South."[11] Faulkner's character looks to the battle of the Wilderness in Virginia in 1864, and the sanguinary turns of fate that went against the South, particularly when Confederate Lt. Gen. James Longstreet was nearly killed in a friendly fire incident: *"and that same Longstreet shot out of saddle by his own men in the dark by mistake just as Jackson was. His face to us? His face to us?"* (italics in original).[12]

With the license afforded an artist, Faulkner leaves the matter as a rhetorical question. It seems to me, though, that Abraham Lincoln grappled with the same question in his second inaugural address. "His face to us?" he might have asked. Perhaps not. Lincoln, who was never a church member and read theology only occasionally and informally, posits a way of coming to terms with the war's cause, length, casualties, aftermath, and legacy. Lincoln was not above skepticism. It is to Lincoln that historian Mark Noll ascribes the same sense of doubt and discomfort with doubt that Nathaniel Hawthorne ascribes to Herman Melville: "He can neither believe, nor be comfortable in his unbelief; and he is too honest and courageous not to try to do one or the other."[13] Nevertheless, just 41 days before his assassination, Lincoln offered a sublime benediction to the country by dint of his second inaugural address. It is a "peerless work of political theology," as historian Lewis E. Lehrman describes it, that is steeped in scriptural language and allusions.[14] Lincoln's counsel to the nation, North and South, is to act with compassion, with the full knowledge that one may be acting in the presence of one enemies (Psalm 23:5), and that a man's foes may well "be those of his own household" (Matthew 10:36). His summation is well known:

> With malice toward none, with charity for all, with firmness in the right as God gives us to see the right, let us strive on to finish the work we are in, to bind up the nation's wounds, to care for him who shall have borne the battle and for his widow and his orphan, to do all which may achieve and cherish a just and lasting peace among ourselves and with all nations.

Lincoln makes no claim of understanding the ways of Providence in bringing about the war to the American landscape; he resists any temptation to triumphalize the war's end as a Northern victory or a Southern defeat; he refrains from speculating on the ways of Providence in permitting war to continue for so long. Indeed, Lincoln found only a consuming inscrutability in his search for God. However, as historian Anthony Guelzo observes, "this was not an excuse for passivity, but was rather a call for chastity of purpose."[15] That the reunited nation should undertake this redemptive initiative on behalf of all its citizens is what Lincoln preaches.

Lincoln's counsel in the second inaugural address is respected and revered, even venerated, but it continues to go unheeded. True, no civil war has erupted in America since 1861: some form of perpetual disequilibrium has kept the country in tenuous balance since then. There is friction, yes, but not war. Lincoln's cosmic skepticism precluded his advancing the same contention as that which is inscribed at the base—the plinth—of a Tennessee Civil War monument: "IS. 53:6," it reads. Isaiah 53:6 is an accusation and condemnation: it takes terse but pointed measure of the prophet Isaiah's generation, and it has applications to the generations that follow: "All of us like sheep have gone astray," the prophet avers. "Each of us has turned to his own way; / But the LORD has caused the iniquity of us all / To fall on Him." The prophet saw redemption for his people's failings only by way of a transcendent instrument—a messiah.

How should we, in the twenty-first century, come to terms with the Confederate monument on the Virginia landscape? What is the message? No family is spared sorrow. None eludes strife or suffering. That the "foe should be of one's own household" is an accusation that could find resonance in any family, within any culture or nation, of any generation. The Civil War monument is a testimony to that failing, but Lincoln's call is still in the air. The country failed in 1861. Its people failed. The momentum toward war could not be stayed. In some ways, it was wanted. To the extent that we in the twenty-first century fail to find "a just and lasting peace" with the past, as Lincoln advised, we will fail to bring peace to this generation and time as fully as those who went to war failed their generation and time in 1861.

Lincoln advises concrete action: "binding up the nation's wounds." It may seem ironic that he would advance that counsel, since so many lives were taken and so many men and women suffered in the war that spanned the breadth of his presidency. However, it may also be the case that Lincoln, at the center of the conflict, was by temperament, circumstance, and sublime insight best suited to advance the idea that the proverbial Good Samaritan's mercy toward an erstwhile enemy was the imperative now that the war was nearing its end. His rhetoric was lofty, the import transcendent, but the advice has practical applications: the call it seems is to work on the landscape in the daily, mundane, vital tasks of education, health care, highway maintenance, building, food production, governance, et al. This is arguably the postwar "unfinished work" that Lincoln also exhorted the nation to fulfill in the Gettysburg Address.

Looking at the broad sweep of Virginia's monumentation text leads me to conclude that the monument makers accomplished two things. First, they proclaimed reconciliation: the words "Our Confederate Dead," inscribed on a courthouse monument place the war firmly in the past and the dead in permanent commemoration. Done. Second, they also placed the commemoration of the Confederate soldier in public space. In important ways, this was a service. By erecting a monument to commend the service of citizen soldiers, they served as an archetype that was followed by subsequent generations when they commemorated citizens called to service in subsequent wars in the twentieth and twenty-first centuries. None of the conflicts was without controversy, but the service men and women were deemed worthy of remembrance nevertheless.

However, in the wake of recent events, it seems clear that the political consensus to erect these monuments came at a price. The place of monuments on courthouse grounds or public parks has and will subject them to the currents of political favor, tolerance, conviction, and convenience.

I do not doubt the general goodwill of the public. Monuments are a testament to it. The enduring presence of the Confederate monument is a testament to tolerance, especially if they are interpreted as commemorations of individuals—e.g., King George (1867) lists 97 names; Nottoway (1893) lists 532 names; Front Royal (1911) lists some six hundred; the Tappahannock monument (1909) lists 772; and the Hanover courthouse monument (1914) lists 1,119 names.

In addition, I do not doubt that there are men and women of goodwill in public office. However, there is no assurance that sentiment, convictions, aesthetics, integrity, and historic sensibility will persuade them to maintain public space Confederate monuments in perpetuity. One could hope that this historic public archive of commemoration will be preserved in public space, in the same way that the monuments to the service men and women of World War One, World War Two, the Korean War, the Vietnam War, or the gulf wars should

be preserved. If not, those who live to regret that public monuments are removed may find consolation in the fact that those who remove them will also pass from the public scene—"the way of all flesh"—as surely as the monuments they dismantle, and that, for better or worse, another generation will come along to judge their legacy and then make their own mark on the landscape.

As for the Virginia Confederate monument looking out on Confederate cemeteries, it is hallowed ground. Let the dead rest in peace—*Requiescat in pace*. Let the veterans and those who cared for them rest in peace. Let the cemetery monuments do the work of remembrance that the monument makers desired.

Timothy Sedore
May 2018

Notes

1. Wilkinson further observes, "At the time of the collapse of France in 1870, there were exactly nine statues of illustrious French men and women in Paris. Thirty years later there were 110." Burke Wilkinson, *The Life and Works of Augustus Saint Gaudens* (New York: Dover, 1985), 94.

2. "The *Apollo Belvedere* is not only beautiful but enormously influential. . . . Almost every standing figure, draped or undraped, in any form of movement, from the sixteenth century to the nineteenth, is derived from the contrapposto pose of the Apollo." Philippi de Montebello, qtd. in Wilkinson, *Life and Works*, 346.

3. James Robertson Jr., Lecture, Civil War Preservation Trust, Blacksburg, Virginia, July 24, 2003.

4. John Keegan, *The Second World War* (New York: Penguin, 1998), 25.

5. Thayer Tolles, "Daniel Chester French, 1850–1931; *The Minute Man*, 1771–1775; this cast, around 1875–1876," Traditional Fine Arts Organization, http://www.tfaoi.com. Accessed August 12, 2017.

6. Eleanor Jones Harvey, *The Civil War and American Art* (New Haven: Yale University Press, 2012), 1.

7. John Keegan, *The American Civil War: A Military History* (New York: Random House, 2009), large print, 611.

8. "A Forum with Ken Burns," Public Broadcasting System, http://www.pbs.org/lewisandclark /forum/. Accessed September 8, 2017.

9. Daniel Aaron, *The Unwritten War: American Writers and the Civil War* (New York: Alfred A. Knopf, 1973), 340.

10. Walt Whitman, "Specimen Days," qtd. in Louis Mazur, ed., *"The Real War Will Never Get in the Books": Selections from Writers during the Civil War* (New York: Oxford University Press, 1993), 286.

11. Stephan Cushman, *Bloody Promenade: Reflections on a Civil War Battle* (Charlottesville: University Press of Virginia, 1999), 186.

12. William Faulkner, *Go Down, Moses* (New York: Vintage Press, 1973), 286.

13. Mark Noll, *America's God: From Jonathan Edwards to Abraham Lincoln* (New York: Oxford University Press, 2005), 436; cf. Anthony Guelzo, *Abraham Lincoln: Redeemer President* (New York: Simon and Schuster, 1999), 446.

14. Lewis E. Lehrman, "Lincoln's Second Inaugural," The Gilder Lehrman Institute of American History, https://www.gilderlehrman.org/history-by-era/american-civil-war/essays/lincoln's-second-inaugural. Accessed September 27, 2017.

15. Guelzo, *Abraham Lincoln: Redeemer President*, 420.

Virginia Regions

1. The Shenandoah Valley
   and Northwest Virginia
2. Southwest Virginia
3. Richmond, Northern Virginia, and
   the Piedmont
4. The Northern Neck, Middle Peninsula,
   Eastern Shore, and Eastern Southside
5. Petersburg, the Southside West of
   Petersburg, and Central Virginia
   West of Richmond

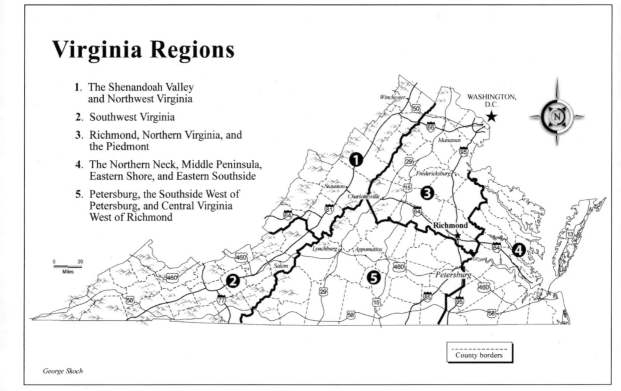

George Skoch

County borders

Preface to the Cloth Edition

This is a book about the Civil War in Virginia and the monuments in Virginia that commemorate that conflict. It draws from travel, research, and photography over the course of several years to every Virginia county and several hundred of Virginia's towns and cities. This research began with a curiosity about monument inscriptions by this author, someone who takes an abiding interest in the way words serve their purpose in the world. It was sustained by the conviction that every monument is distinctive—where it is, what it says, how it appears, how it represents the cause that was fought for and the price that was paid.

I paid close attention to visual features: materials (stone, granite, bronze); forms and formats (obelisk, shaft, pyramid, pillar, statuary, frieze, relief); and many other details (fonts, for example, and the presence of other architectural details, like columns). I also made every effort to do justice to what was written at these sites and thus to reproduce the monument inscriptions as accurately as possible. It should be noted that since there are 360 sites described here—including many sites with more than one monument—the styles vary a good deal. Some, in fact, are highly irregular. They are transcribed as is, from top to bottom, line by line, all sides as appropriate.

This survey is organized geographically. Following an introductory chapter, the tour, so to speak, moves north to south, from the Shenandoah Valley and northwest Virginia (chapter 1) to the southwestern highlands (chapter 2); then from northern Virginia (chapter 3, the Washington suburbs, Richmond, northern Virginia, and the Piedmont) across eastern Virginia (chapter 4, the Northern Neck, Middle Peninsula, Eastern Shore, and eastern Southside) to Virginia's Southside (chapter 5, Petersburg, the Southside west of Petersburg, and central Virginia west of Richmond). An appendix follows. A list of works consulted in the preparation of this book is available on the Southern Illinois University Press website, www.siupress.com.

There is, of course, no way to recreate the experience of actually visiting these sites, and certainly no sure way to capture the sense of loss, remembrance, defiance, bitterness, or mourning that is presented. In these pages, however, we are confronted with the testimony of those for whom the war was more than an event, a cause, or a remembrance. In some way—for better or worse—they represent what William Faulkner famously observed, that the "past is never dead. It's not even past."

Acknowledgments

The author gratefully acknowledges the support, in the form of grants, of the Research Foundation of the City University of New York during the course of this project.

Thanks are extended to several anonymous readers who read and critiqued early manuscript versions of this book.

ABBREVIATIONS

B.R.   business route
C.H.   courthouse
C.R.   county route
C.S.A. Confederate States of America
L.M.A. Ladies Memorial Association
N.B.P. National Battlefield Park
N.H.P. National Historic Park
S.C.V. Sons of Confederate Veterans
U.D.C. United Daughters of the Confederacy
U.S.   U.S. route
V.M.I. Virginia Military Institute
V.R.   Virginia state route

An Illustrated Guide to Virginia's Confederate Monuments

INTRODUCTION

This book offers a guide to Virginia's outdoor Civil War monuments and markers to Confederate soldiers. Over three hundred monuments or markers—courthouse, town or city square, cemetery, highway, and battlefield examples—stand in the commonwealth, ranging from the Cumberland Gap near Kentucky to the Eastern Shore, and from the northern Virginia suburbs of Washington, D.C. to the South Side near North Carolina. The monument commemoration movement began in 1861, peaked around 1913, and continues to this day.

Other forms of media dominate public attention today, but these monuments still command public space in the way generations of Southerners wanted the war to be remembered. Confederate monuments are tangible physical reminders of a conflict that shaped America and yet still defies understanding. "If the South has a symbol," landscape historian John Fraser Hart observes, "it is the statue of the Confederate soldier which stands in the county seat. Hands resting on the barrel of his grounded rifle, knapsack and blanket roll on his back, he stares in stony silence to the north whence came the invading Yankee armies." It is this vision of the South—and Virginia in particular—that occasions this book.

Virginia's monuments have never been collectively surveyed. There are good reasons for this: they are scattered across nearly forty thousand square miles of the commonwealth. It required several years and several thousand miles of travel to confirm my suspicion that no monument duplicates another. It took no time to recognize that the monuments offer a means of exploring the contrast of contemporary conceptions of tragic irony with timeless private anguish, and the conflict of intimate personal loss with the need to present enduring, affecting public remembrance.

There was much to remember, record, and declare about the war. The challenge each monument committee or town or sculptor had was to evoke great meaning in a finite space. Their success varied, but the statistics, though horrific, are clear enough: the war took about 623,000 lives from among three million soldiers from a nation with a antebellum population of about thirty-one million people. Some 471,000 were wounded. Among the last states to secede from the Union, Virginia was a reluctant member of the Confederate States of America. Secession, however justified, carried a high price: seventeen thousand Virginians were killed. The Virginia campaigns were the largest ever in the Americas: twenty-six major battles along with some four hundred other clashes. Though the Confederacy lasted but a short time as a nation, it fielded one of the finest armies ever; yet that army met its end—symbolically, if not militarily—in Virginia. The story of the nation and its army is told in the monuments.

The legacy of the war was shaped in Virginia. The Museum of the Confederacy was established in Richmond. So, too, was the national headquarters of the United Daughters of the Confederacy and Battle Abbey, home to the Confederate Memorial Association, which merged with the Virginia Historical Society in 1946. The Southern Historical Society—a bulwark of Lost Cause ideology and justification—met in Virginia. The Monument Avenue statues of Robert E. Lee, Thomas J. "Stonewall" Jackson, Jefferson F. Davis, and James E. "J. E. B." Stuart retain the grandeur and pomp of a shadow-nation capital city, and there are more monuments in Virginia than in any other state of the former Confederacy. Moreover, Jefferson Davis, the Confederacy's only president, is buried in Virginia, as are many of the nation's most illustrious soldiers—Lee, Jackson, Stuart, among them. But it is the common soldier that drew the attention of many monument builders and is the focus of much of this book. Small town monuments, in particular, reflect the intimacy of war and the utterly personal nature of its effects. It was far from battlefields that most families grieved, lost, faced uncertainty and separation, or weighed commitment. In that sense, the battles of Spotsylvania and

Chancellorsville were also fought at Eastville on the Eastern Shore or Bristol on the Tennessee state line, as well as thousands of Virginia villages, towns, and homes.

Chauvinism about this subject is readily gratified. It is easy to claim that the soldiers are not always artful, that they often look stiff or frozen, and that the inscriptions seem terse and routine. It does not help that mass production of the statues meant that many Confederate soldiers looked virtually identical to their Union counterparts or "that they all look basically the same."

I do not find these arguments convincing. After all, the same claim can be applied to Civil War battles—so many, so similar—or to American cities, or to luggage in airport carousels, or to just about anything that is complex, plural and unfamiliar. There are patterns and trends in monuments, but there are no types. Novelist F. Scott Fitzgerald puts it this way: "Begin with an individual," he avers, "and before you know it you find that you have created a type; begin with a type, and you find that you have created—nothing. . . . There are no types, no plurals."

They may look similar, but they are different, if only slightly—if only in setting, ornamentation, inscription, sponsorship, or maker. They are, moreover, as distinct as the communities they represent. Those differences—like two individuals—deserve attention: the challenge is to recognize the distinctions and the opportunity they offer to understand how a host of communities came to terms with a war whose meaning is still debated. It was not an academic issue. It was arguably quasi-religious. As a body of rhetoric, the ten-thousand-word text inscribed on markers across Virginia is cryptic and revealing—variously hopeful, affectionate, inspiring, vexing, banal, and provocative. The inscriptions often seem clear enough. The phrases "Our Confederate Soldiers," or "Our Confederate Heroes" are etched on monuments across the South, but the need to claim those ties and to ensure that those words would outlast the generation that professed them is profound. "Our Confederate Dead," the women of the United Daughters of

the Confederacy declare on the granite shaft at Marshall, dedicated in 1928, claiming the dead for their own, even sixty-three years after the war's end. This book explores that need to display those convictions and claims. This author has been repeatedly impressed by the attempts to effect a reconciliation between intimate, private mourning and abstract ideology: between the loss of child, parent, spouse, friend, or sibling in the war, and the rhetorical effort to rationalize that loss and sustain adherence to the Lost Cause and other ideologies that emerged from that war.[1] Impressed, but I should not be: rhetorician Richard Weaver avers that "every use of speech, oral and written, exhibits an attitude, and an attitude implies an act. . . . Every utterance is an attempt to make others see the world in a particular way and to accept the values implicit in that point of view."

The monuments in this book have proven to me, however, that efforts to justify the cause or mediate bereavement in this medium are not always successful. I attribute something of the irony or cynicism in twentieth- and twenty-first-century American thought to the various claims made in Civil War monuments. Their claims are often so unabashed or fervent that the modernist or postmodern era would find that they lack credibility. A distinctive kind of triumphalism—or "glorious contentment," as historian Stuart McConnell puts it—is declared in many Northern Civil War monuments, but defiant glory and apologetics—arguments in defense of Southern participation in the war—or rationales are common in Southern monuments. In *The Great War and Modern Memory*, Paul Fussell contends "that there seems to be one dominating form of modern understanding; that it is essentially ironic; and that it originates largely in the application of mind and memory to the events of the Great War." Fussell arguably overstates the case when he makes claims to one dominating form, but to the extent that perceptions of irony prevail, the foundations for that perspective were laid in part during the American Civil War and are present and discernible in the monuments described here.

History

Civil War monuments are often classified by the year they were erected. The categories are deceptively neat; the years 1861–1889 have been called the "Bereavement and Funereal Era," those from 1890 to 1920 the "Reconciliation" or "Celebration Era,", and those from 1920 to the present the "Commemorative Era."

The monument movement began early. A marble shaft was erected to Francis S. Bartow at Manassas on September 4, 1861, only a few months after the war's first major battle. The shaft was placed on the site where Bartow was killed at the head of his brigade. (Union troops destroyed the monument when the Confederates retreated, but a vestige remains to this day.) The first courthouse monument was erected at King George Courthouse in 1867. Lynchburg claims the first cemetery monument, in Old City Cemetery, dedicated May 10, 1868.

The neoclassical movement had origins in Greek and Roman culture. It was common practice in Greek city-states to use stone slabs and bronze plaques to display public records, including laws, decrees, treaties, religious notices, and war memorials. It was only natural then, that in the Bereavement and Funereal Era, 1861–1889, the need to retrieve, identify, and bury the dead occasioned many memorials in a style that nineteenth-century Americans admired and emulated.

Monuments often presided over mass burials. Violent death was so common and pervasive that the war finally ended the prevailing rural cemetery decorum and romanticization of death. The mid-nineteenth-century American focus on death may seem odd, even perverse today, but it led to dozens of parklike, "rural" cemeteries' being opened across America in the 1830s and 1840s. The sites were modeled along the lines of Mount Auburn Cemetery, in Cambridge, Massachusetts, as a place for the memorialization of the dead in a dignified, picturesque garden landscape—indeed as a place to fulfill a desire to idealize death. But death as a pleasant easing into another world—a kind of edenic dream fulfilled—became an outmoded concept with the coming of the war. The rituals of honoring the dead were simplified, often eliminated—even as the methods of killing became simpler and more efficient. Grim, linear rows of graves were practical, pragmatic, and necessary. Unless families could intervene or an officer of high rank or popularity had been killed, orderly disposal was the best that could be expected or hoped for. In the immediate postwar era, enormous efforts were made to collect, identify, and rebury the dead, and to place monuments over them with attendant ceremonies. The degree of ornamentation of monuments varied, from utter restraint to Victorian extravagance, but most common was an obelisk, often with an urn or drape on top. Although a common symbol in the South was the Confederate battle flag, religious import often took precedence. The inscriptions had a grim tone. The 1884 Lexington obelisk to "Southern Soldiers," for example, offered "no tuneful choir" for its Confederate dead but only "a rest remains long denied us here."

In the Reconciliation or Celebration Era, 1890–1920, mourning became celebration, but celebration in the fullest sense of the word: "The word comes from Latin and means 'much frequented,' suggesting continuity of involvement," according to art historian Donald M. Reynolds. "To celebrate a monument properly, then, is to incorporate it into the everyday life of our society at all levels." So it was that the peak of monument development occurred in these years. County seats, city centers, and parks and battlefields were chosen more often as sites than cemeteries were. In small towns and rural counties, the courthouse remained at the center of political, social, legal, and commercial activity. It was here, not the cemetery, where sculptures of Confederate common soldiers and inscriptions of Lost Cause homilies were placed. By 1920, nearly every courthouse in Virginia had a Confederate monument. The dedication rituals changed as well, with more emphasis on exuberant speeches, parades, and festivities rather than religious rites, sermonizing, and solemnity. The semicentennial of the war, 1911 to 1915, served as an impetus, as was the Spanish-American War–era of reconciliation between North and South, the nationalist fervor aroused during World War I, and the maturity or passing of the first generation of descendents and the deaths of most of the veterans. By 1914, according to Charles Reagan Wilson, over a thousand monuments had been erected in the South.

Other changes included a wider use of battlefield memorial sites and highway guideposts. Most battlefields reverted to prewar uses after 1865 and initially drew little attention apart from efforts to recover the dead and place monuments over battlefield cemeteries. The largest monuments were to individuals: for Jackson at Chancellorsville (1888) and for Stuart at Yellow Tavern (1888). Tourism began with veterans returning to survey the ground where they had fought. State and national battlefield parks were established as destinations for travelers. Monuments along the railroad were erected at Fredericksburg—the "Meade" Pyramid near Fredericksburg (1898)—and at Guinea Station—the Stonewall Jackson shaft (1903)—to give notice to travelers of the wartime significance of the places they were passing. A series of twenty-five battlefield tablets furthered that trend in the 1920s, as did the Jefferson Davis Highway markers, also erected in the 1920s. Sixty-two markers describing the campaigns around Richmond—with inscriptions written by historian Douglas Southall Freeman—were placed in the 1920s in large measure for travelers by automobile.

Care should be taken in defining the movement at this time as one of reconciliation. Many monuments made paradoxical, even contradictory claims. Some were radical and even subversive in appearance or rhetoric, yet they were oddly passive and static. The elegists—those who wrote inscriptions on monuments—at once proclaimed that the cause was just, but they did nothing to revivify the Confederacy. They justified the revolution, but they did not resurrect its government. In short, they defined reconciliation in particular ways. Voicing the claim or inscribing it in stone was both provocative and cathartic: inscribing the words "Our Confederate Soldiers" gave vent to a host of sentiments and convictions but did nothing to revive secession. The sculpted weapons were carved in stone: they were potent, but not literally lethal.

The Arlington Cemetery monument, designed by Moses J. Ezekiel, serves as a prime example. Reconciliation has been claimed as its central theme: President Woodrow Wilson delivered a conciliatory address at the dedication ceremonies on June 4, 1914. Union and Confederate veterans placed wreaths on the graves. However, there was no hint that the "Lost Cause" was not laudable, legitimate, or just. The seal of the Confederacy is prominently inscribed; so too is a bas-relief of Minerva, goddess of war, and a shield bearing the word "Constitution." Although Ezekiel called this a "peace monument," this kind of peace and reconciliation had a subversive, militant quality: it meant vindication, one that, as historian Karen L. Cox describes it, "acknowledged military defeat and nothing more."

The Commemorative Era includes monuments from 1921 to the present. In the 1920s and 1930s, many monuments nostalgically commemorated what was thought to be a simpler time. Historical interpretation was the prevailing theme: patriotic tributes or religious rationales were less common. The monuments were modest in scale; the inscriptions were less strident and more spare—a trend that would continue into the 1940s, although World War II interrupted construction from 1941 to 1949. The 1950s and early 1960s were characterized by centennial apologetics and nostalgia, as well as civil rights–era revisionism. Only a few Virginia monuments were erected between 1965 and 1981, in some sense no doubt because of the Vietnam War. However, a resurgence of interest began after the bicentennial of 1976 and continued into the twenty-first century. Many of the monuments erected in the 1980s and 1990s were placed at sites that had been previously overlooked: courthouse sites at Grundy and Gate City; and battlefield sites at Sutherland and Hanging Rock, for example. The inscriptions on these monuments were didactic and instructive, designed to offer a historical perspective rather than strike an emotional chord. In the 1990s, monuments from the states of Alabama and Mississippi were erected at Stonewall Cemetery in Winchester, a plaque was erected at the Fredericksburg Confederate cemetery, and a triptych was erected at Mount Jackson. In the first years of the twenty-first century, new monuments were erected on the courthouse grounds of Abingdon, Appomattox, and Courtland; Richmond's Oakwood and Hollywood cemeteries; and Spotsylvania Court House Battlefield.

Inscriptions

Some ten thousand words are inscribed on monuments in Virginia. Many of the texts are sometimes strikingly simple or declarative, others cryptic, terse, and incisive; still other monuments are decorated with rosters, declarations, and sentiments to the point where they cover virtually every space on the monument.[2]

Elegists have the challenge of balancing inscriptions and adornment: the problem arises of integrating text, setting, and purpose as well as aesthetics with function. Solutions varied, but the pace of American prose that evolved in the nineteenth century led to a new "efficiency" and directness that found expression in a pattern of clipped inscriptions—profound in some cases, profoundly suggestive in others, or profoundly facile, depending on the text and the reader.

Most town, city, or cemetery monument inscriptions begin or end with an evocation or exhortation: "To the Confederate Soldier" or "In Memory of Our Confederate Soldiers." The Louisa courthouse monument is erected "In Memory of the Courage, Patriotism and Devotion of the Confederate Soldiers of Louisa County."

Proverbs or aphorisms, sometimes in Latin, are common. The seal of the Confederacy, with the motto "Deo Vindice"—"God will avenge"— is often superimposed. So, too, is the phrase "Sic Semper Tyrannis"—the Latin phrase on the seal of Virginia, which is translated as "Thus Ever to Tyrants."

Apologetics—arguments in defense of the cause of the South or the Confederacy—are arguably the most strident elements of inscrip-

tions. The Sussex County monument declares of "Our Confederate Soldiers," that "The Principles for Which They Fought Live Eternally." The Charles City courthouse obelisk is dedicated to "Defenders of Constitutional Liberty and the Right of Self Government." The county courthouse example in Montross calls attention to those

WHO FELL IN DEFENCE OF VIRGINIA,
AND IN THE CAUSE OF
CONSTITUTIONAL LIBERTY.

The Berryville Courthouse monument is

ERECTED TO THE MEMORY OF
THE SONS OF CLARKE
WHO GAVE THEIR LIVES
IN DEFENSE OF THE RIGHTS
OF THE STATES AND OF CONSTITUTIONAL
GOVERNMENT.

Invocations of the sacrifice of Confederate soldiers made are common. The Marion text praises "The Defenders of State Sovereignty" for being "Faithful Unto Death." It concludes with a claim that these warriors died as martyrs

WHO BORE THE FLAG OF
OUR NATION'S TRUST,
AND FELL IN THE CAUSE
'THO LOST, STILL JUST
AND DIED FOR ME AND YOU."

The Harrisonburg monument (1876) has one of many broad justifications, declaring that the "Confederate Soldiers who lie here. . . . Died in Defence of The Rights of The South." The text invokes "the principles of 1776," and concludes that "The Southern Soldier died for his Country" before noting that "Success is not Patriotism" and "Defeat is not Rebellion." The Front Royal monument (1911) marks those who "Gave Their Lives In Defense of Truth and Right" and declares that "They Died in The Cause of Honor and Justice." The Sussex County monument (1912) declares that "The Principles For Which They Fought Live Eternally." The Lunenburg courthouse monument (1876) declares that "We Fought for the Sovereignty of the States." The Halifax monument (1911) is declared in "Loving Remembrance of

The Confederate Soldiers of Halifax County, Who Fought for Constitutional Liberty."

Sentiments, paeans, or summary tributes also occur. One panel of the Marion monument states: "Glory Sits Beside Our Grief." Another at New Castle: "Invincible In Life[,] Immortal In Death." Another, at Stanardsville: "Dead—yet still they speak." At Washington, Virginia, the elegists praise the soldiers' "unwavering Patriotism[,] faultless fealty."

They often claim to speak for the dead. The Georgia monument at Stonewall Cemetery, Winchester, is perhaps the most obvious example. With a conspicuous parallel to the epitaph for the Spartans killed at the battle of Thermopylae (480 B. C.), it concludes:

> GO, STRANGER, AND TELL IT
> IN GEORGIA, THAT WE DIED HERE
> IN OBEDIENCE TO HER LAWS.
> 1861–1865

In general, Virginia's monuments offer the same two themes that historian Jay Winter observed about monuments commemorating World War I: "war as both noble and uplifting and tragic and unendurably sad." These, he continues, "are present in virtually all postwar war memorials; they differ in the balance struck between them. That balance was never fixed; no enduring formula emerged to express it, though traditional religious images were used repeatedly to do so." Those who erected Virginia's Confederate monuments did not seem to find an enduring formula either. With few exceptions, though, they defended a belief system that held that the cause was just, and that the efforts expended and sacrifices made were honorable.

Taken as a whole, Civil War monuments reflect these changes by intertwining Victorian gestures with sharp declarative simplicity. The inscriptions are often strikingly direct. Richmond's massive Monument Avenue memorial to Robert E. Lee has a text that "merely" states "Lee." The North Carolina obelisk at Stonewall Cemetery in Winchester simply but emphatically declares, "N-C-Confederate Dead." For all the adornment on the Tazewell courthouse monument (1903)—a Confederate

soldier standing at the top and a relief of Robert E. Lee on one of its panels—the inscription is brief, arguably taciturn

> TO THE CONFEDERATE SOLDIERS OF
> TAZEWELL
> 1861–1865

Luray's 1918 monument declares:

> CSA
> CONFEDERATE SOLDIERS
> 1861–1865

The Pulaski monument (1906) is only a bit more elaborate:

> IN MEMORY
> OF THE
> CONFEDERATE SOLDIERS   ———
> OF
> PULASKI COUNTY
> 1861–1865

Not all monuments are so spare, of course. Many courthouse and cemetery monuments have rosters of service units, veterans, those killed in service, survivors, or casualties—the latter term defined as killed or wounded. The Hillsville courthouse monument (1908) lists twenty-two engagements and battles, from Gettysburg to Cotton Mountain, and specifies that the county contributed sixteen companies of infantry and cavalry. The Fincastle courthouse monument (1901) lists twelve companies and an array of reserves and civilian contributions to the cause. It also honors the "Women of Botetourt" for their "Constant Encouragement" and "Steadfast Devotion." The courthouse monument at Nottoway (1893) lists 532 names, Tappahannock (1909) lists 772, and Hanover (1914) lists 1,119.

But brevity usually prevails, with such cryptic phrases as "Confederate Soldiers" or "Our Confederate Dead" often serving as summary statements.

Design

Typical postwar monuments or markers are made of bronze, white bronze, marble, or granite. Iron, copper, limestone, and aluminum as well as common fieldstone were also used. They are either:

- An obelisk: a tall, slender four-sided stone pillar tapering toward a peaked top.
- A slab, tablet, or pillar, sometimes called a stele: an upright stone or plaque set on a stone base.
- A statue: set on a stone pedestal, plinth or base, sometimes with a shaft or dado that displays an inscription; the whole is surmounted by a sculpture of a soldier, usually standing at parade rest.
- A plaque or tablet of bronze, marble, or granite on a wall.
- A shaft or column, sometimes surmounted by a soldier.

Equestrian monuments of Lee are at Richmond and Charlottesville; of Jackson at Richmond, Charlottesville, and Manassas; of Stuart at Richmond. Arches stand at the entryway to the soldiers' section of Lynchburg's Old City Cemetery, Petersburg's Blandford Cemetery, and the officers' section of Hollywood Cemetery. Statues of various officers stand in Richmond and Lynchburg. Like the inscriptions, all

Fig. 0.1. An obelisk, this one a tribute to Col. John S. Mosby dedicated June 26, 1920. A granite plinth, base, dado, and obelisk with bronze plaque and relief of Mosby.

of these forms have neoclassical derivations. In fact, the basic forms of the public monument—the arch, column, obelisk, and equestrian statue—were established in Rome two thousand years ago.

Fig. 0.2. A granite shaft: the Stonewall Jackson tablet, erected 1903, at the Stonewall Jackson Shrine at Guinea. An upright stone, slab, tablet or plaque set on a stone base.

Fig. 0.3. A Virginia courthouse soldier standing on Main Street at the Pearisburg courthouse, dedicated July 3, 1909: a private soldier, in bronze, standing at parade rest surmounting a granite shaft, dado, and base.

Fig. 0.4. The Norfolk column at Commercial Place, dedicated May 16, 1907, of granite and bronze by Couper Marble Works: granite plinth, base, dado, and column surmounted by Confederate private soldier, in bronze, standing with flag, bearing a sword.

Fig. 0.5. A plaque: in bronze on the Sutherlin Mansion at Danville, circa 1920s. Example of a monument on a tablet of bronze, marble or granite set on a wall.

Nearly two hundred sculptures of private or common soldiers stand atop monuments in Virginia. Historian Wayne Craven asserts that this idealization of the "ordinary soldier" is a distinctively American phenomenon. Craven writes that "Prior to the Civil War it was the custom to erect monuments of officers only—to the generals, admirals, colonels and so on." Civil War monument practices were different: at "battlefields, in the town parks and public squares throughout the nation, there arose memorials to the common soldier or to his regiment which had fought so bravely."

Who he was and what he fought for would be defined and redefined from decade to decade, but the soldier's appearance was fairly consistent. He was usually armed but never bellicose. He was common in the best sense: unexceptional, unbowed, vigilant, and thoughtful. Ironically the archetypal figure may have originated in the north. Two possibilities have been argued for: the earliest was an 1867 sculpture of an infantryman leaning on his rifle—a lifelike, relaxed figure by Martin Milmore. Milmore's sculpture, which stands at Forest Hills Cemetery, Massachusetts, has neoclassical origins in Roman genre sculpture from 60 to 30 B.C. The other possibility is the U.S. Soldier Monument at Antietam National Cemetery, a granite soldier standing at parade rest atop a pedestal. That design was adopted on September 16, 1867, and proved to be an archetype: the soldier stands with one foot forward, the butt of his rifle between his feet, hands grasping the muzzle, left over right, and the coat's hood draped across his shoulders like a cape.

A related facet was their manufacture: the making of monuments became an industry in the postwar era. Only four companies made statuary in the United States before the Civil War; in 1915 there were sixty-three. Standard models evolved, but individual community distinctions were preserved. These statues were individually made, usually employing a standard model that was modified to suit a sponsoring organization's specifications. Many were manufactured in the north: the Monumental Bronze Company of Connecticut produced the soldiers at Hillsville, Tazewell, Floyd, Fredericksburg, Portsmouth, Chester, Manassas, and Suffolk: a "white bronze" soldier—zinc really—at parade rest. (The medium is called white bronze but is actually pure zinc. White bronze fell from fashion shortly after its introduction and has not been used for over eighty years.) Thomas Delahunty produced the Virginia obelisk and the unknown soldiers' monument at Stonewall Cemetery, Winchester. Southern manufacturers included the McNeel Marble Company of Marietta, Georgia, the Muldoon Company of Louisville, Kentucky, and the J. H. Brown Company of Richmond.

Many communities contracted with sculptors for statues. Some were local artisans; others had national or international reputations. Among those with one or more commissions were Herbert Barbee, Solon H. Borglum, Caspar Buberl, William L. Couper, Moses J. Ezekiel, Frederick Moynihan, Frederick W. Sievers, William L. Sheppard, and Edward V. Valentine.

Ceremonies

Dedication ceremonies concluded a process that sometimes extended for decades. Fundraising initiatives included bazaars, ice cream socials, fairs, concerts, dinners, and sales of various mementoes. These affairs raised thousands of dollars at a time of acute economic hardship in the South. Monuments ranged in cost: from a shaft or plaque at a few hundred dollars, to common soldiers monuments costing from one to eight thousand dollars, up to one hundred thousand dollars for the Lee monument in Richmond.

Attendance at the ceremonies was often enormous. Crowds estimated in the hundreds of thousands gathered for the Lee and Davis monument dedications in Richmond around the turn of the twentieth century. On the other hand, there was no ceremony at all for others, such as the Texas Brigade monument on the Wilderness battlefield in 1964. Most common were small town gatherings, which were so popular that they often represented the largest peacetime assemblies to this day. Reports on the ceremonies were published in *Confederate Veteran,* the *Southern Historical Society Papers,* local newspapers, and pamphlets. The

ceremonies included a parade or procession, with the participants including soldiers and veterans groups, politicians, women's groups, children, and bands. The town was decorated with banners. The "Programme" for the Louisiana Monument at Stonewall Cemetery in Winchester, dedicated July 4, 1896, is typical:

> *Procession*
> *Music*
> *Address of welcome*
> *Prayer*
> *Presentation of monument*
> *Unveiling of monument by Miss Virginia Nicholls*
> *Poem*
> *Oration*
> *Delivery of Monument*
> *Benediction*

Dedication speeches were highly anticipated and were often published and sold in pamphlets as part of the fundraising process. The Southern Historical Society published some in their entirety. Newspapers covered them, and excerpts appeared in *Confederate Veteran.*

Conversely, once a monument was erected and the ceremonies were over, little public mention was made of them thereafter. They took their place in the community, as it were, and, barring accident, dislocation, relocation, or repair, they have remained a part of their community to this day.

The role that women have played in the monument movement cannot be overlooked. They were fundamental to its vigor and success. Many chapters of the Ladies Memorial Association—in many cases an extension of women's wartime relief societies—took the initiative in organizing committees and identifying, collecting, and burying the dead. The United Daughters of the Confederacy, founded in 1895, continued in and expanded that role. Women initiated and sustained the fundraising for most monument projects—often for decades until completion—and they organized the cleanup of cemeteries, set dates for decorating graves, and collected and distributed flowers. Women's groups eventually controlled virtually all aspects of the process: conception, initiation, fundraising, monument design, and dedication ceremonies. They blended strains of solemnity and festivity, restraint and extravagance in doing so. Of extravagant sentiment it is worth noting that several monuments had a prominent place for the poetry of Father Abram Ryan (1838–1886), a Roman Catholic priest known as the "Poet Priest of the Lost Cause." That a Catholic priest and prelate (as well as a Confederate veteran who lost a brother in the war) was so highly regarded in a predominantly Protestant land is surprising. Ryan, however, evidently struck a chord in the Protestant South, as did other postwar poets such as Father John Bannister Tabb (1845–1909). There was something worshipful, meditative, exalting, and ultimately quasi-religious about the movement, so much so that the scale, ornamentation, and effusive rhetoric that was wanted could perhaps only be met by the kind of theatrical rhetoric and iconography of Roman Catholic traditions, as opposed to the relatively spare and restrained Protestantism of Virginian religious traditions. Further, in the soldier there is something of an American Eucharist: the ceremony of dedication was a veritable anointing, a bonding of the past with the present.

Slavery

There is no explicit mention of slavery in Virginia monuments. Arguably, a racial dominance is a principle theme, and the fact is that self-rule left much of the political leadership in charge that would have led an independent Confederacy. The dedication address at the Millwood Cemetery monument by Col. Richard Henry Lee is typical in denouncing those who claimed that slavery was a cause to fight for.

> It is stated in books and papers [that Southerners fought] to preserve human slavery, and that their defeat was necessary for free government and the welfare of the human family . . . As a Confederate soldier and as a citizen of Virginia I deny the charge, and denounce it as a calumny. We were not rebels; we did not fight to perpetuate human slavery,

but for our rights and privileges under a government established over us by our fathers and in defenses of our homes.

Historian Kirk Savage concludes that this rhetoric reflects the idealization of a "normative white body, a 'race' of white men." There is truth in Savage's assertions, although neither Northern nor Southern monuments made an issue of slavery, and the charge may be laid against the sponsors of Northern monuments as much as the sponsors of Southern monuments. In Virginia that racial dominance was not unchallenged: two African American soldiers appear on Virginia monuments. Moses Ezekiel's Confederate monument at Arlington Cemetery displays a frieze of life-sized figures of mythical gods together with Southern soldiers and civilians, among them a Black Confederate soldier. Norfolk's West Point Cemetery of Elmwood Cemetery has the only tribute to Union soldiers erected by Southerners in Virginia, and the only monument to Black Civil War troops in Virginia. These men, as the inscription declares, are "Our Heroes 1861–1865."

The Eastville courthouse monument (1913) praises the "Soldiers of the Confederacy" who "Died Bravely In War, or In Peace Lived Nobly to Rehabilitate Their Country." The use of monuments as a means of interpreting the postwar era, implicit elsewhere, is explicit here: for several decades the wartime generation set the course of reconstruction, dominating the South's economic, political, and social life The achievements and shortcomings of the reconstruction generation are many, and well beyond the scope of this text, but they include the failure of reconstruction to fully emancipate Southern Blacks. "The Yankees helped free us, so they say," an eighty-one-year-old former slave concluded, "but they let us be put back in slavery again."

Parameters

Included in this study are outdoor courthouse and town monuments, cemetery and city monuments, and battlefield monuments or markers. Due diligence was done to document every site, but this study may have inadvertently overlooked monuments. Corrections or additions are welcome.

I made some deliberate exclusions, such as the state historical highway markers (described in John S. Salmon's *Guidebook to Virginia's Historical Markers*), the Jefferson Davis Highway markers, the Virginia Civil War Trails markers, and the Civil War Preservation Trust's battlefield narratives. I excluded tributes to Union soldiers, although there are several of these. I did not include tributes to war horses, although their service and deaths are commemorated at several sites. I excluded some plaques, including sixty-two cast iron markers describing the campaigns around Richmond, which are essentially narrative guides.

The largest deliberate exclusion is tombstones, a study that could run to volumes. As tempting as it was to include the Lee Chapel, the Davis or Stuart tombstones at Hollywood, or the Sally Tompkins tribute at Mathews, I did not deem it fair to exclude others—by the thousands—who were equally worthy of attention by dint of service or sacrifice. I admit to some arbitrariness: I included public shrines, as it were, where two generals are interred, so the A. P. Hill statue in Richmond and the Jackson statue at Lexington are included. This study also precludes comprehensive detailing. Sculptures of tree stumps, symbolizing the brevity of life, are common features but are not included, and laurel leaf wreaths—which represent victory, distinction, eternity, or immortality—are not always noted either.

At any rate, I undertook a broad portrait: I looked at this subject in terms of distinctive and typical monuments, unusual and typical inscriptions, and background history. Of the last, the record is strikingly lacking in depth and breadth. As prominent and venerable as the monuments are, much of the history behind them is incomplete, undocumented, or missing. Virginia is not unique: studies of other states' monuments have found the same unevenness. Many women's or veterans' committee records have disappeared, although there is no knowing what remains undiscovered in some Virginia attic or basement somewhere. It may be that committee minutes, correspondence, and contracts were simply not thought to be relevant once a monument was completed. The records are uneven: other monuments are amply documented and fill in gaps of understanding for the ways in which undocumented monuments came to be. Larger cities are apt to have better records. There are four boxes—168 files and three bound volumes of materials—on Richmond's Soldiers and Sailors memorial in the archives of the Museum of the Confederacy, and the Monument Avenue sculptures are amply documented as well. Similarly, although the Hanover courthouse monument archives are extensive and were easily found in the local library, the Bowling Green monument, in the adjacent county, held virtually no documentation, not even the records that the monument inscription assures the viewer are in the archives. Regardless of what I found or what remains undiscovered, the central thread of this subject, I will argue, is the rhetoric: the words communities chose to inscribe on their monuments.

Disclaimer: For the record this author has Southern roots but a Northern upbringing. I am aware that the history behind these monuments is sometimes contentious and provocative. If slavery was a principal cause of the war, it is also true that many men and women, North and South, were simply caught up in events over which they had very limited control, and that there were as many motivations to fight on one side or another as there are monuments in Virginia—ranging from the personal to the altruistic and from the noblest to the basest. That so many monuments claim that the cause of the South was just is not surprising to me: I do not see what alternative is available. Silence, one might suppose, euphemism as a rule, abstraction as a necessity, darkness if you will. Of the latter there is plenty. Time constraints meant that much of my fieldwork exceeded the light in the day and carried into the night. It was then that I was most aware of the import of the mute testimony left to us in carved stone. I realized how enduring, majestic and yet majestically insufficient these monuments are to tell the story of what happened to the generation that lived through the war.

Union officer Charles S. Wainwright recognized early on that the war would be clouded with a host of errant or self-serving interpretations. By 1864, he wrote that the "objects of the war" had completely changed: "the real question of the salvation of the Union ha[s] been so completely overlaid by the insurance of a continuation in power of the Republican party that it is only by digging deep down that I can find the object for which I alone am fighting." He summarized the matter best when he wrote that the "Almighty alone knows what will be the real issue to the country of this contest."

Three final notes:

- Many if not most of these monuments are on public property or in cemeteries with public access, but not all of them. If you go, private property should be respected at all events.
- GPS coordinates have greatly simplified the challenge of finding the monuments described in this book but have not eliminated it. Excellent maps are available and continue to ease the process of locating sites. So, too, is a willing companion, someone to serve as a spotter while the other drives or vice versa, and someone to share the landscape of this history with.
- A list of works consulted in the preparation of this book is available on the Southern Illinois University Press Website, www.siupress.com.

Notes

1. As a matter of convention, I will use the term American Civil War to describe the events of 1861–1865, although the War between the States or other descriptions may be more accurate or preferred and the official term for the conflict is the War of the Rebellion. "Civil War" is rarely used on Virginia monuments, but it reflects common contemporary usage. I will also use the term Confederate monuments or soldiers broadly, although some monument inscriptions deliberately avoid the use of the word.

2. I will use the term inscription to apply to all monument texts—a broader definition than simply engraved texts. Monument texts were also placed in raised lettering, bas-relief, or high relief.

1. The Shenandoah Valley and Northwest Virginia

Geographical Outline. Eleven counties, cities such as Covington, Harrisonburg, Lexington, Staunton, Waynesboro, Winchester: the Shenandoah Valley and far west counties, from Winchester in Frederick County and the West Virginia state line in the north, to Lexington and the James River to the south; from the Blue Ridge Mountains to the east to the West Virginia state line in the west.

Campaigns. Several campaigns took place here, including Maj. Gen. Thomas J. "Stonewall" Jackson's Valley campaign of 1862, with battles and monuments at Winchester, Kernstown, McDowell, Harrisonburg, Port Republic, Cross

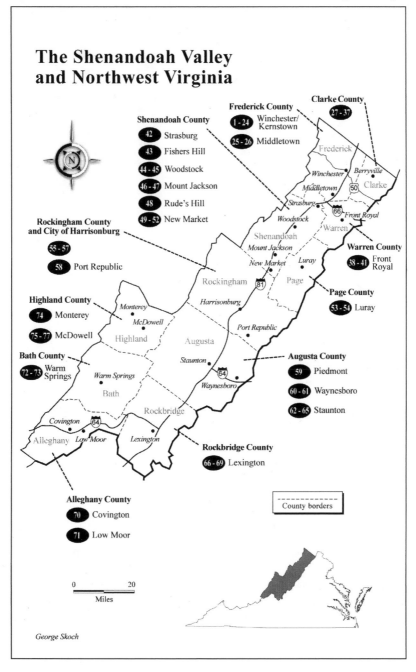

The Shenandoah Valley and Northwest Virginia

Frederick County
- 1 - 24 Winchester/Kernstown
- 25 - 26 Middletown

Clarke County
- 27 - 37

Shenandoah County
- 42 Strasburg
- 43 Fishers Hill
- 44 - 45 Woodstock
- 46 - 47 Mount Jackson
- 48 Rude's Hill
- 49 - 52 New Market

Rockingham County and City of Harrisonburg
- 55 - 57
- 58 Port Republic

Warren County
- 38 - 41 Front Royal

Highland County
- 74 Monterey
- 75 - 77 McDowell

Page County
- 53 - 54 Luray

Bath County
- 72 - 73 Warm Springs

Augusta County
- 59 Piedmont
- 60 - 61 Waynesboro
- 62 - 65 Staunton

Rockbridge County
- 66 - 69 Lexington

Alleghany County
- 70 Covington
- 71 Low Moor

County borders

0   20
Miles

George Skoch

Keys, and Front Royal. The Gettysburg Campaign of 1863 is commemorated with a monument for the battle of Second Winchester. The Valley campaigns of 1864–65 are commemorated with monuments for the battles of Piedmont, New Market, Third Winchester, Second Kernstown, Tom's Brook, Cedar Creek, Cool Spring, Berryville, Fishers Hill, and Waynesboro.

Terrain. The Shenandoah Valley (also called the Valley of Virginia) extends from Winchester to Lexington and is flanked by the Blue Ridge to the east and the Allegheny Mountains to the west. The "Valley" ascends from northeast to southwest; the two forks of the Shenandoah meet at Front Royal and flow north to meet the Potomac River at Harpers Ferry, West Virginia. (In local vernacular, to travel north is to travel "down the Valley"; to travel south is to travel "up the Valley," because the Shenandoah flows south to north.) Massanutten Mountain divides the Luray Valley and the South Fork of the Shenandoah River from the North Fork between Harrisonburg and Front Royal.

Farming gave the Valley strategic significance during the war. The Valley Pike (now U.S. 11) was completed in 1840 and facilitated transportation of the Valley's agricultural output. The Valley also served as an avenue of invasion to the North in 1862, 1863, and 1864.

Commentary. Much of northwest Virginia is visually striking. There "may be lovelier country somewhere," historian Bruce Catton writes, "the Island Vale of Avalon, at a gamble—but when the sunlight lies upon it and the wind puts white clouds racing their shadows the Shenandoah Valley is as good as anything America can show." However, over one hundred military engagements took place in the Valley during the war years. The legacy of the war is evident in the conflicting ways in which it is remembered. About three thousand Confederate soldiers are buried in Stonewall Cemetery in Winchester, for example; more than four thousand Union soldiers are buried across the street, in the national cemetery.

Several collecting points in the Valley served as Confederate hospitals. Cemeteries near some of these sites stand at Winchester, Harrisonburg,

Front Royal, Staunton, Lexington, Waynesboro, Strasburg, Mount Jackson, and New Market. Every county has a Confederate monument. Clifton Forge is the only county seat without a Confederate memorial.

Frederick County and Winchester
Winchester
1. Common Soldier, Winchester Courthouse

Monument is a private soldier, in bronze, surmounting a granite pedestal.
LOCATION: 20 North Loudoun Street, 22601
DATE: November 15, 1916
MEDIA: Bronze, granite
Front

IN LASTING MEMORY

OF

EVERY CONFEDERATE SOLDIER

FROM

WINCHESTER AND FREDERICK COUNTY

WHO FAITHFULLY SERVED THE SOUTH

—

1861–1865

Winchester and the surrounding area were heavily contested during the war. Three major battles were fought at Winchester, along with numerous skirmishes, and the town is said to have changed hands seventy-two times during the course of the war. Loyalties were divided among the residents, and Union forces occupied Winchester during much of the conflict, but this is the northernmost courthouse monument to a Confederate soldier in the United States.

The soldier stands in front of the courthouse, facing west. He is described as an infantryman departing for war with firm, mature resolution: a "Heroic figure in bronze of a Confederate soldier, fully armed and equipped, stand[ing] on a base of polished granite."

- The Winchester courthouse, a Greek revival structure erected in 1840, is now a Civil War museum. It served as a prison and hospital during the war.

2. First Winchester, Battlefield Tablet

Monument is a bronze plaque set between two posts.

LOCATION: 1835 Valley Avenue, 22601 (corner of Jubal Early and Valley Avenue)
DATE: circa 1927
MEDIUM: Bronze

FIRST BATTLE OF WINCHESTER
MAY 25, 1862 BETWEEN
CONFEDERATES UNDER
BRIG. GEN. T. J. "STONEWALL"
JACKSON AND THE FEDERALS
UNDER MAJ. GEN. N. P. BANKS
BEGAN JUST SOUTH OF THIS
SITE. THE FEDERALS WERE
DRIVEN IN RETREAT
THROUGH WINCHESTER'S STREETS WITH
LOSS OF STORES AND MANY PRISONERS.
CONFEDERATES ENGAGED,
16,000, CASUALTIES 400.
FEDERALS ENGAGED, 8,000. CASUALTIES 2017.

Tactical and moral consequences dominate this triumphant narrative. Maj. Gen. Nathaniel

P. Banks's retreating army of about sixty-five hundred men—not the eight thousand that the inscription claims—was driven north along the Valley Pike. They skirmished at Middletown and Newtown on May 24, then were attacked, outflanked, and thoroughly defeated on the south end of Winchester on May 25, by some sixteen thousand troops under the command of Maj. Gen. Thomas J. "Stonewall" Jackson. As a result, the Union Army's ambitions for a drive on Richmond were disrupted, and thousands of troops were diverted to the Shenandoah and the defense of Washington, D.C.

- Jackson is misidentified as a brigadier general. He was promoted to major general October 7, 1861.

3. Second Winchester, Battlefield Tablet

Monument is a bronze tablet set on a fieldstone base.

LOCATION: Northeast corner of East Boscawen and North Cameron streets, 22601
MEDIA: Bronze, fieldstone

SECOND BATTLE OF WINCHESTER
JUNE 13–15, 1863 TOOK PLACE
DURING GEN. LEE'S
ADVANCE TO GETTYSBURG
BETWEEN CONFEDERATES
UNDER GEN. EWELL AND FEDERALS UNDER
GEN. MILROY. THE FEDERALS
OCCUPIED POSITIONS
ON THE HILLS NORTH AND
WEST OF WINCHESTER
NOW CALLED MILROYS [SIC] AND
STAR FORTS FROM WHICH
THEY RETREATED AND A LARGE
PART OF THEIR ARMY
MADE PRISONERS BY THE CONFEDERATES.

Evidently a replacement marker, Second Winchester is described in more momentous terms than its First Winchester counterpart. Maj. Gen. Richard S. Ewell's Second Corps, Army of Northern Virginia, defeated, routed, and nearly destroyed a Federal division under Maj. Gen. Robert Milroy. The action continued north of Winchester, where the Snowden Andrews marker stands.

The larger purpose—Lee's advance during the invasion of the North—is noted, and the Federals seem less inclined to retreat: they occupy positions—Star Fort and Milroy—whose works are still extant. Gettysburg is mentioned. Although the Union Army is described as retreating and the Confederates are again victorious, there is nothing of the lark associated with First Winchester, and the forts remain as scars and reminders of the war to this day.

4. Lt. Col. Richard Snowden Andrews, 1st Maryland Artillery

Monument is a bronze plaque inset on a boulder.
LOCATION: 2732 Martinsburg Pike, Stephenson 22656 (U.S. 11, grounds of Emmanuel United Methodist Church)
DATE: December 4, 1920
MEDIA: Bronze, granite

LIEUT COL RICHARD SNOWDEN ANDREWS
STEPHEN'S DEPOT JUNE 15TH 1863
ANDREWS ARTILLERY BATTALION
1ST MARYLAND BATTERY LIEUT C S CONTEE
[26 NAMES]
[ARTIST'S SIGNATURE]
"I REGARD THIS AS THE
THERMOPYLAE OF MY CAMPAIGN"
GEN R. E. LEE

In the climactic episode of the battle of Second Winchester, troops under Maj. Gen. Edward Johnson blocked the line of retreat of defeated, retreating Union troops under Brig. Gen. Robert H. Milroy. The Confederates stood here, by night, astride the Valley Pike (present day U.S. 11) and the railroad. Milroy attacked; a vicious night action ensued. Two guns of the battery were placed within range of the Union muskets, but the gunners maintained their position until most of them were killed or wounded. Lt. Col. Richard S. Andrews was among the officers wounded. Lieut. C. S. Contee was shot in both legs. Most of the Union force of about twenty-five hundred men was killed, wounded, or taken prisoner. Milroy and about two hundred cavalry escaped. The bronze relief depicts the battery in action, along with a portrait bust of Andrews, whose family sponsored the monument. From here, the Army of Northern Virginia advanced into Pennsylvania, where it later was defeated at Gettysburg.

- The area, site of the surrender of Union troops, is a particularly well-preserved part of the Second Winchester battlefield.

Stonewall Cemetery at Mt. Hebron Cemetery
SITE: Stonewall Cemetery at Mt. Hebron Cemetery
LOCATION: 305 East Boscawen Street, 22601

5. Entry Stone with Plaque
Monument is a bronze plaque set on a boulder.
LOCATION: Southwest corner of grounds
DATE: October 25, 1888
MEDIA: Bronze, granite

STONEWALL CEMETERY
3000 CONFEDERATE
SOLDIERS REST HERE
DEDICATED 1866

Stonewall may be the oldest dedicated postwar Confederate cemetery. The first memorial services were held on June 6, 1865. June 6 was chosen in remembrance of Brig. Gen. Turner Ashby's death on June 6, 1862, and would set a pattern for dedication dates at Stonewall Cemetery over the next hundred and fifty years.

Monuments from the states of South Carolina, North Carolina, Virginia and Georgia are in the first row; Alabama, Maryland, Tennessee, Louisiana, Florida, and Mississippi monuments flank the Unknown Soldier monument in the following rows. Individual tombstones from Arkansas (twenty), Kentucky (three) and Delaware (one) are also set apart, although at this writing no presiding state monument marks them.

In its comparatively small confines, Stonewall Cemetery is more extravagant in monumentation than the much larger and better known Confederate cemeteries at Hollywood, Oakwood, or Blandford. Indeed, the density of monuments here may be greater than any other Confederate cemetery.

- Work began on collecting the dead in the summer or fall of 1865. Records indicate that the remains of each soldier were placed in a separate coffin, and each soldier was placed in a separate grave. Many of the dead were taken from outside Winchester, some from the battlefields at Berryville and Cool Spring in Clarke County.

By one count there were 2,494 in all. On October 25, 1866, eighteen months after the close of the war, the work of removal was completed, and "Stonewall Cemetery" was formally dedicated.
- Winchester National Cemetery, established for Union soldiers, is across the street.
- Confederate generals buried here include Turner Ashby, Archibald C. Godwin, Robert D. Johnston, and John G. Walker. Over 250 other Confederate dead are buried outside Stonewall Cemetery in the larger, surrounding cemetery grounds of Mt. Hebron.

6. South Carolina Obelisk

Monument is a marble obelisk surmounting a granite base and marble plinth and dado.
DATE: June 6, 1899
MEDIA: Granite, marble
Front

[SOUTH CAROLINA SEAL]
SOUTH CAROLINA

—

"LORD GOD OF HOSTS, BE WITH US YET,
LEST WE FORGET—LEST WE FORGET!"

—

THO' LOST IT BE TO MEN,
IT LIVES WITH GOD AGAIN.

—

IN MEMORY OF THE 149
CONFEDERATE DEAD OF
SOUTH CAROLINA.
ALBIN & NAU

South Carolina commemorates 149 soldiers here, although 150 are listed by the local United Daughters of the Confederacy roster. These are described as "Confederate Dead," like the men given tribute on the adjacent North Carolina monument, but in contrast to other state monuments whose dead are cited as dying in defense of their state.

- The excerpt, "Tho' Lost it Be to Men . . ." is taken from a poem by Edward R. Miles, "Lines for Memorial Day, 1871." The poem was published on the occasion of the reinterment of the South Carolina dead from the Battle of Gettysburg.
- The excerpt "Lest We Forget . . ." is taken from Rudyard Kipling's poem "Recessional," first published in 1897, appears on numerous monuments in Virginia.

7. North Carolina Obelisk

Monument is a granite obelisk surmounting a base, plinth, and dado.
DATE: June 6, 1900
MEDIUM: Granite

-N-C-
CONFEDERATE
DEAD

This is arguably the most restrained inscription in Virginia. Note the omissions: there is no mention of 1861–1865, and North Carolina is not even spelled out. The monument stands in a field of 452 graves of soldiers from North Carolina, but no numbers are specified, unlike the nearby South Carolina, Virginia, or Georgia monuments.

The dedication ceremonies struck a different tone. The Reverend James Battle Avirett gave the oration at the laying of the foundation stone on September 17, 1897 (the thirty-fifth anniversary of the battle of Sharpsburg). Avirett—author of a biography of Confederate cavalryman Turner Ashby and a chaplain in Ashby's command—offered a vigorous defense of the Lost Cause, twice making the claim that the Lost Cause was not lost: "Lost Cause! Lost Cause!! Lost Cause!!!" he declared. "If lost, 'twas false—if true, it is not lost." Avirett also took the occasion to claim that the war was nearly won on several occasions:

It is true, aye sadly, tearfully true, dear friends, that the Southern cross shone out with great brilliancy again and again amid the dark clouds of internecine strife. It well nigh breaks the heart to fully realize that so near came we more than once to the very brink of the chasm separating us from the fields of nationality that we inhaled the aroma of the flowers blooming therein, but we could not cross to gather them.

Most provocative, perhaps, was Avirett's defense of slavery, which, he maintained, was biblically warranted and praiseworthy:

Let the world say what it pleases about the institution of slavery, provided for and fully warranted under both Testaments of the Word of God, as well as under the Constitution. Under its peculiarly patriarchal influences—in the War of 1812, in the conflict with Mexico, and in the war between the States, there has been a type of heroism ... which ... challenges the admiration of the world and has won for the South, in dispassionate military circles, the plaudits of marshalled immortality.

These issues are apparently beyond consideration to the elegists. The focus of the inscription is on the loss and the bereaved rather than the reason for the loss, or how the loss might have been mitigated, warranted, justified, avoided, or vindicated.

8. Virginia Obelisk

Monument is a marble obelisk surmounting a funereal urn, the whole standing on a base, plinth, and dado.
DATE: June 6, 1879
MEDIA: Marble, granite
Front

> [SWORD, HIGH RELIEF]
> [SEAL OF VIRGINIA]
> VIRGINIA
> —
> IN MEMORY OF
> THE 398 VIRGINIA SOLDIERS,
> LYING IN THIS CEMETERY,
> WHO FELL IN DEFENCE OF
> CONSTITUTIONAL LIBERTY AND
> THE SOVEREIGNTY OF THEIR STATE,

> FROM 1861 TO 1865. A. D.
> —
> DULCE ET DECORUM EST PRO PATRIA MORI.
> —
> ERECTED BY
> THE LADIES OF THE VIRGINIA
> SHAFT ASSOCIATION OF WINCHESTER,
> JUNE 6TH, 1879.

Several claims appear on this obelisk in the front row of Stonewall Cemetery. Virginia's soldiers—the Confederacy is not mentioned—fell in defense of "Constitutional Liberty" and the "Sovereignty of This State." Like other monuments in Virginia, there is no indication that the defense was not successful. For a contrasting thesis, see the Georgia monument in the adjoining lot. Erected at a cost of fifteen hundred dollars, the shaft is the work of Thomas Delahunty of Philadelphia. His work on the Monument to the Unknown stands nearby.

- The monument is inscribed to 398 Virginians, but the total number of Virginians believed to be interred here is 447, including the Virginia lot addition and other plots.
- The dedication date, June 6, 1879, is the same date as the Monument to the Unknown, which in turn commemorates the death of Brig. Gen. Turner Ashby on June 6, 1862. Ashby is buried here, along with his brother Capt. Richard Ashby. Close by are the Patton brothers, colonels George and Tazewell Patton, whose descendent, Lt. Gen. George S. Patton, would earn a place in history during World War II.

9. Winchester Women Tablet
Monument is a black granite shaft with multicolored images.

LOCATION: Virginia section
DATE: June 6, 1999
MEDIUM: Granite

In Honor
Of
The Women of Winchester
The Ladies Confederate Memorial Association
Organized in 1865
And
Turner Ashby Chapter #184
United Daughters of the Confederacy
Organized 1897
For Five Generations They Have
Cherished the Memory of the
Soldiers Who Lie in The
Stonewall Cemetery
"Love Makes Memory Eternal"
Dedicated June 6, 1999

This women's tribute reflects a late twentieth century trend in tombstones, though not monuments: the use of black granite and colored images. Three images are presented: Stonewall Jackson stands with his horse Little Sorrel, Robert E. Lee stands with Traveler, and they hover, as it were, over a tableau of women in nineteenth-century garb gathered on the grounds of the cemetery.

10. Unknown Virginians Tablet
LOCATION: Virginia section
DATE: June 6, 1967
MEDIUM: Granite

IN MEMORY OF
THE TWENTY CONFEDERATE SOLDIERS
BURIED IN STONEWALL CEMETERY,
WHOSE GRAVES ARE UNMARKED.
ERECTED BY TURNER ASHBY
CHAPTER, NO. 54,
UNITED DAUGHTERS OF THE CONFEDERACY
JUNE 6, 1967

A supplement to the 1879 monument, this marker gives substance and an affecting thoroughness to the U.D.C.'s commemoration of men whose graves cannot be found. Even in 1967—one hundred years after the war—efforts continued to document or remember or find the remains of those who fought.

11. Georgia Obelisk

Monument is a granite obelisk surmounting a base, plinth, and dado.

DATE: June 4, 1884
MEDIUM: Granite
Front

> ERECTED A. D. 1884,
> BY THE PEOPLE OF GEORGIA
> TO 290 OF HER SONS WHO
> LIE IN THIS CEMETERY.
> GEORGIA
> —
> GO, STRANGER, AND TELL IT
> IN GEORGIA, THAT WE DIED HERE
> IN OBEDIENCE TO HER LAWS.
> 1861–1865.
> —
> "WHEN DUTY CALLED, THEY CAME
> WHEN COUNTRY CALLED, THEY DIED."
> —
> "THE BRAVE
> DIE NEVER, BEING DEATHLESS, THEY
> BUT CHANGE THEIR COUNTRY'S ARMS
> FOR MORE—THEIR COUNTRY'S HEART."

The only obelisk in Virginia from Georgia has a particularly acidic accusation at its climax. Sides one—"Erected 1884"—and four—"'The Brave Die Never . . .'"—have the themes and sentiments of late funereal-era monuments. The third side is also sentimental in tone: "When Duty Called They Came When Country Called They Died." The declaration facing south, "Go, Stranger . . ."demands that the beholder go to Georgia to declare that these 290 sons of Georgia are still here. Moreover, it declares that "We Died Here" and that "we" are still in service "to her laws."

- One woman is buried here. Clelia Dau, wife of Lt. Col. B. Edward Stiles, was interred beside her husband in 1887, twenty-two years after his death, in action at Front Royal in 1864.
- The phrases on sides three and four are similar to inscriptions on the Georgia monuments at Gettysburg (1961) and Sharpsburg (1961), though without the implied accusation at this site. The Gettysburg and Sharpsburg monuments each read: "We Sleep Here in Obedience to Law. When Duty Called, We Came. When Country Called, We Died."

12. Alabama Tablet

Monument is a granite shaft set on a base.

DATE: June 6, 1997
MEDIUM: Granite
Front

> [U.D.C. SEAL]
> ALABAMA
> ROSTER OF HER FALLEN HEROES
> [36 NAMES, TWO COLUMNS]
> CONFEDERACY
> —
> UNITED
> —
> [35 NAMES IN TWO COLUMNS,
> INCLUDING ONE LISTED AS UNKNOWN]
> IN MEMORY OF
> ALABAMAS CONFEDERATE SONS
> DEO VINDICE
> DAUGHTERS
> —
> OF THE

The Alabama plot has seventy-one graves for its "Confederate sons." The 1997 granite shaft is the largest monument from Alabama in Virginia and was sponsored by the Alabama Division of the United Daughters of the Confederacy. It was erected at the prompting of a twelve-year-old girl from Alabama, who had noticed the absence of a monument to Alabama soldiers buried at Winchester.

- The wraparound inscription reads "United Daughters of the Confederacy."

13. Florida Obelisk

Monument is a granite obelisk surmounting a base, plinth, and dado.

DATE: June 6, 1902
MEDIUM: Granite
Front

CSA

1861–1865

FLORIDA

—

THEIR NAMES SHALL NE'ER
FORGOTTEN BE WHILE HONOR
CALLS THE ROLL.

—

[BLANK]

—

FLORIDA'S DAUGHTERS
TO HER BRAVE SONS.

This is the only obelisk from the state of Florida in Virginia. The monument was dedicated in 1902, but a funereal-era affection is apparent in the tribute from Florida's "Daughters to her Brave Sons" that the "Names shall ne'er Forgotten Be."

As is the case with many sites, extant records are incomplete and almost certainly inaccurate: a United Daughters of the Confederacy booklet on Stonewall Cemetery, written in 1962, lists thirty-eight names in the Florida section, representing the 2nd, 3rd, 5th, 8th Florida Infantry, and, in one case, the 20th Florida—although no 20th Florida is listed in any Army of Northern Virginia orders of battle.

14. Maryland Common Soldier

Monument is a marble sculpture of a private soldier standing at parade rest, surmounting a base and shaft.

DATE: June 6, 1880
MEDIUM: Marble
Front

John O'Brian
Sculptor

[MARYLAND SEAL]
[FATTI MASCHII PAROLE FEMINE]
TO
THE MEMORY OF
HER SONS

WHO FELL ON
VIRGINIA'S SOIL
MARYLAND
—

UNHERALDED
UNORGANIZED
UNARMED
THEY CAME FOR
CONSCIENCE SAKE [*SIC*]
AND DIED FOR RIGHT
J. WENMAN & SONS.
BALTIMORE, MD.
—

ALIKE IN BLOOD,
ALIKE IN FAITH;
THEY SLEEP ALIKE
THE LAST SLEEP
OF THE
BRAVE.
—

MANASSAS
1861.
APPOMATTOX
1865.

Fifteen graves mark the Maryland lot, which is dominated by what Emerson's 1911 *Historic Southern Monuments* calls "a superb structure, capped with a statue of a private soldier, by O'Brien, that cost $2,500." The monument is apparently secondhand: the "statue was made on an order that failed and the work was procured at a small percentage of its value."

Maryland was a border state that recognized slavery but did not secede from the Union. The claim that Maryland's Confederate soldiers "Died for Right" is common in Southern monuments. However, more emphasis is given to the Maryland Confederates as iconoclasts among their Southern secessionist brethren: the Marylanders are "Alike in Blood, Alike in Faith" and those who sleep "the Last Sleep of the Brave."

- The state motto, "Fatti maschii parole femine," is translated "manly deeds, womanly words," or as "strong deeds, gentle words."

- The dedication address by Spencer C. Jones, a Confederate veteran and Maryland attorney and politician, took particular note of the inscription:

The monument this day unveiled tells in its inscription tersely, but truly and eloquently, the story of the gallant dead whom we commemorate.

Let us, their surviving comrades, as we leave this place to resume the duties of our diverse careers, as incitement to "the high purpose and the firm resolve," and ever proudly remembering that we are their living representatives, bear with us, inscribed on our hearts, the epitaph of our fallen heroes engraven on their tomb: "Unheralded, unorganized, unarmed. They came for conscience sake and died for right."

15. Mississippi Tablet

Monument is a bronze plaque inset on a local limestone boulder, the whole standing on a granite base.

DATE: June 6, 1998
MEDIA: Bronze, local limestone

MISSISSIPPI
In a tangle of willows without light
The singular screech-owl's tight
Invisible lyric seeds the mind
With the furious murmur of their chivalry

Ode to the Confederate Dead
By Allen Tate
[67 names in four columns,
including two listed as "Unknown"]
DEDICATED JUNE 6, 1998

Sixty-seven soldiers are listed in the Mississippi plot. A letter held in Handley Library, Winchester, dated March 7, 1896, notes that the legislature of the state of Mississippi voted to allocate $231 to purchase headstones for sixty-six soldiers buried here.

"Ode to the Confederate Dead" is an unusual but appropriate choice for a monument inscription erected 133 years after the war's end. The dedication date upholds the century-old Stonewall Cemetery custom of commemorating the date of Turner Ashby's death. Ironically, the excerpt describes a failed effort to come to terms with the presence and sacrifice of the Confederate dead. Allen Tate (1899–1979), a twentieth-century advocate and spokesman for the Southern literary tradition, wrote that the poem is "'about' solipsism . . . a philosophical doctrine which says that we create the world in the act of perceiving it; or about Narcissism, or any other ism that denotes the failure of the human personality to function objectively in nature and society."

16. Louisiana Obelisk
Monument is a granite obelisk surmounting a base, plinth, and dado.
DATE: July 4, 1896
MEDIA: Bronze, granite
Front

[RELIEF OF C.S.A. NATIONAL FLAG]
[RELIEF OF SEAL OF LOUISIANA]
TO THE
SOLDIERS OF LOUISIANA,
WHO DIED FOR THE SOUTH
IN THE VALLEY CAMPAIGN,
THIS MONUMENT HAS BEEN ERECTED
IN MEMORY OF THEIR NOBLE
DARING AND HEROIC ENDURANCE
IN THEIR COUNTRY'S CAUSE.
LOUISIANA
C.S.A.

MULDOON MONT. CO.
LOUISVILLE KY.

—

SLEEP IN PEACE WITH KINDRED ASHES
OF THE NOBLE AND THE TRUE;
HANDS THAT NEVER FAILED THEIR COUNTRY;
HEARTS THAT NEVER BASENESS KNEW.

—

THEY DIED
FOR THE PRINCIPLES
UPON WHICH
ALL TRUE REPUBLICS
ARE FOUNDED.

—

REMEMBER THEIR VALOR,
KEEP HOLY THE SOD!
FOR HONOR TO HEROES
IS GLORY TO GOD!

Seventy gravestones mark the Louisiana lot. The presiding monument—the only obelisk from Louisiana in Virginia—was dedicated

on Independence Day in 1896. The relief of a Confederate national flag is wrapped around the obelisk, with the flag's shaft snapped in two. The bronze relief of a pelican feeding its chicks, from the coat of arms of Louisiana, is displayed in front.

Second-war-of-independence claims are intertwined with an absolution in the inscription. The very soil that wraps these men is sanctified: "Keep Holy the Sod!" The reputation of the Louisiana regiments goes unremarked, but it does them no disservice to mention that they were nicknamed "Tigers," as much for their willingness to fight their fellow Confederates, as to engage in combat with Yankees. Still, high ideals motivated them: "They Died for the Principles Upon which all True Republics are Founded." Death cleanses and purifies: these are "Hearts that Never Baseness Knew."

17. Unknown Confederate Dead, Common Soldier

Monument is a marble sculpture of a private soldier surmounting a base, plinth, dado, and column.
DATE: June 6, 1879
MEDIA: Granite, marble
Front

[SEAL OF THE CONFEDERACY]
TO THE
UNKNOWN AND UNRECORDED
DEAD.
—

[RELIEF OF CROSSED CANNON BARRELS]
ERECTED, A. D. 1879, BY THE
PEOPLE OF THE SOUTH,
TO THE 829 UNKNOWN CONFEDERATE DEAD
WHO LIE BENEATH THIS MOUND;
IN GRATEFUL REMEMBRANCE OF
THEIR HEROIC VIRTUES,
AND THAT THEIR EXAMPLE OF
UNSTINTED DEVOTION
TO DUTY AND COUNTRY MAY
NEVER BE FORGOTTEN.
—

[RELIEF OF TWO TENTS AND
STACKED MUSKETS]
"ON FAME'S ETERNAL CAMPING GROUND

THEIR SILENT TENTS ARE SPREAD;
WHILE GLORY GUARDS WITH SOLEMN ROUND
THIS BIVOUAC OF THE DEAD."
—

[RELIEF OF CROSSED SWORDS AND BUGLE]
WHO THEY WERE, NONE KNOW;
WHAT THEY WERE, ALL KNOW.
T. DELAHUNTY.
LAUREL HILL,
PHILA.

The forty-eight-foot column, surmounted by an aged Confederate soldier, looms over the cemetery and contributes to an atmosphere that is—arguably—as melancholy and evocative as any battlefield or Confederate cemetery in Virginia.

The dedication date, like others here, is the anniversary of Turner Ashby's death. The column, of Italian marble with a base of Richmond granite, was erected at a cost of ten thousand dollars and is said to be the first monument in the world erected to honor unknown war dead, as well as the first Southern soldier monument. This soldier looks older than most of the sculptures erected thereafter: he is aged but unswerving in stance: perpetually in uniform, perpetually in mourning, with rifle held in the arms command that is used for mourning or prayer. Thomas Delahunty is the sculptor and also produced the Virginia monument. The monuments were dedicated on the same day. The *Winchester News* approved of the fact that the monument was made domestically. Although Delahunty was from Philadelphia, the *News* noted that he lost a brother on the Confederate side during the war. Further, it claimed that Delahunty's work was "far superior to any monumental work imported or executed from or in Italy. And as a work of art it will speak for itself and show what Philadelphians can do[,] and Mr. Delahunty is proud to say that no other but home talent has been employed on the work."

The excerpt beginning "On Fame's Eternal Camping . . ." is taken from the first stanza of "The Bivouac of the Dead," by Theodore O'Hara, a Southerner who fought on the Confederate side in the war. The poem extends to nine stanzas, dates from 1847, and was written in commemoration of Americans killed at the Battle of Buena Vista during the Mexican-American War. Stanzas of the poem are also posted in national cemeteries, including the Winchester National Cemetery across the street.

- Excerpt from the dedication address of John T. Morgan:

[T]he west face of the monument . . . looks to the setting sun, "To the unknown and unrecorded dead." But as it is, and as history will record, how honorable is that inscription, and how just are those that follow. On the southern face the legend is this, "Erected A. D. 1879 . . ." To the east this proclamation greets the rising sun with each coming day, "Who they were, none know; what they were, all know." And looking to the North is an appealing tribute, which is addressed to the generous of every clime, and which a Confederate soldier so just paid to his comrades, whom he so soon followed to the tomb: "On Fame's . . ." It must be the task of the historian to collect and authenticate all the great array of facts upon which the vindication of these dead must rest; and it will be a credit to the age if the impartial truth shall thus be revealed to posterity. I believe that it will yet be so.

Four marble slabs surround the Unknown monument. Each is a slab laid face-up and stands on a granite base.

The slabs were added after the 1879 monument was erected. Local sources note that the dead beneath these slabs were not buried according to the battlefields where they fought, contrary to what the inscriptions may imply. Six battles are referenced here: Cool Spring, three battles of Winchester, Cedar Creek, and two battles of Kernstown.

- Battlefield is spelled with two words on these markers.

18. Cool Spring Tablet

Southeast side:

> UNKNOWN DEAD
> FROM THE
> COOL SPRING
> BATTLE FIELD.

19. Winchester Tablet

Northeast side:

> UNKNOWN DEAD
> FROM THE
> WINCHESTER
> BATTLE FIELD.

20. Cedar Creek Tablet

> UNKNOWN DEAD
> FROM THE
> CEDAR CREEK
> BATTLE FIELD.

21. Kernstown Tablet

> UNKNOWN DEAD
> FROM THE
> KERNSTOWN
> BATTLE FIELD.

22. Texas Tablet

Monument is an inscribed stone set on a concrete base.

DATE: June 6, 2005
MEDIUM: Fieldstone

TEXAS

The six Texans buried here were commemorated by the local United Daughters of the Confederacy in this the most recent state monument erected in Stonewall Cemetery. The monument is modest in size—a small local boulder, really—and has the shortest monument inscription in Virginia.

- Another tribute to Texas Confederates in Virginia stands on the Wilderness battlefield.

23. Tennessee Obelisk

24. Kernstown, Battlefield Tablet

Monument is a granite obelisk surmounting a base, plinth, and dado.

DATE: June 6, 1902

MEDIUM: Granite

TENNESSEE

The only obelisk from Tennessee in Virginia presides over twenty-nine graves. It has the most cryptic nineteenth or twentieth-century inscription in Virginia. (The Lee monument in Richmond has two words; the Texas monument nearby was installed in 2005.) There is quite enough space on the monument for more words—all of the other contemporary monuments are more elaborate—but here one word, "Tennessee," is all.

Monument is a bronze tablet set on a limestone base.

LOCATION: 3239 Valley Pike, 22602

DATE: circa 1927

MEDIA: Bronze, limestone

FIRST BATTLE OF KERNSTOWN
WAS FOUGHT HERE SUNDAY MARCH 23, 1862
CONFEDRATES UNDER GEN. T.
J. "STONEWALL" JACKSON
ATTACKED FEDERALS UNDER
GEN. JAMES SHIELDS
THE FIGHTING WAS CHIEFLY
WEST OF THE ROAD
AND CONTINUED FROM EARLY
AFTERNOON UNTIL
NIGHTFALL WHEN JACKSON RETIRED WITH
HIS FIRST AND ONLY REVERSE
CONFEDERATES ENGAGED,
3,000, CASUALTIES, 718.
FEDERALS ENGAGED, 8,000, CASUALTIES 590.

This monument is unusual for noting the day of the week when the battle was fought. Jackson, of strong Presbyterian Christian convictions, was allegedly loath to fight on Sunday. At Kernstown, as well as elsewhere, he made an exception. Attacking what turned out to be superior numbers west of the Valley Pike (present-day U.S. 11), Jackson suffered his only defeat. The elegists choose to call it a "reverse." Jackson "retired," the text observes, justly implying that Jackson yielded the initiative. He would reclaim it by May 1862.

25. Middletown, Battlefield Tablet

Monument is a bronze tablet set on a granite base.

LOCATION: U.S. 11, south of Middletown, 22645

DATE: circa 1927

MEDIA: Bronze, granite

> THE BATTLE OF CEDAR CREEK
> FOUGHT ON THESE HILLS AND
> FIELDS, OCT. 19, 1864.
> GEN. JUBAL A. EARLY'S 22,000 CONFEDERATES
> ATTACKED GEN. PHILIP H.
> SHERIDANS [*SIC*] 60,000
> FEDERALS. THE FIRST ASSAULT[,]
> A SURPRISE FLANK
> MOVEMENT BY GEN. JOHN B. GORDON, WAS A
> CONFEDERATE SUCCESS. THIS
> ADVANTAGE NOT
> BEING FOLLOWED UP, ENABLED
> GEN. SHERIDAN
> TO RALLY AND WIN THE VICTORY.

The Union victory at Cedar Creek is well noted in this monument, but the emphasis on numbers—that the Confederates were outnumbered nearly three to one—is emphasized. There are no recriminations for the "advantage not being followed up" by the Confederates, but Lt. Gen. Jubal A. Early bears the legacy of having been in command that day. The Southern custom of naming battles after the nearest town or city, Middletown, is not followed here. Instead, the Union name, Cedar Creek, is used. Further, prominence is given to Maj. Gen. John B. Gordon, Early's subordinate and rival in memory. Gordon is credited only with success—leaving Early with the responsibility of the defeat.

The battle was a turning point in the war. Despite being surprised and routed, Federal forces under generals Horatio G. Wright and Philip H. Sheridan rallied to launch a victorious counterattack. The defeat was decisive for the Confederate army in the Shenandoah Valley and was, apart from the battle of Nashville, as complete a Union victory as was fought during the war. Moreover, the timing of the victory gave support to Lincoln's presidential reelection campaign that fall and was arguably pivotal: by some accounts it gave Lincoln full confidence that his bid for a second term would be successful. With that victory, the Confederacy's prospects for life dimmed.

- The numbers listed are exaggerated. More evenhanded accounts list thirty thousand Federal troops at Cedar Creek opposed by seventeen thousand Confederates.

26. Maj. Gen. Stephen Ramseur Column

Monument is a granite plinth, dado, and column, with a bronze plaque on the dado.

LOCATION: South of Middletown on U.S. 11, 22645

DATE: September 16, 1920

MEDIA: Bronze, granite

ESSE QUAM VIDERI
NORTHWEST OF THIS TABLET 800 YARDS,
IS THE BELLE GROVE HOUSE IN
WHICH DIED, OCTOBER 20, 1864,
OF WOUNDS RECEIVED AT CEDAR
CREEK OCTOBER 19, 1864,
MAJ.-GEN. STEPHEN DODSON RAMSEUR, C.S.A.
A NATIVE OF NORTH CAROLINA
HE RESIGNED FROM
THE UNITED STATES ARMY IN
1861, AND ENTERING
THE CONFEDERATE STATES
ARMY AS A LIEUTENANT,
ROSE TO THE RANK OF MAJOR
GENERAL AT THE AGE OF 27.
ERECTED 1919 BY
THE NORTH CAROLINA
HISTORICAL COMMISSION
THE NORTH CAROLINA DIVISION, U.D.C.

Stephen Dodson Ramseur was said to have an insatiable appetite for fighting. His boyish appearance belied the wild aggressiveness he was capable of in combat, and officers and enlisted men alike recognized his leadership qualities. Ramseur was mortally wounded while trying to rally Confederate troops after the defeat at the battle of Cedar Creek. He was the highest-ranking officer who died on this field.

The wounded Ramseur was taken prisoner by Union troops during the retreat after the battle and was attended by friends on the Union side, among them generals George A. Custer and Wesley Merritt. Ramseur died at Belle Grove, near here, on the grounds behind the monument. He was eulogized as one who "died as became a Confederate soldier and true believer."

- North Carolina has relatively few monuments in Virginia, although a similar monument is close by, this one to Brig. Gen. James J. Pettigrew, mortally wounded ten days after the Battle of Gettysburg. It stands off U.S. 11, across the state line in present-day West Virginia. The Ramseur and Pettigrew monuments were dedicated one day apart, September 16 and 17, 1921. Among the speakers at the Ramseur dedication was former Union officer and Medal of Honor winner Henry A. Du-Pont, who also attended to him when he was wounded and captured.
- The Latin expression, "Esse Quam Videri," meaning "To be rather than to seem," was adopted as the North Carolina state motto in 1893 and is also inscribed on the North Carolina monument at Appomattox (chapter 5).

Clarke County

27. Berryville, Courthouse Common Soldier

Monument is a granite sculpture of a common soldier surmounting a plinth, pedestal, dado, and cap.
LOCATION: 104 North Church Street, 22611
DATE: April 26, 1880
MEDIUM: Granite
Front

1861 1865
ERECTED
TO THE MEMORY OF
THE SONS OF CLARKE
WHO GAVE THEIR LIVES
IN DEFENSE OF THE
RIGHTS OF THE STATES
AND OF CONSTITUTIONAL
GOVERNMENT.

FATE DENIED THEM SUCCESS,
BUT THEY ACHIEVED
IMPERISHABLE FAME.

—

CO. D. 6TH. VA. REGT. CAV.
[29 NAMES]

—

2ND. VA. INF. STONEWALL BRIG.
[2 NAMES]
CO C.
[18 NAMES]
CO I.
[24 NAMES]

—

OTHER COMMANDS
[34 NAMES]

Berryville's Confederate monument stands twenty feet above the courthouse grounds. The eight-foot-tall soldier is called a "Son of Clarke" on the inscription. "He" is manifestly not a Confederate, and his cause is a matter of principle—the "rights of the states" and "constitutional government," not the Confederacy. He has his hat in his hand and a pensive countenance, not unlike the Mount Jackson and Alexandria soldiers. He has no weapon and carries no cartridge box or cap box, one observer notes. Further, his haversack and canteen are on the wrong side of his body.

The granite for the monument was quarried from Petersburg, the records indicate, from a site "within a few yards of the spot where Gen. Hill fell a martyr to his State." A contemporary account describes the monument this way:

The base is four feet square, and with the pedestal, is twelve feet in height. Surmounting these is a heroic figure, eight feet high, . . . standing with arms folded, with bare head and eyes cast down, the embodiment in stone of one who, after having given up home, friends, and country in defence of principles, now that the struggle is over and all lost, almost as in a dream begins to realize the situation. And yet there is something of hope in the expression of the face—a hope which has found fruition in the part the sol-

diers of the Lost Cause have played in the progress and advancement of our united country since the close of the war.

- The ceremonies: "The address was delivered by Hon. James Marshall, himself an old soldier. The monument was unveiled by Miss Washington Gold, president of the Stonewall Chapter. The J. E. B. Stuart Camp, assisted by the Stonewall Chapter, entertained the visiting Camps and all old soldiers and a great many others, providing a bountiful feast. The large crowd who attended on that occasion testified to the desire of the people to do honor to the Confederate Soldier and the cause he represented."

28. Millwood, Burwell Cemetery Shaft at Old Chapel

Monument is a plinth, base, shaft, and cap.
LOCATION: Intersection of V.R. 255 and U.S. 340, 22646
DATE: 1892
MEDIUM: Granite
Front

STONEWALL BRIGADE
2ND VA. INFANTRY
[2 NAMES]

COMP C
[19 NAMES]
WM. N. NELSON
1ST CAPT. CO. C
2ND VA. INFANTRY
CONFEDERATE DEAD
—
1861–1865
CO I
[20 NAMES]
—
[24 NAMES]
—
CLARKE CAVALRY
[23 NAMES]

The work of Deahl Messrs. & Bros., this is one of the few Valley monuments dedicated exclusively to individual units. The Stonewall Brigade was largely raised in Shenandoah Valley and was initially led by Col. Thomas J. Jackson. The Clarke Cavalry became Company D of the 6th Virginia Cavalry.

• Excerpt from the dedication address by Col. Richard Henry Lee:

We are met in this place to look for the first time on a monument erected by loving hearts in honor, first, of the Confederate dead from this country, whose names adorn yon monument; second of all Confederate dead, no matter who they are, who have been committed in this county to the keeping of their mother earth.

No more appropriate place for a Confederate monument could have been selected within the valley of Virginia. . . . It was in this county, too, that the great rebel of America, George Washington, developed his young manhood. . . . Within this cemetery repose the remains of Edmund Randolph, one of the authors and defenders of the Constitution of the United States, in defense of which those in whose memory yon monument has been erected died.

• The Old Chapel on these grounds, a plain coursed rubble limestone edifice, dates from 1793 and is the oldest Episcopal church west of the Blue Ridge
• Southern novelist and Confederate soldier John Esten Cooke is also buried here.

SITE: Battlefield markers
Monuments are shafts set at roadside locations.

The J. E. B. Stuart Camp of Confederate Veterans erected ten granite shafts in Clarke County in the 1890s. (One cannot be located and may not be extant.) Most of the markers commemorate victories; several describe actions of Mosby's men in 1864–65 and clashes related to the Shenandoah campaign of 1864. The themes are Southern victories and partisan resistance to incursion. Federal troops are always defeated in these actions, and Southern casualties are minor or incidental.

Sons of Confederate Veterans, Clarke County Tablets

29. Morgan's Lane Shaft

LOCATION: From Berryville east on V.R. 7 and south to Pashall Lane (C.R. 608), 22611

COL. MORGAN'S LANE
AUG. 19, 1864
MOSBY'S ATTACK ON
CUSTER'S HOUSE
BURNERS.
NO PRISONERS.

After a detachment of "Mosby's men" attacked a Fifth Michigan Cavalry picket post, Michigan Brigade commander Brig. Gen. George A. Custer retaliated by ordering the burning of houses in the area. Rangers commanded by Capt. William Chapman in turn attacked Custer's troopers here—Mosby was not present. Chapman ordered that no prisoners be taken. About thirty of the detachment were killed, but the climactic phrase "No Prisoners" emphasizes Southern vindication.

30. Cool Spring Shaft

LOCATION: C.R. 603 north of V.R. 7 west of the Shenandoah River, 22611

BATTLE OF
COOL SPRING
JULY 18, 1864
EARLY & CROOK

Cool Spring was a late war Confederate victory fought on July 17–18, 1864. The action occurred during the Federal pursuit of Lt. Gen. Jubal A. Early's Army of the Valley in the aftermath of the latter's raid against the Baltimore and Ohio Railroad and Washington, D.C. The Federals passed through Snickers Gap and crossed the Shenandoah (to the present-day grounds of Holy Cross Abbey) before they were attacked and forced back.

Some four hundred casualties were incurred among the Confederate force of eight thousand men. Arguably, the engagement was neither crucial nor a turning point. In fact, the narratives of recent decades—Douglas Southall Freeman, Bruce Catton, Shelby Foote, James McPherson—give it little or no attention. Still, "it was fought," as historian Peter Meany observes, "men were killed or wounded, and nothing is ever wasted." In this case, Cool Spring was vital for the Confederates to keep Union attention and resources on the Valley. For the Federals, it was evident that the battle for control of the Shenandoah would have to be "fought to a finish," and Cool Spring thus anticipated the Valley campaign of 1864.

31. Double Tollgate Shaft

LOCATION: On U.S. 340, west side, north of U.S. 522 and 340, 22663

DOUBLE TOLLGATE
FIGHT
AUG. 11, 1864
IMBODEN & U. S.
CAVALRY.

Among many skirmishes during Confederate troops' movements in the 1864 raid into Pennsylvania under Jubal A. Early's overall command, a "sharp engagement" developed here between Confederate cavalry under Brig. Gen. John D. Imboden and Union cavalry under Brig. Gen. George A. Custer. The county history says that Imboden's troopers drove back the Federals. The state marker notes only that they clashed here.

- Double Tollgate refers to tollgates that served the Nineveh, Newton, and Berrys Ferry turnpikes. The roads connected Front Royal, Winchester, present-day Stephens City, and the Shenandoah River.

32. Battle of Berryville Marker

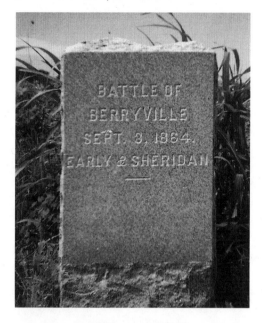

LOCATION: Bus. V.R. 7, west of U.S. 340, 22611

BATTLE OF
BERRYVILLE
SEPT. 3, 1864
EARLY & SHERIDAN

The action here, September 3–4, 1864, was one of the first engagements of the Valley campaign of 1864. Federal troops under Maj. Gen. Philip H. Sheridan moved west from Washington, D.C. reached Berryville and clashed with Lt. Gen. Richard H. Anderson's (Kershaw's) division under Lt. Gen. Jubal A. Early's command. An estimated five hundred casualties were incurred between the two sides. The results were judged "inconclusive," by the National Park Service narrative of this battle, but the county history calls it a Confederate victory.

33. Buck Marsh Fight Marker

LOCATION: Northwest of intersection of U.S. 340 and V.R. 7, 22611

BUCK MARSH FIGHT
SEPT. 13, 1864,
MOSBY'S ATTACK ON
SHERIDAN'S WAGON
TRAINS.

On August 13, 1864—not September 13—Mosby's men ambushed Sheridan's supply train of wagons coming from Harpers Ferry, which was guarded by a combined force of infantry, artillery, and cavalry. The action took place at Buck Marsh Run, about a mile north of Berryville. The rangers captured or destroyed seventy-five wagons, and took two hundred beef cattle, between five and six hundred horses and mules, and two hundred prisoners—all of this in addition to plunder taken by Mosby's men. (Mosby, however, made a point of not partaking of plunder himself.)

34. Mt. Airy Fight Marker

LOCATION: Intersection of V.R. 7 and Blueridge Mountain Road C.R. 601, 22611

MT. AIRY FIGHT
SEPT. 16, 1864
MOSBY & U. S.
CAVALRY

Elements of the 8th New York Cavalry were resting here in the midst of a raid whose purpose was to go "after Mosby and to burn and destroy," according to Southern accounts. They were set upon and defeated by rangers led by Capt. Samuel F. Chapman. Col. Mosby was not present, despite what the inscription implies.

35. Vinyard Fight Marker

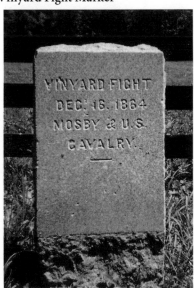

LOCATION: East of Millwood on C.R. 723, 22646

VINYARD [SIC] FIGHT
DEC. 16, 1864
MOSBY & U. S.
CAVALRY.

Heavy casualties were taken by about one hundred troopers of the 14th Pennsylvania Cavalry who were ambushed on December 15, 1864, in this late-war small-unit action. Sixty rangers under Lt. John Russell suffered no losses. Col. Mosby, though mentioned in the inscription, was not present.

- The marker stands east of Millwood on C.R. 723 (east for two miles to the granite marker on the left side of the highway); west from U.S. 17/50 it stands northwest on C.R. 723.

36. Mt. Carmel Fight Marker

LOCATION: Just east of intersection of (U.S. 17/50) and Mt. Carmel Road (C.R. 606), north side of highway, 22646

MT. CARMEL FIGHT
FEB. 19, 1865
MOSBY & U. S.
CAVALRY

Federal cavalry was ambushed here by a band of outnumbered Confederates in a short, sharp skirmish. The Federals were scattered and driven back to the Shenandoah River. Thirteen Union soldiers were killed and some sixty-three captured, of a total of around two hundred engaged.

37. Gold's Farm Fight Marker

LOCATION: West side of U.S. 340, just north of C.R. 657, 22611

FIGHT AT
GOLD'S FARM
SEPT. 3, 1864
MOSBY & 6TH N.Y.
CAVALRY

Lead elements of an advance by the 6th New York Cavalry were ambushed here by rangers in an action fought on the same day as the battle of Berryville. The Southerners were led by Capt. Samuel F. Chapman: Mosby was not present.

Warren County
Front Royal

38. Common Soldier, Warren County Courthouse

Monument is a private soldier standing at parade rest surmounting a plinth, base, dado, pedestal, and shaft.

LOCATION: 1 East Main Street, 22630
DATE: July 4, 1911
MEDIA: Bronze, granite
Front

CSA
1861
[CROSSED C.S.A. NATIONAL
FLAG AND BATTLE FLAG]
1865
UNVEILED
JULY 4, 1911
THIS MONUMENT WAS ERECTED
TO COMMEMORATE THE COURAGE
AND PATRIOTISM OF THE MEN
FROM WARREN COUNTY, WHO
SERVED HONORABLY IN THE
CONFEDERATE ARMY.
"TO THOSE WHO FOUGHT AND
LIVED, AND TO THOSE
WHO FOUGHT AND DIED. TO THOSE
WHO GAVE MUCH
AND THOSE WHO GAVE ALL."
—
VIRGINIA
BULL RUN
SEVEN PINES   CHICKAMAUGA
FRONT ROYAL   MURFREESBORO
MANASSAS   SHARPSBURG
FREDERICKSBURG   CHANCELLORSVILLE
CO A 23 VA CAV
[27 NAMES]
CO B 17 VA INF
[101 NAMES]
CO D 23 VA INF
[42 NAMES]
CO D 49 VA INF
[20 NAMES]
—
CSA
GETTYSBURG
NEW MARKET   SHILOH
PORT REPUBLIC   FISHERS HILL
ATLANTA   CEDAR MOUNTAIN
WILDERNESS   RESACA
COMPANY D 49 VIRG INFANTRY
[82 NAMES]

CO E 7 VIRG CAV
[79 NAMES]
CO E 12 VIRG CAV
[57 NAMES]
—
VIRGINIA
FRANKLIN ·
WINCHESTER VA   MALVERN HILL
PETERSBURG   PERRYVILLE
KENNESAW MOUNTAIN   NASHVILLE
BRANDY STATION   VICKSBURG
CO I 12 VIRG CAV
[74 NAMES]
MOSBY'S 43 VIRG BATT CAV
[29 NAMES]
WHITE'S 35 BATT VIRG CAV
[15 NAMES]
CHEW'S VIRG BATT
[4 NAMES]
COMP A 39 BATT CAV
[2 NAMES]
1 MISSOURI INF
[2 NAMES]
2 MISSOURI INF
[3 NAMES]
MISC.
[32 NAMES]

This "consecrated column, a voice from the storied past," according to a local history, was erected during the semicentennial of the war. The monument, by the McNeel Marble Works, is one of several monuments in Virginia with inscriptions designed, it seems, with the ambition of compressing as much detail onto the stone façade as possible. (Hanover, Hillsville, King William, and Tappahannock are among the others.) This one was erected through a collaboration of the Warren Rifles Chapter of the United Daughters of the Confederacy, the Ladies' Warren Memorial Association, the William Richardson Camp of United Confederate Veterans, and the Warren Blues Camp of the Sons of Confederate Veterans. The cost of the monument was twenty-nine hundred dollars, raised by public subscription, along with an appropriation by the county. Newspaper accounts estimated the crowd attending the dedication ceremonies at between six and seven thousand people. Mrs. Eleanor W. Richardson, aged ninety, unveiled the monument. She was the eldest mother of a Confederate soldier then living in Warren County. Among the speakers at the ceremonies was Robert E. Lee, Jr., "son of the Confederate military chieftain."

- Veterans who were still living as well as those who had died are inscribed on the monument. The intention was to list all six hundred men from Warren County who fought. As is often the case with such efforts (e. g., the Pennsylvania monument at Gettysburg, the Vietnam memorial in Washington, D.C.), the list is not complete: later research revealed other soldiers from Warren County.

39. Front Royal, Battlefield Tablet

Monument is a bronze tablet set on a granite base.
LOCATION: U.S. 340 (Royal Avenue), corner of Chester Street, 22630
DATE: May 23, 1927
MEDIA: Bronze, granite

BATTLE OF FRONT ROYAL
MAY 23, 1862. GENERAL JACKSON SURPRISED

GENERAL BANKS' FORCES IN
AND AROUND FRONT
ROYAL, CAPTURING MANY
PRISONERS AND ARMY
SUPPLIES AND FORCING BANKS
TO FLEE IN DISORDER
OUT OF THE SHENANDOAH
VALLEY INTO MARYLAND.
THIS WAS THE FIRST MOVE IN
JACKSON'S CELEBRATED
VALLEY CAMPAIGN
ERECTED BY WM. RICHARDSON CAMP, U. C. V.
1927

Dedicated on the sixty-fifth anniversary of the battle of Front Royal, this United Confederate Veterans is one of the series of battlefield tablets erected in Virginia in the 1920s. This U. C. V. inscription, written by Confederate veteran William A. Compton, is more strident in tone than the other markers in the series, especially those by the United Daughters of the Confederacy.

- The battle was fought by forces under Brig. Gen. Thomas J. "Stonewall" Jackson against a Union garrison under the immediate command of Col. John R. Kenly. Outnumbered and surprised, the victory here was nearly total and forced Union troops under Maj. Gen. Nathaniel Banks at Strasburg, posted west of here, into a retreat as well. They withdrew to Winchester where Jackson's men in the battle of First Winchester defeated them on May 25, 1862.
- Jackson—justly—is given great credit here. He is mentioned twice in this short text: it is Jackson who "surprised" the Union army, and the action was fought during his "Celebrated Valley Campaign."

Prospect Hill Cemetery
LOCATION: 200 W. Prospect Street, 22630

40. Mosby's Command Obelisk
Monument is an obelisk set on a plinth, base, and dado.
DATE: September 23, 1899
MEDIUM: Granite

Front

ERECTED
1899
BY THE SURVIVORS OF
MOSBY'S COMMAND
IN MEMORY OF
SEVEN COMRADES
EXECUTED
WHILE PRISONERS OF WAR
NEAR THIS SPOT,
SEPTEMBER 23RD, 1864.
MOSBY'S MEN
—
[C.S.A. BATTLE FLAG]
DULCE ET DECORUM EST
PRO PATRIA MORI.
—
IN
EVERLASTING HONOR
OF
THOMAS E. ANDERSON

—— CARTER
DAVID L. JONES
LUCIEN LOVE
WILLIAM THOMAS OVERBY
HENRY C. RHODES
ALBERT C. WILLIS
43RD. BATTALION VA. CAVALRY
MOSBY'S COMMAND
C.S.A.

"All roads led to Front Royal on September 23, 1899, when some 5,000 people converged on the town for an important event": the dedication for this tribute to "Seven Martyrs" under Mosby's command. The dedication date, September 23, 1899, was the thirty-fifth anniversary of the day they were executed.

Six men were taken during a raid on Front Royal: two were hanged; four were shot. Willis, the seventh, was captured and hanged three weeks later. Blame was ascribed to Custer for the executions, although this allegation has never been definitively proved. No matter. Mosby took revenge the following November, hanging three of Custer's soldiers near Berryville, before an agreement was reached between Sheridan and Mosby to treat those captured on both sides as prisoners of war.

The cost of the monument was one thousand dollars. Charles Broadway Rouss of Winchester, a Confederate veteran and postwar merchant, contributed six hundred dollars. Designed by the Alexandria Marble Works, it is, according to a local history, "a handsome, rough-hewn obelisk of dark Vermont granite, 25 feet high. . . . Broad flights of stone steps lead up to the monument, located on a beautifully terraced approach at the brow of the cemetery." From here, the record says, "one can stand and look down on the three different places at which the six Rangers were executed."

- Two thirty-pounder Parrott Rifles flank the monument.
- Excerpt from the dedication address by Maj. A. E. Richards:

Let it not be supposed that we desire to rekindle the passions of sectional strife.

There is no longer any bitterness between the soldiers of the North and the soldiers of the South. Whatever of prejudice may have been engendered between the two sections while the war lasted has ceased to exist.

41. Soldier's Circle Obelisk

Monument is an obelisk with a funereal urn and drape atop, the whole surmounting a plinth, base and shaft.
DATE: August 24, 1882
MEDIUM: Granite
Front

ERECTED BY THE LADIES
WARREN MEMORIAL
ASSOCIATION AUGUST 24TH
1882.
ALBIN & BRO.
WIN'R VA.

—

IN MEMORY OF THE ONE
HUNDRED AND EIGHTYSIX
HONORED MEN WHO LIE

BURIED HERE, FROM THIS
AND OTHER SOUTHERN
STATES. THEY GAVE THEIR
LIVES IN DEFENSE OF
TRUTH AND RIGHT.
—
VIRGINIA HONORS THE BRAVE.
—
THEY DIED IN THE CAUSE
OF HONOR AND JUSTICE.

This gray obelisk was erected in tribute to 276 Southern dead collected from sites across Warren County. Ninety are identified and interred with marble headstones; a common grave inters 186 unidentified dead in "Soldiers Circle." The hill was an artillery position during the battle of Front Royal, and Maj. Gen. Thomas J. "Stonewall" Jackson observed the attack by Confederate troops on the town from here.

This is a postwar cemetery. There was no community cemetery at Front Royal when the war began. Soldiers who died in local military hospitals or who were killed in the battle of Front Royal and other skirmishes in the area were buried in various locations. Their remains were collected and reinterred here by the local Ladies Memorial Association, chartered November 7, 1868. The monument, headstones, and ornamental iron fence cost twenty-four hundred dollars. The obelisk, of Italian marble by Albin & Bro. in Winchester, was erected at a cost of eleven hundred dollars and was carved by John B. Graver. The ornamentation is simple: many monuments have carvings representing the branches of service in the Confederate army. In this case, carved on the south side is an infantry sword and belt, which look as if they had just been hung up by a soldier.

The war and its outcome are not mentioned; neither is the Confederacy. States rights—Virginia—is the issue. The inscription is grim, but the dedication ceremonies were festive and culminated three days of events which concluded with an unveiling of the monument by thirteen girls, representing Southern states, dressed in white with black sashes and black ribbons in their straw hats.

Shenandoah County

42. Strasburg, Cemetery Obelisk

Monument is an obelisk surmounting a plinth, base, and dado.
LOCATION: Strasburg Presbyterian Church, 325 South Holliday Street, 22657
DATE: May 30, 1896
MEDIUM: Granite
Front

1896
ERECTED
BY
STOVER CAMP NO. 20
CONFEDERATE
VETERANS
IN MEMORY OF OUR FALLEN COMRADES
NUMBERING 136

Like many Valley towns, Strasburg was a place of conflict during the war. Skirmishing near Strasburg occurred several times, and the pursuit of Confederate forces after the battle of Cedar Creek continued here. The monument is unusual in not being sponsored by women, although the United Daughters of the Confederacy of Strasburg has cared for the grounds since 1904. "Yankees and Confederates" are buried here, one U.D.C. member told the author, taken from different farms and shallow graves in the area, some of them known, many of them unknown. Still, they are all judged as "Our Comrades."

The church edifice, dedicated May 16, 1839, has a plaque stating that the structure was used as a hospital by both sides during the "War Between the States."

43. Fishers Hill Battlefield Tablet

Monument is a bronze tablet set on a fieldstone base.

LOCATION: West side of U.S. 11, south of Strasburg, 22626
DATE: circa 1927
MEDIA: Bronze, fieldstone

> THE BATTLE OF FISHERS HILL
> WAS FOUGHT ON THESE BLUFFS
> SEPTEMBER 22, 1864
> GEN. PHILIP H. SHERIDAN'S 60,000 FEDERALS
> ATTACKED GEN. JUBAL A. EARLY'S 18,000
> CONFEDERATES. THROUGH
> THE ADVANTAGE OF
> OVERWHELMING NUMBERS, THE FEDERALS
> WON THE VICTORY.

This is another of a series of markers placed at twenty-five Virginia battlefields under the overall sponsorship of the Virginia Statewide Battlefields Markers' Association. The markers often present narratives of valiant Confederate soldiers defeating superior numbers. The Federals are acknowledged to have won the victory in this case, but the narrative reflects the postwar conviction that overwhelming numbers and resources defeated the Confederacy. That claim is partially justified: outnumbered by a factor of about three to one, Lt. Gen. Jubal A. Early's army of some ninety-five hundred men was outflanked and nearly routed here against a force under Maj. Gen. Philip H. Sheridan of about thirty thousand. The Confederate positions were strong, but the army seemed shaken by the defeat at the battle of Third Winchester on September 19, only three days earlier. In the face of a flanking movement, Confederate cavalry offered little resistance; in turn the Southern infantry proved unable to resist the attackers.

44. Woodstock, Massanutten Cemetery Obelisk

Monument is an obelisk surmounting a plinth, base, and dado.

LOCATION: Benchoff Drive, grounds west of Massanutten Military Academy, 22664
DATE: October 19, 1899
MEDIUM: Marble
Front

ERECTED
BY THE
SHENANDOAH CHAPTER
UNITED DAUGHTERS
OF THE
CONFEDERACY.
IN MEMORY
OF THE CONFEDERATE
SOLDIERS BURIED IN
WOODSTOCK
VA.
1899

Snyder
Woodstock Va.

—

CAST DOWN, BUT
NOT DESTROYED;
2 COR. 4 C. 9 V.
HONOR AND FAME
THE RECORD KEEP.
1861

—

SONS OF
VIRGINIA
N. CAROLINA
GEORGIA
S. CAROLINA
MISSISSIPPI
ALABAMA
LOUISIANA.
Could bleed and die, but
Not with HONOR part
C.S.A.

—

UNKNOWN
THIS VOICELESS
STONE IN DEATHLESS
SONG SHALL TELL,
THE STORY HOW YE FELL.
1865

The cemetery opened in 1898, and in 1899, approximately seventy Confederate soldiers who had died at field hospitals around Wood-

stock were disinterred and reburied here at what is known as Holly Circle.

The monument stands on a grave mound surrounded by trees. The quotation, "Cast Down, but not Destroyed; 2 Cor. 4 C. 9 V." is drawn from the apostle Paul's letter to the Corinthians, which was written in part to encourage the just "saints" in their suffering in a corrupt, debased world. The "saintly" Corinthians were not perfect, as Paul makes clear, but they had promises of a far better life to come. That prospect is implied for the Confederate soldiers interred at Woodstock.

The monument was rededicated on October 19, 1999. The original dedication date, October 19, 1899, was the thirty-fifth anniversary of the battle of Cedar Creek. Many Confederate victories were won in the Valley, but Cedar Creek, a Southern defeat, resolved the issue of control of the Valley with its dramatic turn of events, from near victory to a virtual rout. That day served as a threshold on the postwar world that emerged without an independent Confederacy: its people were "cast down but not destroyed."

The passage beginning with "This Voiceless Stone" is taken from Theodore O'Hara's "Bivouac of the Dead." The larger stanza reads:

Yon marble minstrel's voiceless stone
In deathless song shall tell,
When many a vanquished age hath flown,
The story how ye fell.
Nor wreck, nor change, nor winter's blight,
Nor time's remorseless doom,
Shall dim one ray of glory's light
That gilds your deathless tomb.

45. Lt. Col. Alexander S. Pendleton Tablet
Monument is a granite shaft displaying bronze reliefs of Pendleton and the Murphy house.
LOCATION: 156 South Muhlenberg Street at Dingledine, west of Main Street, 22664
MEDIUM: Granite

[RELIEF OF PENDLETON]
LIEUTENANT COLONEL
A. S. "SANDIE" PENDLETON

C.S.A.
WHILE SERVING AS JUBAL EARLY'S CHIEF OF
STAFF AND DIRECTING THE
REAR-GUARD OF THE
2ND CORP. [SIC] OF THE ARMY
OF NORTHERN VIRGINIA
AFTER THE BATTLE OF FISHERS
HILL, LT. COL. A. S.
PENDLETON WAS WOUNDED
SEPT. 22, 1864, NEAR
THE FOUR-MILE HOUSE AT
MT. PROSPECT ON THE
VALLEY PIKE. HE WAS TAKEN
TO DR. MURPHY'S
HOUSE AND ATTENDED BY MRS. MURPHY, THE
MURPHY DAUGHTERS, AND DRS.
HUNTER H. MCGUIRE,
BLACK AND MAGRUDER. ON THE EVENING OF
SEPT. 23, PENDLETON PASSED
AWAY, JUST FIVE DAYS
BEFORE HIS 24TH BIRTHDAY.
HE WAS BURIED IN
THE WOODSTOCK LUTHERAN
CEMETERY. AFTER
GEN. SHERIDAN'S ARMY HAD
WITHDRAWN NORTH
OF CEDAR CREEK, HIS REMAINS
WERE REMOVED TO
LEXINGTON WHERE HIS FAMILY
RESIDED. ON OCT. 25,
FOLLOWING FUNERAL SERVICES AT GRACE
EPISCOPAL CHURCH, PENDLETON WAS
REINTERRED IN THE LEXINGTON

CEMETERY NEAR THE GRAVE OF
HIS FORMER COMMANDER, GEN.
THOMAS "STONEWALL" JACKSON.
[RELIEF OF HOUSE]

—

ERECTED TO HONOR THOSE WHO
SERVED THE CONFEDERACY
STONEWALL BRIGADE FOUNDATION
STOVER CAMP CHAPTER, DAUGHTERS
OF THE CONFEDERACY
STRASBURG GUARD, SONS OF THE
CONFEDERATE VETERANS

Lt. Col. Alexander S. "Sandie" Pendleton received a gunshot wound to the abdomen after the battle of Fishers Hill. He was shot while piecing together a rear guard to ward off the Union pursuit after the battle. He was taken to the house at this site and tended by Drs. Hunter H. McGuire, Harvey Black, and Magruder. McGuire and Black had also attended to Stonewall Jackson when he was wounded at the battle of Chancellorsville.

Pendleton's wound proved fatal. Buried near the battlefield, his body was later exhumed and sent to his family in Lexington, Virginia. His parents—his father was Confederate Brig. Gen. William Nelson Pendleton—and his wife of nine months attended his reburial near Jackson's grave in what is now Stonewall Cemetery. One month later his only child, a son, was born.

The house no longer stands; the monument stands near the Woodstock United Methodist Church.

Mount Jackson

46. Common Soldier, Our Soldiers Cemetery
Monument is a private soldier facing east, standing with arms crossed, surmounting a base, pedestal, and cap.
LOCATION: U.S. 11, Main Street to corner of Nelson Street, 22842
DATE: May 1903
MEDIA: Granite, marble
Front

> [RELIEF OF C.S.A. FIRST NATIONAL
> FLAG WITH ELEVEN STARS]
> ERECTED BY
> MOUNT JACKSON CHAPTER OF
> THE U.D.C.
> MAY 1903
> TO ALL CONFEDERATES
>
> —
>
> "NE'ER BRAVER BLED FOR A BRIGHTER
> LAND
> NOR BRIGHTER LAND HAD A CAUSE SO
> GRAND."
>
> —
>
> SOLDIERS BURIED HERE FROM
> VIRGINIA   GEORGIA
> NO. CAROLINA   SO. CAROLINA
> ALABAMA   TENNESSEE
> MARYLAND   LOUISIANA
> TEXAS
>
> —
>
> "AND NOW, LORD
> WHAT I WAIT FOR
> MY HOPE IS IN THEE."
> 1861–1865
>
> —
>
> "NOR SHALL YOUR GLORY BE FORGOT
> WHILE FAME HER RECORD KEEPS."

The sculpture of the U.D.C.-sponsored Confederate soldier is a brooding, meditative figure facing east, six and one-half feet tall, "sculptured in Rome," contemporary notes observe, appearing "to be leaning against a stump, hat in hand, looking downward in meditative mood . . . denot[ing] respect for his fallen comrades who lie around him." Built at a cost of fifteen hundred dollars, it presides over "359 Confederate heroes," the records note. Of these 238 were identified at the time, but recent research, as displayed in the 1998 monument below, has remedied that. Unlike the statues at Berryville and Alexandria, which are also figures of mourning and loss, this one still has his weapon at hand.

Confederate Veteran called it a "handsome monument stand[ing] in our cemetery, surmounted by the statue of a Confederate soldier. He looks down pathetically, with head uncovered in respect to his fallen comrades."

The first excerpt ("brighter land . . . cause so grand") is taken from "The Sword of Robert Lee" by Abram Joseph Ryan. The third excerpt ("while fame her record keeps") is taken from Theodore O'Hara's "Bivouac of the Dead," although in this context it can be read as a Lost Cause patriotic note. The second excerpt is taken from Psalm 39:7: "And now, Lord, what wait I for? My hope is in thee." The choice suits the monument, but it is unusually self-questioning: the whole of Psalm 39 is a commentary on the brevity and apparent meaninglessness of life. David, the psalm's warrior-poet author, writes further that "verily every man at his best state is altogether vanity. Surely every man walketh in a vain shew."

"Our Soldiers Cemetery" was established in 1861, although it was not formally dedicated until May 10, 1866, the third anniversary of Stonewall Jackson's death. The whole community, including the nearby towns of New Market and Edinburg, participated in the dedication ceremonies. A wreath of flowers was placed on each of the graves. The ceremonies included an address by Col. Henry Kyd Douglas, staff officer to Stonewall Jackson. The U.D.C. chapter at Mount Jackson was organized in 1897.

47. Our Soldiers Cemetery, Triptych

Monument is three adjoining granite tablets with six bronze plaques affixed, two to each tablet.

DATE: 1998

MEDIA: Bronze, granite

Bronze plaque

HERE LIE THE CONFEDERATE
SOLDIERS NAMED BELOW
ALABAMA
[38 NAMES]
FLORIDA
[4 NAMES]
GEORGIA
[80 NAMES]
LOUISIANA
[9 NAMES]
MARYLAND
[4 NAMES]
MISSISSIPPI
[5 NAMES]

Bronze plaque

HERE LIE THE CONFEDERATE
SOLDIERS NAMED BELOW
ALABAMA
[4 NAMES]
FLORIDA
[1 NAME]
GEORGIA
[7 NAMES]
LOUISIANA

[1 NAME]
NORTH CAROLINA
[19 NAMES]

Center

CSA
[BAS-RELIEF, HOSPITAL]
CONFEDERATE HOSPITAL
MT. JACKSON VA.
G. CASTEEL
'97

THE CONFEDERATE HOSPITAL WAS ES-
TABLISHED AT MOUNT JACKSON UNDER
THE DIRECTION OF DR. ANDREW RUSSELL
MEEM BY ORDER OF THE CONFEDERATE
MEDICAL DEPARTMENT IN RICHMOND,
VIRGINIA ABOUT SEPTEMBER 15, 1861.
DR. MEEM, A NATIVE OF THE AREA, WAS
A GRADUATE OF PRINCETON UNIVERSITY
AND THE UNIVERSITY OF PENNSYLVANIA
MEDICAL COLLEGE.

DR. MEEM, ON A VISIT TO HARRISON-
BURG FEBRUARY 26, 1865, BECAME ILL
WITH AN UNKNOWN AILMENT AND DIED
AT THE AGE OF 41.

THE HOSPITAL CONSISTED OF THREE
TWO-STORY BUILDINGS, 150 FEET LONG,
ACCOMMODATING UP TO 500 PATIENTS.
A CEMETERY WAS ESTABLISHED ACROSS
THE VALLEY PIKE ON THE WEST SIDE,
ON LAND BELONGING TO COLONEL LEVI
RINKER.

IN THE SUMMER OF 1865, THE 192ND
OHIO VOLUNTEER MILITIA TORE DOWN
THE HOSPITAL AND BUILT A LARGE
VILLAGE, INCLUDING A COURTHOUSE,
GUARDHOUSE, BALLROOM AND GAL-
LOWS, AT RUDE'S HILL, THREE MILES
SOUTH OF MOUNT JACKSON. FEDERAL OC-
CUPATION FORCES USED THESE BUILD-
INGS THROUGHOUT THE RECONSTRUC-
TION PERIOD. WHEN RECONSTRUCTION
ENDED IN 1875, THE STRUCTURES WERE
REMOVED.

Bronze plaque

HERE LIE THE CONFEDERATE
SOLDIERS NAMED BELOW
NORTH CAROLINA
[77 NAMES]
SOUTH CAROLINA
[28 NAMES]
TENNESSEE
[4 NAMES]
TEXAS
[1 NAME]
VIRGINIA
[70 NAMES]

Bronze plaque

HERE LIE THE CONFEDERATE
SOLDIERS NAMED BELOW
SOUTH CAROLINA
[15 NAMES]
VIRGINIA
[10 NAMES]
STATE & UNIT UNKNOWN
[1 NAME]

The roster of the dead on this triptych, the
work of Gary Casteel, reflects efforts to document the names of the Confederate soldiers
buried here—a trend of recent decades among
local historians or researchers (in this case D.
Coiner Rosen) that has also led to other monuments and public rosters, such as the memorial wall at Warrenton Cemetery (chapter 3).
Reportedly, the roster is complete and there
are no longer any unknowns. The monument
serves as a kind of supplement or enhance-
ment of the monument it stands behind, like
the 2000 Appomattox and 1999 tablets. This

triptych's form and inscription is at eye level
and has some of the same features as Washington, D.C.'s Vietnam War Memorial (1982).

48. Rude's Hill Tablet

Monument is a bronze plaque set on a field-
stone base.
LOCATION: U.S. 11 north of New Market,
22844
DATE: 1927
MEDIA: Bronze, granite
RUDE'S HILL
STONEWALL JACKSON'S CAMP GROUND [SIC]
APRIL 2–16, 1862
HIS HEADQUARTERS AT THE
FOOT OF THIS HILL.
COLONEL JOHN FRANCIS NEFF, COMMANDER
33RD. REGIMENT, STONEWALL BRIGADE
BORN AND BURIED NEAR HERE.
ERECTED BY THE SHENANDOAH
CHAPTER, U. D. C [SIC]
1927

No major battles were fought at Rude's Hill,
but this seemingly modest ridge had tactical
and strategic value in the Shenandoah Valley
and was the site of extensive activity during
the war. Rude's Hill is a range of highlands
overlooking the North Fork of the Shenandoah
River. The river makes several abrupt turns in
this vicinity. A single wooden bridge of the
Valley Turnpike spanned the river, and the road
passed through bottomland within easy artillery range of the ridge.

Lt. Col. Turner Ashby's cavalry fought Federal forces under Maj. Gen. Nathaniel P. Banks
here in 1862; skirmishing occurred here after
the battle of New Market in 1864, and forces

under Lt. Gen. Jubal A. Early fought Sheridan's cavalry on November 22, 1864, just months before the war's end. None of these actions bears mention. Instead, this monument commemorates the hopeful days of the Shenandoah Valley campaign of 1862, when Jackson's army dealt repeated defeats to the Northern armies.

- John Francis Neff, killed in action at Second Manassas, was respected as a promising young officer, and popular enough with his men for them to elect him colonel of the 33rd Virginia Infantry.

49. Summers-Koontz Column

Monument is a marble column surmounting a plinth, base, and dado.

LOCATION: U.S. 11, four miles north of New Market at C.R. 828, 22844
DATE: 1927
MEDIUM: Marble
Front

> Capt. Geo. W. SUMMERS
> AND
> Serg. NEWTON KOONTZ
> Company D, 7th Virginia Cavalry,
> Were here executed on
> June 27, 1865, By order of
> Lt. Col. Huzzy [SIC], 192d O.V.M.I.
>
> —
>
> Without the privilege of an-
> y kind of trial; they hav-
> ing been arrested at their
> homes in Page Co., brought
> here and shot.
>
> W. N. COX

> —
> [blank]
> —
> Erected in 1893 by
> Friends, under the
> supervision of
> Capt. T. J. ADAMS

This Italian marble, nine-and-a-half-foot-high obelisk stands in a pasture four miles north of New Market. The grounds are owned by the Shenandoah Valley Battlefields Foundation and were recently renovated to permit visitor access.

The memorial indicts Lt. Col. "Huzzy" (actually Lt. Col. Cyrus Hussey) of the 192nd Ohio Infantry for an arbitrary and unjust execution of two men for stealing horses. The theft is omitted from the inscription (and the horses were later returned), but is duly reported on the state plaque beside the road. The pathos of the death of Summers and Koontz, which took place just after the war's end, was described by Summers's father, George Summers, in *Confederate Veteran* some forty years later. The elder Summers wrote that "They yielded at last to their fate, and knelt to be shot to death the very day of their arrest. . . . He was my only son."

New Market
50. St. Matthews Cemetery Obelisk

Monument is an obelisk surmounting a plinth, base, and dado.

LOCATION: Reformation Lutheran Church, 9283 North Congress Street, 22844

DATE: May 12, 1898

MEDIUM: Granite

Front

> A GRATEFUL TRIBUTE
> TO THE
> SOUTHERN SOLDIERS
> AND
> V.M.I. CADETS
> WHO FELL IN THE BATTLE
> OF NEW MARKET, VA.,
> MAY 15, 1864.
> CONFEDERATE
> MEMORIAL
> —
> FELL IN THE BATTLE
> OF NEW MARKET
> AND RESTING
> IN HER CEMETERIES
> 62D. VA. REGT.
> [11 NAMES]
> 30TH. VA. REGT.
> [2 NAMES]
> 26TH. VA. BATTN.
> [3 NAMES]
> —
> 23D. VA. CAVALRY
> [4 NAMES]
> 22D. VA. REGT.
> [1 NAME]
> LOWRY'S BATTERY.
> [1 NAME]
> CHAPMAN'S BATTERY.
> [1 NAME]
> 53D. N. C. REGT.
> [1 NAME]
> REGIMENT UNKNOWN.
> [8 NAMES]
> EIGHT UNKNOWN.
> [2 NAMES]
> ERECTED BY
> THE WOMEN'S MEMORIAL SOCIETY
> OF THE LOST CAUSE.
> NEW MARKET, VA. A. D. 1898.
> W. N. COX & CO.

> —
> 1861–65.
> OUR
> CONFEDERATE
> HEROES
> SLEEPING BUT GLORIOUS

Although they commemorate the same event, this 1898 obelisk is not as conspicuous as the nearby Hall of Valor, erected in 1967. Its focus is not on the cadets of the Virginia Military Institute, who formed only a fraction of the Confederate troops who fought here, but on thirty-four of the estimated five hundred and forty casualties. The use of the phrase "Lost Cause" is unusual, despite its prominence in the postwar era and even today. The tribute, "Sleeping but Glorious," may be a reference to the Pauline passage that assures Christians that they "shall not all sleep" (1 Cor. 15:52).

- Excerpt from the dedication address by John N. Upshur (1848–1924), a physician and member of the V.M.I. Class of 1867.

This is a day long to be remembered in the history of this school of soldiers. We have assembled to do homage to that battalion of young soldiers, who more than a generation ago received their baptism of fire and won immortal glory upon the memorable field of New Market. The first and only time in history, I believe, when in solid phalanx, undaunted and invincible, as a battalion, testimony was borne to the discipline and training of any military school.

New Market Battlefield State Historic Park

SITE: New Market Battlefield State Historical Park

8895 George Collins Parkway, 22844

51. Battlefield Tablet

Monument is a bronze tablet set on a granite base with two flanking cannon barrels.
LOCATION: Collins Parkway
DATE: May 15, 1926
MEDIA: Bronze, granite

THE BATTLE OF NEW MARKET
WAS FOUGHT HERE SUNDAY MORNING
MAY 15, 1864
THE CONFEDERATES UNDER
GEN. J. C. BRECKINRIDGE
WERE VICTORIOUS
OVER THE FEDERALS UNDER
GEN. FRANZ SIGEL
THE DECISIVE INCIDENT OF THE BATTLE
WAS THE HEROIC CAPTURE OF
THE FEDERAL BATTERY
BY THE V.M.I. CADETS

The Confederate victory here is the most venerated battlefield in the Valley and one of the most celebrated and well memorialized battlefields in Virginia, notwithstanding the fact that Interstate 81 runs through the middle of the grounds where the fighting took place.

Here a Confederate army of about forty-one hundred men led by Maj. Gen. John C. Breckinridge defeated a Union army of about six thousand men under Maj. Gen. Franz Sigel. The latter force included 257 cadets from the Virginia Military Institute. Using the Corps of Cadets gave the battle a lasting legacy for V.M.I., although the practical military effects were temporary. The engagement's relative significance may be compared to the monuments at Waynesboro and Piedmont only a few miles away.

52. Woodson, 1st Missouri Tablet

Monument is an inscribed bolder.
LOCATION: Collins Parkway
DATE: 1905
MEDIUM: Fieldstone

This rustic pile
The simple tale will tell:
It marks the spot
Where Woodson's heroes fell.

This rough-hewn monument was erected in 1905 by two veterans of Company A, 1st Missouri Cavalry, which was commanded by Capt. Charles H. Woodson. Composed of paroled prisoners captured at Port Gibson, Mississippi, who were released at Richmond, this unit had no formal connection to the regular First Missouri Cavalry. Serving with the 62nd Virginia Infantry, the unit's casualties at New Market were five killed and thirty-five wounded from a total of sixty-five men.

- This is one of only two soldier monuments on the field; the other is to the 54th Pennsylvania Infantry.

Page County
Luray
53. Common Soldier, Campbell Avenue

Monument is a private soldier standing at parade rest surmounting a base, four columns supporting a shaft and pedestal.

LOCATION: Campbell, Broad and Virginia avenues, 22835
DATE: July 20, 1918
MEDIUM: Marble
Front

CSA
CONFEDERATE SOLDIERS
1861—1865

—

CSA
CONFEDERATE SOLDIERS
1861—1865

Luray is the only Virginia county seat of its size with two town square–type Confederate monuments. This standard-issue 1918 McNeel Marble Company model is more restrained than the 1898 custom-made design located less than a mile to the east.

The monument stands twenty feet high and cost eight thousand dollars. Bronze tablets were planned for the monument along the inside and outside but were never installed. The "soldier figure" was to

> be of Imported Italian marble and the rest of the structure [of] silver gray Georgia marble, quarried at Marietta, Ga. . . . a standard monument marble being free from iron which in time discolors all stones in which it is to be found. . . . On the inside of the monument will be a tablet inscribed to the women of Page county who at their homes sustained and cheered the heroes at the front.

Space on the monument was left to inscribe up to eight hundred names, or for the names of the companies that volunteered from Page County, but none of these additions was made. A fountain sponsored by the Women's Christian Temperance Union, erected in 1913, was displaced and removed when the monument was erected.

No reason is cited for having a second Confederate monument in Luray, but this soldier is younger in appearance than his cross-town counterpart and is of the type intended to serve as a role model, the kind that led Confeder-

ate General Stephen D. Lee to assert that they are "for the sake of the living, that in this busy industrial age these stones to the Confederate soldier may stand like great interrogation marks to the soul of each beholder. Are you also ready to die for your country?" Lee concluded. "Is your life worthy to be remembered along with theirs?"

54. Common Soldier, Main Street

Monument is a base and pedestal surmounted by private soldier, with musket pointed downward.
LOCATION: B.R. 211 (Main Street) at Reservoir, 22835
DATE: July 21, 1898
MEDIA: Limestone, marble
Front

[BAS-RELIEF OF ROBERT E. LEE]

GLORY CROWNED.
1861–1865.

—

TO THE HEROES,
BOTH PRIVATE & CHIEF, OF THE
SOUTHERN CONFEDERACY,
IS THIS TRIBUTE
AFFECTIONATELY INSCRIBED.

—

WOULD IT NOT BE A BLAME FOR US
IF THEIR MEMORIES PART
FROM OUR LAND & HEART,

AND A WRONG TO THEM & A SHAME FOR US,
THE GLORIES THEY WON SHALL
NOT WANE FOR US
IN LEGEND & LAY
OUR HEROES IN GRAY
SHALL FOREVER LIVE OVER AGAIN FOR US.
RYAN

This is the better known, more sentimental, more senior monument in Luray. The affection and reverence for the Confederate officer and common soldier is lavish: "Glory crown[s]" them, the inscription declares, whether they are "private" or "chief."

The monument, erected at a cost of $4,890, was "the result of the persistent efforts and the patriotic zeal of the sculptor, Mr. Herbert Barbee," according to a contemporary account. Barbee (1847–1936) was the sculptor of the Little Fork Church and Washington, Virginia memorials and possibly the Warrenton Cemetery monument as well. He took evident pride in this monument's Southern origins, declaring at the dedication ceremonies that:

> Everything about the monument is Southern. The site upon which it is built was presented to me by wealthy Southerners. The marble was given by one of Mosby's men. . . . The men employed were Southern; therefore it cannot be said that foreign aid was necessary to build a tribute to Southern heroism.

The soldier, he wrote, is a "typical Confederate picket":

> His well-worn shoes reveal sockless feet and protruding toes; his garments are wind-blown and his wild hat shades his far-seeing, determined eye; acoutered with his cartridge box, bayonet, and canteen, buckled around the waist, he stands gun in hand, ready for duty—a vigorous embodiment of soldier and patriot.

- The excerpt beginning "Would it not be . . ." is by Abram Ryan. Other excerpts from Ryan's poetry are inscribed at Little Fork Church, Mount Jackson, and Isle of Wight.

Rockingham County and City of Harrisonburg

Harrisonburg

55. Woodbine Cemetery Obelisk
Monument is a marble obelisk surmounting a plinth, base, and dado.
LOCATION: 301 South Willow Street, 22801

DATE: April 26, 1876
MEDIUM: Marble
Front

THIS
Monument is erected by the
LADIES MEMORIAL ASSOCIATION
in grateful remembrance of the
gallant Confederate Soldiers,
who lie here.
THEY DIED IN DEFENSE OF THE RIGHTS
OF THE SOUTH,
in the war between the States,
from 1861 to 1865.

—

1876.
In memory of men,
who with their lives
vindicated
the principles of
1776.
G. D. ANTHONY

FECIT,

Harrisonburg, VA.

—

BATTLES

of the Valley of the Shenandoah,

McDOWELL,

Piedmont, Cross Keys,

Port Republic,

New Market, Cedar Creek,

Kernstown,

Harrisonburg, Winchester,

Harper's Ferry [sic].

—

THE

Southern Soldier

Died for his Country.

Success is not Patriotism.

Defeat is not Rebellion.

The marble of this 1876 obelisk is weathered, but at the dedication ceremonies "this was a handsome . . . shaft rising to the height of 20 feet," according to *Historic Southern Monuments,* which notes that "For many years the women of the Memorial Association, organized in 1868, labored early and late to raise funds to erect this memorial."

Dedicated in the national centennial year, 1876, on the Confederate memorial day, the inscription holds that the Southern lives sacrificed in the war "vindicated the principles of 1776." The other claim—"Success is not Patriotism. Defeat is not Rebellion"—affirm the faith of a Lost Cause community and subversion of the reunited republic.

- Other notes from *Historic Southern Monuments,* published in 1911:

On Friday, June 19, 1868, the ladies of Rockingham County met in Harrisonburg and formed an association for care and preservation of the graves of Confederate buried in Rockingham County. Mr. Samuel Shacklett of Harrisonburg gave an acre of ground for a cemetery, and the Association went to work. The bodies of soldiers already resting in the local cemetery were removed to the Confederate section, and also many others were brought from adjacent battlefields

or small towns throughout the county, making a total of 245 Confederates who now sleep in Woodbine Cemetery. . . .

- Editorial note: The rear—side 3—panel displays a list of military engagements in the Shenandoah Valley. McDowell is inscribed with prominent upper case lettering. No pattern of victory, loss, casualty, or chronology is apparent in the list of battles: just one Kernstown, one Winchester, no Fishers Hill or Tom's Brook. And no Front Royal, as one commentator observes, the only 1862 action not mentioned.
- The Latin expression on side 2, "Fecit," is translated as "designer."
- Also buried here: Brig. Gen. John R. Jones and Maj. Joseph W. Latimer (1834–1863), called the "Boy Major," mortally wounded at the Battle of Gettysburg.

56. Ashby Memorial and Battlefield Tablet

Monument is a bronze tablet set on a concrete base.

LOCATION: South Main Street (U.S. 11) and Port Republic Road, 22801

DATE: 1926

MEDIA: Bronze, concrete

A MILE AND A HALF SOUTHEAST

OF THIS SPOT

GENERAL TURNER ASHBY OF FAUQUIER,

"KNIGHT OF THE VALLEY,"

WAS KILLED IN BATTLE

JUNE 6, 1862.
TO HONOR HIM
AND ALL OF ROCKINGHAM'S ENLISTED MEN
1861–1865
THIS TABLET IS ERECTED
1926

Listed as one of the twenty-five monuments sponsored by the Association on Civil War Battlefields, this is the only battlefield monument in that series that is devoted to Turner Ashby, the "Knight of the Valley." Rockingham's enlisted men are given a tribute, but chivalric terms are applied to Ashby—a charismatic leader but a poor disciplinarian, especially in the eyes of his commander, Stonewall Jackson. The battle of Harrisonburg, in which he was killed, is indirectly mentioned; Ashby was the only Confederate general killed during the 1862 Valley campaign.

57. Gen. Turner Ashby Tablet

Monument is a granite shaft set on a base.
LOCATION: From Harrisonburg east on Virginia 659 (Port Republic Road), north (left) on Neff Avenue, left on Turner Ashby Lane, 22801
DATE: June 6, 1898
MEDIUM: Granite

GEN. TURNER ASHBY.
C.S.A.

WAS KILLED ON
THIS SPOT.
JUNE 6, 1862.
GALLANTLY LEADING
A CHARGE

Apart from Stonewall Jackson and Robert E. Lee, Turner Ashby (1828–1862) may be the most beloved Confederate soldier in the Valley. Ashby was legendary even before his death. Historian Douglas Southall Freeman writes that Jackson's cavalry commander was "strange almost mysterious," and that in the early days of the war, he was "so flawlessly courageous in the presence of the enemy that he attract[ed] to him every boy in the Shenandoah Valley who love[d] horses and crave[d] adventure." Ashby was promoted to general only ten days before his death, an irony noted in the inscription. His impetuosity led him here, to Chestnut Ridge during the battle of Harrisonburg just east of the city; he did not have command of the units engaged. Ashby's horse was shot from under him, and he was said to be moving forward on foot when he was fatally wounded. His last words were said to be, "Forward, my brave men."

- Jackson said of him in the official report: "His daring was proverbial, his powers of endurance almost incredible, his character heroic, and his sagacity almost intuitive in divining the purposes and movements of the enemy."
- The Turner Ashby Chapter of the United Daughters of the Confederacy is credited with sponsoring the monument. However, the collaborative nature of many memorial projects is reflected in the list of charter members of the Turner Ashby Memorial Association: the S. B. Gibbons Camp of Confederate Veterans, the Turner Ashby Chapter of the U.D.C., the Ladies' Memorial Association, and the Turner Ashby Camp of Confederate Veterans.
- Ashby is interred in Stonewall Cemetery, Winchester, with his brother Frank, who was killed in action in July 1861.
- Emerson's *Historic Southern Monuments*

describes the setting for the dedication ceremonies: "To the east stretch the Massanutta [*sic*] Mountains, while far to the west the Alleghanies can be seen. Such was the crowd on the da[y] of the unveiling that when the first carriage was halted in front of the monument others were still leaving the town."

Rockingham County

58. Port Republic, Battlefield Tablet

Monument is a bronze tablet set on a fieldstone base.

LOCATION: U.S. 340 at Ore Bank Road, 24471

DATE: circa 1927

MEDIA: Bronze, fieldstone

> PORT REPUBLIC BATTLEFIELD
> HERE, JUNE 9, 1862
> GEN. T. J. "STONEWALL" JACKSON
> DEFEATED GEN. J. SHIELD'S [*SIC*] VANGUARD
> ADVANCING FROM ELKTON
> UNDER GEN. R. O. TYLER.
> FEDERALS ENGAGED, 4500
> KILLED, WOUNDED AND MISSING,
> 551, CAPTURED, 450
> CONFEDERATES ENGAGED, 6000
> KILLED AND WOUNDED, 804

This battle summary understates the importance of the action near the still small village of Port Republic. The climax of Jackson's Valley campaign occurred here: the defeat of two separate Union armies, one here, the other at Cross Keys. Brig. Gen. James Shields commanded Federal troops here. The twin victories, fought on the same day, left Jackson in control of most of the Shenandoah Valley, and the Jackson legend was firmly established. Jackson is the central figure: "Here Jackson defeated . . ."

- The figures for Union troops are at variance with other sources. The National Park Service lists thirty-five hundred Union troops opposed by six thousand Confederates, with 1,002 Federal and 816 Confederate casualties.
- The Elkton area was known as Conrad's Store during the war. "Gen. R. O. Tyler" is Union brigadier general Erastus B. Tyler.

Augusta County and Cities of Waynesboro and Staunton

59. Piedmont, Battlefield Tablet

Monument is a bronze tablet set on a cement base.

LOCATION: C.R. 608, about one half mile north of New Hope, 24469

DATE: circa 1927

MEDIA: Bronze, granite

> PIEDMONT BATTLEFIELD
> HERE ON JUNE 5, 1864, WAS
> FOUGHT THE BATTLE OF
> PIEDMONT FOR THE POSSESSION
> OF STAUNTON
> UNION FORCES UNDER GEN.
> DAVID HUNTER 12,015 MEN
> AND SUFFERED A LOSS OF
> 130 KILLED AND 650
> WOUNDED, CONFEDERATE
> FORCES NUMBERING 5,600
> MEN UNDER GEN. W. E. JONES

DEFEATED WITH LOSS
460 KILLED, 1,450 WOUNDED
AND 1,000 PRISONERS.
GEN. JONES WAS KILLED NEAR THIS SPOT.

Although less well known than the battle of New Market, this Union victory followed that engagement by a few weeks and undid its effects. By now Brig. Gen. David Hunter had replaced Brig. Gen. Franz Sigel who was in command of Union forces at New Market. Advancing south, Hunter engaged an ad hoc Confederate force assembled here and commanded by Brig. Gen. William E. Jones. After heavy fighting, a Federal assault found a gap in the Confederate lines, and the Southerners gave way. While trying to stem the retreat, Jones was killed, and the retreat became a rout. Hunter occupied Staunton on June 6 and Lexington on June 11. Confederate troops under Lt. Gen. Jubal A. Early finally stopped Hunter's advance outside Lynchburg on June 17–18, 1864.

The plaque is another of the series of battlefield markers erected statewide in the 1920s. Grim narratives of valiant, outnumbered Confederates are a hallmark of the memorials. The word defeat is not used often, but it occurs here: the Confederates are "defeated" with heavy losses.

Waynesboro

60. Riverview Cemetery Obelisk

Monument is a four-sided granite shaft with a decorative cap, set on a granite base.
LOCATION: 420 Rosser Avenue, 22980
DATE: May 24, 1906
MEDIUM: Granite
Front

CSA
OUR CONFEDERATE DEAD
1861–1865
—
CSA
VIRGINIA
[20 NAMES]
TWO UNKNOWN SOLDIERS
—
CSA
[6 NAMES]
—
CSA
GEORGIA
[2 NAMES]
LOUISIANA
[1 NAME]
MARYLAND
[1 NAME]

This simple shaft, despite its restrained tone and modest appearance, was, like many monuments, the subject of great celebration when it was dedicated in 1906. A parade assembled on Wayne Avenue and marched along Main Street, with the Stonewall Brigade veterans leading, followed by students of the Fishburne Military School, other veterans, sons of veterans, the Waynesboro Fire Department, carriages with speakers, and floats with the ladies who were a part of the afternoon ceremonies of prayers, speeches, unveiling, speeches, benediction, and salute.

Historian James I. Robertson Jr. identifies this as a battlefield monument, although there is no mention of the battle on the inscription. Still, the field is nearby, and it may, as such, be said to testify to the courage of those who stood by the colors in the last days of the war. The battle of Waynesboro, March 2, 1865, is overlooked by the decisiveness of the battle of Cedar Creek, but Waynesboro is the site of the last chapter of the Valley campaigns.

After a brief standoff, two Union cavalry divisions under Sheridan, which had ridden up the Valley from Winchester, turned the Confederate right flank and scattered Lt. Gen. Jubal A. Early's "army of observation" of about sixteen hundred men. "I went to the top of a hill to reconnoitre," wrote Early, "and had the mortification of seeing the greater part of my command being carried off as prisoners." Early and a small escort evaded capture and escaped over Rockfish Gap. For his part, Early took no blame for the debacle:

> I did not intend making my final stand on this ground . . . yet I was satisfied that if my men would fight, which I had no reason to doubt, I could hold the enemy in check until night, and then cross the river and take position in Rockfish Gap; for I had done more difficult things than that during the war. ——

No great credit is extended to these men by Early, but their loyalty exceeded the bonds of mortality: they are still here.

61. Col. William H. Harman Tablet

Monument is a granite shaft on a base, the whole surrounded by a rail fence.
LOCATION: Main Street to McElroy to Constitution Park
MEDIUM: Granite

WILLIAM H. HARMAN
COLONEL, C.S.A.
Born Feb. 17, 1828
Killed in action at
Waynesboro Mar. 2, 1865.
He was lieutenant of a company from Augusta County in the Mexican War; afterwards Brig-General in the

Virginia Militia; appointed
Lieut Col. 5th Virginia Inft.
C.S.A. May 7, 1861; Col. And
A. D. C. on staff of Maj. General Edward Johnson,
May 17, 1862.
A Gallant Soldier

A native of Waynesboro, William H. Harman lived in Staunton and served as the commonwealth's attorney of Augusta County from 1851 to 1863. Harman was attacked by five Union soldiers at the foot of Main Street hill in the confusion after the battle of Waynesboro, and is said to have fought to the death. His body was interred at Thornrose Cemetery, Staunton.

- The monument was moved several times before being placed here. A plaque at the base reads:

THIS RAIL CONTRIBUTED
JEB STUART CHAPTER
UDC STAUNTON, VA.
OCTOBER 18TH, 1926

Staunton, Thornrose Cemetery
LOCATION: 1041 West Beverley Street, 24401

62. Entryway Plaque
Monument is a bronze plaque set on a limestone tower near the gateway to the cemetery.
DATE: circa 1904
MEDIUM: Bronze

THIS BRONZE
COMMEMORATES TO GENERATIONS
WHICH KNEW THEM NOT,
THE VIRGINIA VOLUNTEERS
FROM AUGUSTA IN THE ARMY
OF THE CONFEDERATE STATES.
TWENTY-TWO COMPANIES FROM
HERE FOLLOWED JACKSON AND
STUART, WITH MANY IN OTHER
COMMANDS.
NO REBELS THEY, BUT WORTHY
SONS OF PATRIOTIC SIRES, WHO
TOOK UP ARMS IN THE HOUR
OF THEIR STATE'S EXTREMITY,
WHEN ARGUMENT FOR PEACE WAS
ENDED, TO DEFEND THE SOIL,
THE HOMES AND THE CONSTI-
TUTIONAL RIGHTS WON BY
THEIR FATHERS. THE WORLD
HAS SEEN NO BRAVER NOR
TRUER SOLDIERY THAN THE
YEOMEN WHOSE DEEDS MADE
GLORIOUS THIS VALLEY OF THE
SHENANDOAH, AND THEIR FAME
RESTS SECURE AS THEIR NATIVE HILLS
IF THEY JUSTIFIED NOT THE
CAUSE FOR WHICH THEY WERE
READY TO DIE, THEY ENNOBLED
THEMSELVES, AND MAY BE
"FORGIVEN BY THE SONS OF
MEN WHO FOR CONSCIENCE
SAKE FOUGHT AGAINST THEIR
GOVERNMENT AT LEXINGTON
AND BUNKER HILL."

Thornrose Cemetery was founded in 1849, the Augusta Memorial Association in 1870. This majestic statement on the gateway to the cemetery grounds praises the "Virginia Volunteers" from Augusta who fought for their soil, homes, and constitutional rights. Certitude about the justice of their cause is not ventured, but the plaque claims a connection between their "glorious deeds" in conscience and nobility of purpose to those who fought in the first American War of Independence. Lexington and Bunker Hill are invoked as revolutionary victories "against their government," but Yorktown—and final victory—is not.

- Confederate generals John Echols and Robert D. Lilley are interred in this cemetery, as is Maj. Jedediah Hotchkiss, mapmaker and staff aide to Stonewall Jackson.

63. Common Soldier

Monument is a base and shaft surmounted by private soldier standing at parade rest.
DATE: September 25, 1888
MEDIA: Granite, marble
Front

[RELIEF OF CROSSED MUSKETS]
HONOR TO THE BRAVE.
870 LIE HERE,
RECORDED BY NAME, COMPANY & REGIMENT:
FROM
VIRGINIA 305, N. CAROLINA
176, S. CAROLINA 59,
GEORGIA 208, ALABAMA 49, FLORIDA 8,
MISSISSIPPI 11, LOUISIANA 19, TENNESSEE 12,
ARKANSAS 20, TEXAS 3,
AND 207
RECORDED BY NAME ONLY.
CONFEDERATE DEAD
—

[RELIEF OF CROSSED SWORDS]

"THERE IS A TRUE GLORY AND A TRUE HONOR;
THE GLORY OF DUTY DONE;
THE HONOR OF THE INTEGRITY
OF PRINCIPLE."
ROBERT E. LEE.

—
[RELIEF OF ENGINEERING TOOLS]
"AS UNKNOWN AND YET WELL KNOWN."
AROUND THIS SHAFT
ARE GATHERED ALSO THE REMAINS OF
ABOUT 700 CONFEDERATE SOLDIERS,
NOT RECORDED BY NAME,
FROM FIELDS OF ALLEGHANY, MCDOWELL,
CROSS KEYS, PORT REPUBLIC & C.
VIRGINIA FORGETS NOT ANY,
WHO DIED IN HER DEFENSE.

—
[RELIEF OF CROSSED CANNON BARRELS]
WEIGH NOT THEIR WORTH
BY THE BALANCE OF BATTLE:
THESE HAVE GLORIFED THEIR CAUSE
BY THE RECORD OF NOBLE SACRIFICE,
THE SIMPLE MANHOOD OF THEIR LIVES,
THE PATIENT ENDURING OF SUFFERING,
AND THE HEROISM OF DEATH.
MAY SUCH FIDELITY AND PATRIOTISM
ENDURE FOREVER

Thousands of Confederate troops traveled through Staunton during the war. Stage, and railroad access made it a collection site for supplies, reinforcements, and casualties. The city's Deaf, Dumb, and Blind Institute and the Western Lunatic Asylum were eventually pressed into service as military hospitals along with private businesses and homes.

No system of recording burials was in place until March 1862. As early as March 1866, several women of Staunton began volunteer work at Thornrose. Efforts to maintain the individual gravesites continued into the twentieth century. The effects were not permanent. Today the graves are unmarked apart from a few modern markers, and most of these were installed without knowledge of the actual burial sites of the named soldiers."

A monument committee was organized June 9, 1883. The presiding edifice is thirty feet high, of Italian marble, and is the work of Victor Pathia, of Correggio, Italy. It was installed by Charles M. Ehmann and stands at the highest point in the cemetery. Over eighteen hundred soldiers are interred here. The sculpture was commissioned by the Augusta Memorial As-sociation and the Ladies' Auxiliary. Nearly four thousand people attended the unveiling on September 25, 1888, including Governor W. H. Fitzhugh Lee, Jubal A. Early, and Jed Hotchkiss.

The tribute beginning "Weigh not" is attributed to William Henry Trescot and also appears on the Confederate monument on the South Carolina state capitol grounds. The quotation by Robert E. Lee—"Duty Done . . . Integrity of Principle"—is taken from his private correspondence and has been understood as representing his code of life.

The battles inscribed on the rear panel were fought in the early years of the war. Alleghany and McDowell, west of Staunton, were fought in 1861 and 1862, respectively. Port Republic and Cross Keys, east of Staunton, were also fought in 1862. Later actions—New Market, Piedmont, and Waynesboro—are incorporated as "& c"—e. g., the rest.

- A bronze plaque at the base of the sculpture reads:

"THIS SITE MAINTAINED BY
5TH VIRGINIA
COMPANY E RE-ENACTORS
'LESS WE FORGET'" [SIC]

64. Tablet with Plaque, "Mirabeau"

Monument is a bronze plaque inset on a granite shaft and set on a stone base, on the west side of the Confederate cemetery.
DATE: circa 1920s
MEDIA: Bronze, granite

"CROWN ME WITH FLOWERS," CRIED
MIRABEAU, IN HIS LAST HOUR, AND LOVING
FRIENDS BROUGHT THEM. LONG MAY THE
GRAVES OF THESE CONFEDERATE SOLDIERS
BE STREWN WITH THE FIRST FLOWERS OF
SPRINGTIME AS A FITTING TRIBUTE TO
MATCHLESS VALOR AND EXALTED WORTH.
"HERE ARE THEY WHO MARCHED AWAY
FOLLOWED BY OUR HOPES AND FEARS,
NOBLER NEVER WENT THAN THEY
TO A BLOODIER, MADDER FRAY,
IN THE LAPSE OF ALL THE YEARS.
GARLANDS STILL SHALL
WREATHE THE SWORDS
THAT THEY DREW AMID OUR CHEERS;
CHILDREN'S LISPINGS, WOMEN'S WORDS,
SUNSHINE, AND THE SONG OF BIRDS
GREET THEM HERE THROUGH
ALL THE YEARS."

The "first" American Revolution and the
Civil War as the Second American Revolution are invoked or implied on several Virginia
monuments. This monument offers the only
direct reference to the French Revolution. The
inscription is by Armistead C. Gordon from
his poem, "The Garden of Death." The poem
was read at the unveiling of the Confederate
statue here. "Mirabeau" is Honoré Gabriel Ri-
quetti, comte de Mirabeau (1749–1791), a del-
egate of the third estate for the States General
of 1789, and an eloquent speaker.

65. Tablet with Plaque, "McKim"
Monument is a bronze plaque inset on a gran-
ite shaft, on the east side of the Confederate
cemetery.
DATE: circa 1920
MEDIA: Bronze, granite

IN MEMORY
OF THE
CONFEDERATE SOLDIERS
FROM
STAUNTON AND AUGUSTA
COUNTY
1861–1865
"NOT FOR FAME OR REWARD, NOT FOR PLACE
OR RANK, NOT LURED BY
AMBITION OR GOADED

BY NECESSITY, BUT IN SIMPLE OBEDIENCE TO
DUTY, AS THEY UNDERSTOOD
IT, THESE MEN SUF-
FERED ALL, SACRIFICED ALL,
DARED ALL—AND DIED!
NO STATELY ABBEY WILL EVER
COVER THEIR RE-
MAINS. THEIR DUST WILL
NEVER REPOSE BENEATH
FRETTED OR FRESCOED ROOF.
NO COSTLY BRONZE
WILL EVER BLAZON THEIR
NAMES FOR POSTERITY
TO HONOR—BUT THE POTOMAC
AND THE RAPPA-
HANNOCK, THE JAMES AND CHICKAHOMINY,
THE CUMBERLAND AND THE TENNESSEE, THE
MISSISSIPPI AND THE RIO
GRANDE, AS THEY RUN
THEIR LONG RACE FROM THE
MOUNTAINS TO THE
SEA, WILL SING OF THEIR
PROWESS FOREVERMORE."

This is still another approach to memorial-
izing at Thornrose: this one—"In Memory of
the Confederate Soldiers From Staunton and
Augusta County"—hazards a blunt recognition of "These Men [who] Died" not for principles or rights, as is so often proclaimed, but
in "Simple Obedience to Duty."

The quotation is attributed to Reverend Randolph Harrison McKim, a Confederate veteran (2nd Virginia Cavalry) and longtime pastor of Epiphany Church in Washington, D.C. The passage is taken from a speech he gave to a United Confederate Veterans reunion at Nashville, Tennessee, on June 14, 1904. An excerpt also appears on the Confederate monument at Arlington Cemetery.

Rockbridge County and Lexington

Lexington, Virginia Military Institute

66. Thomas J. "Stonewall" Jackson Statue

Monument is a granite pedestal surmounted by bronze figure.
LOCATION: Virginia Military Institute parade ground, Letcher Avenue, 24450
DATE: June 19, 1912
MEDIA: Bronze, granite

STONEWALL JACKSON
THE
VIRGINIA MILITARY
INSTITUTE
WILL-BE-HEARD-FROM
TO-DAY
GENERAL-JACKSON
AT-CHANCELLORSVILLE
MAY 3, 1863

Jackson dominates the campus parade ground of the college where he served as an instructor. The sculptor is Moses Ezekiel, who is also credited with the New Market monument here. The interpretation is distinctive: the Jackson figure is wearing a wide-brimmed hat, not the fatigue cap, as was his custom; he also appears to be standing in high wind, to judge by the tousled appearance of his frock coat and hat.

The quotation attributed to Jackson may represent the high water mark of the Confederacy. It is not quite accurate. "Ready for battle," the Virginia Military Institute archives note, Jackson "was surrounded by former students and colleagues from his years at V.M.I.; they were now his officers and comrades-in-arms. Overcome by emotion, Jackson said, 'the Institute will be heard from today.'" The Army of Northern Virginia never looked as capable, even triumphant as it did on the afternoon of May 2, 1863, during the battle of Chancellorsville (not May 3, as the monument has it). It was also the day Jackson was shot—a few hours after making this remark, by night, in a case of friendly fire.

- A replica of this monument stands on the grounds of the state capitol at Charleston, West Virginia.
- The remains of Little Sorrel, Jackson's warhorse, were interred here in 1997.

67. New Market Memorial, Statue, Virginia Mourning

Monument is a bronze sculpture of a woman, "Virginia," set on a granite base and pedestal with bronze tablets.
DATE: June 23, 1903
MEDIA: Bronze, granite

Front

COMPANY A
[13 NAMES]
[52 NAMES]
ROLL OF HONOR
KILLED
[10 NAMES]
WOUNDED
[49 NAMES]
—

COMPANY C
[12 NAMES]
[60 NAMES]
—

COMPANY D
[12 NAMES]
[60 NAMES]
NEW MARKET, VIRGINIA, MAY 15, 1864
FIELD AND STAFF
[6 NAMES]
NON-COMMISSIONED STAFF
[3 NAMES]
MUSICIANS
[3 NAMES]
—

COMPANY B
[12 NAMES]
[63 NAMES]

The statue of a bereaved woman, titled "Virginia Mourning Her Dead" and sculpted by Moses Ezekiel, presides over four bronze plaques with a litany of names of the cadet corps at the time of the battle of New Market. "Virginia" is said to be watching over the Corps and the Corps' wartime casualties. Ezekiel, an alumnus of V.M.I. and a cadet at the time of the battle, describes her this way: "the chain mail clad female figure is seated mourning upon a piece of breast work and her foot rests upon a broken cannon over grown with ivy, and she holds a reversed lance in her hands." There is no narrative and no mention of the war, although neither is necessary, of course: the campus has numerous tributes and reminders of both.

The number of cadets listed is 275. Of these, 257 were directly engaged in the battle; ten were killed, forty-nine wounded. Eighteen cadets served as artillery or wagon guards, or were left at the Institute to act as guards.

The archives note the following about the unveiling:

The statue was dedicated on Alumni Day, June 23, 1903, following a morning parade and guard mount. Alumni began arriving on June 15, 1903 and the population of Lexington was doubled at the time of the ceremonies!

At 10:30 A.M. a prayer by Dr. R. J. McBride began the ceremony. There was a commemorative ode by the Honorable A. E. Gordon, and an address by Dr. John N. Upshur VMI 1867, a New Market veteran.

The attendees at the ceremonies included a reunion of cadets from 1839 to 1903. The archives record that "Men whose locks were white and whose forms were bent with years seemed now to step with the agility of youth again and to walk erect, as in days of yore, when they marched to the beat of the drum."

• Individual headstones mark the graves of the cadets interred here, but the remains are actually buried in a copper box set into the foundation of the monument.

Bronze wall plaque:

IN MEMORIAM
TO THE CADETS WHO GAVE THEIR
LIVES IN THE BATTLE OF NEW MARKET
MAY 15, 1864
AND LIE BURIED ELSEWHERE
[4 NAMES]
THIS PLAQUE PLACED BY
THE VMI ALUMNI ASSOCIATION

Stonewall Cemetery

68. Confederate Memorial, Obelisk
Monument is an obelisk surmounted by funereal urn.

LOCATION: White and Main Street, 24450
DATE: 1884
MEDIUM: Granite
Front

ERECTED
TO THE MEMORY OF OUR
SOUTHERN SOLDIERS,
1884.
Welcome peaceful bed
When our camps expired
Though no tears be shed,
Though no tuneful choir,
Chant in mournful strains
While around our bier:
Yet a rest remains
Long denied us here.
—
[10 NAMES]
—
UNKNOWN
Let us gather sweet flowers,
and garland the simple stone,
that marks the spot where someone lies.
In a strange land unknown.
—
[22 NAMES]

Some four hundred Confederate soldiers are buried here, most of them in family plots. This is the collective monument to them. The Jackson statue dominates these grounds and draws the most visitors, and this unobtrusive obelisk is hard to find and little known, but it stands northwest of the Jackson plot.

This memorial is particularly grim: the ground is unsanctified—"a strange land unknown." The funereal tone is relentless: "no tears . . . no tuneful choir . . . mournful strains . . ." Stonewall Cemetery is rich with epitaphs that testify to religious faith or comfort, but here none is offered—only a surcease from conflict and the rest to be obtained in death that was not afforded these men in life.

- Also buried in Stonewall Cemetery: generals Elisha F. Paxton, William N. Pendleton, Chief of Artillery of the Army of Northern Virginia; Edwin G. Lee.
- Lee Chapel inters members of the Lee family on the grounds of Washington and Lee University. The remains of Traveller, Lee's warhorse, are interred just outside its doors.

69. Thomas J. "Stonewall" Jackson Statue

Monument is a figure sculpted in bronze surmounting a granite pedestal.

DATE: July 21, 1891

MEDIA: Bronze, granite

JACKSON
1824–1863

—

STONEWALL

Thomas J. "Stonewall" Jackson was reinterred here beneath this statue sculpted by Edward V. Valentine, which was unveiled with elaborate ceremonies in 1891. Valentine also sculpted the statue of Robert E. Lee inside the Lee Chapel nearby.

This is arguably the central monument in Lexington: Jackson's presence is commanding and preeminent.

A bronze plaque on the pedestal reads:

FIELD MARSHAL THE RIGHT HONORABLE
VISCOUNT WOLSELEY, K. P., G.
C. B., G. M., G. C. M. G.
BRITISH SOLDIER OF THE HIGHEST RANK,
SAYS:
The fame of Stonewall Jackson is no longer
The exclusive property of Virginia and the South;
it has become the birthright of every man
privileged to call himself an American"
THIS TABLET PLACED BY THE
CAMP FRANK PAXTON, S.C.V.,
MARY CUSTIS LEE CHAPTER, U.D.C.. [SIC]

Field Marshal Garnet Joseph Wolseley (1833–1913) was a highly decorated British Army officer and writer, of wide service and extensive combat experience, known for his efficiency and competence.

Among those present at the dedication ceremonies: generals Jubal A. Early, Wade Hampton, P. G. T. Beauregard, John B. Gordon, Thomas L. Rosser, W. H. Payne, and James A. Walker. The assembly also included five hundred veterans of the Stonewall Brigade, along with contingents of the R. E. Lee Camp of Richmond, the Stonewall Camp of Veterans from Winchester, and organizations from Baltimore, New Orleans, and Salisbury, North Carolina. Veterans of the Rockbridge Artillery fired a general's salute of seventeen guns.

- Stonewall Jackson Memorial Cemetery is said to have begun as the burial ground for the old Lexington Presbyterian Church in 1789.
- Jackson's body was originally interred about one hundred feet from this site.

Alleghany County and Covington

70. Covington, Courthouse Common Soldier

Monument is a private soldier standing at parade rest surmounting a shaft, set on a base and plinth.
LOCATION: 266 West Main Street, 24426
DATE: September 15, 1911
MEDIUM: Granite
Front

[C.S.A. NATIONAL AND BATTLE FLAGS]
TO THE
CONFEDERATE
SOLDIERS OF
ALLEGHANY
COUNTY.

—

"THEY FOUGHT FOR LIBERTY,
HOME AND THOSE THEY LOVED,
THEIR NAMES ARE BORNE
ON HONOR'S SHIELD AND
THEIR RECORD IS WITH GOD."
ERECTED IN LOVING TRIBUTE
BY THE
ALLEGHANY
CHAPTER, U.D.C.

—

ALLEGHANY COUNTY
FURNISHED MORE
SOLDIERS TO THE
CONFEDERATE CAUSE
THAN SHE HAD VOTERS.
1861–1865

—

"FATE DENIED THEM VICTORY,
BUT CROWNED THEM WITH
GLORIOUS IMMORTALITY."
UNVEILED
SEPTEMBER 15,
1911.

Covington's monument was dedicated during the semicentennial of the war and displays the same lofty, celebratory grandeur of other monuments erected in that peak year of the movement. The ceremonies coincided with the dedication of a new courthouse. Some seven thousand people were present, crowding the courthouse grounds and the surrounding blocks.

The claim that "Their Names are Borne on Honor's Shield and their Record is with God," has the confidence of the Confederate national motto, "Deo Vindice." The reference to voters on the third (rear) panel was inscribed before women's suffrage and implies that the wartime generation—especially the younger men, those not of age to vote—are role models for generations of "true" Confederates to come.

71. Low Moor, Oakland Church Common Soldier

Monument is a private soldier standing at parade rest, at eye level, atop a marble pedestal.
LOCATION: I-64, Exit 21, east of Low Moor on B.R. 60–220, to Oakland Church, 24457
DATE: 1930s (estimated)
MEDIA: Faux granite, marble
Front

THIS STONE IS ERECTED TO
COMMEMORATE THE GLORY OF
THOSE HEROES WHO WERE
HONORED AND LOVED BY THE
PEOPLE OF ALLEGHANY CO.
AND OF THOSE TO US UNKNOWN
BUT KNOWN TO FAME.

HONORED BY MEN AND LOVED
OF GOD MAY THE NAMES OF ALL
BE WRITTEN IN THE "LAMBS
BOOK OF LIFE."

—

[7 NAMES]

—

[BLANK]

—

[7 NAMES]

This church cemetery monument stands near Interstate 64. Erected circa 1847, Oakland Grove Presbyterian Church, east of Low Moor, is the oldest known ecclesiastical structure in Alleghany County. It appears isolated today, but in the nineteenth century it had a prime location near the Jackson River, a railroad (still in service), and an east-west turnpike. A plaque placed by the Jackson Chapter of the United Daughters of the Confederacy notes that the building served as a hospital for Stonewall Jackson's troops during the Shenandoah Valley campaign of 1862. At least twelve members of a Tennessee regiment are known to have been buried here. Other dead soldiers—men under Stonewall Jackson's command—were buried

here as well. A restoration of the church and the grounds was recently completed, but little data is extant about the monument, and it remains an obscure site for Civil War commemoration.

- The monument is not dated, but the style is similar to monuments erected in the 1930s. The soldier is hollow and may be a cast stone design to create the appearance of granite.
- The inscription does not refer to the war, and no great cause to die for is declared. The reference to the "Lambs Book of Life" is apocalyptic, and is excerpted from Revelation 21:27.
- The Oakland Church was dissolved on December 23, 1962. The Low Moor Presbyterian Church provides upkeep for the site; occasional services are still held there.

Bath County, Warm Springs

72. Courthouse Common Soldier

Monument surmounts a pedestal, dado, plinth, and base.

LOCATION: U.S. 220 and V.R. 39, 24484
DATE: June 20, 1923
MEDIUM: Granite

[SEAL OF THE CONFEDERACY]
CONFEDERATE
SOLDIERS
1861–1865
"LEST WE FORGET."
ERECTED BY
BATH CO. CHAPTER
U.D.C. 1922

The Warm Springs elegy, a McNeel Marble sculpture, is a latter-stage courthouse monument. Little is known about it, although no other monument of its size or scale stands in Bath County. The monument is significant for its confidence. No apologetic or rationale for the war is offered, and its presence in this small, quiet town suggests a sentinel-like defiance of any possibility that the soldier's status will ever be diminished or forgotten. The traditional monition or caution, "Lest we forget," seems the more earnest a claim to make in what is an otherwise tranquil, rural mountain valley landscape.

- A local story holds that boys playing on the statue in the 1950s broke the bayonet on the soldier's weapon.
- Another local story—probably apocryphal—holds that the monument originally delivered for the dedication date ceremonies was a Union soldier, to the surprise of all in attendance when he was unveiled. That soldier was speedily replaced with the present one. No local copies of the *Bath County Enterprise* could confirm the tale; the United Daughters of the Confederacy chapter disbanded many years ago, and no U.D.C. records are known to exist.
- Numerous skirmishes and maneuvers occurred in the area, and Confederate hospitals were established at the various springs and resorts including Bath Alum, Healing Springs, Hot Springs, and Warm Springs.

73. Cemetery Tablet

Monument is a bronze tablet set on a fieldstone base.
LOCATION: U.S. 220, south of V.R. 39, marker at cemetery hilltop intersection
MEDIA: Bronze, fieldstone

THIRTY
UNIDENTIFIED SOLDIERS
OF THE ARMY
OF THE CONFEDERACY
WHO DIED ON ACTIVE DUTY
ARE BURIED
NEAR THIS MARKER

This site has commanding views of the surrounding valleys and hills. The sponsor is unknown, and indeed local residents were unaware of its existence. It is thought to be related to local military hospitals. Of them the limited data reveals that Warm Springs Hospital, owned by George Mayse, became a Confederate hospital by July 1861 and remained in operation until at least June 1863. On October 12, 1861, ten officers and 450 enlisted men were in the hospital. At least forty-eight deaths occurred here between July and December 1861.

Highland County

74. Common Soldier, Monterey Courthouse
Monument is a private soldier standing at parade rest, in marble, surmounting a granite plinth, base, and dado.
LOCATION: 165 West Main Street, 24465
DATE: July 4, 1919
MEDIA: Granite, marble
Front

TO THE
CONFEDERATE SOLDIERS

OF
HIGHLAND COUNTY
A LOVING TRIBUTE TO
THE PAST, THE PRESENT,
AND THE FUTURE.

—

ERECTED BY
HIGHLAND CHAPTER
UNITED DAUGHTERS OF
THE CONFEDERACY
1918

The monument was erected just after World War I and, thus, late in the reconciliation era. The sculpture of the young Confederate soldier, a product of the A. M. Kerr Marble Works of Staunton, faces north, with one hand holding a weapon and the other hand raised above his eyes to gaze into the distance, as if to continue the vigil against threats of incursion from the north.

The statue, of marble imported from Italy, was erected on a cement circular base surrounded by a ring of grass. It stands approximately thirteen feet high, and cost about fifteen hundred dollars. The sculptor is unknown.

The dedication festivities began with a parade at 10 A. M., on July 4, 1919. The morning and afternoon programs included band selections, an address, readings, speeches, and singing. A crowd of approximately five thousand people was present, including about forty Confederate veterans. The U.D.C. chapter president, Mrs. J. B. Bradshaw, performed the unveiling of the monument.

75. McDowell, Battlefield Tablet

Monument is a bronze tablet set on a fieldstone shaft.

LOCATION: U.S. 220 east of McDowell, 24458
DATE: 1917
MEDIA: Bronze, fieldstone

COMMEMORATING
THE BATTLE OF MCDOWELL
MAY 8, 1862
FEDERALS
IN ACTION 4000—KILLED AND WOUNDED 256
CONFEDERATES
IN ACTION 2500—KILLED AND WOUNDED 498
CONFEDERATE OFFICERS KILLED
CAPTAINS   LIEUTENANTS
[FOUR NAMES]   [FOUR NAMES]
ALL OF THE 12TH GEORGIA REGIMENT
[ROSTER OF EIGHT OFFICERS
FROM SEVEN VIRGINIA REGIMENTS]
ERECTED BY
THE HIGHLAND CHAPTER
UNITED DAUGHTERS OF THE CONFEDERACY
1917

This is one of several U.D.C. monuments in this area erected under the leadership of Mrs. J. B. Bradshaw, the "leading spirit" among a group of women of Highland County who met at the Mansion House in McDowell, on Thursday, May 8, 1913, the fifty-first anniversary of the battle of McDowell, for the purpose of organizing a chapter of the United Daughters of the Confederacy."

Fought on May 8, 1862, during the 1862 Valley campaign, Maj. Gen. Thomas J. Jackson with six thousand Confederate troops advanced west from Staunton and clashed with two Union brigades of Maj. Gen. John C. Frémont's force, about sixty-five hundred men under brigadier generals Robert H. Milroy and Robert C. Schenck, who were advancing on the Shenandoah Valley. Milroy's troops assaulted the Confederate position on Sitlington's Hill east of the town but were repulsed after heavy fighting. The Federals retreated west in the aftermath, and Jackson pursued to Monterey before turning his army east to face Nathaniel Banks's army near Strasburg. The monument states the facts of the action—the aggregates and casualties—but it makes no mention of the outcome of the battle as a Confederate victory.

76. McDowell Church, Battlefield Tablet

Monument is a bronze tablet set on a fieldstone base.
LOCATION: Highland Turnpike (U.S. 250) and Bullpasture Road, 24458
DATE: 1926
MEDIA: Bronze, granite, fieldstone

BATTLE OF MCDOWELL
MAY 8, 1862, ONE MILE SOUTHEAST,
JACKSON AND EDWARD JOHNSON, C.S.A.
DEFEATED MILROY AND SCHENCK, U.S.A.
THIS CHURCH SERVED BOTH BLUE AND GRAY

AS A HOSPITAL
THIS MARKER ERECTED 1926

This United Daughters of the Confederacy monument summarizes the action that is detailed in the monument across the Bullpasture River. It is listed as one of the twenty-five battlefield markers of the Virginia Statewide Battlefield Markers Association. This tablet gives particular attention to the McDowell Presbyterian Church and its role in serving as a hospital that served the wounded on both sides of the battle. The inscription gives equal status to the United States and the Confederacy, although the Confederacy was never formally recognized by the United States. However, it also notes that the church hospital made no such distinctions among the casualties.

77. McDowell, Church Cemetery Tablet

Monument is a granite tablet set in concrete on a fieldstone base.
LOCATION: Highland Turnpike (U.S. 250) and Bullpasture Road, 24458
DATE: circa 1930s
MEDIA: Fieldstone, granite

IN THIS AREA ARE BURIED
CONFEDERATE AND UNION
SOLDIERS WHO DIED AT
MCDOWELL VA MAY 8 1862

This church cemetery marker, of anonymous origins, located across the road from the church/hospital site, indicates that the dead—both blue and gray—are buried together in unmarked graves. It provides the final public notice of the presence of these dead, whose interment here would likely have been forgotten otherwise.

2. Southwest Virginia

Geographical Outline. Twenty counties, independent cities such as Bristol, Roanoke, and Salem: the West Virginia state line or James River to the north; the Kentucky state line to the west; the Tennessee state line to the south, and the line of the Blue Ridge to the east and northeast.

Campaigns. Several campaigns took place in the Southwestern Highlands over control of the Cumberland Gap and the Virginia and Tennessee Railroad. Union forces also assailed the mineral works at the aptly named Saltville and the lead works around Wytheville. Partisan activities on both sides were common. Nonpartisan criminal opportunism was not unknown.

Terrain: By some accounts, southwest Virginia is a world to itself, although the railroad, along with interstates 81 and 77, and U.S. 460, 58, and 11, provide ready avenues of access into most of the mountains and valleys. Roanoke is the largest city, and has the largest concentration of monuments in the southwest.

Commentary. There are few battlefield monuments in southwest Virginia: Hanging Rock in Roanoke County, Cranesnest in Wise County, and Cove Mountain in Wythe County are the exceptions. No monuments commemorate the two battles of Saltville or the Cloyd's Mountain battlefield near Dublin.

Courthouse monuments extend along the railroad towns—e. g., Roanoke, Marion, Abingdon, and Bristol—as well as the southernmost tier of county seats at Floyd, Hillsville, and Independence. Southern sentiments do not stop at the state lines. Confederate monuments also stand in West Virginia at the county seats of Hinton (Summers), Union (Monroe), and Lewisburg (Greenbrier), as well as at the former resort springs and military hospital at Red Sulphur Springs (Monroe County).

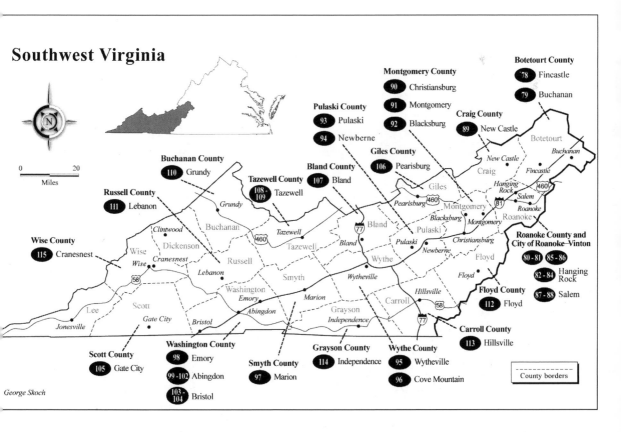

Southwest Virginia

George Skoch

As one travels west in Virginia there are fewer monuments. Only two county seat monuments stand west of the Clinch River Valley: Gate City's 1988 plaque and Grundy's 1998 tablet. None stand at the far western seats of Lee, Dickinson, or Wise counties. Every other county seat has a monument.

Some seventeen thousand men from southwestern Virginia served in Confederate armies, of whom an estimated forty-five hundred died. Meanwhile, the rule of law in this region virtually disappeared: crime went unpunished, army deserters often found sanctuary, and bushwhackers wandered unchecked throughout the country, taking advantage of travelers, the elderly, and the isolated.

Botetourt County

78. Fincastle, Courthouse Obelisk

Monument is a granite plinth, base, dado, and obelisk.
LOCATION: 20 East Back Street, 24090
DATE: October 27, 1904
MEDIUM: Granite
Front

ERECTED A. D. 1904.
TO COMMEMORATE
THE DEEDS AND SERVICES
OF THE
TWELVE VOLUNTEER COMPANIES,
—NAMED HEREUNDER—
THAT WENT TO THE WAR
FROM BOTETOURT COUNTY.
THE FINCASTLE RIFLES,
CO. D. 11 REG'T. VA. INFANTRY.
THE BOTETOURT DRAGOONS,
CO. C. 2 REG'T. VA. CAVALRY.
THE MOUNTAIN RIFLES,
CO. H. 28 REG'T. VA. INFANTRY,
ANDERSON'S BATTERY—THE
BOTETOURT ARTILLERY.
1861 C.S.A. 1865.
—

TO
THE WOMEN OF BOTETOURT
IN REMEMBRANCE OF
THEIR CONSTANT ENCOURAGEMENT,
STEADFAST DEVOTION,
TENDER MINISTRATIONS AND
UNFAILING PROVIDENCE AND CARE,
DURING THE WAR
AND IN THE
DARK RECONSTRUCTION YEARS.
THE ROARING-RUN COMPANY,
CO. K. 11 REG'T. VA. INFANTRY.
THE BOTETOURT GUARDS,
CO. K 57 REG'T. VA. INFANTRY.
THE OSCEOLA GUARDS,
CO. K 60 REG'T. VA. INFANTRY.
A. J. WRAY,
RICH D. VA.
—

IN HONOR OF
THOSE MEN OF BOTETOURT,
—OF THE PERIOD 1861–1865,—
WHO FAITHFULLY DID DUTY
IN THE
CIVIL AND MILITARY SERVICE OF
VIRGINIA,
AND OF
THE CONFEDERATE STATES.
IN RECOGNITION OF
THOSE WHO GAVE, AND OF
THOSE WHO WORKED AND SERVED,
TO SUPPORT OUR SOLDIERS,
AND FOR THE COMFORT AND
SAFETY OF THEIR FAMILIES.

THE BOTETOURT HEAVY ARTILLERY,
CO. C. 20 BAT'N. VA. H'VY. ART'Y.
THE BOTETOURT SENIOR RESERVES,
CO.—4 REG'T. VA. RESERVES.
THE BOTETOURT JUNIOR RESERVES,
CO. E. 2 BAT'N. VA. RESERVES.

—

IN MEMORY OF
OUR BRAVE AND LOYAL
OFFICERS AND ENLISTED MEN
WHO WERE KILLED IN BATTLE,
AND WHO
DIED FROM WOUNDS AND DISEASE,
DURING THE WAR,
AND OF
OUR FAITHFUL COMRADES
WHO HAVE DIED SINCE THE WAR.
THE BLUE RIDGE RIFLES,
CO. A. 28 REG'T. VA. INFANTRY.
THE BOTETOURT SPRINGS COMPANY,
CO. E. 28 REG'T. VA. INFANTRY.
THE BRECKENRIDGE INFANTRY,
CO. K. 28 REG'T. VA. INFANTRY.

The sponsorship for this monument is not cited and at this writing is unknown. Andrew Wray, of Richmond, received the commission. A county history notes that "One of the largest crowds ever assembled [was] here" for the ceremonies and that "Lady 'sponsors' wearing white dresses and beautiful hats assisted in removing the veil covering the monument."

Standing outside the 1848 courthouse, this monument is similar in style, content, and features to the Botetourt Artillery obelisk at Buchanan, some ten miles to the east. Here, as at Buchanan, elaborate tributes and service notes are inscribed. The Fincastle tribute is unique in making direct reference to the continuing service of women after the war—the "Dark Reconstruction Years."

Everyone in Botetourt who contributed to the war effort, it seems, is given tribute: the "Women of Botetourt"; the men who provided "Civil" service; and anyone "Who Worked and Served to Support Our Soldiers and for the Comfort and Safety of their Families." The *Richmond Times-Dispatch* observed that this "splendid granite shaft" was unveiled on a day

that was "bright and beautiful, cool and bracing." Of the dedication ceremonies they wrote:

> The town was in gale [sic] attire, the colors and flags of the Confederacy being mingled with those of a united country. . . . The principal address of the day was by Attorney-General Anderson, whose oration was magnificent and in every way suited to the occasion. After the address the old veterans were formed in line and marched to the town hall where a beautiful dinner was served. . . . The exercises during the day were greatly enlivened by the Alpine Band from Clifton Forge.

- Editorial note: periods missing from the format of two of the "Co K's."

79. Buchanan, Botetourt Artillery Obelisk

Monument is a granite plinth, base, dado, and obelisk.

LOCATION: Buchanan Presbyterian Church, 19559 Main Street, 24066
DATE: July 20, 1902
MEDIUM: Granite
FRONT

C.S.A.
ERECTED BY
THE BOTETOURT ARTILLERY
MONUMENT ASSOCIATION
A. D. 1902
IN COMMEMORATION OF
THE DEEDS AND SERVICES OF
THE BUCHANAN COMPANY.
ORGANIZED OCT. 1859, AS
THE MOUNTAIN RIFLES
VIRGINIA VOLUNTEERS.
ENLISTED MAY 1861, IN THE CONFEDERATE
STATES ARMY, FOR TWELVE MONTHS, AS
CO I-H- 28 REGIMENT VIRGINIA INFANTRY.
REENLISTED NOV. 1861, FOR THE WAR, AS
ANDERSON'S BATTERY LIGHT ARTILLERY.
RENAMED, MARCH 1863, AS
THE BOTETOURT ARTILLERY.
1861–1865
THE
BOTETOURT ARTILLERY

—

TO
OUR OFFICERS AND MEN
WHO WERE KILLED IN BATTLE,
AND
WHO DIED FROM WOUNDS AND DISEASE,
DURING THE WAR.

—

TO OUR COMRADES
WHO HAVE DIED SINCE THE WAR,
AND
TO THE SURVIVORS OF OUR COMPANY.

—

TO
OUR LOVING, SELF-SACRIFICING,
CONFEDERATE WOMEN.

Monuments to individual Confederate units are uncommon in southwest Virginia. This unit served as infantry and artillery as well as in several different theatres of the war, from First Manassas as Co. I, 28th Virginia Infantry, then as the Botetourt Artillery in Kentucky and Vicksburg. The unit surrendered at Vicksburg, was reconstituted, served in western Virginia, and finally disbanded at Christiansburg in 1865. The only Virginia monument on the Vicksburg battlefield is dedicated to the Botetourt Artillery.

Roanoke County and Cities of Roanoke and Salem
Mt. View Cemetery, Vinton

80. Sundial and Shaft, 1954

Monument is an inscribed granite shaft with a sundial set atop and with an adjoining bench.
LOCATION: Mountain View Road, 24179
DATE: May 29, 1954
MEDIA: Bronze, granite

IN MEMORY OF
ALL CONFEDERATE SOLDIERS
BURIED IN THIS CEMETERY,
AND THEIR STRUGGLE FOR

OUR CONSTITUTIONAL RIGHTS.
ROANOKE CHAPTER
UNITED DAUGHTERS OF THE
CONFEDERACY
1954

SUNDIAL inscription, granite:

WE LIVE IN DEEDS, NOT IN YEARS

Vinton's shaft and the unusual sundial monument offer a bulwark of affirmation that these Confederates died for a communal "we": for "Our" constitutional rights. The monument was erected early in the civil rights era, indeed in the same year as the Supreme Court's Brown vs. Board of Education decision. In this instance, the struggle for "Our Constitutional Rights" is arguably displayed as part of a polemical continuum extending from "Their Struggle" to the present.

The sundial has raised Roman numerals and a zero. The raised letter pronouncement, "We Live in Deeds . . ." is attributed to Aristotle. The larger context reads, in part:

> We live in deeds, not years: in thoughts not breaths; in feelings, not in figures on a dial. We should count time by heart throbs. He most lives who thinks most, feels the noblest, acts the best.

81. Tablet, Roster

Monument is a bronze plaque set on a granite shaft.

MEDIUM: Granite

IN MEMORY OF THE SOLDIERS
OF
THE WAR BETWEEN THE STATES
BURIED IN THIS CEMETERY
[43 NAMES]
BY
MAJOR WILLIAM F. GRAVES CHAPTER
UNITED DAUGHTERS OF THE CONFEDERACY
VINTON, VIRGINIA
—
[CHRISTIAN CROSS]

William F. Graves (1832–1923) served as lieutenant colonel of the 2nd Virginia Cavalry and is buried in Mountain View. Graves's dedication address at the Bedford Courthouse monument is excerpted in chapter 5. The large Christian cross on the reverse side of this monument deserves notice. Small crosses are displayed on the University of Virginia tablets; of the few, this is certainly the largest cross on a Confederate monument in Virginia.

Hanging Rock, Battlefield
S. R. 419 to S. R. 311 north, Salem

82. Battlefield Pyramid, 1932
MONUMENT is a four-sided pyramid set on a base and plinth.

LOCATION: V.R. 311, 24153
DATE: June 3, 1932
MEDIUM: Granite

COMMEMORATING
BATTLE OF HANGING ROCK
JUNE 21, 1864.
ERECTED BY
SOUTHERN CROSS CHAPTER
U.D.C.
JUNE 3 1932

Proximity was a factor in the proliferation of monuments at this site. The battle of Hanging Rock was the only engagement of any size fought in Roanoke County during the war. The word battle overstates its scale. Union troops under David Hunter were intercepted by Confederate forces under John McCausland during the former's retreat to West Virginia after the battle of Lynchburg. The Federals were harassed here, not routed or defeated. Some sources state that there were no casualties, but Confederate Veteran reports that the Confederates lost two men with several wounded, while the Union forces lost eight to ten men, with about forty to fifty wounded. Small as it was, Hanging Rock conformed to the ideal of victory for the Confederate cause, and its monuments are similar to Confederate victory sites like Trevilians and New Market.

The ceremonies for this pyramid reflected the commemorative-era nostalgia for the war years. *Confederate Veteran* notes that "The girls who unveiled the monument wore costumes of the 1860s. Flags of the Confederacy, United States and Virginia were carried by Sons of Confederate Veterans, and the salute was fired by three members of the American legion."

- The pyramid is constructed of native granite; it was originally topped with a cannon ball found on the Garst farm some years after the battle. Upon her death in 1960, Miss Massie Garst bequeathed the Hanging Rock site to the Virginia Division of the United Daughters of the Confederacy.
- The dedication date, June 3, commemorates Jefferson Davis's birthday.

83. Battlefield Pyramid, 1964

Monument is a four-sided pyramid set on a base and plinth.
LOCATION: Northwest entrance of southbound I-81, Exit 141, 24153
DATE: June 21, 1964
MEDIUM: Granite

COMMEMORATING THE 100TH
ANNIVERSARY OF THE
SKIRMISH OF HANGING ROCK
JUNE 21, 1864
ERECTED BY THE WILLIAM WATTS CHAPTER
U.D.C.
JUNE 21, 1964

This centennial-era monument is identical in materials and appearance to the United Daughters of the Confederacy monument of 1932. It is, however, located on high ground just off Interstate 81 and is the only Virginia monument on the bank of an interstate highway grade. Unlike the 1932 monument, the more accurate word "skirmish" is used to describe the action here.

84. Pvt. George Morgan Jones Statue

Monument is a figure dressed as an officer, in bronze, surmounting a fieldstone pedestal and granite base, plinth, and pedestal.

LOCATION: C.R. 819 off S. R. 419, 24153

DATE: 1911

MEDIA: Bronze, fieldstone, granite

IN HONOR OF
GEORGE MORGAN JONES
CITIZEN SOLDIER
PHILANTHROPIST

This is a duplicate of the 1911 original statue of George Morgan Jones that stands at Randolph-Macon Women's College. Its placement is incongruous, although the casual visitor has no reason to think so. Neither Jones, nor the 2nd Virginia Cavalry in which he served as a private, was present for the action at Hanging Rock. The statue was erected in Salem in 1999 at a time when this battlefield was being developed as a park and historical destination. Originally it stood on the grounds of the former Jones Memorial Library in Lynchburg, but the library relocated, and the site became part of the Patrick Henry Institute.

Roanoke

85. City Courthouse Shaft to Gen. Robert E. Lee

Monument is a shaft set on a base, plinth, and dado.

LOCATION: Lee Plaza: 315 West Church Avenue S. W., 24016

DATE: October 4, 1960

MEDIUM: Granite

Front

[C.S.A. FLAGS: CROSSED STARS
AND BARS AND NATIONAL]
C.S.A.
ROBERT EDWARD LEE
SUPERINTENDENT, U. S. MILITARY ACADEMY
1852–1855
COMMANDER, ARMY OF NORTHERN VIRGINIA
1862–1865
COMMANDER-IN-CHIEF,
CONFEDERATE ARMIES
1865

PRESIDENT, WASHINGTON COLLEGE
1865–1870
ERECTED BY
ROANOKE CHAPTER—WILLIAM
WATTS CHAPTER
UNITED DAUGHTERS OF THE CONFEDERACY
DEDICATED OCTOBER 4, 1960

The inscription on this civil rights and centennial-era monument does not focus on Robert E. Lee (1807–1870) as a legend or leader, but on his civil and military service. Lee offers a presiding example of a steady, devoted public servant, one who is sanctified from any issues of his oath of allegiance—despite the fact that his decision to side with Virginia and the South against the U.S. remains one of the paradoxes of a man for whom duty and constancy were held sacred. The location outside the Federal courthouse—and the time, 1960—suggest that the heroes of the Confederacy left a benign and instructive heritage.

86. Fair View Cemetery Tablet

Monument is a shaft set on a base and plinth.
LOCATION: 3300 Melrose Avenue N. W., 24017
DATE: May 30, 1939
MEDIUM: Granite
Front

[U.D.C. SEAL]
SOUTHERN CROSS OF HONOR

1861
1865
TO THE MEMORY OF
ALL CONFEDERATE VETERANS
BURIED IN FAIR VIEW CEMETERY.
LOVE MAKES MEMORY ETERNAL
ERECTED BY WILLIAM WATTS CHAPTER
UNITED DAUGHTERS OF THE CONFEDERACY
ROANOKE, VA. MAY 30, 1939

The monument at Fair View, dedicated to three hundred Confederate veterans whose remains are buried here, was unveiled by James W. Gwaltney, aged 94, of the 34th Virginia Infantry and included ceremonies by a group of Veterans of Foreign Wars attendees. This is another of the series of nostalgic 1930s monuments. The sentiment, "Love Makes Memory Eternal," is also inscribed on the New Castle and Pearisburg courthouse monuments and at Tazewell's Jeffersonville Cemetery.

Salem

87. Courthouse Common Soldier

Monument is a private soldier standing at parade rest, in marble, surmounting a granite plinth, base, pedestal, and shaft.

LOCATION: Main Street and College Avenue, 24153
DATE: June 3, 1910
MEDIA: Granite, marble
Front

[CROSSED C.S.A. NATIONAL FLAGS]
IN MEMORY OF THE
CONFEDERATE SOLDIERS OF
ROANOKE COUNTY
1861–1865
LOVE MAKES MEMORY ETERNAL
—

[BLANK]
—

[U.D.C. SEAL]
ERECTED BY
SOUTHERN CROSS
CHAPTER U.D.C.
SALEM VA. 1909
—

[BLANK]

This twenty-eight-foot Barre granite monument stands where the Salem Artillery was mustered into service in 1861. The "Salem Flying Artillery Battery," originally Company A, 9th Virginia Infantry, served throughout the war and surrendered at Appomattox.

The courthouse was dedicated in April 1910 —coincident with the erection of the monument, which was dedicated on the anniversary of Jefferson Davis's birthday. The simple, confident tribute is similar to other southwestern monuments at Lebanon, Abingdon, Gate City, Marion, and Pulaski. The regional claim, "Love Makes Memory Eternal," was first inscribed here, but the soldier is more boyish than the Frederick W. Sievers figures at Pulaski or Abingdon or the monument at New Castle.

- Of the ceremonies the "handsome monument'" drew notice in the Confederate Veteran issue of February 1911:

Both chapter and Camp give great honor to the indefatigable Mrs. E. E. Evans for this monument. It was carved after her design, and it was largely due to her that the necessary money was raised.

On a raised platform near the veiled monument were seated the speakers of the day [including former Governor Claude A. Swanson], members of Chapters Southern Cross, of Salem, and William Watts, of Roanoke, and Camp Hupp-Deyeirie, of Salem.

At the conclusion of his address the members of the Salem Chapter of the Daughters of the Confederacy, dressed in white and carrying Confederate flags, marched to the monument, and, surrounding it, each took one of the twenty-six ribbons which, being drawn, revealed the beautiful monument.

- The courthouse building was sold to Roanoke College in 1987 and is now West Hall, but the county retains ownership of the monument site.

88. East Hill Cemetery Tablet

Monument is a granite tablet set on a base.
LOCATION: East Main Street and Lynchburg-Salem Turnpike, 24153
DATE: May 30, 1935
MEDIUM: Granite

[U.D.C. SEAL]
TO HONOR OUR
CONFEDERATE SOLDIERS
1861 C.S.A. 1865
ERECTED BY
SOUTHERN CROSS CHAPTER
U.D.C.
MAY 30, 1935

The United Daughters of the Confederacy tribute was dedicated on Decoration Day, 1935, in the midst of the Great Depression. The elegant, though modestly sized tablet at this hilltop cemetery represents a peak of nostalgic, pre–World War II monumentation.

- This is one of the few references to the Southern Cross in Virginia, which was conceived by the U.D.C. in 1899 and appears on Confederate soldier grave markers across the South.

Craig County

89. New Castle, Courthouse Common Soldier

Monument is a private soldier standing at parade rest surmounting a plinth, base, pedestal, and shaft.

LOCATION: 182 Main Street, 24127
DATE: May 1915
MEDIUM: Granite
Front

CSA
[RELIEF OF CROSSED FLAGS]
TO THE
CONFEDERATE SOLDIERS
OF CRAIG COUNTY,
1861–1865.
—

INVINCIBLE IN LIFE
IMMORTAL IN DEATH.
—

LOVE MAKES
MEMORY ETERNAL.
—

THE GREATEST GIFT
A HERO LEAVES HIS RACE,
IS TO HAVE BEEN A HERO.

The New Castle Confederate soldier stands on a pedestal that rises almost twenty-three feet in this small county seat in the Virginia highlands. Like many other Confederate memorials in western Virginia, it is the largest outdoor monument in the county.

The sculptor is unknown. The ornamentation—a relief of crossed flags—is modest. The tribute—"Invincible In Life . . ."—offers an example of the fact that grand claims are not necessarily logical. Note the paradox in the assertion that Confederate soldiers who, being invincible, cannot die will, by their deaths, be immortal.

The phrase beginning "The Greatest Gift . . ." is a rare, explicit reference to race. It may be less provocative—and intended to be more inspirational—than it seems, but the chauvinism is apparent.

Hunter's Union army passed through New Castle in June 1864, after the battle of Lynchburg and skirmish at Hanging Rock.

Montgomery County

90. Christiansburg, Courthouse Obelisk
Monument is an obelisk set on a base, plinth, and pedestal.
LOCATION: 1 East Main Street, 24073
DATE: 1883
MEDIUM: Granite
Front

TO THE MEMORY
OF MONTGOMERY'S SONS
WHO FELL IN THE
LOST CAUSE
AND TO ALL
THE CONFEDERATE DEAD
WHO LIE BENEATH HER SOIL
THIS MONUMENT

IS ERECTED BY HER DAUGHTERS
1861–1865
—

ERECTED 1883
—

IN THIS COUNTY
LIE THE REMAINS OF
300 CONFEDERATE SOLDIERS
FROM
SISTER SOUTHERN STATES
WHOSE SACRIFICE THIS
STONE ALSO COMMEMORATES

The modest fifteen-foot courthouse lawn elegy is distinctive for its explicit mention of the "Lost Cause"—the only site where that phrase occurs in the southwest. Sponsored by the local Ladies Memorial Association, the balance of affection and solemn awareness of mortality is also notable. Although the diction marks this as a very feminine text (e. g., "her daughters," "Sister Southern States,"), the sense of mortality—grim even by the standards of funereal monumentation—is pervasive, especially given its courthouse grounds location: "Sons Who Fell," "Confederate Dead," "Lie the Remains of 300 Confederate Soldiers," "Whose Sacrifice," "Lie Beneath Her Soil."

91. Montgomery, Montgomery White Sulphur Springs Obelisk

Monument is a marble obelisk set on a base, plinth, and pedestal.
LOCATION: C.R. 641 off U.S. 11–460, 24073
DATE: 1889
MEDIUM: Marble

IN MEMORY OF
CONFEDERATE HEROES
WHO DIED HERE
1861–1865.
ERECTED IN 1889.

This was once a popular leisure destination, but today it is one of the least heralded Civil War sites in Virginia. In the nineteenth century this quiet, wooded valley east of Blacksburg was full of activity—festive music, dancing, and general revelry—as a well-known health spa. The resort was one of dozens that emerged in the Shenandoah Valley and the Blue Ridge in the early and mid-nineteenth century, many aided by railroad access, rising middle-class incomes, and the belief that "taking the waters"—"hydrotherapy," as it was also called—was part of a healthy lifestyle.

During the war this vacation spot, like many resorts, became a military hospital. Catholic nuns from Richmond came to serve here. The Confederate cemetery is located about a mile from C.R. 641. Wooden crosses were placed at 265 gravesites in 1873, but no vestige of the site is discernible, and the grounds are on private property. The United Daughters of the Confederacy cemetery plot was purchased for private use in 1949, and the monument was moved from the cemetery to its present roadside location above the site of the resort.

Reunions of veterans took place at Montgomery White Sulphur Springs for several decades. The Southern Historical Society was reorganized here in 1873, with Jefferson Davis giving the principal address. The recession of 1893 doomed the resort; a flood in 1902 finished it. Only a few pottery shards were left of this site at the time of this writing; even discerning where the buildings once stood is difficult.

- Other resorts converted to Confederate hospitals include Huguenot Springs (chapter 3).

92. Blacksburg, Westview Cemetery Obelisk

Monument is an obelisk set on a base, plinth, and pedestal.
LOCATION: 2700 Prosperity Road, 24060
DATE: 1901
MEDIA: Granite, marble
Front

TO THE
MEMORY OF THE
CONFEDERATE
DEAD
OF BLACKSBURG
AND VICINITY.
1861–1865
—
ERECTED BY THE
HARVEY BLACK
CHAPTER
OF THE UNITED
DAUGHTERS OF THE
CONFEDERACY
[UNREADABLE]

The United Daughters of the Confederacy chapter, founded in 1896, is named for Dr. Harvey Black, surgeon in the Army of Northern Virginia, a founder of Virginia Polytechnic Institute and State University, and a descendent of the founders of Blacksburg. Black served as one of Stonewall Jackson's surgeons and participated in the amputation of Jackson's arm following the general's wounding at the battle of Chancellorsville. Black is buried in Westview.

The slender obelisk is located in the town cemetery on a hillside east of the main campus of Virginia Tech. The obelisk faces northeast; two postwar, breech-loading cannon flank the monument. The site marks a contrast to the off-campus residential neighborhood surrounding it, but the war's legacies are well integrated into the history of this postwar institute. The federal Morrill Act for land grant colleges facilitated the establishment of the college (now Virginia Tech) in 1872. Antipathy to the federal government at the college was so strong that only the Virginia State Color flew on campus between 1872 and 1876. Federal authorities resorted to threats to withdraw financial support if the college did not fly the National Color. The college acceded.

Many ex-Confederates or their sons became students, administrators, or faculty here. Charles Landon Minor, Virginia Tech's first president, served as a captain in the Confederate Army. The legacy is also evident in the name of prominent buildings on campus. Mc-Bryde Hall is named for John M. McBryde, who served as college president, 1891–1907, and who also served in the 1st South Carolina Infantry and the 1st South Carolina Cavalry. Lane Hall is named for James Lane, Commandant of Cadets, and a general in the Army of Northern Virginia. Other former Confederate soldiers associated with the college, cavalrymen all, include generals Fitzhugh Lee, William H. F. Lee, and Lunsford Lomax, the latter serving as college president, 1886–91.

Pulaski County

93. Pulaski, Courthouse Common Soldier

Monument is a private soldier, in bronze, with musket held at waist level, pointed forward surmounting a plinth, base, and pedestal.
LOCATION: City park west of courthouse on Washington Street, 24301
DATE: 1906
MEDIA: Bronze, granite

IN MEMORY
OF THE
CONFEDERATE SOLDIERS
OF
PULASKI COUNTY
1861–1865

Pulaski is a railroad and manufacturing town and county seat formerly known as Central Depot. The county soldier's sculptor is Frederick W. Sievers, who also designed the Abingdon courthouse monument. The pose of this soldier is identical to that at Abingdon, including the same tear in the pant leg on the right calf. "His" countenance and deportment suggest that he is alert but not threatening, capable and confident, but not menacing.

That he faces east belies the myth that Civil War monuments necessarily face north or south. In fact, the Pulaski figure faces the railroad station (now a museum) across the street and justly anticipates the flux and rapid communications that would characterize the twentieth century.

94. Newberne, Cemetery Shaft

Monument is a shaft and cap surmounting a base and plinth.
LOCATION: C.R. 682 (Newbern [sic] Road); east from Interstate 81, exit 98, 24126
DATE: 1904
MEDIUM: Granite

CONFEDERATE DEAD
1861–1865
ERECTED BY THE PULASKI CHAPTER U.D.C.
1904

Like the Wytheville monument in the adjacent county, this is a modest marker. Grim proclamation—the declaration of "Confederate Dead"—is clear in the first line. Cause and duration—1861–1865—are invoked in the second line. Women, however, control the rhetoric and memory and thus have the most prominent place. By 1904, with the war nearly forty years in the past, preeminence was passing to those who mourned rather than the mourned.

Wythe County

95. Wytheville, East End Cemetery Obelisk

Monument is an obelisk surmounting a plinth, base, and dado.
LOCATION: U.S. 11 (Main Street) to Goodwin Lane, 24382
DATE: May 30, 1900
MEDIUM: Granite

Front

OUR
CONFEDERATE
DEAD.
C.S.A.
—
[CROSSED SWORDS]
—
TO THE HEROES
OF
1861–1865.
DEFENDERS OF STATE
SOVEREIGNTY.
—

[C.S.A. BATTLE FLAG]

There is no courthouse monument in Wytheville. The sponsors of this eighteen-foot obelisk, erected in 1900, resisted the trend of the time to place memorials on courthouse grounds or city or town centers. Here the hilltop town cemetery remains the center of remembrance. Although the Confederate soldiers are given a celebratory tribute as "Heroes," there is, too, an almost grim proclamation that these are "Our Confederate Dead."

- Historic Southern Monuments reports that "twenty-five or more Confederate soldiers are interred in the center of a square" and that "Many, very many, who fell in battle or died of wounds and disease in hospitals, lie buried here." Among the dedication speakers was the Confederate veteran, the "inimitable and irresistible 'cyclone,' Jim Marshall [who] appeared before the cheering assembly, and moved his hearers at his will with 'wit, wisdom, and eloquence.'"
- Of the women of the Wythe Grey Chapter, United Daughters of the Confederacy it was noted in Confederate Veteran:

This noble band of women has gathered up the remains of all who died in hospitals and reinterred them in a mound, in the center of a square, in the beautiful cemetery on the hill, and at a cost of about $500 placed over them a shaft "To the Unknown Dead," simple, unostentatious, but touchingly pathetic.

- Also buried here: General James A. Walker.

96. Cove Mountain Battlefield Tablet

Monument is a bronze tablet set on a granite base.

LOCATION: C.R. 600 east of C.R. 603, 24382

DATE: 1990

MEDIA: Bronze, granite

> War Between The States Marker
>
> The Battle of Cove Mountain
>
> May 10, 1864
>
> The two sides met at the Gap of Crocketts Cove about two miles southwest of here. When darkness fell General W. W. Averell and his Union Troops retreated leaving 114 dead and wounded. Seventeen of the wounded were left at this church where the local families fed them and attended to their injuries. There are no documented accounts of the number of Confederate casualties.
>
> Erected by Wythe-Grey Chapter, UDC
>
> August 25, 1990

This scenic valley was the site of a battle along the Raleigh and Grayson Turnpike, today known as C.R. 600 and 610. Some two thousand Union cavalry advancing south under Brig. Gen. William W. Averell clashed with a combined force of Confederate infantry and cavalry under Brig. Gen. John Hunt Morgan and Brig. Gen. William E. Jones. The Confederates blocked Averell's troops from the mineral works at Wytheville and Saltville and held the battlefield in the aftermath.

The Crockett's Grove Church on this site served as a hospital. The Greek revival–style building, erected in 1858, is the oldest church in continuous use in the county.

- The traditional designation of the "War Between the States" continues here. Citing the monument as a "Marker" seems redundant, although Richmond's Soldiers and Sailors monument also calls itself a monument.

Smyth County

97. Marion, Courthouse Common Soldier

Monument is a private soldier standing at parade rest surmounting a plinth, base, pedestal, and shaft.

LOCATION: 109 West Main Street, 24354

DATE: July 4, 1903

MEDIUM: Granite

Front

1861 CSA 1865
[SEAL OF VIRGINIA]
CONFEDERATE DEAD
ERECTED
1903
—
TO THE
DEFENDERS
OF
STATE SOVEREIGNTY.
FAITHFUL UNTO DEATH
—

[C.S.A. BATTLE FLAG]
—
GLORY SITS
BESIDE
OUR GRIEF.
LEST WE FORGET

Marion's courthouse monument was unveiled on the Fourth of July 1903 "with elaborate ceremony in the presence of a big crowd," the local paper reported. The speakers included Robert E. Lee Jr. and John Warwick Daniel. All "enjoyed the nice spread" afterwards.

The Richmond Times-Dispatch described it as the product of "the work of noble women." Marion's claim of loyalty to the Confederacy is comparable only to the Hillsville monument in southwest monuments.

- The phrase "Faithful Unto Death" is taken from Revelation 2:10, the letter to the "faithful church" at Smyrna, which intimates that that community's trials have a divine purpose and that redemption is in prospect.
- The apologetic, "Defenders of State Sovereignty," is also used at East End Cemetery, Wytheville.

Washington County and City of Bristol

98. Emory, Confederate Cemetery Obelisk
Monument is an obelisk set on a base, plinth, and dado; bronze plaques with rosters.
LOCATION: Holston Conference Emory and Henry Cemetery, Linden Street near Oxford Avenue (C.R. 866), 24327

DATE: circa 1900s
MEDIA: Bronze, marble
Front

206
SOUTHERN SOLDIERS
WAR 1861–1865
OUR CONFEDERATE DEAD

ALABAMA	GEORGIA
[19 NAMES]	[27 NAMES]
GEORGIA	FLORIDA
[4 NAMES]	[1 NAME]

J. W. VERMILLION
—

KENTUCKY	NORTH CAROLINA
[17 NAMES]	[6 NAMES]
LOUISIANA	SOUTH CAROLINA
[4 NAMES]	[8 NAMES]
MISSISSIPPI	TENNESSEE
[4 NAMES]	[10 NAMES]

TENNESSEE CONT'D	VIRGINIA
[5 NAMES]	[27 NAMES]

TEXAS
[3 NAMES]
VIRGINIA
[18 NAMES]
—
VIRGINIA CONT'D   VIRGINIA CONT'D
[26 NAMES]   [3 NAMES]
STATE UNKNOWN
[21 NAMES, 2 LISTED AS UNKNOWN]
INSCRIPTION ON TWO BENCHES:
1861–1865

This is one of the few wartime Confederate cemeteries in southwest Virginia. Unlike the cemeteries at Sinking Springs or Tazewell, most of the dead here are identified. Although the surface of this hilltop monument is mottled and neglected, the bronze roster of names conveys the impression of a precisely described assembly. Two benches, each inscribed with the war years, "1861–1865," on the seat, overlook the cemetery.

The Confederacy commandeered the campus of Emory and Henry College in December 1862 and converted its main building into a hospital. Although the hospital was established for the treatment of wounded Confederates, the hospital staff treated wounded Union soldiers as well.

This site—a hilltop location near the college campus—was established as the hospital cemetery. The inscription mentions 206 soldiers, but the bronze plaque rosters total 205. The names inscribed—with two unknowns—include casualties at the two battles of Saltville in 1864. The first, a Confederate victory, was fought on October 2, 1864. The second, a Union victory, was fought during the course of Maj. Gen. George Stoneman's cavalry raid into southwest Virginia on December 20–21, 1864.

99. Abingdon, Courthouse Common Soldier

Monument is a private soldier, in bronze, with musket held at waist level, pointed forward, surmounting a granite plinth, base, dado, and pedestal.
LOCATION: 191 East Main Street, 24210
DATE: May 30, 1907
MEDIA: Bronze, granite

Front

TO THE
CONFEDERATE SOLDIERS
OF
WASHINGTON COUNTY
VIRGINIA.
ERECTED MAY 30, 1907.
—
1861 1865
[SEAL OF VIRGINIA]
FORTITUDE
ET
PECTE
PRO PATRIA
—
[BLANK]
—
OUR MOTHERS   DAUGHTERS
WIVES AND
SISTERS
[AT BASE WITH TWO LAUREL WREATHS:]
AMOR PATRIE
["F. W. SIEVERS 1907" AT BASE]

The reconciliation-era courthouse monument focuses on the sentiments of Confederate veterans, was sponsored by them, and is, in part, a self-tribute. The Latin proverb "Fortitude et Pecte pro Patria" may be translated as "Courage and Strength for Country." Tributes from Confederate soldiers to their women are

also given. However, the expression "Amor Patrie"—"Love for Country"—is the last word. (This is the only Latin phrase inscribed on a southwest monument.) The young women are barefoot, stern, resolute. The soldier, standing eight feet high, is a little more relaxed: armed and ready, but casual in his deportment.

Several bronze reliefs are mounted on the base. One depicts a woman bearing a shield in her left hand and a sword in right hand. A Confederate battle flag waves behind her, the state seal is on the shield, and "CSA" is inscribed on the belt buckle. On the opposite side a woman displays an unfurled battle flag.

- Frederick William Sievers, the sculptor, was born in Fort Wayne, Indiana, in 1872. He was raised in Richmond, studied sculpture in Rome and Paris, and had studios in New York and Richmond. This was his first major public commission. The soldier is, to all appearances, identical to his design at Pulaski. Confederate monuments at Gettysburg, Leesburg, and Richmond are also credited to him.
- The monument, erected at a cost of four thousand dollars, stands "where our boys were mustered in when they enlisted," a local history reports. The pedestal is of Virginia granite, the eight-foot soldier of bronze.
- Judge John A. Buchanan accepted the monument from the W. E. Jones Camp of Confederate Veterans. It was in turn presented to the Anne Stonewall Chapter, United Daughters of the Confederacy. Buchanan assured the ex-soldiers that "You veterans of the Camp can feel assured that your gift will be sacredly cared for and your trust faithfully executed. . . ." In his remarks, Judge Buchanan gave an extended oration on the meaning of the "dauntless mien of that figure." He concluded:

The orator of the occasion is the monument itself. No living lips, however eloquent, could awaken the memories and touch the hearts of the surviving men and women of 1861–65 as does the pathetic utterance of that silent figure.

- The Virginia Historical Highway marker cites a dedication date of May 10, 1907.

100. Abingdon, Courthouse, General Officers Tablet

Monument is a shaft and cap set on a base.
LOCATION: Courthouse grounds, 191 East Main Street, 24210
DATE: August 7, 1999
MEDIUM: Granite

A MEMORIAL TO THE GENERALS
FROM WASHINGTON COUNTY WHO
SERVED IN THE WAR OF 1861–1865
GENERAL JOSEPH E. JOHNSTON

ARMY OF THE POTOMAC
COMMANDER—DEPT. OF THE WEST
ARMY OF TENNESSEE
BRIG. GENERAL WILLIAM E.
"GRUMBLE" JONES
COMMANDER 1ST & 7TH VA. CALVARY [SIC]
DEPT. OF SOUTHWEST VA.
AND EAST TENNESSEE
BRIG. GENERAL JOHN PRESTON
SUPERINTENDANT—CONSCRIPTION
BRIG. GENERAL W. Y. C. HUMES
ARMY OF TENNESSEE
BRIG. GENERAL JOHN B. FLOYD
DEPT. OF SOUTHWEST VA. & EAST TN.

Four Confederate generals are commemorated in this recent monument. Johnston, listed first, rose highest in rank; Jones and Preston were solid combat officers; Humes held staff positions; and Floyd, though a general, is least reputable.

Joseph Johnston (1807–1891) was born near Farmville but was raised in Abingdon. He held many positions but is associated here with what would become the Army of Northern Virginia, which he commanded until he was wounded and replaced by Robert E. Lee. W. E. Jones (1824–1864) is given the nickname "Grumble." It is a false note of intimacy: no nicknames are invoked with the other officers, such as "Ole Joe" with Johnston. Jones was killed in action at the battle of Piedmont. He is buried at the Glade Spring Presbyterian Church in Glade Spring, beside the remains of his wife.

W. Y. C. Humes (1830–1883) entered the Confederate army as a lieutenant of artillery in June 1861. In March 1865, he was commissioned major general. John S. Preston (1809–1881) served on Gen. P. G. T. Beauregard's staff, rose to the rank of brigadier general, and was put in charge of the bureau of conscription.

John B. Floyd is dutifully listed, but his standing in history as a political operative and opportunist is unflattering. L. C. Angle, in the dedication address for the monument, diplomatically admitted that Floyd "had a most remarkable, if controversial, career." He is the only one of these four generals buried in Abingdon.

101. Unknown Confederate Dead Tablet

Monument is a shaft set on a base.
SITE: Sinking Spring Cemetery
LOCATION: From Main Street, north on Russell Road, 24210
DATE: September 30, 1961
MEDIUM: Granite
Front

1861 CSA 1865
[CROSSED C.S.A. STARS AND
BARS AND BATTLE FLAG]
UNKNOWN CONFEDERATE DEAD
DEDICATED BY THE
ANNA STONEWALL JACKSON CHAPTER
U.D.C.
SEPT. 30, 1961

In addition to combat and disease, the mass movement of troops was another hazard of the war. Railroad service in the Confederacy was chronically underserviced and unreliable, and moving troops on the lines was often dangerous. Here it was lethal. This Confederate cemetery was founded in September 1861, when seventeen Louisiana soldiers, killed in a train accident on the Virginia and Tennessee Railroad near Abingdon, were interred here.

102. Confederate Cemetery Tablet

Monument is an obelisk set on a base and dado.
DATE: July 4, 2002
MEDIUM: Granite

[47 NAMES]
ERECTED IN HONOR OF SOLDIERS
WHO FOUGHT IN THE
WAR OF 1861–1865,
WHOSE GRAVES ARE IN THE
SINKING SPRINGS CEMETERY.
[CROSSED C.S.A. BATTLE FLAGS]
DEDICATED JULY 4, 2002, BY
THE SONS OF CONFEDERATE
VETERANS.
—
[C.S.A. BATTLE FLAG]
—
DONATED BY
JAMES
&
CHARLOTTE
PITTS
—
[C.S.A. BATTLE FLAG]

Sinking Spring Cemetery dates from the eighteenth century. This modest obelisk stands adjacent to the section for the Unknown Confederate Dead. Apart from the battle flag display, it is a comparatively nonpartisan monument, one that appears to include Confederate and Union soldiers in its tribute, although the roster of soldiers is restricted to Confederates. The war is not the "War Between the States" a traditional Southern designation, but the more neutral "War of 1861–1865."

Bristol

103. Courthouse Common Soldier

Monument is a private soldier standing at parade rest surmounting a shaft, dado, plinth, and base.
LOCATION: State and Randall streets, 24201
DATE: May 27, 1920
MEDIUM: Marble

[BAS RELIEF OF C.S.A. BATTLE FLAG]
PRESENTED BY
COL. J. M. BARKER

OF BRISTOL, TENN.
TO THE CHAPTER OF THE U.D.C.,
IN MEMORY OF THE BRAVE MEN
AND NOBLE WOMEN OF
TENNESSEE AND VIRGINIA FROM
1861 TO 1865
ERECTED 1920
[RELIEF OF CROSSED SWORDS]

This twenty-five-foot-high monument stands near the Virginia-Tennessee state line with a tribute extended to citizens in both states—all of them, not just local and not just the men. The sculptor is unknown. The monument formerly stood at the courthouse but was moved to this site, near the former railroad station, when a new courthouse was erected. It was originally dedicated and unveiled May 27, 1920, in the presence of a crowd of some five thousand people. Confederate Veteran proclaimed that it was erected "with the hope that it would 'keep alive all noble feelings that characterized those living and acting in 1861–65.'" The eight-foot-tall figure is one of the few statues of a Confederate soldier ever carved in Italy by an Italian sculptor of Italian marble.

- The sponsor, James M. Barker, was thirteen when the Civil War broke out, but he served as a soldier in the Confederacy for over two years. His title as colonel was conferred after the war, when he also served as mayor of Bristol and was a businessman.
- The arch proclaiming "Bristol" behind the monument was erected in 1910.
- Excerpt from the dedication address by W. H. Rouse:

Monuments are never needed by those for whom they are erected. It was regarded as necessary to inscribe on the Bunker Hill Monument only the word "Here" indicating the place. No work of praise or recital of deed was needed to perpetuate knowledge or memory of the great event. Can any luster be added to the memory of the great event. Can any luster be added to the name of Washington, Lincoln, Lee, Jackson, John Howard Payne, or to confederate armies or the Mothers of the Confederacy by monumental shaft? Oh, no, their lives and deeds and sacrifices and services are recorded in history and country and character and memory more lasting than if in marble and carved wood, yet monuments are erected as a visible, tangible mark of our recognition and veneration of high emprise and in the hope that little children will stop and ask and learn the story and emulate and grow in mental and moral stature. A monument after all is history and love and admiration and inspiration.

That figure of the lonely rebel up there at the top is tongue-less and voiceless and silent, yet so eloquent that across the stretch of almost sixty years we hear the tramp of serried columns and footsore battalions, and the drum beat of a hundred battle fields and the sorrowing and suffering wail of many mothers and wives and sisters and daughters in Confederate homes scattered all the way from Maryland down through these hills and valleys, on down through palmetto and pine, the cotton and the corn, to Texas and the Gulf; hence here are story and history and tragedy and oration and poem and song and sermon and funeral dirge loudly proclaimed.

104. East Hill Cemetery Tablet

Monument is a bronze plaque set on a concrete base.

LOCATION: U.S. 421 to State Street to hilltop

DATE: 1995
MEDIA: Bronze, stone

CONFEDERATE MEMORIAL
1861–1865
ERECTED BY
ANN CARTER LEE CHAPTER
UNITED DAUGHTERS OF THE CONFEDERACY
AND
JUDGE J. C. BELL
OF MISSISSIPPI
1995

This hilltop cemetery, founded in 1857, straddles Bristol, Tennessee, and Bristol, Virginia. The site is just above the United Daughters of the Confederacy monument and overlooks the city. With the railway nearby, several military hospitals were established in Bristol during the war. The dead—some three hundred—were interred here.

Scott County

105. Gate City, Courthouse Plaque

Monument is a bronze plaque set against a brick wall background on a concrete base.
LOCATION: 202 West Jackson Street, 24251
DATE: October 1988
MEDIUM: Bronze

SONS OF CONFEDERATE VETERANS
[S.C.V. emblem]

[1896]
Dedicated to the Confederate
Soldiers of Scott County by the Sons
of Confederate Veterans.
Let not ignorance of fact or time
overshadow their acts of patriotism,
bravery, and courage for Virginia
and the Confederacy.
C.S.A.
"DEO VINDICE"
Erected 16, October 1988
John S. Mosby, Camp #1409

Gate City, formerly known as Estillville, stands near Moccasin Gap in Clinch Mountain, just a few miles north of the Tennessee state line. Virginia's county monuments west of Bristol—just two, at Grundy and here—were erected late in the twentieth century. This, the 1988 example, is especially focused on countering any "ignorance" which may "overshadow [the] acts of patriotism" of Confederate soldiers.

Giles County

106. Pearisburg, Courthouse Common Soldier

Monument is a private soldier, in bronze, standing at parade rest surmounting a granite shaft, dado, and base.
LOCATION: 120 North Main Street, 24134

DATE: July 3, 1909
MEDIA: Bronze, granite
Front

1861–1865
TO THE
CONFEDERATE SOLDIERS
OF
GILES COUNTY.
[LAUREL WREATH, HIGH RELIEF]
OUR HEROES
—

GILES CO. FURNISHED SEVEN
VOLUNTEER COMPANIES NUMBERING
ABOUT 800 MEN AS FOLLOWS:
CO D 7TH REGIMENT INFANTRY
" F 24 " "
" H 36 " "
" I 36 " "
" H 37 " CAVALRY
MCCOMAS—FRENCH ARTILLERY
STARKE'S BATN. WISE BRIG.
GILES CO. RESERVES.
4TH BATTALION BRIGADE
LEST WE FORGET
—

IT IS THE DUTY WE OWE TO
THE DEAD WHO DIED FOR US,
BUT WHOSE MEMORIES CAN
NEVER DIE
IT IS A DUTY WE OWE TO POSTERITY
TO SEE THAT OUR CHILDREN
SHALL KNOW THE VIRTUES AND
RISE WORTHY OF THEIR SIRES.
JEFFERSON DAVIS.
LOVE MAKES MEMORY ETERNAL
—

THIS MONUMENT IS THE GIFT
OF THOSE WHO REVERE
THE MEMORY OF
THE CONFEDERATE SOLDIER
ERECTED BY MCCOMAS CHAPTER
UNITED DAUGHTERS OF THE CONFEDERACY
JULY 3, 1909

Of this monument Confederate Veteran enthused that it stands "in the heart of the mountains[,] for the world honors the Confederate soldiers, and all Confederate soldiers honored the boys from Giles." The monument is crowded with detail and staunch in its apologetic. The memorial offers the assurance that the county's population was wholly committed to the cause of the Confederacy, in this case proclaiming that Craig County "Furnished Seven Volunteer Companies . . . 800 Men As Follows. . . ."

The Jefferson Davis quotation is taken from speech given in New Orleans on April 25, 1882, and published in the *New York Times* on April 30, 1882. The *Times* called the speech a "long harangue" but noted that Davis was received with "wild and enthusiastic response" and that Davis expressed "a willingness to share Lee, Jackson and Johnson [sic] with the 'enemy.'" The use of the Davis quotation is unusual. Outside of the former national capitals, Richmond and Danville, this is the only direct reference to Davis in Virginia.

Bland County

107. Bland, Courthouse Common Soldier

Monument is a private soldier, in marble, standing at parade rest surmounting a granite shaft, dado, plinth, and base.

LOCATION: 612 Main Street, 24315
DATE: August 15, 1911
MEDIA: Marble, granite
Front

1861–1865
ERECTED BY BLAND CHAPTER U.D.C.
AS A LASTING MEMORIAL
TO THE GALLANT SONS OF BLAND COUNTY
WHO GAVE THEIR LIVES IN DEFENSE OF
THEIR BELOVED SOUTHLAND.
OUR HEROES
—
CO. F. 51ST. VA. INF.
CO. G. 36TH. VA. INF.
CO. F. 45TH. VA. INF.
—
[BLANK]
—
CO. B. 47TH. VA. BAT.
CO. F. 8TH. VA. CAV.
FATE DENIED THEM VICTORY
BUT CROWNED THEM WITH
GLORIOUS IMMORTALITY.

Few Virginia monuments mention defeat; some imply victory. Bland County's twenty-two foot elegy focuses on the "Gallant Sons" of the county who died, not for the Confederacy, but in defense of the "Beloved Southland."

This soaring, semicentennial monument is set in the valley between Walker and Brushy mountains. The small town is adjacent to Interstate 77, but the area retains its remote, rural character.

The Confederate soldier, whose sculptor is unknown, faces north, as does the courthouse, erected in 1889. The tribute, "To The Gallant Sons . . ." is similar to the one at Hillsville, some forty miles to the south.

Tazewell County

108. Tazewell, Courthouse Common Soldier

Monument is a white bronze private soldier standing at parade rest surmounting a shaft, dado, plinth, and base.

LOCATION: Main Street, 24651
DATE: 1903
MEDIUM: White bronze

TO THE CONFEDERATE
SOLDIER OF TAZEWELL
1861–1865

The inscription on this white bronze monument is strikingly direct, even militant and is suggestive of an ideal Tazewell soldier whose individual resolve and conviction transcends defeat. The statue faces north, with a prominent place in front of the county courthouse (erected in 1874, rebuilt in 1914). The soldier's stance is paradoxical: aggressive in pose, yet static in form and legacy—he keeps vigil, but "he" is not going anywhere.

- A similar white bronze model stands at Floyd (1904) and Hillsville (1907), as well as Hinton, West Virginia.

109. Jeffersonville Cemetery Shaft

Monument is a bronze tablet set into a field-stone base, shaft, and cap.
LOCATION: B.R. 460–19, 24651
DATE: 1892
MEDIA: Bronze, fieldstone

TO THE MEMORY
OF OUR
CONFEDERATE DEAD
1861–1865
"LOVE MAKES MEMORY ETERNAL."

Jeffersonville's monument predates the courthouse monument, which—with its white bronze materials—would have been considered more progressive, modern in design, and prominently defiant than this early reconciliation example.

The county history describes the "Unknown Confederate Graveyard" as the county's "most sacred shrine." No court records mark its boundary lines. The site began as a temporary repository for the bodies of Confederate soldiers who were killed in battle or died from other causes. Some of the bodies were later claimed by relatives for reinterment at home; an unknown number remain. After the war it was known as the "Unknown Confederate Graveyard." The Brown-Harman Camp of Confederate Veterans held their annual commemorative service on this plot until the camp disbanded. The local U.D.C. chapter succeeded them.

Buchanan County

110. Grundy, Courthouse Tablet

Monument is a granite tablet on a base.
LOCATION: 1012 Walnut Street, 24614
DATE: 1998
MEDIUM: Granite

TO THE GALLANT CONFEDERATE
SOLDIERS OF BUCHANAN COUNTY
VIRGINIA 1861–1865
10TH KENTUCKY CAVALRY—CO.'S F. G. H. & I
21ST VIRGINIA CAVALRY—CO. F
21ST VIRGINIA INFANTRY BATTALION CO. E
22ND VIRGINIA CAVALRY—CO. B
34TH VIRGINIA CAVALRY
BATTALION—CO.'S A & C
2ND VIRGINIA STATE LINE CO.'S B. D. & E
COUNTS PARTISAN BATTALION COLLEY'S CO.
LT. COL. V. A. WITCHER CAMP NO. 1863
SONS OF CONFEDERATE VETERANS—1998

The Grundy elegy is a typical late-twentieth-century commemoration: the scale is modest, the adjectives are few, and unit rosters are emphasized. Local contributions to the Confederate military are displayed. Grundy has a 1987 memorial in bronze and granite to workers in the coal industry, surmounted by a coal miner and titled "Today's Miner." Although it is much larger, ten years older, and more elaborate, it has the same conception of lauded, workmanlike fortitude as is presented in the Confederate elegy.

Russell County

111. Lebanon, Courthouse Common Soldier

Monument is a private soldier standing at "shoulder arms" surmounting a plinth, base, dado, and shaft.

LOCATION: 121 East Main Street, 24266

DATE: 1914

MEDIUM: Marble

FRONT

1861

[RELIEF OF CROSSED FLAGS]

1865

CSA

[RELIEF OF CROSSED FLAGS]

—

ERECTED

1914

—

"TO THE

CONFEDERATE

SOLDIERS

OF RUSSELL COUNTY.

A LOVING TRIBUTE TO THE

PAST, PRESENT AND FUTURE"

The twenty-two-foot Lebanon monument has a celebratory-era simplicity. The memorial is confident and assured. The tone is sentimen-

tal rather than defiant, wistful rather than bereaved. The whole of the imagined community of Russell County extends its "loving tribute" to its Confederate soldiers, along with the hope that the Confederacy's legacy will endure to perpetuity. The monument was erected in 1914—the same year that World War I erupted, but well before the United States entered in 1917.

- The phrase beginning "A Loving Tribute," is also inscribed on the Monterey courthouse monument.
- The monument has been relocated from the middle of Main Street.

Floyd County

112. Floyd, Courthouse Common Soldier

Monument is a private soldier standing at parade rest, surmounting a plinth, base, dado, and shaft.

-

LOCATION: 100 East Main Street, 24091
DATE: July 4, 1904
MEDIUM: White bronze
Front

[BAS RELIEF OF ROBERT E. LEE]
STOOP ANGELS, HITHER
FROM THE SKIES;
THERE IS NO HOLIER
SPOT OF GROUND
THAN WHERE DEFEATED
VALOR LIES BY MOURNING BEAUTY
CROWNED.
BULL RUN
MANASSAS
—

ERECTED
BY THE
FLOYD CHAPTER
OF
DAUGHTERS
OF THE
CONFEDERACY
NO. 723,
IN THE YEAR
1904.
CEDAR RUN
CHICKAMAUGA
—

FLOYD COUNTY
TO
THE ARMY
OF THE CONFEDERACY
DRURYS [SIC] BLUFF
COLD HARBOR
—

IN MEMORY
OF OUR
FALLEN BRAVES,
THE
CONFEDERATE SOLDIERS,
FROM
1861 TO 1865.
SEVEN PINES
FREDERICKSBURG

The white bronze statue stands in front of the 1950 courthouse. The excerpt on the front panel was written by Henry Timrod (1828–1867), Confederate soldier and poet, who was known during the war as the "Laureate of the Confederacy." The passage is taken from his "Ode Sung at Magnolia Cemetery," written in 1867, and composed on the occasion of the decoration of the graves of the Confederate dead in Magnolia Cemetery, Charleston, South Carolina.

Timrod is one of the few Southern poets of the era who still has a place in contemporary literary anthologies. A writer of love and nature poetry before the war, Timrod was influenced by English Romantic movement poets such as Wordsworth and Tennyson. The war, however, moved Timrod to write with the kind of secessionist sentiment and nationalistic fervor of poets such as Father Abram Ryan and Father John Bannister Tabb. He enlisted in a South Carolina regiment but poor health precluded service; he died of tuberculosis shortly after this poem's composition.

The larger context reads:

> Sleep sweetly in your humble graves,
> Sleep, martyrs of a fallen Cause;
> Though yet no marble column craves
> The pilgrim here to pause. . . .

The third panel is explicitly inscribed to soldiers from Floyd County. That they are "Our Fallen Braves" may be a means of ascribing a youthful, sporting, Lost Cause mystique to them.

Battles are commemorated on all four sides. Like the Hillsville monument in the adjacent county, many landmark engagements are not included while other actions are prominent, and some are mentioned twice. Chancellorsville, Appomattox, and Petersburg, for example, are unmentioned, but "Drury's Bluff" (Drewry's) and Cold Harbor are. Cedar Run (1862) is also known as Cedar Mountain or Slaughter's Mountain. Bull Run and Manassas are usually described as being the same engagement, and Bull Run is the Union designation for the battle.

- The monument is inscribed with the year 1904, but June 3, 1906, the anniversary of Jefferson Davis's birthday, is listed by some sources.

Carroll County

113. Hillsville, Courthouse Common Soldier

Monument is a private soldier standing at parade rest, surmounting a plinth, base, dado, and shaft.

LOCATION: 605 Pine Street, 24343
DATE: July 4, 1907
MEDIUM: White bronze
Front

[BAS-RELIEF OF R. E. LEE]
CONFEDERATE DEAD.

1861–1865.
"FATE DENIED THEM VICTORY
BUT CROWNED THEM WITH
GLORIOUS IMMORTALITY."
ERECTED 1908 BY THE CARROLL CHAPTER
DAUGHTERS OF THE CONFEDERACY, AS A
LASTING MEMORIAL TO THE GALLANT SONS
OF CARROLL COUNTY WHO GAVE THEIR LIVES
IN DEFENSE OF THEIR
BELOVED SOUTHLAND.
"THOUGH MEN DESERVE, THEY MAY NOT
WIN SUCCESS; THE BRAVE WILL
HONOR THE BRAVE,
VANQUISHED NONE THE LESS."
GETTYSBURG
—

CO. C, 24TH VA. INFANTRY
CO. E, 45TH VA. INFANTRY
CO. I, 45TH VA. INFANTRY
CO. C, 29TH VA. INFANTRY
CO. D, 29TH VA. INFANTRY
CO. E, 29TH VA. INFANTRY
CO. F, 29TH VA. INFANTRY
CO. G, 54TH VA. INFANTRY
CO. I, 63RD VA. INFANTRY
CO. F, 5TH VA. INFANTRY
RESERVES.
PART CO. I, 50 VA. INFANTRY
PART CO. H, 51 INFANTRY.
FRANKLIN
—

PART OF CO. C, 8TH VA. CAVALRY
PART OF CO. H, 8TH VA. CAVALRY
PART OF CO. K, 25TH VA. CAVALRY
PART OF CO. G, 22ND VA. CAVALRY
PART OF CO. I, 26TH VA. CAVALRY
PART OF CO. E, 27TH VA. CAVALRY
CHICKAMAUGA
—

1ST MANASSAS
WILLIAMSBURG;
SEVEN PINES, FRAZIER'S FARM,
CARNAFAX FERRY [SIC], COTTON MOUNTAIN,
LEWISBURG, FAYETTE C. H., SHARPSBURG,
FREDERICKSBURG, COLD HARBOR,
FORT DONELSON, CLOYD'S FARM,
CEDAR CREEK, CHATTANOOGA,
LOOKOUT MOUNTAIN, MISSIONARY RIDGE,

RESACA, MURFREESBORO, DREWRY'S BLUFF,
WILDERNESS, PIEDMONT, DALTON,
WINCHESTER, MIDDLE CREEK,
MOREFIELD, PLYMOUTH,
NEWMARKET, ATLANTA,
FIVE FORKS, DINWIDDIE C. H., BENTONVILLE
2ND MANASSAS

Made "of beautiful white bronze," Hillsville's courthouse monument was erected at a cost of at thirteen hundred dollars and was dedicated on the Fourth of July in 1907. The Confederate Veteran description notes that the monument "stands where the companies were formed and whence the brave fellows marched away, the majority of whom never returned. The soldier, vigilant yet at rest, keeps his vigil and ever shields that Southland so dear to every Virginian."

The selection of the thirty-six engagements on the fourth panel is idiosyncratic. Late war actions at Five Forks, Bentonville, and Dinwiddie are mentioned, but Appomattox and Petersburg are not. Sharpsburg is inscribed but not South Mountain; Wilderness but not Spotsylvania; Franklin but not Nashville; Gettysburg but not Vicksburg; Fredericksburg but not Chancellorsville. The Atlanta campaign—at least four separate battles—is aptly summarized as Atlanta, although Resaca and Dalton, also part of that campaign, are mentioned as well. Cloyd's Mountain is called Cloyd's Farm; New Market is inscribed as one word—Newmarket—referring either to the battle of New Market in the Shenandoah in 1864 or, less likely, New Market Heights near Richmond in 1864, and Carnifex is spelled Carnafax.

- The twenty-foot monument was originally installed in the middle of Main Street, in front of the courthouse. It was moved in the 1930s when Main Street was widened as part of a Civilian Conservation Corps (C.C.C.) project.
- Variations on the Lost Cause theme of "Fate Denying Them" also appear on the Berryville, Bland, and King and Queen courthouse monuments and the Charlottesville university cemetery.

Grayson County

114. Independence, Courthouse Common Soldier

Monument is a private soldier, in marble, standing at parade rest, surmounting a granite plinth, base, dado, and shaft.
LOCATION: Court and Main streets, 24348
DATE: 1911
MEDIA: Granite, marble

1861
[CROSSED C.S.A. BATTLE FLAGS]
1865
VIRGINIA
TO OUR
SOLDIERS
OF THE
CONFEDERACY
GRAYSON COUNTY

The Independence monument offers a stylistic contrast to the profusely decorated Hillsville monument twenty-three miles to the east. Here restraint, even elegance prevails. Three panels on this monument are blank. The fourth—the front—displays the only ornamentation: a relief of crossed battle flags on the shaft, and cannons crossed with an olive wreath.

The courthouse, built in 1908, was construct-ed in one of the few counties, if not the only one, with no rail service. Ox- or horse-drawn wagons were almost certainly used to transport the forty-five-thousand-pound monument, but this well-tended bulwark looks as new as the day it was dedicated.

The monument stands twenty-five feet with a six-foot soldier. The soldier, of white Italian marble from a studio in Carrara, Italy, was sculpted from drawings executed by the designer and builder of the monument, J. Henry Brown of Richmond. The pedestal, base, die, caps, and shaft are of "Confederate Gray Granite" from a quarry north of Richmond.

The date the monument was erected is uncertain, but hundreds of people are said to have been in attendance for the unveiling. Anne Cox and Ossie Gentry pulled the cords to drop the veil. An undated news clipping observes that the granite for the monument "was quarried from right beneath the old trenches and re-doubts [sic] which protected the Confederate Capitol throughout the stern years of 1861–65. Over it having screamed the shells, and whistled and whispered the hail of death from northern guns."

Wise County

115. Cranesnest Battlefield Tablet
Monument is a granite tablet set on a granite base.
LOCATION: Coeburn Mountain Road off V.R. 72, Cranes Nest Road 24293
DATE: November 10, 1998
MEDIUM: Granite

CRANES NEST BATTLEFIELD
NOVEMBER 4, 1864
DEDICATED TO THE MEN
WHO FOUGHT AND DIED
IN THE SERVICE OF THEIR STATE

At this site a Virginia Home Guard of Union soldiers clashed with approximately three hundred Confederate mounted troops at the head of the Cranesnest River. "Battlefield" is something of an overstatement by comparison to the scale of eastern conflicts involving hundreds of thousands of troops, but many of those involved at Cranes Nest were from this region and thus the "brother-against-brother" war had literal meaning. Here the Confederates defeated the Union troops, and at least eight Virginia Yankees were killed.

- David Vanover, a Clintwood, Virginia businessman, sponsored this monument.

3. RICHMOND, NORTHERN VIRGINIA, AND THE PIEDMONT

Geographical Outline. Eighteen counties, independent cities at Alexandria, Charlottesville, Fairfax, Fredericksburg, Manassas, and Richmond; the Potomac River to the north, the Chesapeake Bay to the east, the James River to the south, and the Blue Ridge to the West.

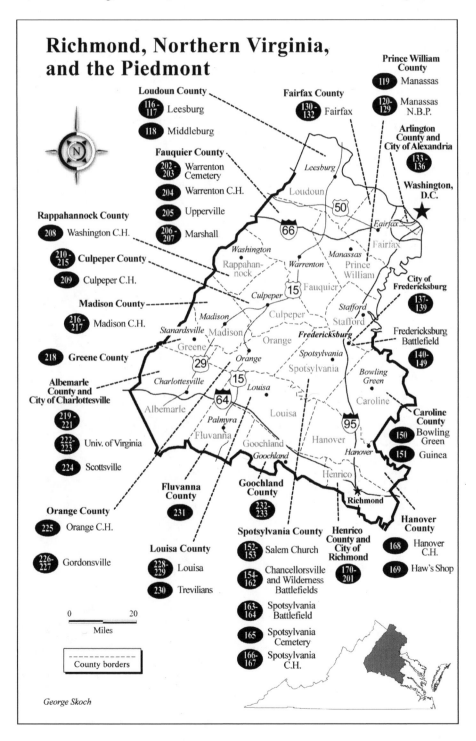

Richmond, Northern Virginia, and the Piedmont

Prince William County
- 119 Manassas

Loudoun County
- 116-117 Leesburg
- 118 Middleburg

Fairfax County
- 130-132 Fairfax

- 120-129 Manassas N.B.P.

Arlington County and City of Alexandria
- 133-136

Fauquier County
- 202-203 Warrenton Cemetery
- 204 Warrenton C.H.
- 205 Upperville
- 206-207 Marshall

Rappahannock County
- 208 Washington C.H.

Culpeper County
- 210-215
- 209 Culpeper C.H.

Madison County
- 216-217 Madison C.H.

- 218 Greene County

Albemarle County and City of Charlottesville
- 219-221
- 222-223 Univ. of Virginia
- 224 Scottsville

Washington, D.C.

City of Fredericksburg
- 137-139

Fredericksburg Battlefield
- 140-149

Caroline County
- 150 Bowling Green
- 151 Guinea

Orange County
- 225 Orange C.H.
- 226-227 Gordonsville

Fluvanna County
- 231

Goochland County
- 232-233

Louisa County
- 228-229 Louisa
- 230 Trevilians

Spotsylvania County
- 152-153 Salem Church
- 154-162 Chancellorsville and Wilderness Battlefields
- 163-164 Spotsylvania Battlefield
- 165 Spotsylvania Cemetery
- 166-167 Spotsylvania C.H.

Henrico County and City of Richmond
- 170-201

Hanover County
- 168 Hanover C.H.
- 169 Haw's Shop

0   20
Miles

County borders

George Skoch

Campaigns. Numerous and bloody, from 1861 to 1865. Richmond, Northern Virginia, and the Piedmont have the most violent legacy on the American continent, with battles, skirmishes, encampments, and movements that are almost beyond counting. The opposing capitals, Richmond and Washington, D.C., are only 110 miles apart, and enormous, unprecedented casualties resulted from the efforts to attack and defend them. Major campaigns culminated in battles and ultimately monuments at Manassas (or Bull Run) in 1861 and again in 1862, as well as Cedar Mountain. First Fredericksburg was fought in 1862; and the battles of Chancellorsville, Salem Church, and Second Fredericksburg were fought in 1863. Cavalry battles of the Gettysburg Campaign took place at Brandy Station, Middleburg, and Upperville in June 1863, and monuments stand there as well. Other battlefield sites from 1862–64 where no Confederate monuments stand at present include Aldie, Bristoe Station, Chantilly, Mine Run, North Anna, Rappahannock Station, Thoroughfare Gap, Todd's Tavern, and Cold Harbor. Kelly's Ford is marked with two monuments, both to Major John Pelham. The Overland Campaign of 1864 included major battles at Wilderness and Spotsylvania, as well as cavalry actions at Haw's Shop, Trevilians, and Yellow Tavern. There were other clashes, of course, but monuments stand at each of the above locations.

Numerous military hospitals were established behind the lines; monuments at these sites stand at Charlottesville, Richmond, Madison, Scottsville, and Gordonsville.

Southern battlefield memorials are comparatively few in number. None approaches the scale of Sharpsburg or Gettysburg, but virtually every county seat in this region (Stafford and Warsaw excepted) has a public monument.

Terrain. Northern Virginia's rolling fields have largely been subsumed by decades of housing, office, and retail development. Shopping centers, housing, offices and four-lane highways, for example, have overtaken the battlefield at Chantilly, though a one-acre memorial parcel has been preserved. Development continues to swell around other sites—e. g., Manassas, Chancellorsville, and Fredericksburg. Nevertheless, the terrain and road network retain elements of their nineteenth-century contours. Too, the Blue Ridge foothills and the Piedmont still have something of their nineteenth-century rural character, although corridors of development continue to change the landscape along U.S. 211, 15, 17, and 29, and V.R. 3.

Richmond's symbolic importance is singular in the United States. Monument Avenue gives the appearance of a city with the formality and aura of a phantasmagoric national capital. The elegies there and throughout the city are staid, solemn, and subversive. The price paid for that aura and status is evident: some thirty-six thousand Confederate soldiers are buried in Oakwood, Hebrew, Shockoe Hill, and Hollywood cemeteries.

Loudoun County
Leesburg

116. Courthouse Common Soldier

Monument is a private soldier, in bronze, surmounting a granite plinth, base, pedestal, and
dado.

LOCATION: 18 East Market Street, 20176
DATE: May 28, 1908
MEDIA: Bronze, granite

> IN MEMORY OF THE
> CONFEDERATE SOLDIERS
> OF LOUDOUN COUNTY VA.
> ERECTED MAY 28 1908

The Loudoun Chapter, United Daughters of
the Confederacy, erected this confident-look-
ing monument. It stands in front of the Greek
revival courthouse of 1895. The dedication ceremonies included addresses by Senator John
Warwick Daniel and ex-governor Claude A.
Swanson. The soldier is a Frederick W. Sievers
design. Sievers describes the sculpture, which
is similar to his Pulaski and Abingdon monuments, as a

> Confederate Infantryman standing [in
> the] act of cocking [a] musket. The sta-
> tue of [a] Confederate Infantry man in
> the act of cocking his musket is that
> of a beardless young man in complete
> Confederate costume. He stands with
> left foot forward, with weight of body
> equally divided over each leg.

Extensive wartime activity took place here,
especially during the first two years of the war
but also when this part of Virginia was called
"Mosby's Confederacy." The terse phrasing is at
once perfunctory and suggestive: perfunctory
in that the tribute is common in courthouse
monuments, varying only in the name of the
county, but provocative in that Leesburg is
only a few miles from the Potomac River and
former national border.

- "Copyright 1907 by Wm Sievers" is inscribed the right side of the base, "F W
  Sievers Sculptor 1907" on the left side.

117. Union Cemetery Obelisk

Monument is a marble obelisk set on a plinth,
base, and dado.

LOCATION: 323 North King Street, 20176
DATE: October 21, 1877
MEDIUM: Marble
Front

> TO THE
> UNKNOWN CONFEDERATE DEAD
> who lie near this monument
> and to the many
> noble Sons of Loudoun who
> fell and were
> left on the field of battle.
>
> —
>
> HAUD PLURIBUS IMPARE.
> At Ball's Bluff, near this town, on
> the threshold of Virginia and the
> Confederacy, the invading army
> of the North was, on Oct. 21st 1861, utterly
> defeated and driven into the Potomac.
> This monument is erected to the

memory of those who died in defence
of the Lost Cause by their late
comrades in arms and a grateful
and admiring people. Oct. 21st 1877.

—

Stoop, angels, hither from the skies!
There is no holier spot of ground
Than where defeated valor lies,
By mourning beauty crowned.

—

The gallant soldiers whose memory this
monument is intended to perpetuate
were attached chiefly to the following
commands viz:
8th, & 17th, Va. Inf.
Loudoun Artillery
White's 42nd, Batt. Va. Cav.
Mosby's 43rd, Batt. Va. Cav.
13th, 17th, 18th, & 21st Miss. Inf.
NO SOUND CAN AWAKE THEM
TO GLORY AGAIN.

This sixteen-foot-high obelisk was erected
in the area where Mississippians were garri-
soned and buried their dead in late 1861 and
early 1862. By 1877, all of the markers that had
identified each of the Leesburg garrison dead
had apparently disappeared. Burials of veterans took place here as well as of wartime dead
from disease, and the dead from the battles of
Ball's Bluff and Gettysburg and other engagements.

- "Haud Pluribus Impar" is translated as
"To no one equal." The excerpt beginning
"Stoop, angels . . ." was written by Henry
Timrod and also appears, in slightly different form, on the courthouse monument at Floyd.
- Who "White" is with the "42nd Va. Cav."
is not clear. Col. Elijah V. White commanded the 35th Battalion of Virginia
Cavalry, not the "42nd Batt. Va. Cav.
(Washington)." William T. Robins was
lieutenant colonel of the 42nd Virginia Cavalry. Major, later Lt. Col. Robert
White was commander of the 41st Virginia Cavalry.

Middleburg

118. Sharon Cemetery Obelisk

Monument is a granite obelisk with a bronze
plaque set on a base and plinth.
LOCATION: Jay Street, 20117
DATE: 1910
MEDIA: Bronze, granite
Front

TO THE UNKNOWN DEAD.

—

THE PERPETUAL CARE
OF THIS HALLOWED SPOT
IS THE GIFT OF THE
MIDDLEBURG CHAPTER
UNITED DAUGHTERS
OF THE CONFEDERACY

Little is known about this site. Extant local
and Virginia United Daughters of the Confederacy chapter and division records have no
mention of it; neither do extant local newspapers. The U.D.C. chapter disbanded years ago,
and no cemetery records exist.

The monument is incongruent with the pros-
perous small town that surrounds it today, but

here Union cavalry clashed with Confederate cavalry under Maj. Gen. J. E. B. Stuart during the Gettysburg Campaign. No mention of the battle is made in the memorial, and wounded men from Second Manassas—some twelve hundred—were also cared for here in local churches and private homes.

The interred are not "Confederate Dead" but "Unknown Dead." They are sanctified to a "Hallowed Spot" and the "Perpetual Care" of the U.D.C.

Prince William County and City of Manassas

119. Manassas City Cemetery, Common Soldier

Monument is a white bronze private soldier standing at parade rest, surmounting an ex-

tended granite shaft, the whole set on a plinth, base, and dado.

LOCATION: 9027 Center Street, 20110
DATE: August 30, 1889
MEDIA: Granite, white bronze

[SEAL OF VIRGINIA]
SIC SEMPER TYRANNIS.
VIRGINIA
DEDICATED BY THE LADIES
MEMORIAL ASSOCIATION
OF MANASSAS,
ON AUGUST 30, 1889, TO THE HEROES
OF VIRGINIA AND HER SISTER STATES,
WHO YIELDED THEIR LIVES
ON JULY 18–21, 1861 &
AUGUST 28, 29 & 30, 1862,
IN DEFENSE OF THE SOUTHERN CAUSE
J. R. TILLETT,
CO. H, 15 VA. CAV.
BUILDER.

MANASSEH
LODGE NO 182 AE&M
AL 3888
JUNE 20 A. D. 1888
G. P. WRIGHT. W. M.

The dedication date of this monument commemorates the culmination of the Army of Northern Virginia's 1862 campaign in northern Virginia. Two major actions were fought near here: First Manassas was the first major land battle of the war and a Confederate victory. Second Manassas, another Confederate victory, led Southern arms to the brink of Washington, D.C. August 30 commemorates the second day of the battle, when the Army of Northern Virginia resisted sustained Union attacks and then undertook an onslaught against the Federal left that surprised and nearly routed the Union Army. In the end, the Confederates were victorious, but on Sunday, August 31, 1862, they were left with a battlefield covered with some fifteen thousand wounded and three thousand dead.

The "Southern Cause" is cited as a noble, sacred enterprise. Unspecified is the outcome of the war, but there is no indication that the "Defense of the Southern Cause" was not successful.

As with other monuments, the fundraising process was lengthy, but the Memorial Association history notes that eventually "our efforts were crowned with success, [and] the monument to the Confederate Dead was unveiled on August 31, 1889." W. H. Fitzhugh Lee and John Warwick Daniel were among the speakers at the ceremonies. The figure of a soldier is a later addition—another Monumental Bronze product from Connecticut.

Manassas National Battlefield Park
6511 Sudley Road, 20109

120. Brig. Gen. Thomas J. Jackson, Equestrian Statue

Monument is a bronze equestrian figure surmounting a granite pedestal and base.
LOCATION: Henry Hill
DATE: August 31, 1940
MEDIA: Bronze, granite
Front

THOMAS JONATHAN
JACKSON
1824 1863
—
"THERE STANDS JACKSON
LIKE A STONE WALL"
—
ERECTED BY
THE STATE OF VIRGINIA
UNDER ACT OF 1938
GOVERNORS

[2 NAMES]
SPONSORS
[3 NAMES]
—

FIRST BATTLE OF MANASSAS, JULY 21, 1861
NYC
J. P. POLLIA

A spontaneous call led to this imposing monument. Although the Confederate army at First Manassas was commanded by generals Joseph E. Johnston and P. G. T. Beauregard, it is Brig. Gen. Thomas J. Jackson whose statue stands here and who ultimately emerged as a national hero, earning the nom de guerre "Stonewall," when Brig. Gen. Barnard Bee, in the heat of battle, made the claim cited here.

The Depression-era sculpture was funded with an appropriation of twenty-five thousand dollars by the Virginia General Assembly in anticipation of the seventy-fifth anniversary of First Manassas, although it was dedicated on the anniversary of Second Manassas. The statue is large; the inscription is spare. The words "Stone Wall" are associated with Jackson without being applied to his name.

A design specification of the sponsoring committee was that Jackson be depicted on his horse Little Sorrel. There was disappointment, even bitterness especially among veterans, about the Monument Avenue statue of Jackson in Richmond and the use of a better-looking horse as a model rather than Little Sorrel. Jackson is absolutely resolute, standing like a one-man bulwark against an ominous, invisible host, as if anticipating their pending incarnation. It is an irony of the commemorative sculpture style of the 1930s, however, that he has the out-sized features that are reminiscent of the social realism of Soviet-style monumentation and that Jackson, a devout Christian, is interpreted by those standards. Another unusual feature is his dress—winter uniform and cape on a July battlefield.

• National Park Service Historian Theodore C. Mahr writes that the monument was placed near the site of the "Jackson cedar," which was previously used to mark the spot near where Jackson placed his line of battle. Today, however, historians believe Jackson's line was south of the present monument.

121. Brig. Gen. Barnard Bee Shaft

Monument is a granite shaft set on a base and plinth.

DATE: July 21, 1939
MEDIUM: Granite

GENERAL
BARNARD ELLIOTT BEE,
OF SOUTH CAROLINA,
COMMANDER, THIRD BRIGADE,
ARMY OF THE SHENANDOAH,
WAS KILLED HERE JULY 21, 1861.
JUST BEFORE HIS DEATH,
TO RALLY HIS SCATTERED TROOPS,
HE GAVE THE COMMAND:
"FORM, FORM, THERE STANDS JACKSON
LIKE A STONE WALL;
RALLY BEHIND THE VIRGINIANS."
PRESENTED BY
THE MARY TALIAFERRO THOMPSON
SOUTHERN MEMORIAL ASSN.
OF WASHINGTON, D.C.—JULY 21, 1939.
—
[5 NAMES]

The Bee monument, like the adjacent Jackson statue, was erected to commemorate the seventy-fifth anniversary of the battle of First Manassas. Brig. Gen. Barnard E. Bee's place in history rests almost entirely on the above quotation. The consensus of interpretation is that Bee was lauding Jackson's stalwartness, but the remark has sometimes been read as an aspersion on Jackson's rigidity in the midst of the flux and confusion on Henry Hill. Since Bee was shot shortly after making his claim there is no confirming the interpretation. He died the following morning and was buried in the family plot at Pendleton, South Carolina.

- How the claim drew attention and was recollected in all the noise and confusion of the battle is not clear, and some doubts have been voiced over the years about what was actually said. Historian James I. Robertson Jr. notes that Hunter McGuire combined several versions in having Bee shout: 'There stands Jackson like a stonewall! Rally behind the Virginians.'" Douglas Southall Freeman uses a contemporary newspaper account of Bee shouting: "There is Jackson standing like a stone wall. Let us determine to die here and we will conquer. Follow me."

122. Brig. Gen. Francis Bartow Tablet

Monument is a bronze plaque set in a granite shaft on a granite base.

DATE: 1936
MEDIA: Bronze, granite

BRIGADIER GENERAL
FRANCIS STEBBINGS BARTOW
BORN SAVANNAH GEORGIA, SEPT. 16, 1816

MORTALLY WOUNDED ON THIS SPOT,
JULY 21, 1861
COMMANDED 7TH, 8TH, 9TH,
& 11TH GEORGIA &
1ST KENTUCKY REGIMENTS
THE FIRST CONFEDERATE OFFICER
TO GIVE HIS LIFE ON THE FIELD.
W. P. A. 1936 (GA. DIV.) U.D.C.

The largest Henry Hill monuments were erected within a three-year period in the 1930s. This is the earliest of the three and is apparently the only Confederate monument in Virginia erected by the federal Works Progress Administration (W.P.A.). It is functional in design by comparison to the elegant, stylized Jackson and Bee monuments erected only a few years later. It replaced what may have been the war's first monument, also to Francis Bartow, erected by Confederate soldiers on September 4, 1861. A vestige remains only a few feet away, among the trees. The first Bartow monument was vandalized and destroyed by Union soldiers after the Southerners retreated in March 1862.

Bartow officially ranked as a colonel; at First Manassas he was serving as an "acting general." He was one of many promising young Confederate officers killed early in the war. At the time of his death he had risen to brigade command along with Barnard Bee, Stonewall Jackson, and Arnold Elzey.

123. 7th Georgia Infantry, Rickett's Battery

Monument is a marble shaft.
LOCATION: Henry Hill
DATE: circa 1903
MEDIUM: Marble

POSITION
7TH GA. REGT.
CAPTURED RICKETTS BATTERY
JULY 21, 1861.

Veterans of the 7th Georgia Infantry erected at least six markers, as part of an effort to systematically document the various movements of the regiment on this field of battle. The effort met with partial success: two survive; the other stands near a trail some 350 yards distant. Col. Francis Bartow was killed while leading the 7th Georgia at the above marker.

124. 7th Georgia Infantry, 5th Position Tablet

Monument is a marble shaft.
LOCATION: Henry Hill
DATE: circa 1903
MEDIUM: Marble

5TH POSITION
7TH GA. REGT.
JULY 21, 1861.

This marker stands southeast of the Henry House near the First Manassas Trail. The 7th Georgia participated in the campaigns of the Army of Northern Virginia from the Seven Days Battles in 1862 to Cold Harbor in 1864. It served with Lt. Gen. James Longstreet's First

Corps at Suffolk, Virginia, in Georgia, and in Tennessee. The regiment reported 153 casualties from among the 580 men present at First Manassas. At Appomattox, it surrendered with twenty-four officers and 164 men.

125. Pvt. George T. Stovall, 8th Georgia Infantry Tablet

Monument is a marble tablet set upon a concrete base.
LOCATION: Sudley Road, Matthews Hill
MEDIA: Concrete, marble

THIS MARBLE
MARKS THE SPOT
WHERE FELL
GEORGE T. STOVALL
OF THE ROME LIGHT GUARDS,
8TH REGT GEORGIA VOLUNTEERS
AT THE BATTLE OF JULY 21, 1861
BORN AT AUGUSTA GA.
APRIL 25, 1835
HIS LIFE HE DEVOTED TO HIS GOD
AND SACRIFICED IN HIS COUNTRY'S DEFENSE
HIS LAST WORDS WERE I AM GOING
TO HEAVEN

Records are incomplete on this marker, which stands along the Matthews Hill Loop Trail, near the intersection with the First Manassas Stone Bridge Loop Trail. Letters in the possession of the Museum of the Confederacy indicate that Stovall was shot while carrying his wounded brother from the field of battle. The brother

evidently survived the war. At his death in 1907, the torn coat of George Stovall was draped over his body.

- Stovall's knapsack and canteen are held in the archives of the Museum of the Confederacy. So, too, is the piece of shell from his mortal wounding.

126. First Manassas Battlefield Tablet

Monument is a bronze tablet set on a fieldstone base.
LOCATION: U.S. 29 and V.R. 234
DATE: July 21, 1928
MEDIA: Bronze, fieldstone

BATTLEFIELD OF BULL RUN OR
FIRST MANASSAS
JULY 21, 1861
CONFEDERATES UNDER
GENERAL BEAUREGARD
DEFEATED FEDERALS UNDER
GENERAL MCDOWELL.
GENERAL JACKSON GIVEN
NAME OF "STONEWALL"
ON THIS FIELD. GENERALS BEE
AND BARTOW KILLED.
OLD STONE HOUSE USED AS HOSPITAL
THIS MARKER ERECTED
JULY 21, 1928

The two Manassas battlefield markers were the last of the series of twenty-five monuments placed by the Association on Civil War Battlefields throughout the state. The United Daughters of the Confederacy sponsored the Manassas markers. Standing at the corner of the wartime Warrenton Pike and the Manassas-Sudley Road, this monument does not review the battle it commemorates; nor does it remark on the significance of this action as a

Southern victory or the first major land battle of the war. It stands, however, in the middle of a field of action that saw a battle of unforeseen carnage, ferocity, and consequences. Some sixty thousand troops were involved, with casualties of about forty-seven hundred men. P. G. T. Beauregard is given due notice as field commander in the inscription, although Gen. Joseph E. Johnston, the other principal field commander, is omitted, but it remarks on Jackson's nom de guerre. The deaths of Bee and Bartow—for whom monuments were erected only a few years after this one—merit mention after Jackson. The stone house, still standing, provides closure to the narrative, placing its present-day status in context with its wartime use as a hospital.

127. Groveton Cemetery Obelisk

Monument is an obelisk set on a plinth, base, and dado.
LOCATION: U.S. 29 near C.R. 622
DATE: August 30, 1904
MEDIA: Granite, marble
Front

[C.S.A. BATTLE FLAG]
DULCE ET DECORUM
EST PRO PATRIA MORI.

ERECTED
BY THE
UNITED DAUGHTERS
OF THE
CONFEDERACY
TO THE
CONFEDERATE
DEAD.
WE CARE NOT WHENCE THEY CAME,
DEAR IN THEIR LIFELESS CLAY!
WHETHER UNKNOWN, OR KNOWN TO FAME,
THEIR CAUSE AND COUNTRY STILL THE SAME.
THEY DIED—AND WORE THE GRAY.
—
THEY SLEEP WELL
IN THEIR UNKNOWN
GRAVES ON THE FAR-AWAY
BATTLE FIELD.
—
THEY GAVE THEIR
LIVES IN DEFENCE OF
THEIR COUNTRY, ON
THE FIELDS OF THE
FIRST AND SECOND
BATTLES OF MANASSAS.
—
BUT FOR THEM THE
COUNTING OF TIME
IS NOT: FOR THEY
DWELL IN THE CITY
OF GOD.

The Groveton and Bull Run Memorial Association was formed on April 27, 1867, to acquire land for the site of the Confederate cemetery at Groveton. The cemetery was established sometime prior to 1869. Thereafter a Mr. Benson L. Pridmore contracted to gather the soldiers' remains and reinter them. Pridmore was paid fifty cents for each reinterment, and remains were taken from sites scattered across the countryside. Ultimately, some five hundred soldiers were buried here, of whom only two were fully identified.

The reference to the "City of God"—Jerusalem—probably derives from the New Testament book of Revelation 3:12 ("Him that overcometh will I make a pillar in the temple of the city of my God, which is new Jerusalem . . . ').

"We care not . . ." is taken from "March of the Deathless Dead" by Father Ryan and is also excerpted at Spotsylvania. The larger context reads:

> Gather the corpses strewn O'er many a battle
>   plain;
> From many a grave that lies so lone,
> Without a name and without a stone,
> Gather the Southern slain. . . .

- Shafts surrounding the monument are inscribed, from left to right: Virginia, North Carolina, South Carolina, Georgia, Florida, Alabama, Mississippi, Louisiana, Texas, Arkansas, Missouri, Tennessee, Kentucky, and Maryland, respectively.
- The Timothy Dunklin memorial, which may or may not be a gravesite, stands across from Brawner's Farm on private property.

128. Second Manassas Battlefield Tablet

Monument is a bronze tablet set on a fieldstone base.
LOCATION: Adjacent Groveton Cemetery off U.S. 29
DATE: July 21, 1928
MEDIA: Bronze, fieldstone

GROVETON
SECOND BATTLE OF BULL RUN
AUGUST 30, 1862
CONFEDERATES UNDER
GENERALS LEE, JACKSON
AND LONGRSTREET DEFEATED
FEDERALS UNDER
GENERAL POPE. GENERAL LONGSTREET DINED

AT OLD DOGAN HOUSE. FIERCE
FIGHT OF R. R. CUT
HALF MILE NORTHWEST.
THIS MARKER ERECTED
JULY 21, 1928

The memorial aptly summarizes the action here, in which the troops under these three Confederate generals defeated the Union forces under Maj. Gen. John Pope. The Dogan House is one of three surviving period houses in the park; the railroad cut was a principal feature of the Confederate defense line.

- The two Bull Run battlefield monuments were dedicated on the same day, July 21, 1928, under the auspices of the Manassas and Bull Run chapters of the United Daughters of the Confederacy.
- The monument was dismantled and removed from its original site next to the Old Dogan House in 1978; it was reerected in June 1987 in the parking area for the Confederate cemetery.

129. Lee, Jackson, Longstreet Meeting Tablet

Monument is a bronze plaque set on a fieldstone base and tablet.
LOCATION: Two miles west of intersection of Sudley Road (V.R. 234) and Lee Highway (U.S. 29) adjacent Conway-Robinson State Forest
DATE: circa 1917
MEDIA: Bronze, fieldstone

THIS MARKER, ERECTED BY THE
HAYMARKET AGRICULTURAL CLUB,
INDICATES THE SPOT WHERE

GEN. R. E. LEE,
GENERAL LONGSTREET,
AND GENERAL JACKSON,
MET ON AUGUST 29.TH, 1862,
ABOUT 12.30 P:M. AS CERTIFIED BY
LIEUT, COL. EDMUND BERKELY.
SOLE SURVIVOR OF THE MEETING,
WHO SERVED THAT DAY ON
GENERAL LONGSTREET'S STAFF
BY SPECIAL ORDER.

Memory is the focus here: the date, time and place of this momentous meeting are "certified" by this rough-hewn monument, but what was decided and why Lee, Longstreet, and Jackson met are not mentioned. Historian Douglas Southall Freeman styles this meeting as an episode in the "Gallant Rivalry of Manassas." Like the Lee-Jackson bivouac, it marks the site of a dramatic battlefield conference that changed the course of events: in this case with Longstreet's men turning the Federal left flank, gaining the field from the Northerners, and bringing Southern arms to the outskirts of Washington, D.C.

- The monument was originally erected circa 1917, sometime before the death of Edmund Berkely of the 8th Virginia Infantry, who was present at this meeting. The monument has been moved to accommodate traffic and road widening. It now stands near the grounds of the Conway-Robinson State Forest.
- The memorial has unusually erratic punctuation.

Fairfax County and City of Fairfax

130. Fairfax, Courthouse Obelisk
Monument is an obelisk set on a base and plinth.
LOCATION: 10455 Armstrong Street, 22030
DATE: June 1, 1904
MEDIUM: Granite

THIS STONE MARKS
THE SCENE OF THE
OPENING CONFLICT
OF THE WAR OF
1861–1865, WHEN

JOHN Q. MARR,
CAPT. OF THE WARRENTON
RIFLES, WHO WAS THE
FIRST SOLDIER KILLED
IN ACTION, FELL 800 FT
S. 46* W (MAG.) OF THIS
SPOT, JUNE 1ST, 1861.
ERECTED BY MARR CAMP, C. V.
JUNE 1, 1904

Six weeks after Fort Sumter was fired upon, John Q. Marr was shot by Union cavalry in a field of clover in an area that now bears extensive development. Marr's death presaged the killing that would continue for the next four years. He was the first Southern soldier killed.

The memorial describes Marr's service and sacrifice like that of a citizen or civil servant—e. g., a police officer or fire fighter—who gave his life for his community. Marr is called a soldier, not a Confederate soldier, since he was not in Confederate service; he was captain of the Warrenton Rifles, a militia unit. His remains are in Warrenton cemetery.

131. City Cemetery Obelisk

Monument is an obelisk set on a base, plinth, and dado.

LOCATION: 10567 Main Street, 22030
DATE: 1890
MEDIUM: Granite
Front

> FROM FAIRFAX TO
> APPOMATTOX.
> 1861–1865.
> ERECTED TO THE MEMORY OF THE
> GALLANT SONS OF FAIRFAX, WHOSE
> NAMES ARE INSCRIBED ON THIS
> MONUMENT; BUT WHOSE BODIES LIE
> BURIED ON DISTANT BATTLE-FIELDS;
> AND TO THE MEMORY OF THEIR 200
> UNKNOWN COMRADES WHOSE REMAINS
> ARE AT REST BENEATH THIS MOUND.
> "THESE WERE MEN WHOM DEATH
> COULD NOT TERRIFY;—WHOM DEFEAT
> COULD NOT DISHONOR."
> CONFEDERATE
> DEAD
>
> —
>
> 8TH VA. INFANTRY.
> [1 NAME]

CO G.
[26 NAMES]
17TH VA. INFANTRY.
CO. D.
[20 NAMES]
J. F. MANNING
WASH, D.C.

—

17TH VA. INFANTRY.
CO. A.
[1 NAME]
CO. F.
[1 NAME]
CO. K
[1 NAME]
7TH VA. INFANTRY. CO. E.
[2 NAMES]
49TH VA. INFANTRY.
[1 NAME]
19TH GA. INFANTRY CO. K.
[5 NAMES]
ARTILLERY.
STUARTS HORSE.
[1 NAME]
KEMPER'S BATTERY.
[1 NAME]
DANVILLE.
[2 NAMES]
NAVY
[2 NAMES]

—

1ST VA. CAVALRY.
[1 NAME]
4TH VA.
[4 NAMES]
6TH VA. CO. A.
[1 NAME]
CO. F.
[4 NAMES]
CO. K.
[2 NAMES]
11TH VA. CO. I.
[12 NAMES]
MOSBY'S CAVALRY.
[11 NAMES]

This Richmond gray granite shaft was erected to commemorate the dead from nearby battles as well as the dead from the local community. Today the site is bleak, even forbidding, set at the center of an asphalt circle beneath which lie two hundred unknown dead.

The inscription is attributed to South Carolina diplomat and historian William Henry Trescot and also appears on the state house grounds Confederate monument at Columbia, South Carolina, dedicated in 1878. The larger context reads:

> Let the stranger, who in future times read this inscription, recognize that these were men whom power could not corrupt, whom death could not terrify, whom defeat could not dishonor, and let their virtues plead for just judgment of the cause in which they perished . . . Let the South Carolinian of another generation remember that the state taught them how to live and how to die, and that from her broken fortunes she has preserved for her children the priceless treasures of her memories, teaching all who may claim the same birthright that truth, courage and patriotism endure forever.

An adjacent plaque lists the names of six Union and 156 Confederate soldiers buried here.

- Periods are applied inconsistently in this inscription format. "Mosby's Cavalry" status is distinctive—not Partisan Rangers, as they were designated December 7, 1864, nor 43rd Virginia Cavalry Battalion, as they were first designated, but a cavalry unto itself.

132. Pvt. Peyton Anderson Tablet
Monument is a bronze tablet set on a granite base.
LOCATION: Fairfax Blvd (Lee Highway) (U.S. 50/29) west of Fairfax Circle (U.S. 29)
DATE: May 27, 1927
MEDIA: Bronze, granite

PEYTON ANDERSON OF THE RAPPAHANNOCK
CAVALRY WAS SEVERELY
WOUNDED ON PICKET DUTY
122 FT. N. W. OF THIS SPOT MAY 27, 1861
THE FIRST SOLDIER OF THE SOUTH TO
SHED HIS BLOOD FOR THE CONFEDERACY

ERECTED BY FAIRFAX CHAPTER,

U.D.C. MAY 27, 1927

First blood is cited here. Peyton L. Anderson Jr. and William Lillard of the 6th Virginia Cavalry were stationed here as pickets in the early weeks of the war in Virginia. Anderson would find a place in history when he was shot in the arm in an encounter with Federal troops but later recovered and eventually served with Mosby's Rangers. Lillard was captured. Anderson enlisted in the Rappahannock Cavalry, which was later mustered into Company B of the Sixth Virginia Cavalry.

- Anderson survived the war; he did not live to see this monument completed. Present at the monument dedication ceremonies were Anderson's widow, Luemma, and many of his descendants.
- The marker was moved during the widening of the Lee Highway; thus the "122 ft. N. W. of this spot" is no longer accurate.

Arlington County and City of Alexandria

133. Alexandria, Courthouse Common Soldier

Monument is a private soldier, in bronze, standing with arms crossed, surmounting a granite plinth, base, dado, and pedestal.
LOCATION: Washington and Prince streets, 22320
DATE: May 24, 1889
MEDIA: Bronze, granite
Front

> ERECTED
> TO THE MEMORY OF THE
> CONFEDERATE DEAD
> OF ALEXANDRIA VA.
> BY THEIR
> SURVIVING COMRADES.
> MAY 24TH 1889
> THIS MONUMENT MARKS THE SPOT FROM
> WHICH THE ALEXANDRIA TROOPS LEFT TO
> JOIN THE CONFEDERATE FORCES
> MAY 24, 1861

> —
> THEY DIED IN THE
> CONSCIOUSNESS OF DUTY
> FAITHFULLY PERFORMED.
> ALEXANDRIA ARTILLERY
> [9 NAMES]
> [22 OTHER NAMES]
> —

> SEVENTEENTH VIRGINIA INFANTRY

CO. A	CO. G
[16 NAMES]	[11 NAMES]
CO. E	CO. H
[16 NAMES]	[22 NAMES]

> CO. I
> [3 NAMES]

The title of the pensive private in the middle of Washington and Prince Streets is "Appomattox," based on a period painting by John A. Elder (1833–1895). Caspar Buberl was the sculptor of the resulting statue. The Confederate soldier is similar to the statues at Mount Jackson and Berryville.

The R. E. Lee Camp of United Confederate Veterans raised much of the money for the monument—two thousand dollars for the figure, one thousand dollars for the Georgia granite base. The Women's Auxiliary of the Lee Camp also staged a fundraising lecture series and several fairs.

The monument was dedicated on the twenty-eighth anniversary of the vote for secession by Virginia—May 23, 1861. Militiamen mustered at this site shortly thereafter and departed to form part of what became the 17th Virginia Infantry, which served throughout the war and surrendered at Appomattox. The memorial lists ninety-nine names, fifty-eight of them from the 17th Virginia.

Legislation in 1890 to secure this site for perpetuity was used to block efforts in the 1930s to move the statue because of traffic concerns. It was invoked again in the 1970s, because of its provocative subject matter. It remains at the place where it was originally erected.

• Excerpt from the dedication address by John Elder:

My friends, the cause cannot be made odious, for which a million christian woman [*sic*] suffered famine for four long years, and gave up their dear ones to slaughter, while their constant prayer ascended like incense to Almighty God for its success, the cause whose exponents and exemplars were such men as Stuart, and Johnston and Jackson, and Lee, and ex-president Jefferson Davis.

134. Christ Church Cemetery Tablet

Monument is a marble tablet set on a matching stone.

LOCATION: 118 North Washington Street, 22314

DATE: December 27, 1889

MEDIUM: Marble

> "How sleep the brave who sink to rest
> By all their country's wishes blest"
> Beneath this mound lie the remains of thirty-four
> CONFEDERATE SOLDIERS
> Which were disinterred from
> the Alexandria Soldiers'
> And reinterred in this ground on the 27th
> day of December 1879, under the /auspices
> Of the Southern Memorial
> Association of Alexandria, Va.
> [roster: 33 names, one unknown]
> These men were prisoners of war, who
> died in Federal Hospitals in this city.
> RESURGEMUS.
> ''ORIGINAL STONE LIES UNDERNEATH''

MILITARY ORDER OF

STARS AND BARS

SAMUEL COOPER CHAPTER

T. A. SULLIVAN & SON, ARL., VA.
MADE BY JOSEPH R. POLDIAK
SEPTEMBER 2002

The tablet and mound mark the graves of Confederate soldiers from Mississippi, South Carolina, North Carolina, Tennessee, Georgia, and Virginia, including one Virginian listed as a "Partizan Ranger." The men were wounded prisoners from Petersburg brought to Alexandria by boat who died in hospital. The bodies were moved Christmas night 1879, and the church cemetery site was dedicated two days later. The original marble tablet was replaced in 2002.

- The colonial Georgian-style church was erected in 1773 from a design by James Wren. George Washington and Robert E. Lee were regular worshippers; many presidents and foreign dignitaries have attended services here as well.

135. Arlington National Cemetery, Confederate Section Sculpture

Monument is a bronze sculpture standing on a granite base and plinth.

LOCATION: Jackson Circle, Fort Myer, 22211

DATE: June 4, 1914

MEDIA: Bronze, granite

Front

> [SEAL OF THE CONFEDERACY]
> [ON SHIELD]
> CONSTITUTION

—TO-OUR-DEAD-HEROES—BY-
THE-UNITED-DAUGHTERS-OF-THE-
CONFEDERACY—VICTRIX-CAUSA-DIIS-
PLACUIT—SED-VICTA-CATONI
—NOT-FOR-FAME-OR-REWARD—
NOT-FOR-PLACE-OR-FOR-RANK
—NOT-LURED-BY-AMBITION—OR-GOADED-
BY-NECESSITY—BUT-IN-SIMPLE-OBEDIENCE-
TO-DUTY—AS-THEY-UNDERSTOOD-
IT—THESE-MEN-SUFFERED-ALL
—SACRIFICED-ALL—DARED-ALL-AND-DIED
RANDOLPH HARRISON MCKIM
AND THEY SHALL BEAT THEIR SWORDS
INTO PLOUGHSHARES AND THEIR SPEARS
INTO PRUNING HOOKS
ALABAMA FLORIDA STATE OF GEORGIA
UNION JUSTICE
MISSOURI VIRGINIA
TEXAS ARKANSAS NORTH CAROLINA
TENNESSEE SOUTH CAROLINA MISSISSIPPI

MADE BY
AKHEN GESELLSCAFT GUIDENBECK
BRONZE FOUNDRY
BERLIN-FRIEDRICHSHAGEN GERMANY
M. EZEKIEL SCULPTER
ROME MCMXII
ATREA
VA
CSA

The most richly decorated elegy in northern Virginia offers a celebratory contrast to the somber, funereal-era cemetery memorials at Manassas, Fairfax, and Warrenton. The designer/sculptor was Moses Ezekiel (1844–1917), a graduate of the Virginia Military Institute, and a participant, with the Corps of Cadets, in the battle of New Market, where he was wounded. Ezekiel also sculpted the Stonewall Jackson monument, the New Market memorial on the V. M. I. campus in Lexington, and the John Warwick Daniels monument in Lynchburg.

Ezekiel accepted the commission of the United Daughters of the Confederacy for the monument on condition that he would retain control of the design. Lavish visual elements predominate: the thirty-two-foot monument is surmounted by a larger-than-life figure of a woman representing the South. The woman's head is crowned with olive leaves. Her left hand extends a laurel wreath toward the South, a gesture recognizing the sacrifice of her sons to her cause. Her right hand holds a pruning hook resting on a plow stock in a gesture of peace and reconciliation. A panoply of vignettes illustrates the effect of the war on various Southerners. The thirty-two figures include a black slave following his young master; an officer kissing his infant child who is held by the child's black caregiver; a young woman binding a sword and sash on her departing soldier; a blacksmith leaving his workshop as his wife looks on; and a young officer standing alone. Another frieze of life-sized figures depicts mythical gods together with Southern soldiers. Included in the frieze is a Black Confederate soldier.

- A reconciliation milestone occurred when Congress authorized the Confederate section in 1900; numerous reinterments followed. Secretary of War William Howard Taft supported the project; President Woodrow Wilson spoke at the dedication ceremonies. Among the 482 persons buried here are 396 soldiers, 58 wives, 15 civilians, and 12 unknown.
- Four cinerary urns symbolize the four years of the Civil War. A frieze of fourteen shields, each depicting the coat of arms of one of the thirteen Confederate states and Maryland. Unlike the commemorative listing of the other Southern states, Georgia is prefaced with the words "State of."
- An early design for the monument depicted Lee at the Wilderness.
- The quotation beginning, "Not for fame . . ." is attributed to Reverend Randolph Harrison McKim, a minister of Epiphany Church in Washington, D.C., and a Confederate veteran. A larger excerpt is inscribed at Thornrose Cemetery, Staunton.
- The Latin quotation "Victrix Causa Diis Placuit Sed Victa Caton" is translated as "The victorious cause was pleasing to the gods but the lost cause to Cato."
- Ezekiel, the first Jewish cadet to attend the Virginia Military Institute, graduated from V. M. I., lived abroad for many years, and went on to earn an international

reputation as an artist. Ezekiel received numerous honors, including being decorated by King Umberto I of Italy and knighted by King Victor Emmanuel III of Italy.

His tombstone, at the base of the monument, makes no mention of his achievements or status, only his time as a cadet:

MOSES J. EZEKIEL
SERGEANT OF COMPANY C, BATTALION
OF CADETS OF THE
VIRGINIA MILITARY INSTITUTE

- Also buried in Arlington Cemetery: Gen. Joseph Wheeler.

136. Upton Hill Tablet

Monument is a bronze plaque set on a boulder.
LOCATION: 5900 Wilson Boulevard, 22205
DATE: June 13, 1980
MEDIA: Bronze, fieldstone

[OAK LEAF CARVING AND THE NUMBER 7]
THIS RED OAK AND STONE
WERE PLACED HERE AS A
BICENTENNIAL MEMORIAL TO
THE MEN IN GRAY WHO
SERVED ON UPTON HILL
BY ARLINGTON CHAPTER
UNITED DAUGHTERS
OF THE CONFEDERACY

Upton's Hill's location at the intersection of several roads as well as its height, which offered an excellent observation point, gave it tactical value in the early months of the war. In the summer of 1861, Confederate troops built fortifications here; they withdrew in the fall, and Union troops moved in and established an observation tower.

This small marker—a boulder taken from the excavation for Washington's Metro subway construction—is distinctive for offering the only reference to the 1976 bicentennial on a Virginia monument. Like the 1876 centennial, the 1976 bicentennial had an influence on the monument movement: a revival of interest and consequent wave of monumentation began at about this time and continued into the twenty-first century.

- The marker stands in front of the Sunrise Retirement Home, at Bluemont Park, across from the old Washington and Old Dominion Railroad line, at Wilson and Manchester.

City of Fredericksburg

137. Confederate Cemetery, Soldier
Monument is a private soldier, in white bronze, standing at parade rest surmounting a plinth, base, and shaft with bronze plaque.
LOCATION: William Street and Washington Avenue, 22401
DATE: 1884
MEDIA: Bronze, granite, white bronze
Front

TO THE CONFEDERATE DEAD
S. CAROLINA   VIRGINIA   N. CAROLINA
—

MISSOURI   KENTUCKY
TENNESSEE   ARKANSAS
—

LOUISIANA   MISSISSIPPI   TEXAS
—

GEORGIA   FLORIDA   ALABAMA

Bronze plaque supplements of 1985 (below) and 1992 (at the entrance) add detail, as is typical with commemorative-era monuments:

Over three thousand Confederate soldiers repose here, including six generals. Only 330 have been identified. The Fredericksburg Ladies Memorial Association organized in 1866, purchased land for the cemetery in 1867 and began reinterring soldiers from the surrounding area. This plaque notes that the dead were taken from four battlefields, presumably Chancellorsville, Fredericksburg, Wilderness, and Spotsylvania. Other actions, lethal but less well known, can be assumed, as can deaths from illness or accidents. Headstones supplied by various Southern states replaced the original cedar posts.

An irony to the placement of the cemeteries at Fredericksburg is that the Confederates are buried on ground that was behind Union lines during the battle, while the National Cemetery is on Marye's Heights, where no Union soldiers trod in the December 1862 battle. It is no irony, though, that the Confederate soldiers are interred in the community that took them in and buried them, while Union soldiers are in the National Cemetery—on the outskirts of the town and under federal auspices.

Fredericksburg Lodge No. 4, A. F. & A. M., of the Masons of Virginia, laid the cornerstone, from the James River Quarry, June 4, 1874. The base was dedicated June 9, 1881. The sculpture, cast by the Monumental Bronze Company, was dedicated on June 10, 1891.

Generals buried here: Seth M. Barton, Dabney H. Maury, Abner M. Perrin, Daniel Ruggles, Henry H. Sibley, Carter L. Stevenson.

• This bronze plaque is set on the brick cemetery wall:

138. Barton Street Cemetery Tablet

Monument is a bronze tablet set on a granite shaft.
LOCATION: Barton and George streets, 22401
DATE: April 18, 2009
MEDIA: Bronze, granite

THE REV. ALFRED M. RANDOLPH OF
ST. GEORGE'S EPISCOPAL CHURCH
OFFICIATED AT THE BURIALS.
ALABAMA   NORTH CAROLINA
[FIFTEEN NAMES]   [ELEVEN NAMES]
ARKANSAS   TENNESSEE
[SIX NAMES]   [ONE NAME]
GEORGIA   TEXAS
[SEVEN NAMES]   [SEVEN NAMES]
VIRGINIA
[3 NAMES]
—
DEDICATED APRIL 18, 2009
SCV CAMP 1722

Fifty-one soldiers are believed to be interred at this site, which is now an athletic field, parking lot, and former schoolhouse; there is no record of the graves ever being moved.

The soldiers came from seven states—Alabama, Arkansas, Georgia, North Carolina, Tennessee, Texas, and Virginia—and rest in a former potter's field given over to military burials by the Fredericksburg City Council. The interments took place from 1861 until 1862 for nonbattle deaths before the Battle of Fredericksburg.

The Sons of Confederate Veterans Matthew Fontaine Maury Camp 1722 in Fredericksburg raised more than two thousand dollars for a granite monument erected in 2009.

139. U.D.C. Presbyterian Church Plaque

Monument is a marble plaque set into a brick wall.
LOCATION: 810 Princess Anne Street, 22401-5820

DATE: 1924
MEDIUM: Marble

GEN. STONEWALL JACKSON,
BY GEN. LEE'S REQUEST, ON
THIS CORNER, PLANNED THE
BATTLE OF FREDERICKSBURG.
NOV. 27, 1862. U.D.C.

James Power Smith identified this location, and the U.D.C. followed up by installing this marble marker in a wall of the Presbyterian Church of Fredericksburg, at the corner of Princess Anne and George streets. Smith served as the pastor of the church 1869–91. In 1862, he served on Jackson's staff as an aide-de-camp. On Sunday morning, November 30, 1862, Smith recalled, he accompanied the general into the deserted city of Fredericksburg. There they sat their horses and Jackson surveyed the area where the battle was to take place only fifteen days later.

It is in an overstatement to say that Jackson "planned the battle" here, but fair enough perhaps to commemorate the fact that Jackson gave consideration to the fight that could take place there. National Park Service historian Donald Pfanz, however, states that the tablet is completely inaccurate. Jackson was nowhere near Fredericksburg on November 27, 1862, and had no reason and no known order to plan a defense at this site.

Fredericksburg Battlefield
1013 Lafayette Boulevard,
Fredericksburg, 22401

140. Fredericksburg Battlefield Tablet

Monument is a bronze tablet set on a granite base.

LOCATION: Hanover Street and Sunken Road, 22401
DATE: May 3, 1927
MEDIA: Bronze, granite

BATTLE OF FREDERICKSBURG
DECEMBER 13, 1862 THE
CONFEDERATES UNDER LEE
DEFEATED THE FEDERALS
UNDER BURNSIDE IN A
SANGUINARY CONFLICT MARKED
BY EXTRAORDINARY
BRAVERY ON BOTH SIDES. IN
A SERIES OF GALLANT
CHARGES THE FEDERAL ARMY
SUSTAINED HEAVY
LOSSES AND BURNSIDE WAS
FORCED TO RE-CROSS
THE RAPPAHANNOCK
ERECTED 1927 BY THE
FREDERICKSBURG AND SPOTSYLVANIA
CHAPTERS, U.D.C.
J. ARTHUR LIMERICK CO. FDR'S BALTO.

This is another of the series of twenty-five battlefield markers erected by the United Daughters of the Confederacy in 1927. The tablet offers a cogent, balanced summary of the action that took place December 11–15, 1862. The "Gallant" charges—fourteen of them in front of Marye's Heights, where the monument stands—were arguably no more tragic than Confederate charges at Franklin or Gettysburg, but the charges here were widely judged to be of no more purpose than to demonstrate the resolve of the Union soldier to fight under the most trying conditions, including gross mismanagement by Maj. Gen. Ambrose E. Burnside. The estimated casualties: Union 12,653 of 114,000; Confederate 5,309 of 72,000.

Responsibility—justly—is imputed to Burnside. The "Federal Army Sustained Heavy Losses," but it is Burnside who "Was Forced to Re-cross the Rappahannock." It is not the army that was defeated but Burnside.

141. Sgt. Richard R. Kirkland Sculpture

Monument is a bronze sculpture of Kirkland giving water to a Union soldier set on a black granite base.

LOCATION: Sunken Road
DATE: September 29, 1965
MEDIA: Bronze, granite
Front

IN MEMORIUM
RICHARD ROWLAND KIRKLAND
CO. G, 2ND SOUTH CAROLINA VOLUNTEERS
C.S.A.
AT THE RISK OF HIS LIFE, THIS AMERICAN
SOLDIER OF SUBLIME COMPASSION BROUGHT
WATER TO HIS WOUNDED FOES AT
FREDERICKSBURG. THE FIGHTING MEN ON
· BOTH SIDES OF THE LINE CALLED HIM
"THE ANGEL OF MARYE'S HEIGHTS."
FELIX DE WELDON
SC. 1965.

—

DEDICATED
TO
NATIONAL UNITY
AND THE
BROTHERHOOD OF MAN

—

ERECTED BY
THE STATE OF SOUTH CAROLINA
THE COMMONWEALTH OF VIRGINIA
COLLATERAL DESCENDENTS OF

RICHARD KIRKLAND
CITIZENS OF THE UNITED STATES
DR. RICHARD NUNN LANIER
EXECUTIVE DIRECTOR
OF THE
RICHARD ROWLAND KIRKLAND
MEMORIAL FOUNDATION
1964
—

BORN, KERSHAW COUNTY, S. C., AUGUST, 1843
SERGEANT AT FREDERICKSBURG,
DECEMBER, 1862
KILLED IN ACTION AT CHICKAMAUGA,
SEPTEMBER, 1863

Dr. Richard Nunn Lanier, of South Carolina, conceived the monument, built at a cost of twenty-four thousand dollars. The sculptor, Felix De Weldon, also designed the Iwo Jima memorial at Washington, D.C.

The Kirkland account has been questioned, but the substance of Southern soldiers bringing aid to wounded Northern soldiers is described by several sources, including Maj. Gen. Joseph B. Kershaw. Richard Rowland Kirkland served with Company G, of the 2nd South Carolina Infantry and saw action at the battles of 1st Manassas, Savage Station, Maryland Heights, and Antietam. At the battle of Fredericksburg on December 13, 1862, Kirkland's unit was posted behind the Stone Wall at the base of Marye's Heights and assisted in the slaughter of successive waves of assaulting Union troops. About eight thousand Union soldiers were shot in front of the wall. The wounded who were able made their way to the rear after dark; others were retrieved by their fellow Federal soldiers. However, many of the wounded—disabled, helpless—remained where they had fallen between the lines all night. Kirkland, according to several accounts, stepped into the field the following day and risked his life in bringing succor—water and clothing—to them.

Kirkland went on to fight at the battles of Chancellorsville and Gettysburg. He was killed at the battle of Chickamauga, on September 20, 1863. In 1909, his remains were interred at Quaker Cemetery in Camden, South Carolina, a few feet from the grave of Maj. Gen. Kershaw.

142. Brig. Gen. Thomas R. R. Cobb Tablet

Monument is a granite shaft.
LOCATION: Sunken Road
DATE: circa 1888
MEDIUM: Granite

ON THIS SPOT
GEN. THOMAS R. R. COBB
OF GEORGIA
FELL IN BATTLE
DEC. 13, 1862.
—

COBB

Although he had no military experience before the war, Thomas Reade Rootes Cobb (1823–1862) rose to the rank of brigadier general and earned the praise of Robert E. Lee. At the battle of Fredericksburg, he was struck by a shell fragment and bled to death. His passing, Lee wrote in tribute, "left a gap in the army which his military aptitude and skill renders . . . hard to fill." Cobb, who was also a member of the provisional Congress, is buried in Georgia. Cobb family members erected the memorial. His older brother, Howell Cobb, was governor of Georgia and a general in the Confederate army.

143. Martha Stevens Tablet

Monument is a granite tablet.
LOCATION: Sunken Road
DATE: December 18, 1917
MEDIUM: Granite

> HERE LIVED
> MRS. MARTHA STEVENS
> FRIEND OF THE
> CONFEDERATE SOLDIER,
> 1861–1865

The Martha Stevens stone was sponsored by the United Daughters of the Confederacy for a woman whose house stood along the Sunken Road. Local tradition holds that Stevens stayed here throughout the battle and cared for the wounded.

144. Second Battle of Fredericksburg, Parker's Battery Tablet

Monument is a granite tablet.

LOCATION: Marye's Heights, National Cemetery
DATE: May 3, 1973
MEDIUM: Granite

> MAY 3, 1973
> IN THIS VICINITY THE MEN OF PARKER'S
> CONFEDERATE BATTERY (THE
> "BOY COMPANY")
> UNDER LT. J. THOMPSON BROWN FOUGHT
> TWO GUNS, TWICE GALLANTLY ASSISTED IN
> REPULSING THE UNION VI CORPS BEFORE
> BEING OUTFLANKED AND OVERWHELMED

Fifteen thousand Union soldiers are buried on the grounds behind this monument. This is the only Confederate monument on these heights, called Willis Hill at the time of the battle, which is dominated by the national cemetery. It is also the only monument on this field dedicated to the Second Battle of Fredericksburg.

This marker omits the battle and year when the action took place. Five months after the Union defeat at the battle of Fredericksburg, Union troops attacked Marye's Heights again during the Chancellorsville campaign. On May 3, 1863, Union forces—Sixth Corps, Maj. Gen. John Sedgwick—took this hill, held by an outnumbered force under Maj. Gen. Jubal A. Early, and captured seven guns. The guns included two pieces of Capt. William Parker's Virginia Battery (one section, under Lt. J. Thompson Brown) posted here. Parker—one of the "boys"—was twenty-five years old when he commanded the battery.

145. Lee's Hill Tablet

Monument is a granite shaft.
LOCATION: Crest of hill off Lee Drive
DATE: 1903
MEDIUM: Granite

LEE'S HILL
BATTLE OF FREDERICKSBURG
DEC. 12–13, 1862.

Lee and other senior officers of the Army of Northern Virginia watched the battle of Fredericksburg from this site, which was called Telegraph Hill in 1862. The monument, erected by James Power Smith, originally stood off U.S. 1, but was moved in the 1960s with the development of the Lee Hill Exhibit Shelter site and trail at Lee's Hill. It was here, as the National Park Service plaque notes, that Lee was witness to such slaughter as to stir him to remark, "It is well this is so terrible! We would grow too fond of it."

146. The "Meade" Pyramid

Monument is a granite pyramid.
LOCATION: Lee Drive in the Fredericksburg and Spotsylvania National Military Park, off Lansdowne Road
DATE: March 31, 1898
MEDIUM: Granite

MARCH 31, 1898
CORNERSTONE
1862
1898

The Meade Pyramid stands within sight of the railroad on the grounds of the First Battle of Fredericksburg. Sponsored by the Confederate Memorial Literary Society and built by the Richmond, Fredericksburg, and Potomac Railroad, the pyramid has a thirty-foot-square base, stands about twenty-four feet high, and is composed of Virginia granite rubble. The monument is unusual but not unique: the design was modeled after the 1869 Hollywood Cemetery pyramid.

The monument's name is misleading and uncertain in origin. The structure is commonly called the "Meade Pyramid," since it stands near where troops under Union Maj. Gen. George G. Meade's line rushed through a gap in the Confederate line. Whether the monument was originally intended to mark this event is still a matter of dispute.

It was designed as a visual experience for passing railroad passengers. The marker only references the battle and the date when the pyramid was erected. To this day, direct access to the monument is difficult, and observing the pyramid from a distance is recommended. The railroad is still in use, and copperhead snakes in the fields surrounding the monument have been a source of caution to visitors.

147. Jackson on the Field Tablet

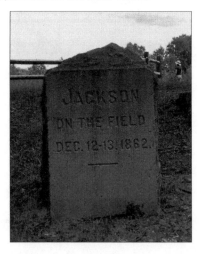

Monument is a granite shaft.
LOCATION: Lee Drive at Prospect Hill
DATE: August 1903
MEDIUM: Granite

JACKSON
ON THE FIELD
DEC. 12–13. 1862

Lt. Gen. Thomas J. "Stonewall" Jackson commanded the right wing of the Army of Northern Virginia at the battle of Fredericksburg and observed the deployment of the Union army from this site. This monument, erected by James Power Smith, has a dynamic tone, making Jackson an active force in the action, one whose very presence is noteworthy.

- The monument originally stood along Mine Road near the tracks of the railroad but was moved with the construction of Lee Drive by the Park Service.

Other Fredericksburg Battlefield Monuments

148. Lee's Winter Headquarters, Tablet

Monument is a granite shaft.
LOCATION: Mine Road (C.R. 636) and Ironwood Lane (C.R. 1251)
DATE: August 1903
MEDIUM: Granite

LEE'S
HEAD QUARTERS [SIC]
WINTER OF 1862–3.

General Lee established his headquarters near here after the battle of Fredericksburg. The site, marked by James Power Smith, is approximate: the best available evidence places the actual location some 250 yards south of Mine Road. Its modesty has been remarked upon: the army's headquarters was in a small clearing in the woods with only a few tents and a single flag to indicate what it was. Lee remained at the site until late March 1863, when a throat infection moved him to take refuge at Thomas Yerby's house nearby.

149. Maj. John Pelham Tablet

Monument is a granite shaft.
LOCATION: Tidewater Trail (V.R. 2–U.S. 17) and Benchmark Road (C.R. 608), south of Fredericksburg
DATE: 1903
MEDIUM: Granite

STUART AND PELHAM
BATTLE OF
FREDERICKSBURG.
DEC. 13, 1862.

This marker, erected by James Power Smith, was placed in the area where a section of Maj. Gen. J. E. B. Stuart's horse artillery under Maj. John Pelham harassed advancing Union troops in the early stages of the battle of Fredericksburg. Pelham's fortitude and skill earned him the sobriquet from Lee, the "Gallant Pelham." Despite the killing power of Union artillery, Pelham's gun and crew proved too elusive to hit. Lee said of him: "It is glorious to see such courage in one so young!" Pelham was killed in a fight with Union cavalry at Kelly's Ford less than four months later.

Caroline County

150. Bowling Green, Courthouse Common Soldier

Monument is a private soldier, in marble, standing at parade rest surmounting a granite plinth, base, dado, and shaft.
LOCATION: 111 Ennis Street, 22427
DATE: April 26, 1906
MEDIA: Granite, marble
Front

1861
1865
[CROSSED C.S.A. BATTLE FLAGS]
ERECTED BY THE PEOPLE OF
CAROLINE COUNTY
TO COMMEMORATE THE VALOR
AND ENDURANCE OF ITS SOLDIERS
FURNISHED TO THE ARMY OF THE
CONFEDERATE STATES OF AMERICA
1861–1865.
CAROLINE CO. VA.

—

NAMES OF SOLDIERS OF RECORD
IN THE CLERK'S OFFICE.

—

30TH REGIMENT VA. INFANTRY

COMPANIES E. F. G. AND H.
47TH REGIMENT VA. INFANTRY
COMPANIES B. G. H. AND K.

—

9TH REGIMENT VA. CAVALRY COMPANY B.
24TH REGIMENT VA. CAVALRY COMPANY F.
THORNTON'S ARTILLERY COMPANY.

The willing suspension of individual choice to a larger purpose is a theme of the Bowling Green memorial underneath the J. Henry Brown sculpture: Caroline County's soldiers were "Furnished" by the community to the army of the Confederacy, a tribute to the soldiers' stolidity and fidelity. The text has no explicit apologetic, but it represents a typical reconciliation-era claim that the Confederate soldiers completed their work and closure was obtained. No victory is claimed, but there is nothing to suggest that the "Soldiers Furnished" were unsuccessful.

Declaring that the monument was "Erected by the People" is unusual. Almost invariably government support and approval was necessary. Public appeals for funds were always made, but city or state usually completed the financial arrangements. "Seldom would governmental support be openly acknowledged," notes historian Sarah Driggs, "since the statue would always be described as coming from 'the people.'"

- The roster of "Soldiers of Record" could not be found in the courthouse and may have been lost in one of several fires that have occurred in the town.

151. Guinea, Stonewall Jackson Tablet

Monument is a granite shaft.

LOCATION: The Stonewall Jackson Shrine, National Park Service, 12019 Stonewall Jackson Road, 22580

DATE: 1903

MEDIUM: Granite

> STONEWALL JACKSON.
> DIED
> MAY 10, 1863.
> BURIED
> LEXINGTON, VA.

This is another monument erected by James Power Smith, staff officer under Jackson, and one of a series he sponsored in this area. Jackson died here, near the rail station (Guiney Station at the time), from complications of his wounds at the battle of Chancellorsville.

This marker was originally posted beside the tracks of the former Richmond, Fredericksburg, and Potomac Railroad ("RF&P") but was moved in front of the National Park Service parking lot in the 1960s. The words "Buried Lexington, Va." were added to clarify the fact that Jackson is not interred here.

Spotsylvania County
Salem Church

152. Salem Church Battlefield Tablet

Monument is a bronze tablet set on a limestone base.

LOCATION: 4054 Plank Road, 22407

DATE: May 3, 1927

MEDIA: Bronze, limestone

> BATTLE OF SALEM CHURCH
> OF MAY 3, 4, 1863 FOUGHT
> BY LEE AND HOOKER,
> CONCLUDED THE CHANCELLORSVILLE

> CAMPAIGN.
> HERE, THE FOLLOWERS OF
> LEE, IN IMPERISHABLE
> BRONZE RESPOND TO THE
> NOBLE SENTIMENT OF
> THE FOLLOWERS OF GRANT AND PAY HIGHEST
> TRIBUTE TO THE PATRIOTISM OF BOTH.
> ERECTED BY THE
> FREDERICKSBURG AND SPOTSYLVANIA
> CHAPTERS, U.D.C.
> 1927

Moving west from Fredericksburg to join the main body of the Army of the Potomac during the battle of Chancellorsville, troops under Maj. Gen. John Sedgwick were denied that union by a Southern force. Most of the action took place on or near this site. Some five thousand casualties were incurred to the opposing sides.

The area is very heavily developed and trafficked; it bears no resemblance to its rural past, but the church still stands on the low ridge on which Confederate forces made their stand.

Both sides receive tributes in the memorial, although Sedgwick, who led the advance, is not mentioned, and Lt. Gen. Ulysses S. Grant, who was not present, is mentioned. Maj. Gen. Joseph Hooker had overall command of the Army of the Potomac but was not on the field. Lee missed the opening of the battle but was on the field thereafter.

153. Salem Church Shaft—Smith

Monument is a granite shaft.
DATE: August 1903
MEDIUM: Granite

BATTLE OF
SALEM CHURCH
MAY 3, 1863.
BROOKS—NEWTON
VS
WILCOX—SEMMES
MAHONE.

This James Power Smith marker offers an evenhanded commentary on the battle. The victors, significance, or higher levels of command in this apparent contest—"VS"—are excluded. At Salem Church, Confederate forces under Brig. Gen. Cadmus M. Wilcox blocked the advance of Union Maj. Gen. John Sedgwick's Sixth Corps. Sedgwick is not referred to, but his division commanders are, Maj. Gen. John Newton and Brig. Gen. William T. H. Brooks, as are the Army of Northern Virginia's First Corps brigade commanders, Wilcox and generals Paul J. Semmes and William Mahone.

- The monument was moved when the intersection was altered.

Chancellorsville Battlefield
9001 Plank Road 22553

154. Gen. Thomas J. Jackson Shaft

Monument is a shaft and cap surmounting a base and plinth.

LOCATION: Chancellorsville Visitors Center, 9001 Plank Road, 22553
DATE: June 13, 1888
MEDIUM: Granite
Front

ON THIS SPOT
FELL
MORTALLY WOUNDED
THOMAS J. JACKSON
LT: GEN: C.S.A.
MAY 2ND 1863
JACKSON
—
THERE IS JACKSON STANDING
LIKE A
STONE WALL.
BEE AT MANASSAS.
—
COULD I HAVE DIRECTED EVENTS,
I SHOULD HAVE CHOSEN FOR
THE GOOD OF THE
COUNTRY, TO HAVE BEEN
DISABLED IN YOUR STEAD.
I CONGRATULATE YOU UPON
THE VICTORY, WHICH
IS TO YOUR SKILL AND ENERGY.
R. E. LEE, GENERAL
—
LET US PASS OVER THE RIVER AND
REST UNDER THE SHADE OF THE TREES.
HIS LAST WORDS.

This area was the most contested ground in North American history, with major battlefields at Spotsylvania, Fredericksburg, and Wilderness, in addition to Chancellorsville, which was arguably Lee's greatest victory. Relatively few Confederate monuments have been erected, but this is one of four devoted to Jackson, who was shot near here on the night of May 2, while he was scouting between the lines.

- Jackson's nom de guerre, Stonewall, is not mentioned, but Bee's tribute is. Lee's tribute is excerpted from a letter written to Jackson while the latter was at a field hospital at Wilderness Tavern.
- There seems to be no doubt about Jackson's last words, spoken on his deathbed at Guiney Station and cited here. They

were attested to by Jackson's physician, Hunter McGuire; Jackson's wife, Mary Anna Jackson; and staff officer, James Power Smith.

- A group that included the reverends Beverly Tucker Lacy and James Power Smith placed the unmarked quartz stone here between 1876 and 1883. The monuments mark where Jackson was tended, rather than where he was wounded, and were placed by the roadside; the actual site where Jackson was shot is several yards north.

155. Brig. Gen. Elisha F. Paxton Tablet

Monument is a bronze plaque inset on a granite shaft.
LOCATION: Stuart Avenue, south of Plank Road (V.R. 3)
DATE: 1980
MEDIA: Bronze, granite

IN THIS VICINITY
BRIG. GEN. E. F. PAXTON, C.S.A.
AGED 35 YEARS, OF ROCKBRIDGE COUNTY, VA.
WAS KILLED ON THE MORNING OF MAY 3, 1863
WHILE LEADING HIS COMMAND, THE
STONEWALL BRIGADE
IN THE ATTACK ON FAIRVIEW

Sponsored by a descendent of Brigadier General Elisha Franklin "Bull" Paxton, the monument cites Paxton's place as commander of the elite Stonewall Brigade. Paxton was highly respected as a man and a leader by Stonewall Jackson. Both men were Presbyterians; both had roots in Lexington, Virginia. Neither survived the battle of Chancellorsville; both are buried in Lexington's Stonewall Cemetery.

156. Lee-Jackson Bivouac Shaft—Smith

Monument is a granite shaft.
LOCATION: Intersection of Furnace (Jackson Trail) and Old Plank roads
DATE: August 1903
MEDIUM: Granite

BIVOUAC
LEE AND JACKSON
NIGHT OF
MAY 1, 1863

This Smith marker gives notice of this site's importance in a turning point in the war, as well as American military history. At or near this site generals Lee and Jackson met and planned the flanking movement around the Union Army of the Potomac, commanded by Maj. Gen. Joseph Hooker, during the battle of Chancellorsville. The scheme was intended to "out-wit and disgrace Fighting Joe," as Capt. William W. Parker of Parker's Battery, a key eyewitness, put it. It was a momentous, brilliant gambit that succeeded.

The bivouac conversation took place in this vicinity over a half hour's time period. Some of the details of this conference have been disputed, but historian Robert E. Krick finds the overall evidence persuasive.

157. Lee-Jackson Bivouac Tablet

Monument is a bronze plaque on a stone base lying flush with the ground.
DATE: October 23, 1937
MEDIA: Bronze, fieldstone

> THESE CEDARS
> PLANTED OCTOBER 23, 1937,
> COMMEMORATE
> THE LAST CONFERENCE
> OF LEE AND JACKSON
> THE STAFF
> OF THE FREDERICKSBURG AND
> SPOTSYLVANIA NATIONAL
> MILITARY PARK

This small plaque, funded by park employees, also marks the site of the last meeting between Lee and Jackson. It stands at the foot of two cedar trees, still standing, which were planted when the monument was erected and which were intended to represent Lee and Jackson. The marker was dedicated as part of the tenth anniversary celebration of the Fredericksburg and Spotsylvania National Military Park.

158. Jackson's Arm, Ellwood Tablet

Monument is a granite shaft.
LOCATION: V.R. 3 to V.R. 20 to Ellwood, National Park Service grounds
DATE: 1903
MEDIUM: Granite

> ARM OF
> STONEWALL JACKSON
> MAY 3, 1863.

The veneration of Jackson's memory includes this James Power Smith shaft marking the site where the general's amputated arm is buried. It stands in a family cemetery about one mile from the field hospital where Jackson was first taken after his wounding. The Reverend Beverly Tucker Lacy buried the arm here, at the Ellwood House, part of the Lacy family estate. The Union army would use the house during the battle of the Wilderness in 1864.

- Access to this site is by request, but permission can be readily obtained at the Chancellorsville Battlefield Visitors Center at 9001 Plank Road.

Wilderness Battlefield

159. Wilderness Battlefield Tablet

Monument is a bronze tablet set on a limestone base.
LOCATION: V.R. 20 and Lee-Ewell Drive, west of Saunders Field
DATE: May 3, 1927
MEDIA: Bronze, limestone

> BATTLE OF THE WILDERNESS
> HERE MAY 5, 6, 1864, 70,000

CONFEDERATES UNDER
LEE DEFEATED 120,000
FEDERALS UNDER GRANT.
CONFEDERATE LOSS 11,500. FEDERAL 18,000.
THIS BATTLE, FOUGHT WITH
CONSPICUOUS BRAVERY,
IN A WILDERNESS ON FIRE, WILL
TAKE IT'S [SIC] PLACE
AMONG THE GREAT BATTLES
OF THE CIVIL WAR.
ERECTED BY THE 13, VIRGINIA
REGIMENT, CHAPTER, U.D.C.
1927
J. ARTHUR LIMERICK CO
FDR'S BALTO.

The narrative on this United Daughters of the Confederacy plaque overstates the numbers of Lt. Gen. Ulysses S. Grant's army (101,895 according to National Park Service accounts; technically Maj. Gen. George G. Meade's Army of the Potomac and Maj. Gen. Ambrose E. Burnside's Ninth Corps) in this opening battle of the 1864 Overland Campaign, but in other respects it is consistent with accounts. The phrase "Wilderness on Fire" is literally true. Several fires occurred in these woods during the course of fighting so fierce and confusing that its full details remain elusive and were so even to the participants.

The narrative claims victory for the Confederates under Lee, but Grant did not retreat as other Union generals had done before. On May 7, 1864, the Federals advanced upon the crossroads of Spotsylvania Courthouse.

- The apostrophe in line 6 and the comma in line 8 are not necessary.
- The monument once stood adjacent to V.R. 20. It was moved when Hill-Ewell Drive was established and moved again when V.R. 20 was widened.

160. Col. James D. Nance Tablet
Monument is a granite shaft.
LOCATION: East side of Orange Plank Road (C.R. 621) near the Widow Tapp Farm, National Park Service grounds
DATE: August 16, 1912
MEDIUM: Granite

COL. JAMES D. NANCE
3RD REG. S.C.V.
KERSHAW'S BRIGADE
KILLED ON THIS SPOT
MAY 6, 1864

As a leader James D. Nance (1837–1864) was a strict disciplinarian, but he had the high regard of his men as well as other officers, including Robert E. Lee. Generals Lee, Longstreet, and Joseph B. Kershaw recommended Nance to take Kershaw's place as brigade commander, when Kershaw was wounded. On the second day of the battle of the Wilderness, Nance was standing behind breastworks near this site encouraging his men when five bullets struck him.

Little was known about this monument until historian Donald Pfanz found records indicating that two 3rd South Carolina veterans, Sgt. W. G. Peterson and Capt. Thomas H. Pitts, erected it. The two men set the marker with the assistance of local residents. The party apparently had the novel experience of being driven out to the Wilderness battlefield by automobile in order to set the monument.

- Today automobile traffic impedes direct access to this monument. It is advisable to dismount one's vehicle and proceed on foot from either the "Lee-to-the-Rear" monuments on the Widow Tapp Farm or from the corner of Hill-Ewell Drive and Orange Plank Road.

161. Texas Brigade Shaft

Monument is a granite shaft set on a pedestal.
LOCATION: Widow Tapp Farm, Orange
Plank Road (C.R. 621)
DATE: 1964
MEDIA: Granite, brass

[STAR OF TEXAS WITH WREATH, IN BRASS]
TEXAS
REMEMBERS THE VALOR AND DEVOTION OF
HER SONS WHO SERVED AT THE WILDERNESS
MAY 6, 1864
FROM NEAR THIS SPOT THE TEXAS BRIGADE
PLEADED WITH GENERAL LEE NOT TO
EXPOSE HIMSELF TO FEDERAL FIRE AND
THEN, AFTER SEEING HIM TO SAFETY,
LAUNCHED A VIGOROUS COUNTERATTACK
THAT STEMMED THE ADVANCE OF HANCOCK'S
CORPS AND SAVED THE RIGHT FLANK OF
THE CONFEDERATE ARMY.
OF APPROXIMATELY
800 TROOPS INVOLVED, THE TEXAS BRIGADE
COUNTED OVER 500 CASUALTIES.
TEXAS TROOPS AT THE WILDERNESS WERE:
1ST TEXAS INFANTRY REGIMENT, LT. COL.

F. S. BASS, 4TH TEXAS INFANTRY REGIMENT,
COL. J. P. BANE; 5TH TEXAS INFANTRY
REGIMENT, LT. COL. K. BRYAN, THE TEXAS
BRIGADE INCLUDED THE THIRD ARKANSAS
INFANTRY REGIMENT.
(BRIG. GEN. JOHN GREGG'S TEXAS BRIGADE
MAJ. GEN. CHARLES W. FIELD'S DIVISION,
LT. GEN. JAMES LONGSTREET'S CORPS).
A MEMORIAL TO TEXANS
WHO SERVED THE CONFEDERACY
ERECTED BY THE STATE OF TEXAS 1964

———

TEXANS
AT THE WILDERNESS
"WHO ARE YOU MY BOYS?" LEE CRIED AS HE
SAW THEM GATHERING.
"TEXAS BOYS," THEY YELLED, THEIR NUMBER
MULTIPLYING EVERY SECOND.
THE TEXANS—HOOD'S TEXANS, OF
LONGSTREET'S CORPS, JUST AT THE RIGHT
PLACE AND AT THE RIGHT MOMENT! AFTER
THE STRAIN OF THE DAWN, THE SIGHT OF
THESE GRENADIER GUARDS OF THE SOUTH
WAS TOO MUCH FOR LEE. FOR ONCE THE
DIGNITY OF THE COMMANDING GENERAL WAS
SHATTERED, FOR ONCE HIS
POISE WAS SHAKEN.
"HURRAH FOR TEXAS," HE SHOUTED, WAVING
HIS HAT, "HURRAH FOR TEXAS."
THE WILLING VETERANS SPRANG INTO
POSITION . . . HE WOULD LEAD THEM IN THE
COUNTERCHARGE . . . HE
SPURRED . . . TRAVELLER
ON THE HEELS OF THE INFANTRY MEN.
. . ."GO BACK, GENERAL LEE, GO BACK!"
THEY CRIED
. . ."WE WON'T GO ON UNLESS YOU GO BACK!"
DOUGLAS SOUTHALL FREEMAN

The sunset-red granite slab, one of a series
of centennial monuments sponsored by the
state of Texas, is copious in detail but wholly
reliant on a twentieth-century source—Douglas Southall Freeman's *Lee's Lieutenants,* published in 1942–44. The memorial is a tribute to
Freeman's writing but also a measure of how
far removed the elegists are from the events
described that they rely on a secondary source
to describe them.

- Eleven markers of this design were erected across the South between 1963 and 1965. Other sites: Gettysburg, Pennsylvania; Sharpsburg, Maryland; Bentonville, North Carolina; Chickamauga and Kennesaw Mountain, Georgia; Mansfield, Louisiana; Pea Ridge, Arkansas; Shiloh, Tennessee; Anthony, Texas; and Vicksburg, Mississippi. Each inscription begins with the phrase, "Texas Remembers." Unlike most monuments, there were no dedication ceremonies.
- Gregg, brigade commander, led the Texans (and Arkansans) here but was killed in action on October 7, 1864, off New Market Road.

162. "Lee to the Rear" Tablet

Monument is a granite shaft.
LOCATION: Widow Tapp Farm, Orange Plank Road (C.R. 621)
DATE: 1903
MEDIUM: Granite

> LEE TO THE REAR!
> CRIED THE TEXANS.
> MAY 6, 1864.

There is no better example of the contrast between commemorative and reconciliation-era elegies than the two monuments on the Widow Tapp Farm site: the 1964 Texas monument, with its profuse detail and extended narrative, and this shaft from 1891, with its cryptic reference—another of the ten markers placed by James Power Smith.

The "Lee-to-the-Rear" incident is now standard in narratives of the Wilderness and is aptly summarized in the Texas monument, but various accounts of the incident are recorded. Douglas Southall Freeman concludes that the facts of the episode are "singularly difficult to establish . . . chiefly because most of those who recorded [it] did so long afterwards, when much telling had put a robe of rhetoric over the actual happenings." The account of Charles Venable, of Lee's staff, has prevailed, and historian Robert K. Krick reports that none of thirty-eight quotes or allusions about the incident deviates markedly from the Venable's story of Texans imploring Lee to leave the field.

- Contemporary accounts of this tablet mention that some forty Confederate Texans are buried in this area. Several telling depressions remain to this day.

Spotsylvania Battlefield

163. Ramseur's Brigade Tablet

Monument is a shaft set on a pedestal.
LOCATION: Near the "Bloody Angle," one hundred yards northwest of McCoull House off Anderson and Gordon drives
DATE: September 2001
MEDIUM: Granite

[C.S.A. BATTLE FLAG]
RAMSEUR'S BRIGADE
2ND NORTH CAROLINA STATE TROOPS
COL. WILLIAM R. COX
4TH NORTH CAROLINA STATE TROOPS
COL. BRYAN GRIMES
14TH NORTH CAROLINA STATE TROOPS
COL. R. TYLER BENNETT
30TH NORTH CAROLINA STATE TROOPS
COL. FRANCIS M PARKER [SIC]
AT DAWN, MAY 12, 1864 UNION TROOPS
OVERWHELMED MAJ. GEN. EDWARD
JOHNSON'S DIVISION AT THE MULESHOE
SALIENT. BRIG. GEN. STEPHEN DODSON
RAMSEUR'S NORTH CAROLINA BRIGADE
COUNTERATTACKED ACROSS THESE
EARTHWORKS AND BY 7:30 A. M.
REGAINED THE PORTION OF THE
SALIENT OPPOSITE THIS POINT. FOR
THE NEXT TWENTY HOURS RAMSEUR'S
MEN HELD THEIR GROUND IN THE FACE
OF DETERMINED UNION ASSAULTS. THE
NORTH CAROLINIANS THEN WITHDREW
TO A NEW DEFENSIVE LINE ONE-HALF
MILE TO THE REAR. THIS GALLANT STAND
HELPED THWART THE UNION ADVANCE
AND SAVED LEE'S ARMY FROM DISASTER.
DEO VINDICE
ERECTED BY THE 30TH N. C. TROOPS
(REACTIVATED) CHARLOTTE N. C.
SEPT. 2001

This is the first of only two Confederate unit monuments on the Spotsylvania battlefield. The size, focus, and content are similar to the 1964 Wilderness monument to the Texas Brigade.

This unit has not earned the same fame as the Texas Brigade, but this monument commemorates a bloody feat of arms by troops who, arguably, staved off a decisive defeat of the army. Douglas Southall Freeman observes that seldom "in the war had one Brigade accomplished so much in fast, close fighting," although the survivors were also said to have emerged "black and bloody as hogs," after the twenty-four hours of combat. One officer called the episode the "crowning glory of the career of Ramseur's Brigade."

- Stephen Dodson Ramseur was killed at the battle of Cedar Creek (October 19–20, 1864), where a monument (chapter 1) was erected to him.
- The monument was erected in September 2001; the dedication ceremonies were held on Veterans Day, November 11, 2001.

164. McGowan's Brigade Tablet

Monument is a shaft standing on a base.
LOCATION: The "Bloody Angle," Spotsylvania Battlefield
DATE: May 9, 2009
MEDIUM: Granite

1861 DEO VINDICI 1865
[C.S.A. BATTLE FLAG]
"THE BLOODY ANGLE"
In the rainy gloom of May 12, 1864, Brigadier
General Samuel McGowan's brigade of South
Carolinian's battled their way into the disputed
earthworks here, near the apex of the Muleshoe

Salient. For eighteen hours the 1,300 South Carolinians defended these works against relentless attacks by thousands of Federals, sometimes engaging in hand-to-hand fighting. By battle's end, 451 men of the brigade were killed, wounded, or missing. The slight angle in the works they defended would forever be known as the Bloody Angle.

To the brave and heroic men of

McGowan's Brigade

this monument is dedicated.

Erected by the State of South Carolina and the

Brig. Gen. Samuel McGowan Camp 40 Sons of Confederate Veterans of Laurens County, South Carolina, 2009

—

CSA

SOUTH

CAROLINA

Brig. Gen. Samuel McGowan, Cdr.

[Quarter Moon and Palmetto Tree image]

1st S . C. Inf.

Orr's Rifles

Lt. Col. George McD. Miller

12th S. C. Inf.

Major Thomas F. Clyburne

13th S. C. Inf.

Col. Benjamin T. Brockman

14th S. C. Inf.

Col. Joseph N. Brown

Several Union monuments were erected in this vicinity over a century ago: a 1906 monument to the 15th New Jersey Infantry and a 1902 monument to the 49th New York Infantry.

This, however, is the first Confederate monument to be erected along a line of earthworks known as the "Bloody Angle." The line was held against repeated Union attacks during the battle of Spotsylvania, as the inscription aptly summarizes. A dawn attack by Union troops surprised the Confederates and nearly broke the Southern line, but Confederate counterattacks plugged the gap. McGowan's Brigade was part of a force that held the line for nearly twenty hours until Confederate troops could create a second defensive line.

The twenty-five thousand dollars for the monument was raised privately. Charles Wilson of Laurens, South Carolina, carved the six and a half-ton monument from Georgia granite. National Park Service policy prevents new monuments from being erected at most national battlefields, but the Fredericksburg battlefield, by dint of a congressional provision dating to the park's establishment in 1927, is an exception. The South Carolina legislature supported the project by asking the U.S. Department of the Interior to permit the marker.

- Samuel McGowan, forty-four at the time of the battle, was highly regarded as an officer. He was wounded here and on three other occasions during the conflict but survived the war and lived until 1897. The S.C.V. camp is named for the general, a Laurens County native, who was a lawyer and jurist before and after the war.
- A band of red granite around the base of the monument is notched to catch rainwater. The granite gives water the appearance of blood and thus evokes the battlefield's nickname.

165. Common Soldier, Spotsylvania Cemetery

Monument is a private soldier, in marble, standing at parade rest surmounting a granite plinth, base, dado, and shaft.

LOCATION: V.R. 208, 22553
DATE: May 12, 1918
MEDIA: Granite, marble
Front

CSA

[CROSSED C.S.A. NATIONAL
AND BATTLE FLAGS]

ERECTED AND DEDICATED

MAY 12, 1918,

BY THE SPOTSYLVANIA CHAPTER
UNITED DAUGHTERS OF THE
CONFEDERACY,

CONFEDERATE SOUTHERN
MEMORIAL ASSOCIATION AND
CITIZENS OF SPOTSYLVANIA COUNTY,
TO COMMEMORATE AND
PERPETUATE THE VALOR AND
PATRIOTISM OF THE SONS
OF SPOTSYLVANIA COUNTY,
VIRGINIA, AND OTHER
CONFEDERATE SOLDIERS WHO
REPOSE IN THIS CEMETERY.

1861–1865

CONFEDERATE SOLDIERS

—

"LOVE MAKES MEMORY
ETERNAL."

—

"WE HAVE GATHERED THE
SACRED DUST,
OF WARRIORS TRIED AND TRUE,
WHO BORE THE FLAG OF

OUR NATION'S TRUST,
AND FELL IN THE CAUSE
'THO LOST, STILL JUST,
AND DIED FOR ME AND YOU."

VIRGINIA

1861–1865

—

"LEST WE FORGET."

Local women formed the Spotsylvania Memorial Association and established this five-acre plot northeast of the county seat in 1866. An estimated 570 soldiers were collected from surrounding farms and fields after the war for this site. Only a few names remain unknown. Headstones of Vermont marble replaced the original wooden markers in the 1930s, with financial support from the federal government.

The monument was the result of a thirteen-year campaign by the Ladies Memorial Association, reorganized in 1905 for the purpose of erecting a monument. The Monument Fund was established in 1909, and the Spotsylvania United Daughters of the Confederacy was organized in 1913. "Even in the shadow of the Great War," the records note, "the Ladies apparently were undaunted in the pursuit of their goal." The county's Board of Supervisors appropriated five hundred dollars on May 7, 1917, and the location was approved on July 14, 1917.

The "Erection and Dedication" date, May 12, commemorates the action at the "Bloody Angle" on May 12–13, 1864, as part of the battle of Spotsylvania. The battle, actually a series of actions, was fought May 8–21, 1864, as part of the Overland Campaign. Spotsylvania was, arguably at least, a Confederate defensive victory.

A wartime spirit of unity affected the dedication ceremonies. The principle speaker was U.S. senator Claude A. Swanson of Virginia. The ceremonies closed with the hymn "America," sung by the audience.

The Civil War is not specified, but the Confederacy is mentioned five times. The apologetic is simple: "'The Cause, 'Tho Lost [was] Still Just."

- The excerpt beginning "We Have Gathered . . ." is by Father Abram J. Ryan and is taken from his "March of the Deathless Dead." The larger context reads:

Gather them one and all,

From the private to the chief;

Come they from hovel or princely hall,

They fell for us, and for them should fall

The tears of a Nation's grief.

Gather the corpses strewn

O'er many a battle plain;

From many a grave that lies so lone,

Without a name and without a stone,

Gather the Southern slain.

Granite shafts—with some inconsistencies of punctuation—surround the above monument.

Northwest

GEORGIA

1861.–1865.

GEORGIA

1861.–1865.

UNKNOWN

1861–1865

UNKNOWN

1861–1865

Northeast

VIRGINIA

1861.–1865.

VIRGINIA

1861.–1865.

NORTH CAROLINA

1861–1865.

NORTH CAROLINA

1861.–1865.

East and southeast of monument

MISSISSIPPI

1861–1865

TENNESSEE

1861–1865

TEXAS

1861–1865

South of monument

LOUISIANA

1861–1865

West and southwest of monument

ALABAMA

1861–1865

SOUTH CAROLINA

1861–1865

Spotsylvania Courthouse

166. Battlefield Tablet

Monument is a bronze tablet set on a granite base.

LOCATION: 9111 Courthouse Road, 22553

DATE: May 3, 1927

MEDIA: Bronze, granite

BATTLE OF SPOTSYLVANIA
MAY 12–18, 1864, BETWEEN THE ARMIES OF
LEE AND GRANT IS UNMATCHED FOR ITS
DISPLAY OF UNYIELDING HEROISM AND
DEVOTION TO DUTY AND PRINCIPLE.
HERE THOUSANDS OF VALOROUS MEN,
FIGHTING WITH BAYONETS
AND CLUBBED MUSKETS,
WROTE THEIR IMPERISHABLE EPITAPH.
ERECTED BY THE
FREDERICKSBURG AND SPOTSYLVANIA
CHAPTERS, U.D.C.
1927

There is no courthouse monument here, but the Spotsylvania cemetery is less than a mile up V.R. 208, and this U.D.C. battlefield marker commemorates the series of actions fought in this area. Tribute is given to both sides in the battle between "the armies of Lee and Grant"—as if the contest was personal—but numbers are omitted. Some 152,000 troops were engaged (100,000 Federals and 52,000 Confederates). Of these, an estimated 30,000 became casualties (18,000 Federal; 12,000 Confederate). Their "Imperishable Epitaph" was written here, but monumentation on this field is sparse, and their epitaph, in that sense at least, is brief. "Fighting With Bayonets And Clubbed Muskets," highlights the intensity and personal nature of the fighting and may be an implicit reference to the action at the "Bloody Angle" on May 12–13, 1864, arguably the fiercest fighting of the war.

167. Lee's Headquarters Tablet

Monument is a granite shaft.
LOCATION: 9111 Courthouse Road, corner of
Brock and Fredericksburg roads, 22553
DATE: 1903

LEE'S
HEADQUARTERS
BATTLE OF
SPOTSYLVANIA
MAY 10, 11, 12, 1864
1903 REPLACED 1964

This marker replaced the original Smith
marker, which was damaged beyond repair
when it was struck by a car. No evidence describes Lee having headquarters in Spotsylvania. This marker, like other Smith monuments, may have been placed with an eye to
visitor access rather than geographic precision.

Hanover County

168. Hanover, Courthouse Obelisk
Monument is an obelisk surmounting a plinth,
base, and dado.
LOCATION: 7515 Library Drive, 23069
DATE: August 27, 1914
MEDIA: Granite, marble, bronze
Front

[CROSSED FLAG OF VIRGINIA
AND C.S.A. BATTLE FLAG]
HANOVER
TO HER
CONFEDERATE SOLDIERS
AND TO HER
NOBLE WOMEN
WHO LOVED THEM
1861–65

OFFICERS
ABOVE THE RANK OF LIEUTENANT
[28 NAMES]

—

ARTILLERY
MORRIS' ARTILLERY
COLEMAN'S, PAGE'S,
MONTGOMERY'S BATTERY
[102 NAMES]
HANOVER ARTILLERY (NELSON'S)
[96 NAMES]
ASHLAND ARTILLERY (WOOLFOLK'S)
[57 NAMES]
OTHER NAMES
[101 NAMES]

—

[CROSSED SWORDS, CROSSED
MUSKETS, CANNON BALLS]
CAVALRY
HANOVER TROOP (COMPANY G, 4TH. VA.)
[145 NAMES]
OTHER COMMANDS
[59 NAMES]
INFANTRY

OTHER COMMANDS
[100 NAMES]
—
INFANTRY
15TH. VIRGINIA REGIMENT, COMPANY
C. (PATRICK HENRY RIFLES.)
[117 NAMES]
15TH. VIRGINIA REGIMENT,
COMPANY E. (ASHLAND GRAYS.)
[97 NAMES]
15TH. VIRGINIA REGIMENT,
COMPANY I. (HANOVER GRAYS.)
[101 NAMES]
15TH. VIRGINIA REGIMENT, COMPANY
K. (HARRISON'S GUARD'S.)
[75 NAMES]

Hanover's monument is unique in at least two respects: bronze plaques listing over a thousand names are inscribed on four sides of the monument—the largest roster of soldiers on a Virginia county courthouse monument. In addition, a record of the labor and consideration necessary to create this monument is preserved in fifty-five extant letters at the Hanover Branch of the Pamunkey Regional Library. The correspondence, from October 1913 to June 1914, includes letters by W. C. Noland of the Hanover monument committee and employees of McNeel Marble Company of Marietta, Georgia, as well as the Detroit Mausoleum Equipment Works, Michigan, which apparently did subcontracting work for the bronze tablets.

The correspondence reveals a diligent attention to detail. Among the questions: whether the flag should be square or rectangular; how it should drape; about the service of David B. Moore, "killed at Petersburg," originally classified with artillery but whose name was moved to "Infantry Other Commands," whether his name was D. B. Moore or D. E. Moore or simply D. Moore (surviving relatives were not sure).

"I wish the space between names to be not less than 3/16," instead of only 1/8," as given . . ." Noland wrote in one letter. The Detroit firm countered that "These are very large Tablets and it is an extremely difficult task to cast these properly on account of the extra ordinary

quantity of lettering of small size." Noland apparently insisted. In a subsequent letter he responds, "As to your suggestion to omit comma between names and initials, I cannot agree to that." And again, the same letter: "Note . . . that I insist on the comma between each name and its initial." There was difficulty with making sure that everything fit: a McNeel Marble letter notes that "You will therefore notice that to cut the words, 'Confederate Soldiers' on the base omits any reference to the Women, to whom we understand the monument is also dedicated." Apparently the difficulty was resolved. A place was found.

169. Haw's Shop Obelisk, Enon Church Cemetery

Monument is an obelisk surmounting a plinth, base, and dado.

LOCATION: 6156 Studley Road, 23116

DATE: 1959
MEDIUM: Granite
Front

IN MEMORY OF
27 UNKNOWN
CONFEDERATE
SOLDIERS
KILLED AT THE
BATTLE OF HAW'S SHOP
MAY 28, 1864
AND BURIED IN
THIS CHURCHYARD
—
ERECTED BY THE
VIRGINIA
STATE LIBRARY,
WITH THE
COOPERATION OF THE
HANOVER CHAPTER UDC
1959

The fight at Haw's Shop took place during the 1864 Overland Campaign and was also a prelude to the battle of Cold Harbor on June 4. Cavalry under Maj. Gen. Wade Hampton clashed here with forces under generals David McM. Gregg and George A. Custer. The Confederate troopers withdrew after a six-hour fight, leaving 230 casualties, including 127 dead, some of whom are buried in unmarked graves at this site. Union casualties were about 340 men.

- The Virginia State Library sponsorship seems out of place, but the library, now the Library of Virginia, was responsible for the state highway historical marker program from 1946 to 1966, including the hundreds of state markers that now stand across the state.

Henrico County and City of Richmond

170. Maj. Gen. J. E. B. Stuart, Yellow Tavern Obelisk
Monument is an obelisk surmounting a plinth, base, and dado.
LOCATION: Telegraph Road off Virginia Center Parkway, Glen Allen, 23059
DATE: June 18, 1888

MEDIUM: Granite
Front

[RELIEF, CROSSED SWORDS]
UPON THIS FIELD
MAJ. GEN. J. E. B. STUART
COMMANDING CONFEDERATE CAVALRY
A. N. VA
RECEIVED HIS MORTAL WOUND
MAY 11, 1864.
STUART
—
HE WAS
FEARLESS AND FAITHFUL,
PURE AND POWERFUL,
TENDER AND TRUE.
—
HE SAVED RICHMOND
BUT HE GAVE HIS LIFE.
BORN FEB. 6, 1833;
DIED MAY 12, 1864.
—
THIS STONE IS ERECTED
BY SOME OF HIS COMRADES
TO COMMEMORATE HIS VIRTUES.

This is the largest battlefield monument between Richmond and Spotsylvania. Here Stuart, with forty-five hundred cavalry, interdicted Maj. Gen. Philip H. Sheridan with ten thousand cavalry on May 11, 1864, six miles north of Richmond. Stuart's men were un-

able to withstand the numbers against them, the battle ended as a Confederate defeat, and Stuart took a single shot from an unhorsed Union private at the close of the action. The wound proved fatal. The memorial focuses on his character, doing so with alliteration— "Fearless and Faithful . . ." It also credits Stuart for having "Saved Richmond," although it is arguable whether Sheridan's men could have entered Richmond and there is some question of whether Sheridan wanted to. That Stuart "Gave His Life" to a purpose is true. Sheridan's cavalry reached the outskirts of Richmond after the battle, passed through the outer defenses and skirmished with the city's intermediate defenses while opening an exit route via Meadow Bridge to the east.

- Abandoned at the time of the battle, the inn of Yellow Tavern no longer stands. The Telegraph Road site, now a residential back street, was once a principal road between the north and south. It was supplanted first by U.S. 1 and later by Interstate 95. Vestiges of the old road continue into the woods to the south and disappear.
- The monument stands on a rise above the road. Two additional plaques are on the wall below the monument.

The first:

GEN. J. E. B. STUART
BORN FEB. 6, 1833,
DIED MAY 12, 1864.

The second:

THIS MONUMENT ERECTED IN
MEMORY OF MAJOR GENERAL
JAMES EWELL BROWN STUART,
C.S.A., BY HIS CAVALRY MEN
ABOUT THIRTY FEET FROM THE
SPOT WHERE HE FELL MORTALLY
WOUNDED ON MAY 11, 1864, WAS
DEDICATED JUNE 18, 1888, BY
THE GOVERNOR OF VIRGINIA,
FITZHUGH LEE, A FORMER
DIVISION COMMANDER IN
STUART'S CAVALRY.
RE-DEDICATED MAY 9, 1964,
HENRICO COUNTY CIVIL WAR
CENTENNIAL COMMISSION

171. Emmanuel Church Cemetery Obelisk

Monument is an obelisk surmounted by an olive leaf carving.

LOCATION: 1214 Wilmer Avenue, 23227
DATE: June 18, 1888
MEDIUM: Granite
Front

Pro Patria
[20 NAMES OR SPACES FOR NAMES]
CONFEDERATE DEAD
FROM 1861 TO 1865

—

[18 NAMES OR SPACES FOR NAMES]

—

[22 NAMES OR SPACES FOR NAMES]

—

[22 NAMES OR SPACES FOR NAMES]

The obelisk was dedicated on the same day as the Stuart monument three miles to the north, and a report of the ceremonies was published in the *New York Times*. The *Times* noted that the "mounted military from Richmond and the surrounding country, the R. E. Lee Camp of Confederate Veterans, and old soldiers generally, and a large number of citizens, including many ladies were present at both ceremonies." Afterwards, "A march was . . . made to a point on the Telegraph [R]oad three miles distant where stands Stuart's monument . . ."

The Gothic revival edifice was built in 1860. It survived the war intact, but the Brook Turnpike nearby was a principal north-south route used by armies of both sides, and the churchyard often served as a stopover place for passing troops. In addition, as the church history reports, "typhoid and dysentery played havoc with those poor men (wounded during the fighting) and many of them lie buried at Emmanuel."

- The nationalistic sentiment "Pro patria" is unusual for a church cemetery monument.
- The roster is numbered, an unusual feature. Blank spaces were left for the unknown dead. Twelve names are italicized, but contemporary records do not cite the reason. Church records indicate that eighty Confederate soldiers are marked with eighty slate stones. The first interment was George Vass of Culpeper in May 1862.

172. Lt. Gen. A. P. Hill, Statue

Monument is a bronze statue surmounting a granite plinth, base, and dado.

LOCATION: Laburnum Avenue and Hermitage Road, 23227
DATE: May 30, 1892
MEDIA: Bronze, granite
Front

> A. P. HILL
> BORN IN CULPEPER CO.
> NOVEMBER 9TH 1825
> KILLED BEFORE PETERSBURG
> APRIL 2ND 1865.
>
> —
>
> ERECTED BY PEGRAM
> BATTALION AND HIS
> COMRADES OF THE
> ARMY OF NORTHERN
> VIRGINIA
>
> —
>
> A. P. HILL
> HIS REMAINS
> WERE REINTERRED HERE
> JUNE 24, 1891.
>
> —
>
> LIEUT. GENL. AND COMMANDER
> 3RD CORPS ARMY OF
> NORTHERN VIRGINIA.

This is Ambrose Powell Hill's third burial site. Shot outside Petersburg just hours before the city's fall, the general was buried in a family cemetery south of Richmond as the war ended. (A marker there stands on private property.) His body was then reinterred at Hollywood Cemetery in 1867 for twenty-four years, before being reburied here.

Thomas A. Brander initiated the fundraising movement for the monument, which was erected at a cost of about fifteen thousand dollars. Brander, a major in Pegram's Battalion (Hill's Corps, Army of Northern Virginia), served as major general and commander of the Virginia division of the United Confederate Veterans. The bronze statue is by William L. Sheppard, also a veteran.

- The ceremonies: "Richmond's girls never looked more beautiful than upon this occasion. It seemed that there were fully fifty thousand on Franklin street [sic] alone, besides those in carriages, buggies, and other vehicles, and from the pretty dress of every one fluttered a little souvenir badge . . ."

- Hill was remembered this way:

Loved comrade, brilliant soldier, chivalrous spirit, true-hearted friend, accomplished gentleman, ardent patriot— Ambrose Powell Hill, we dedicate this monument to thy memory as a feeble token of the love of old comrades and a faint expression of the Southern people, for whom you fought and died so bravely."

- "High spirited, impetuous and proud" is the way historian James I. Robertson Jr. describes Hill in his biography. By virtually all accounts, Hill was an excellent division and brigade commander. Historian Mark Weitz concludes that from "4 May 1862, when he led his brigade into battle at Williamsburg, until 2 May 1863, when he went to the aid of a mortally wounded Stonewall Jackson at Chancellorsville, [Hill] performed as well as any commander on either side during the Civil War." He was less successful at corps command when he succeeded Jackson.
- "Killed before Petersburg" implies something of the sacrificial nature of his death, but historian James I. Robertson Jr. concluded that Hill's life and passing meant more than that: "his story is the story of the Southern Confederacy, and his death in the final days of the war was symbolic of the Southern nation's dying hopes."

Monument Avenue Neighborhood

173. Richmond Second Defense Line, Cannon
Monument is a cannon barrel set on a concrete base.
LOCATION: Monument Avenue at Thompson Street
DATE: 1938
MEDIA: Bronze, granite, iron

THIS CANNON MARKS THE LOCATION OF
THE SECOND LINE OF THE
CONFEDERATE DEFENSES
OF RICHMOND
PLACED IN 1938 BY THE CITY OF RICHMOND
AT THE REQUEST OF THE
CONFEDERATE MEMORIAL LITERARY SOCIETY

Erected to commemorate the seventy-fifth anniversary of the war, this monument marks the second, outer line of defense of Richmond. The cannon is a product of the "Revere Cannon Co."

Conscripted slave and military labor built these defenses, which by 1864 formed a triple ring of fortifications around the city and environs. The lines stretched for forty miles, from Richmond to Petersburg and onto the southwest virtually to the Nottoway River. No vestiges of the works are evident here, but large portions are extant east of the city on the grounds of the Richmond National Battlefield Park. The lines effectively deterred Union incursions until the end of the war, when the city was abandoned by Confederate troops.

- The Confederate Memorial Literary Society was chartered May 31, 1890, as an "adjunct" to the Hollywood Memorial Association. The name is euphemistic and was chosen as a result of local legal technicalities that prevented memorial organizations from holding property.

174. Matthew Maury, Statue

Monument is a granite base surmounted by a seated figure, in bronze, posed before a globe, also in bronze.

LOCATION: Belmont Avenue
DATE: November 11, 1929
MEDIA: Bronze, granite

MAURY
PATHFINDER OF THE SEAS

Matthew Fontaine Maury (1806–1873) earned an international reputation as an oceanographer and had a role in the founding of the U.S. Naval Observatory and the U.S. Weather Bureau. Maury wears civilian clothes, and there is no direct reference to the Confederacy. The work of sculptor Frederick W. Sievers, the Maury tribute is said to have begun to change the meaning of the street away from being a "simple" promenade of Confederate heroes.

The sponsors did not see it that way. One U.D.C. history declares that they were "proud to participate in a long-deferred honor—a handsome monument in Richmond—to America's greatest scientist, "the sailor's best friend," honored in many ways by every maritime nation and by almost every nation on the globe, except his own, for he cast his lot with the Southern Confederacy." Mrs. E. E. Moffitt, president of the Matthew Fontaine Maury Association, initiated the project and lived just long enough to see its completion. The cornerstone was laid June 22, 1922, but the completed monument was not dedicated and unveiled until Armistice Day, November 11, 1929. Maury's great-granddaughter, Mary Maury Fitzgerald, performed the unveiling. The dedication ceremonies occurred thirteen days after the stock market crash that inaugurated the Great Depression.

Maury is described as "listening to the voice of a storm. Above him [is] a group of figures of men, women and animals, supporting a large globe, represent[ing] a storm on land and sea, that rages all around the earth, symbolic of the world and its natural elements."

- Sievers's "Explanation of Model for Proposed Maury Monument" reads, in part:

In preparing a design for the proposed Maury monument I have avoided as far as possible borrowing from the ancient classic. . . . The conception at first may seem a bit revolutionary—it is not—neither is it my endeavor to attempt anything vague or extreme. . . . What I have done is to combine a number of symbols in one harmonius whole; a poem as it were, simply drawn from the facts pertaining to Maury's life. . . . On each of the two lower corners of the pedestal is carved an electric ray or torpedo—a deep sea fish suggesting deep sea investigations, and coincidentally symbolic of the electric torpedo—Maury's invention.

- Maury is buried in Hollywood Cemetery at President's Circle. Another monument to Maury stands at Goshen Pass, Virginia; his birthplace is marked on the Furnace Road of the Chancellorsville battlefield. None of the memorials makes direct reference to the war or his service to the Confederacy.

175. Thomas J. "Stonewall" Jackson, Equestrian Statue

Monument is a granite base and pedestal surmounted by a bronze equestrian sculpture.
LOCATION: Monument Avenue at Boulevard
DATE: October 11, 1919
MEDIA: Bronze, granite
Front

STONEWALL JACKSON

—

BORN 1824
KILLED AT CHANCELLORSVILLE
1863

—

STONEWALL JACKSON

The Stonewall Jackson statue was dedicated after World War I, at a time of eased tension between the North and the South. It was regarded, nonetheless, as "thoroughly Confederate." Some two thousand men in uniform paraded at the unveiling exercises, which were, according to *Confederate Veteran*

presided over by Capt. James Power Smith, the sole survivor of Jackson's staff, and little Anna Jackson Preston unveiled the bronze statue of her great-grandfather, assisted by the little son of the sculptor. The orator of the day was Col. Robert E. Lee, grandson of Gen. R. E. Lee. In the parade as escort of honor, was the corps of cadets from the Virginia Military Institute, in which Jackson was instructor before going into the Confederate army. Representatives of the leading families of the Old Dominion and other States had prominent places in this parade, and many military companies of the State and city gave that feature of distinction to the pageant.

Like the 1938 monument to Jackson that stands at Manassas, here Jackson is presented as a quasi-mythical figure: transcendent, but to judge by the brevity of his life, manifestly mortal. Architectural historian Sarah Driggs observes that the sculptor, F. William Sievers, "seemed to draw on Jackson's intense spirituality in the sculpture, in which he seems completely at ease, even serene." Indeed, she concludes that the monument "combines the visual serenity of the Lee Monument with the martial sentiment of the Stuart Monument." The tribute makes no reference to the war, and there is no apologetic. The narrative is simplified and should not be taken literally: Jackson was mortally wounded at Chancellorsville, but he died at Guiney Station.

Veterans and the sculptor disagreed over which direction the statue should face. "Jackson" faces north. Although F. William Sievers preferred that the sculpture face south, toward most oncoming traffic, the veterans overcame Sievers's arguments because they took offense at the idea of having Jackson posed with his back to his northern enemies.

Jackson is not riding Little Sorrel, his warhorse, but a local thoroughbred racehorse, Superior. Veterans objected to this as well, but were overruled. Jackson seems at ease on Superior, although he was reputedly an ungraceful rider.

- Jackson's visage was modeled on the death mask taken by the sculptor Frederick Volk.

176. Jefferson Davis, Statue

Monument is a plinth, base, and risers surmounted by a sculpture of Davis posed in front of a central column; surrounding this display is a colonnade of thirteen Doric columns, terminating at each end with piers bearing tablets.
LOCATION: Monument and Davis avenues
DATE: June 3, 1907
MEDIA: Bronze, granite
Central column

PRO JURE CIVITATUM
PRO ARIS ET FOCIS
JEFFERSON DAVIS
PRESIDENT
OF
THE CONFEDERATE STATES
OF AMERICA
1861–1865

Dado

Front

JEFFERSON DAVIS
EXPONENT OF
CONSTITUTIONAL PRINCIPLES
DEFENDER OF
THE RIGHTS OF STATES
CRESCIT OCCULTO VELUT
ARBOR AEVO FAMA

Left

AS CITIZEN, SOLDIER,

STATESMAN, HE ENHANCED
THE GLORY AND ENLARGED
THE FAME OF THE UNITED
STATES.
WHEN HIS ALLEGIANCE
TO THAT GOVERNMENT WAS
TERMINATED BY HIS SOVEREIGN
STATE, AS PRESIDENT
OF THE CONFEDERATE STATES
HE EXALTED HIS COUNTRY
BEFORE THE NATIONS.

Right

WITH CONSTANCY AND
COURAGE UNSURPASSED,
HE SUSTAINED THE HEAVY
BURDEN LAID UPON HIM BY
HIS PEOPLE.
WHEN THEIR CAUSE WAS
LOST, WITH DIGNITY HE MET
DEFEAT, WITH FORTITUDE
HE ENDURED IMPRISONMENT
AND SUFFERING. WITH EN-
TIRE DEVOTION HE KEPT
THE FAITH.

Bronze medallions, left to right across the arch:

SOUTH CAROLINA, MISSISSIPPI, FLORIDA
ALABAMA, GEORGIA, LOUISIANA, TEXAS,
VIRGINIA, ARKANSAS, NORTH CAROLINA,
TENNESSEE, MISSOURI, MARYLAND

Across the Arch:

"NOT IN HOSTILITY TO
OTHERS, NOT TO INJURE
ANY SECTION OF THE COUNTRY,
NOT EVEN FOR OUR OWN
PECUNIARY BENEFIT, BUT
FROM THE HIGH AND
SOLEMN MOTIVE OF DEFENDING
THE RIGHTS WE
INHERITED, AND WHICH IT IS OUR DUTY TO
TRANSMIT UNSHORN TO OUR CHILDREN."
JEFFERSON DAVIS, U. S. SENATE
JAN. 21ST, 1861

Bronze plaque, left column:

THE ARMY OF
THE
CONFEDERATE

STATES
FROM
SUMTER
TO
APPOMATTOX
FOUR YEARS OF UNFLINCHING
STRUGGLE AGAINST OVERWHELMING
ODDS
GLORY INEFFABLE THESE
AROUND THEIR DEAR LAND
WRAPPING, WRAPT AROUND
THEMSELVES THE PURPLE MANTLE OF DEATH.
DYING, THEY DIED NOT AT ALL,
BUT FROM THE GRAVE AND ITS
SHADOWS, VALOR INVINCIBLE
LIFTS THEM GLORIFIED EVER ON HIGH.

Bronze plaque, right column:

THE NAVY
OF
THE
CONFEDERATE
STATES
GIVING NEW
EXAMPLES OF HEROISM
TEACHING NEW
METHODS OF WARFARE
IT CARRIED
THE
FLAG OF THE SOUTH
TO THE
MOST DISTANT SEAS
IF TO DIE NOBLY BE EVER
THE PROUDEST GLORY OF
VIRTUE, THIS OF ALL MEN
HAS FORTUNE GREATLY
GRANTED TO THEM; FOR,
YEARNING WITH DEEP
DESIRE TO CLOTHE THEIR
COUNTRY WITH FREEDOM
NOW AT THE LAST
THEY REST FULL OF
AN AGELESS FAME

Of all Virginia's monuments, the Jefferson Davis monument may make the strongest claim that the cause of the Confederacy was not lost. Defeat is mentioned in the tribute to Davis, but Davis—imperfect, enduring—came to embody the life, death, and resurrection of the fallen nation. His wartime service as president was troubled by internal strife and questionable judgments, but his postwar imprisonment and release raised his stature to that of a quasi martyr. Davis faces east; his right hand—palm open—is extended toward the state capitol and former national capitol, as if he were still arguing the cause of secession or the Confederacy. The Davis statue is by Edward Valentine. The monument's architect is William C. Noland.

The monument was unveiled on Davis's birthday in 1907. The crowd was estimated at between eighty thousand and two hundred thousand people. The sixty-seven-foot Doric column is crowned with the allegorical figure of a woman ("Vindicatrix," also called "Miss Confederacy") who points heavenward. Davis is at the center of the monument but arguably is not the focus of celebration. Historian Gaines M. Foster rightly observes that the dedication "climaxed the Confederate celebration by honoring the southern hero most directly identified with the righteousness of the Confederate cause. In so grand a celebration around so elaborate a monument to the vicarious sufferer for all southerners, the South vindicated not only Davis and the cause, but itself."

Confederate Veteran described the ceremonies this way:

[It] was all that could have been imagined. Such a sea of human beings was hardly ever seen in the South, and for a Confederate occasion its like is not expected to appear again. . . . Of course it was not expected that the human voice could be heard by the vast throng. . . . rockets were being sent high above . . . balloons with magnificent Confederate flags floating, which fell in different parts of the assembly, and a fine band of music and hundreds of girls were singing about the area of the monument. Such a joyous throng of so great a magnitude must have rarely ever been witnessed on the earth.

- Of the monument, *Confederate Veteran* cites an unnamed "fine critic" as observing that

Stone cannot be given speech; but in this classic group Valentine has demonstrated that it may be made to express feelings almost too deep for word description, and feelings which bring the mind from distant and fabled Troy to another struggle against inexorable fate.

- This may be the most expensive Civil War monument in Virginia. Nearly ten years were required to raise the eighty thousand dollars for the memorial. A three-year effort by the Davis Monument Association to raise the money failed, and responsibility was passed to the United Daughters of the Confederacy. That the process was completed by the U.D.C. represented a significant change. Hereafter women would take the lead as fundraisers and organizers in the monument movement.
- Latin expressions: "Pro Jure Civitatum pro Aris et Focis" is translated as "For the Rights of the Citizens and the Flame of the Altar"; "Pro Jure Civitatum" as "For the law of the commonwealth"; "Pro Aris et Focis" as "For hearth and home"; "Crescit Occulto Velut Arbor Aevo Fama" as "Just as a tree's growth is in unseen increments, [your] public renown will grow through the ages."
- The open book has been interpreted as either a bible or a book on constitutional law.

177. Richmond Inner Defense Line, Cannon

Monument is a cannon barrel set on a granite base.

LOCATION: Monument Avenue at Strawberry Street
DATE: May 31, 1915
MEDIA: Bronze, granite, iron

THIS CANNON MARKS THE SPOT
WHERE IN 1861 A LARGE EARTHWORK
OF THE INNER LINE OF DEFENSE
WAS CONSTRUCTED
PLACED IN 1915 BY THE CITY OF RICHMOND
AT THE REQUEST
OF THE CONFEDERATE LITERARY SOCIETY

Another city-financed public work, this one a semicentennial example marking the earthwork defenses that once surrounded the city. The cannon is the earlier of two such memorials on the avenue, neither of which makes direct reference to the war.

- No vestiges of the earthworks are apparent. Note the dual sponsorship and the implicit claim of the legitimacy of the defense of Richmond against incursion.

178. Robert E. Lee, Equestrian Statue

Monument is a granite plinth, base, and pedestal surmounted by equestrian sculpture, in bronze, facing south.

LOCATION: Monument and Allen avenues
DATE: May 29, 1890
MEDIA: Bronze, granite

LEE
—
LEE

The Lee monument was the first on Monument Avenue and was placed at what was once the far edge of the city's western suburbs. It represents the apex of the Lost Cause adulation of Lee in Virginia. The figure of Lee, by Jean Antonio Mercie from designs by Paul Pujot, was built at a cost of seventy-five thousand dollars. Some twenty years of meetings, fundraising, discussion, squabbling, design, and execution were required to erect the monument. The statue stands taller than the statue of George Washington in Capitol Square—a provocative gesture. The understated simplicity of the Washington memorial's inscription—"just" two words, Washington—parallels that of the Lee memorial—"just" two words, Lee.

Dedication: Over one hundred thousand people attended the ceremonies—the largest crowd for a dedication up to that time. Jubal A. Early, vigorous Lost Cause proponent, was instrumental in the monument movement. Of Lee he declared:

> It is a vain work for us to seek anywhere for a parallel to the great character which has won our admiration and love. . . . Our beloved Chief stand, like some lofty column which rears its head among the highest, in grandeur, simple, pure and sublime, needing no borrowed lustre; and he is all our own." The South should "see that a monument to his glorious memory is erected at the Confederate Capitol, in defence of which his wondrous talents and sublime virtues were displayed."

- French sculptor Jean Antonin Mercie refused to seat Lee on Traveler, contending that Traveler was too slender a horse for a heroic statue. Instead, Mercie, according to the *Richmond Times-Dispatch* mounted Lee on a French hunter in whose veins there was a strain of Percheron blood. He refused, also, to allow his subject to wear a hat, a procedure altogether contrary to the best tradition in equestrian sculpture. Mercie, however, was adamant, declaring that a brow so noble must not be hidden. So General Lee is holding his hat in his hand.

179. J. E. B. Stuart, Equestrian Statue

Monument is a granite plinth, base, and pedestal surmounted by bronze equestrian sculpture.

LOCATION: MONUMENT AND
LOMBARDY NEAR
STUART AVENUE
DATE: MAY 30, 1907
MEDIA: BRONZE, GRANITE

Front

MAJ: GEN: J. E. B. STUART
COMMANDING·CAVALRY·CORPS
ARMY·NORTHERN·VIRGINIA
CONFEDERATE·STATES·OF·AMERICA
THIS·STATUE·ERECTED·BY·HIS·COMRADES
AND·THE·CITY·OF·RICHMOND
A. D. 1906

—
BORN·IN·PATRICK·COUNTY·VA: FEB·6·1833
DIED·IN·RICHMOND·VA: MAY·12·1864
MORTALLY·WOUNDED·IN·THE·BATTLE·
OF·YELLOW·TAVERN
MAY·11·1864
HE·GAVE·HIS·LIFE·FOR·HIS·COUNTRY
AND·SAVED·THIS·CITY·FROM·CAPTURE
—

"HIS·GRATEFUL
COUNTRYMEN
WILL·MOURN·HIS·LOSS
AND·CHERISH
HIS·MEMORY
TO·HIS·COMRADES·IN·ARMS
HE·HAS·LEFT
THE·PROUD·RECOLLECTION
OF·HIS·DEEDS
AND·THE·INSPIRING·INFLUENCE
OF·HIS·EXAMPLE"
GEN: R. E. LEE
ANNOUNCING·THE·DEATH·OF
GEN: STUART
TO·HIS·ARMY—MAY·20·1864
—

"TELL
GEN: STUART
TO·ACT
ON·HIS·OWN·JUDGMENT
AND·DO·WHAT·HE
THINKS·BEST
I·HAVE
IMPLICIT·CONFIDENCE
IN·HIM "
GEN: T. J. 'STONEWALL' JACKSON
IN·TURNING·OVER·THE·COMMAND
OF·HIS·TROOPS
TO·GEN: STUART
AFTER·BEING·WOUNDED
AT·CHANCELLORSVILLE
MAY·3·1863

Stuart was the best-known cavalryman in the Army of Northern Virginia—effective, impetuous, swaggering, aggressive, and popular. He may be the most down-to-earth and accessible of the Monument Avenue cohort.

In consequence, perhaps, the Stuart monument—a fifteen-foot-high bronze statue stand-ing on a seven-and-a-half-foot-high granite pedestal—lacks the mystical qualities ascribed to Jackson and Lee in this neighborhood. Unlike those examples, testimony is inscribed, as if to fully justify his status in the pantheon. The tribute, "Gave His Life," is similar to the inscription at Yellow Tavern. Stuart faces east, a wary eye to the flanks, including those of Lee and Jackson further down the street. Lee's tribute, taken from General Orders Number 44, is particularly effusive—certainly by Lee's prose standards. "He never brought me a false piece of information," Lee said, upon being told of his death. The Jackson quotation—"Tell Gen. Stuart . . ."—may be an elaboration on what he actually said. The narratives of Shelby Foote, Douglas Southall Freeman, and James I. Robertson Jr. do not mention it but agree in recording him as saying, "I don't know. I can't tell. Say to General Stuart that he must do what he thinks best." Lee's eulogy went on to praise Stuart as being "second to none in valor, in zeal, and in unfaltering devotion to his country."

- Stuart's granddaughter, Virginia Stuart Waller, performed the unveiling. The occasion, according to the *Confederate Veteran* account, "caused an outpour of people that must have gratified those who were intimate with the wonderful cavalryman and a man who was so light-hearted and gay, and yet in whose life there were such deep and undying Christian virtues."

- The monument was presented to the city by former Confederate general John B. Gordon and was accepted by Mayor Carlton McCarthy, a Confederate veteran. The dedication was part of a week of events—including the Jefferson Davis statue dedication—coinciding with a reunion of seventeen thousand Confederate veterans in the city.

- Stuart is riding General, the horse he was riding at the time he was mortally wounded. Frederick Moynihan was the sculptor. Some critics believe that Moynihan plagiarized the work of another sculptor, John Foley, with this statue. Moynihan had worked as Foley's assistant, and the statue of Stuart bears a strong resemblance to Moynihan's statue of General Sir James Outram in Calcutta, India (1874).

- Jackson spoke while mortally wounded. Ironically his testimony is to Stuart's ability leading infantry, in which he was relatively untested, but Jackson's faith, by most accounts, was born out: Stuart proved competent. Stuart survived Jackson by one year and two days.

- Editorial note: The ornamental punctuation with bullets or elevated periods marking the spacing between each word is unusual and is similar to classical Greek punctuation, specifically the Greek semicolon.

180. Richmond Howitzers, Common Soldier

Monument is a private soldier, in bronze, an artilleryman, surmounting a granite plinth, base, dado, and pedestal.

LOCATION: Harrison, Grove and Park Avenue, east of Monument Avenue

DATE: May 30, 1907

MEDIA: Bronze, granite

Front

TO COMMEMORATE

THE DEEDS AND SERVICES

OF

THE RICHMOND HOWITZERS
OF THE PERIOD
1861–1865.

—

FROM BETHEL TO
APPOMATTOX

—

[BLANK]

—

CITA MORS AUT
VICTORIA
LAETA
1859

This is the one of the few unit monuments in Richmond and one of a relative handful in Virginia. The sculpture portrays "Number One," a Confederate artilleryman holding a sponge and rammer.

The service record of the Richmond Howitzers began at least as early as November 9, 1859. The battery was reorganized April 10, 1871. Redesignated a number of times, it saw service in World War I and World War II and continues as a unit of the Virginia National Guard.

The monument is the work of Caspar Buberl and William L. Sheppard, the latter a member of the Richmond Howitzers, who also designed the A. P. Hill monument on Hermitage Road and the Soldiers and Sailors monument on Libby Hill. Buberl's work includes the Confederate statues at Charlottesville, Lynchburg, and Alexandria.

- This is another example of a relatively benign monument that is sharply contrasted with provocative dedication remarks. Leigh Robinson's address included references to the "natural supremacy of the white race over the black," and the allegation that "slavery had been forced upon Virginia." Robinson, a veteran of the Richmond Howitzers, further noted "the importation of slaves into the South by Northern merchants," that Virginia had not opposed "gradual emancipation," and that it had been advocated "by Jefferson as early as 1776."

- The Latin expression, "Cita Mors Aut Victoria Laeta," is translated as "A Quick Death or a Sweet Victory."

Monroe Park

181. Williams C. Wickham, Statue

Monument is a bronze statue surmounting a granite plinth, base, dado, and pedestal.
LOCATION: Monroe Park, 23220
DATE: October 29, 1891
MEDIA: Bronze, granite
Front

WICKHAM
"SOLDIER, STATESMAN
PATRIOT, FRIEND."
PRESENTED TO THE CITY OF
RICHMOND BY COMRADES
IN THE CONFEDERATE ARMY
AND EMPLOYEES OF THE
CHESAPEAKE AND OHIO
RAILWAY COMPANY
—
WILLIAMS CARTER WICKHAM
SEPTEMBER 21ST 1820
JULY 23RD 1888

Williams Carter Wickham's role as a Confederate cavalryman with the Army of Northern Virginia earned him his place in history, but his rank as a brigadier general is not mentioned: the memorial simply calls him a "Soldier."

Wickham, like William Mahone, Thomas L. Rosser, and E. Porter Alexander, is an example of relatively young ex-Confederate officers whose leadership and technical acumen led to postwar careers with the railroads in the turbulent era of that medium's greatest growth. The description of him as a "Statesman" and "Patriot" provide a summary note on a man who stood with the Confederacy and fought for secession, but who was not persuaded that the war could be won or that independence was in the best interests of his state. Wickham rose to brigadier general during active service with the Confederate cavalry and was wounded several times.

The bronze sculpture, standing seven feet high, is by Edward V. Valentine and was funded by private subscription. City appropriations provided the base. The total cost of the monument was about fifteen thousand dollars. Valentine also designed the Davis statue on Monument Avenue, the Lee statue in the chapel of Washington and Lee University, Lexington, and the Jackson statue at Stonewall Cemetery, Lexington.

- Wickham is buried in the family cemetery in Hanover County, near Hanover.
- Also in Monroe Park: a statue of Joseph Bryan (1845–1908), Richmond attorney, civic activist, and member of Mosby's Rangers, unveiled with Mosby present on June 10, 1911.
- A granite shaft to Confederate general W. H. Fitzhugh Lee commemorates his service to the United States in the Spanish-American War in 1898–99. An earlier effort to erect a monument for Lee's service in the Civil War was not successful. The cornerstone for the original Davis monument—it was never completed—was dedicated here in 1896.
- Jackson's Virginia Military Institute cadets drilled Confederate recruits in Monroe Park. The park also served as a campground and hospital site.

State Capitol Grounds
1 Capitol Square, 23219

182. William Smith, Statue

Monument is a bronze statue surmounting a granite plinth, base, dado, and pedestal.

DATE: May 30, 1906

MEDIA: Bronze, granite

Front

WILLIAM SMITH.
VIRGINIA.
BORN SEP 6TH 1797 DIED MAY 18TH 1887.
1836–40. 1841–42.
MEMBER OF VIRGINIA SENATE.
1846–49.
GOVERNOR OF VIRGINIA.
1841–43. 1853–61.
MEMBER OF UNITED STATES CONGRESS.
1861–62.
MEMBER OF CONFEDERATE STATES CONGRESS.
1861–62.
COLONEL 49TH VIRGINIA VOLUNTEERS.
1862–63.
BRIG. GENERAL CONFEDERATE STATES ARMY.
1863–64.
MAJOR GENERAL CONFEDERATE
STATES ARMY.

1864–65.
GOVERNOR OF VIRGINIA.

Right side of bronze base of sculpture:

WM SIEVERS, NY WL SHEPPARD DEST
—
A MAN OF STRONG CONVICTIONS,
BRED IN THE STRICT
STATES RIGHTS SCHOOL,
HE YIELDED PARAMOUNT ALLEGIANCE
TO HIS MOTHER STATE,
AND MAINTAINED WITH FEARLESS
AND IMPASSIONED ELOQUENCE,
IN THE CONGRESS OF THE UNITED STATES
THE SOVEREIGNTY OF VIRGINIA.
WHEN THE STORM OF WAR BURST,
"HIS VOICE WAS IN HIS SWORD."
—
THOUGH PAST THREE SCORE
HE ENTERED THE MILITARY SERVICE
AS COLONEL OF VIRGINIA INFANTRY
AND ROSE BY SHEER MERIT
TO THE RANK OF MAJOR GENERAL.
AT FIRST MANASSAS, SEVEN PINES,
THE SEVEN DAYS BATTLE,
CEDAR MOUNTAIN, SECOND MANASSAS,
SHARPSBURG, FREDERICKSBURG,
CHANCELLORSVILLE AND GETTYSBURG
HIS FIERY YET "CHEERFUL COURAGE"
WAS EVERYWHERE CONSPICUOUS
AND THE ONLY FAULT IMPUTED TO HIM
BY HIS SUPERIORS WAS
A TOO RECKLESS EXPOSURE OF HIS PERSON.
THRICE WOUNDED AT SHARPSBURG,
HE REFUSED TO LEAVE THE FIELD, AND
REMAINED IN COMMAND OF HIS REGIMENT
UNTIL THE END OF THAT
SANGUINARY ENGAGEMENT.
—
CALLED FROM THE ARMY
TO GUIDE AGAIN THE DESTINIES
OF THE COMMONWEALTH
DURING 1864–65.
HE DISPLAYED SUCH ENERGY, RESOURCE
AND UNSHAKEN RESOLUTION,
AS DREW TO HIM THE HEART
OF THE WHOLE SOUTHERN PEOPLE.
TRIED BY BOTH EXTREMES OF FORTUNE
HE PROVED EQUAL TO THE TRIAL,

AND DIED AS HE HAD LIVED,
A VIRGINIAN OF VIRGINIANS.
AUBREY BROS CO/FOUNDERS NY

The seven-and-one-half-foot bronze statue of William Smith—twice governor of Virginia, a United States and Confederate States congressman, a state legislator, and a combat officer as commander of the 49th Virginia Infantry—was sculpted by Frederick W. Sievers from a design by William L. Sheppard. It was dedicated on May 30, 1906.

Smith earned the nickname "Extra Billy" by taking advantage of incentives when he held a U.S. government mail-delivery contract in the 1830s. The moniker is almost invariably linked to his name apart from the public monuments here and on his tombstone at Hollywood Cemetery.

- Of Smith's courage Maj. Gen. J. E. B. Stuart observed that he was "dripping blood but fighting valiantly" at the battle of Antietam and that Smith was "conspicuously brave and self-possessed."
- The memorial is copiously detailed (so, too, is his epitaph in Hollywood Cemetery), a not uncommon approach taken by eulogists for figures whose reputation is not well fixed.

183. Thomas J. Jackson, Statue

Monument is a bronze statue surmounting a granite plinth, base, dado, and pedestal.
DATE: October 26, 1875
MEDIA: Bronze, granite

PRESENTED BY ENGLISH GENTLEMEN
AS A TRIBUTE OF ADMIRATION FOR
THE SOLDIER AND PATRIOT
THOMAS J. JACKSON.
AND GRATEFULLY ACCEPTED BY VIRGINIA
IN THE NAME OF THE SOUTHERN PEOPLE.
DONE A. D. 1875.
THE HUNDREDTH YEAR OF
THE COMMONWEALTH
LOOK! THERE IS JACKSON STANDING
LIKE A STONE WALL.
J. H. FOLEY R. A.
SCULPTOR
LONDON 1873

The Jackson statue, by Irish sculptor John H. Foley, was a forerunner of the promenade of quasi-national monuments in the former capital. The status of the sponsors—the "English Gentlemen"—is prominent. The "Gentlemen" take no stand on the issues of the war: there are no apologetics and no mentions of the Confederacy. However, there is irony in the tribute to Jackson as a "Soldier and Patriot," as it gives credence to Second American Revolution ideals associated with the war. It was the first monument to an individual Confederate soldier erected in Richmond.

Proposals for a monument to Jackson began in June 1863 in London just weeks after the general's death. Strong currents of sympathy for the Confederacy were extant in England during the war. Formal fundraising began with a committee of sixteen "Confederate sympathizers," as they were called, including at least two members of Parliament, who formed the British Jackson Monumental Fund. Time passed, fundraising lagged, and Foley, the sculptor, worked at a slow and deliberate pace on the project. In fact, the statue was not completed until shortly before the sculptor's death in August 1874. The results were well received, however. The dedication ceremonies included a procession to Capitol Square and addresses by Governor James L. Kemper and the Reverend Moses D. Hoge. Richmond was "finely decorated," according to a London newspaper account at the time, "the British colours being prominent."

- Excerpt from the dedication address by Rev. Hoge:

Let the spirit and design, with which we erect this memorial to-day, admonish our whole country that the actual reconciliation of the states must come, and, so far as honorably in us lies, shall come; but that its work will never be complete until the equal honor and equal liberties of each section shall be acknowledged, vindicated, and maintained by both.

. . . We have buried the strifes and passions of the past; we now perpetuate impartial honor to whom honor is due. [L]et this statue endure, attesting to the world for us and our children, honor, homage, reverence for the heroism of our past, and at the same time the knightliest fidelity to our obligations of the present and the future.

184. Hunter Holmes McGuire, Statue

Monument is a bronze statue of seated figure surmounting a granite plinth, base, and dado.
DATE: January 7, 1904
MEDIA: Bronze, granite

TO
HUNTER HOLMES MCGUIRE, M.D., LL.D.,
PRESIDENT OF THE AMERICAN MEDICAL
AND OF THE AMERICAN
SURGICAL ASSOCIATIONS;
FOUNDER OF THE UNIVERSITY
COLLEGE OF MEDICINE;
MEDICAL DIRECTOR, JACKSON'S CORPS,
ARMY OF NORTHERN VIRGINIA;
AN EMINENT CIVIL AND MILITARY SURGEON,
AND BELOVED PHYSICIAN;
AN ABLE TEACHER AND VIGOROUS WRITER,
A USEFUL CITIZEN AND BROAD
HUMANITARIAN,
GIFTED IN MIND AND GENEROUS IN HEART,
THIS MONUMENT IS ERECTED
BY HIS MANY FRIENDS.
—
HUNTER HOLMES MCGUIRE
BORN OCT. 11, 1835.
DIED SEPT. 19, 1900.

Hunter Holmes McGuire was chief surgeon of the Second Corps of the Army of Northern Virginia. McGuire tended Jackson on his deathbed, had a role in organizing the Confederate Ambulance Corps, and earned a reputation for extending kindness to wounded Union prisoners. His statue, a seated figure, was designed by William L. Couper, of Norfolk, and was unveiled January 7, 1904. By an act of the Virginia legislature the statue was placed near the Jackson statue erected nearly thirty years earlier. The *Richmond Times-Dispatch* of January 8, 1904, observed that the statue "represents the surgeon seated in his chair, life-like, as he appeared to many who visited his office while he was living."

McGuire's wartime service bears mention, but it is not the theme of the monument: contemporary accounts proclaimed that this "noble and enduring memorial" is dedicated to the "South's great surgeon and one of her most eminent and illustrious sons." Of men like McGuire, the Reverend James Power Smith said in his dedication address that the "Commonwealth is safe and strong when men are true to duty, brave in the time of peril and upright and steadfast in time of peace."

Oakwood Cemetery

185. Central Obelisk

Monument is an obelisk surmounting a plinth, base, and dado.

LOCATION: 3101 Nine Mile Road, 23223
DATE: May 24, 1871
MEDIUM: Granite
Front

IN MEMORY
OF
SIXTEEN THOUSAND
CONFEDERATE SOLDIERS
FROM THIRTEEN STATES
ERECTED BY THE LADIES
OAKWOOD MEMORIAL
ASSOCIATION ORGANIZED
MAY 10TH 1866.

—

MARYLAND.   FLORIDA.
VIRGINIA.
NORTH CAROLINA.
SOUTH CAROLINA.
TENNESSEE.
ARKANSAS.

—

TEXAS.   KENTUCKY.
GEORGIA.
ALABAMA.
MISSISSIPPI.
LOUISIANA.

—

THE EPITAPH OF THE
SOLDIER, WHO FALLS
WITH HIS COUNTRY, IS
WRITTEN IN THE HEARTS
OF THOSE WHO LOVE THE
RIGHT AND HONOR
THE BRAVE.

Located in the northeast outskirts of the city, Oakwood Cemetery does not have the renown of Hollywood Cemetery. There are, however, nearly as many soldiers buried here as in Hollywood. The Oakwood Confederate Cemetery Trust provides upkeep and care at this writing.

This grim obelisk, erected at a cost of five thousand dollars, is the largest of several Confederate monuments at Oakwood. The site is enormous—sixteen thousand men from thirteen states on some seven acres—but the memorial is focused on the imagined, representative individual: "The Epitaph of The Soldier Who Falls with His Country . . ."

The orderly arrangement of the graves does not, of course, reflect the chaotic suffering from wounds and disease, or sudden, violent death the men here endured. The records are incomplete as well: only about a thousand of the dead are identified. Death was so common that the burial teams could not keep pace: there were 540 burials by January 12, 1862; 4,882 by September 1, 1862; 5,483 by October 1, 1862; and 7,120 by January 1863.

186. Entryway Tablet

Monument is a bronze tablet set on a granite base.

DATE: 1930
MEDIA: Bronze, granite

THIS GROUND
IS THE LAST BIVOUAC OF
17,000 CONFEDERATE SOLDIERS
SLAIN IN DEFENSE OF THE SOUTH.
IN GRATITUDE FOR THEIR DEVOTION
THE COMMONWEALTH OF VIRGINIA
BY ACT OF THE ASSEMBLY OF 1930
HAS PROVIDED PERPETUAL CARE FOR
THEIR GRAVES, A SACRED TRUST
WHICH THE CITY OF RICHMOND
REVERENTLY HAS ACCEPTED

Like the marker at the base of the Hollywood Cemetery pyramid, this plaque serves as a summary note on this site. The 1871 obelisk states that there are sixteen thousand interments. The 1930 marker provides a final estimate: seventeen thousand. Martyrdom is intimated by the declaration "Slain in Defense of the South." "Last Bivouac" is an apparent allusion to the poem "The Bivouac of the Dead," which is traditionally posted at national cemeteries. Confederate cemeteries have had state support for upkeep to this day. It is a pittance, as historian John Salmon puts it, but it serves to illustrate the fact that the costs of the war continue to be borne by the commonwealth.

187. Brown's Island Memorial

Monument is a tablet set on a base.
DATE: September 15, 2001
MEDIUM: Granite
Front

IN MEMORY OF THOSE WHO LOST THEIR LIVES
IN THE EXPLOSION OF C. S. LABORATORIES
ON BROWN'S ISLAND—RICHMOND,
VIRGINIA, MARCH 13, 1863
THOUGH THEIR HANDS WERE SMALL
AND NOT HARDENED IN BATTLE

THEIR SERVICE TO THE
CONFEDERACY LOOMS LARGE
MAY THIS STONE SERVE AS A PERPETUAL
MEMORIAL TO THE DEDICATION/
SPONSORSHIP AND SACRIFICE OF THESE
FORGOTTEN AND UNSUNG VICTIMS
"LET US REMEMBER THEM AS
TIME AND TIDE MOVE
ON IN ENDLESS RHYME
WHILE BUD AND BLOSSOM, HILL AND TREE
REMEMBER THEM, SO SHALL WE"
OLIVER REEVES
ERECTED BY VIRGINIA DIVISION,
UNITED DAUGHTERS OF THE CONFEDERACY,
DEDICATED SEPTEMBER 15, 2001

—

[46 NAMES IN TWO COLUMNS]

Forty-six of seventy workers were killed March 13, 1863, in Department 6 of the Confederate States Laboratories, which manufactured small arms and ammunition at Brown's Island on the James River. Most of the victims were young girls. The supervisor, Reverend John Woodcock, was the only person given a funeral and a headstone; the rest were interred in unmarked graves. This monument redresses something of that injustice. The names of two men and forty-four women are inscribed. The youngest girl is ten years old. Five girls are twelve years of age.

This twenty-first-century monument is unusual for invoking a nineteenth-century poem, specifically the last five lines from "Poem for Confederate Memorial Day," by Oliver Reeves.

188. Shockoe Hill Hospital Tablet

LOCATION: Fourth and Hospital Street,
23219
DATE: 1938
MEDIUM: Granite

[C.S.A. BATTLE FLAG]
IN THIS VICINITY ARE BURIED
220 CONFEDERATE
SOLDIERS AND 577 UNION
SOLDIERS THAT ARE
RECORDED AS WELL AS HUNDREDS
OF OTHER SOLDIERS
OF WHOSE BURIAL NO RECORD WAS MADE
ERECTED BY ELLIOTT GRAYS
CHAPTER U.D.C. 1938.

Shockoe Hill's 1938 monument is unusual for
its inclusion of Confederate and Union soldiers.
The dead were taken from Confederate Hospital
Number 1, which was adjacent to this site. The
facility was intended only for wounded Union
prisoners but soon became the first of the large
General Hospitals that developed during the
war. An adjacent 2002 bronze plaque lists 88 of
at least 661 Union soldiers who died and were
buried here as prisoners of war.

That hundreds of interments occurred with
no records extant suggests that the city's medical facilities were overwhelmed and that distinctions were suspended between the casualties of the opposing sides.

- Established as the city's first municipal
  cemetery in 1820, Shockoe Hill's pastoral
  landscaping was influenced by English
  garden cemetery designs of the time but
  also anticipated the rural cemetery movement of the mid-nineteenth century.

189. Hebrew Cemetery Tablet
Monument is a granite shaft with bronze
plaques.
DATE: circa 1950s
MEDIA: Bronze, granite

TO THE GLORY OF GOD
AND
IN MEMORY OF
THE HEBREW CONFEDERATE SOLDIERS
RESTING IN THIS HALLOWED SPOT
[30 NAMES IN THREE COLUMNS]

ERECTED BY
HEBREW LADIES MEMORIAL ASSO.
RICHMOND VA.
ORGANIZED 1866
[PLAQUE]
H. GERSBERG
SHOULD CORRECTLY READ
HENRY GINTZBERGER
[BRONZE PLAQUE IN FRONT]
THIS SECTION PLACED UNDER
PERPETUAL CARE
MAY 15, 1930.
BY
HEBREW LADIES'
MEMORIAL ASSOCIATION

Until World War II this was the only Jewish
military cemetery in the world. Further, until
2006 this was the only monument in Virginia
dedicated to Jewish Confederate soldiers; it was
also the only Virginia monument to Confederate soldiers that is addressed to a particular ethnic or religious group. The thirty-one
graves here are from Virginia, Texas, Louisiana, Mississippi, South Carolina, North Carolina, and Georgia.

The site is enclosed with elaborate wrought ironwork fencing, adorned with swords, olive wreaths, stacked muskets, and shrouds decorated with Confederate battle flags; each fence post is capped—rather informally, almost whimsically—with a sculpted kepi, all designed by William Myers and cast in the Tredegar Iron Works before 1873. The battle flags, sculpted to drape over tombstones, may represent a Lost Cause substitute for a Tallit, or prayer shawl, a symbol widely used on Jewish Victorian tombstones.

Many of the Jews involved in the erection of this monument had come from Europe only a few decades before the war, but their sense of national loss was said to have been fervent. "Pride in their people and grief over the fate of their 'lost cause' combined to further this loving project," according to contemporary observer Rebekah Bettleheim. She wrote that the entire Jewish population of Richmond went to the cemetery every Confederate Memorial Day to set wreaths on the headstones, and stand before the monument with tears in their eyes.

- The Hebrew Ladies Memorial Association gave the care of the plot over to the Hebrew Cemetery Company in the 1930s.
- Individual grave markers were removed during the 1950s, and the central granite marker was erected in their place. Today the section, like the rest of the cemetery, is maintained by Congregation Beth Ahabah.

Libby Hill Park

190. Soldiers and Sailors Column with Common Soldier

Monument is a Confederate private soldier, in bronze, standing at parade rest surmounting a plinth, base, dado, pedestal, and column.
LOCATION: 28th and East Franklin streets, 23298
DATE: May 30, 1894
MEDIA: Bronze, granite
Front

CONFEDERATE
SOLDIERS & SAILORS
MONUMENT.

ERECTED BY THE
CONFEDERATE SOLDIERS & SAILORS
MONUMENT ASSOCIATION
ANNO DOMINI 1887–1894.

The story behind this tribute to the "ordinary" Confederate soldier was typical of some of the wrangling and disputes that occurred in the monument movement. The monument is ninety feet tall: the bronze statue is seventeen feet high, with a pedestal seventy-three feet high. The thirteen stone cylinders represent thirteen Confederate states. The "Private Soldiers' Monument," as it was called, was modeled on Pompey's Pillar in Alexandria, Egypt, erected by Publius, Prefect of Egypt, in honor of the Roman Emperor Diocletian, who conquered Alexandria in 296 A. D.

Fundraising began in 1887, by the Confederate Soldiers and Sailors Monument Association. Committee members included several veterans who had taken a conspicuous place as public servants, including Virginia's governor, W. H. Fitzhugh Lee, mayor and future lieutenant governor J. Taylor Ellyson, Richmond School Board president John B. Cary, and city engineer Wilfred E. Cutshaw. Secretary Carlton McCarthy had served as mayor of Richmond. The unanimous choice of the committee was the artist Moses Ezekiel. Six tempestuous years of disagreements, miscommunication, and intemperate clashes followed. Finally, the committee severed ties with Ezekiel and turned to William L. Sheppard to complete the project. Fundraising lagged, the project proved to be almost too ambitious, but perseverance on the part of veterans and women's groups prevailed.

The dedication ceremonies were extravagant. One hundred thousand spectators saw a parade of ten thousand marchers, which included a procession of girls representing the thirteen Confederate states and one thousand children carrying Confederate flags, as well as militia units, and groups of veterans, and sons of veterans. The soldier overlooks Main Street to the west and the James River to the south. The monument is discernible from the northbound lanes of Interstate 95 and stands over the bustling Shockoe Slip neighborhood.

Monuments like these "no longer simply honored the dead and celebrated the cause," said Moses D. Hoge, Presbyterian minister, who maintained that they would also serve as a forum of instruction for people who did not read, particularly young men. "Books are occasionally opened," Hoge declared, in a fundraising speech for this edifice, but "monuments are seen every day, and the lesson of that lofty figure which is to tower over Libby Hill [is to] 'Live nobly; there is a reward for patriotic duty; republics are not ungrateful.'"

Chimborazo Park

191. Chimborazo Hospital Tablet

Monument is a bronze plaque set on a boulder.
LOCATION: Overlooking the James River on Chimborazo Park Drive at
3215 East Broad Street, 23223
DATE: 1934
MEDIA: Bronze, granite

> ON THIS HILL STOOD
> CHIMBORAZO HOSPITAL
> 1862–1865
> ESTABLISHED BY
> SURGEON GENERAL S. P. MOORE, C.S.A.
> DIRECTED BY DR. JAMES B. MCCAW
> AT THAT TIME, IT WAS THE
> LARGEST MILITARY HOSPITAL
> IN THE WORLD
> IT CONSISTED OF 150 BUILDINGS
> AND 100 TENTS
> AND CARED FOR 76,000 PATIENTS WITH A
> MORTALITY OF LESS THAN 10 PER CENT
> THIS TABLET IS PLACED BY THE
> CONFEDERATE MEMORIAL LITERARY SOCIETY
> 1934

Chimborazo Hospital opened in October 1861 and is recorded as having served a total of 77,889 soldiers. The casualties overwhelmed the facility's staff and resources, and Chimborazo was infamous for its odors: rotting flesh, blood, gore, and filth. The dead were removed to Oakland Cemetery. Something of the South's backward reputation is addressed in this memorial: Chimborazo was relatively successful in its treatment of casualties. The size and scale of the facility are noted, and the mortality rate—an impressively low ten percent—is emphasized (although the Park Service cites twenty percent in its literature).

Today the hospital facilities are gone, and a public park and the Park Service Visitor Center Medical Museum stand on the site.

Hollywood Cemetery
Location: 412 South Cherry Street, 2322

192. The Pyramid and Adjacent Tablets

Monument is a granite pyramid.
DATE: November 8, 1869
MEDIUM: Granite
Front

NUMINI ET PATRIÆ ASTO.

—

TO THE
CONFEDERATE DEAD.

—

MEMORIÂ IN ÆTERNÂ.

—

ERECTED BY THE
HOLLY-WOOD MEMORIAL
ASSOCIATION.
A. D. 1869.

Of the sixty-one thousand interments in the 135-acre grounds of Hollywood Cemetery, nearly one-third are Confederate soldiers. This ninety-foot pyramid of James River granite was erected and dedicated only four years af-

ter the war. In mass and size, it is the largest Confederate monument in Virginia, may be the largest single monument to military dead in North America, and is arguably the quintessential effort to symbolize the scale of the losses the South incurred.

Interments and reinterments were incomplete in 1869, when it was erected. The "Soldiers' Section" began with a two-acre lot that was donated at the outbreak of the war. It was filled by June 1862. By war's end, more than eleven thousand Confederate dead had been buried. One thousand dead were reinterred from Sharpsburg in 1872, and some three thousand dead were exhumed from Gettysburg and reinterred 1872–73. By the time of the dedication of the 1914 memorial to "Confederate Women," there were eighteen thousand interments.

- The Hollywood Memorial Association was formed in May 1866 and ultimately raised some eighteen thousand dollars for the monument. In addition to repairing and decorating the Soldier's Section, the association reinterred the bodies of hundreds of soldiers that had been buried on battlefields around Richmond, with local farmers aiding the association in locating graves.
- Granite slabs surround the pyramid to the east and northeast. The slabs reflect the various postwar projects to collect the dead from other sites: "UNKNOWN"; "CONFEDERATE DEAD"; VIRGINIA DEAD FROM ARLINGTON MAY 20, 1872."; "SOUTH CAROLINA DEAD FROM ARLINGTON"; "FORT HARRISON." North of Confederate Avenue and east of the bandstand: "SEVEN PINES UNKNOWN"; south of the bandstand and the loop: "UNKNOWN"; "UNKNOWN"; "MILITIA UNKNOWN."
- The Latin expression "Numini Et Patriæ Asto" is translated as "United We Stand Before the Gods and Country." The Latin paean, "MEMORI Â IN ÆTERN Â," is translated as "Eternally in Memory."
- Winder and Chimborazo hospitals were the largest of many such wartime facilities in Richmond. Winder was west of the

city, near present-day Maymont. The dead from Winder were interred at Hollywood; Oakwood took those from Chimborazo.

- A tablet at the base of the pyramid reads:

CHARLES HENRY DIMMOCK
(1831–1873)
CAPTAIN, CORPS ENG., CSA
ARCHITECT-ENGINEER-LAWYER
DESIGNED AND SUPERVISED
THE CONSTRUCTION OF THIS MONUMENT

Dimmock, who also designed the Dimmock Line of defenses at Petersburg, is interred in Hollywood in section 79.

193. Confederate Women Tablet

Monument is a bronze tablet set on a granite base.
DATE: 1914
MEDIA: Bronze, granite

[SEAL OF VIRGINIA]
[FOUR C.S.A. FLAGS]
A MEMORIAL TO THE
CONFEDERATE WOMEN
OF VIRGINIA, 1861–1865
THE LEGISLATURE OF VIRGINIA
OF 1914, HAS AT THE
SOLICITATION OF LADIES
HOLLYWOOD
MEMORIAL ASSOCIATION
AND UNITED DAUGHTERS OF
CONFEDERACY OF VIRGINIA
PLACED IN PERPETUAL CARE
THIS SECTION WHERE LIE BURIED
EIGHTEEN THOUSAND
CONFEDERATE SOLDIERS.

Dedicated to the "Confederate Women of Virginia," this modest semicentennial marker stands in front of the 1869 pyramid. The plaque offers the practical assurance that the Confederate burial grounds will have the perpetual care of the Virginia legislature, a status that would ultimately be extended to other Confederate cemeteries across the state, including Oakwood.

194. Obey Battery Obelisk

Monument is an obelisk surmounting a base, plinth, and dado.
LOCATION: On north side of pyramid parallel to Idlewood Avenue
DATE: June 11, 1887
MEDIUM: Granite

> ERECTED
> BY THE
> OTEY BATTERY
> C.S.A.
> TO THE MEMORY OF
> THEIR DEAD COMRADES
> JUNE 11TH 1887.

The Otey Battery organized in March 1862. It served in western Virginia and was present at the battles of Giles Court House, Fayetteville, and Charleston. Its first commander was George Gaston Otey. The battery's seventeen-foot obelisk stands along the fence adjacent Idlewood Avenue.

The commemorative notes call it "a plain but very expressive and imposing monolith, bearing [a] simple inscription[, but it] speaks loudly to the heart through its silence." The dedication ceremonies were a daylong affair for the veterans: a day spent eating, drinking, and socializing, until six in the evening. Then the members "fell in" and marched to the cemetery for the dedication. A large crowd awaited them. The granite obelisk was shrouded with a white veil and the base was decorated with flowers resembling a breastwork and cannon. Among the speakers was one of their own, Pvt. George Savage, who said in part:

> Comrades! our labor of love is ended! At last a monument to the dead of the Obey Battery stands as we would have it stand. Hands of beauty and purity have unveiled it.... Woman has blessed it with her prayers and her tears. We have consecrated it with prayer, poetry, and speech. May it remain here forever! ... It is cold and voiceless, but to us it speaks aloud of Patriotism, Valor, and Devotion, and it bids us believe that the praises of our heroic dead will be proudly sung "Far on in summers that we shall not see.

195. Pickett's Division Cylinder

Monument is a granite base and octagon arch with bronze plaques, the whole surmounted by a funereal urn.
LOCATION: North of pyramid near the Otey Battery obelisk
DATE: October 5, 1888
MEDIA: Bronze, granite

> PICKETT'S DIVISION
> ARMY NORTHERN VIRGINIA
> WHOSE OFFICERS AND MEN
> FOUGHT BRAVELY AND DIED
> NOBLY, AND THOUGH DENIED
> SUCCESS, "ON FAME'S ETERNAL
> LEAF ROLL WORTHIE TO BE
> FYLED."
> WHENEVER FIELD WAS TO BE
> HELD OR WON
> OR HARDSHIP BORNE OR RIGHT
> TO BE MAINTAINED
> OR DANGER MET OR DEED OF
> VALOR DONE
> XXXX [SIC] OR HONOR GLORY GAINED
> WHERE MEN WERE CALLED TO
> FRONT DEATH FACE TO FACE
> XXXX [SIC] THERE WAS ITS
> RIGHTFUL PLACE
> GEORGE E. PICKETT,

MAJOR GENERAL COMMANDING,
BORN IN RICHMOND CITY, VIRGINIA
JAN. 25, 1825,
DIED IN NORFOLK CITY. VIRGINIA
JULY 30, 1875.
VERA CRUZ, CERO GORDO,
CONTRERAS, CHERUBUSCO, MOLINO
DEL REY, CHAPULTEPEC, MEXICO,
SAN JUAN ISLAND 1859,
WILLIAMSBURG, FAIR OAKS,
GAINES' MILL, FREDERICKSBURG,
GETTYSBURG, PLYMOUTH, COLD
HARBOR, CLAY HOUSE, FIVE FORKS,
SAILOR'S [SIC] CREEK, APPOMATTOX C. H.
MAJOR GENERAL C.S.A.
GEORGE E. PICKETT

—

ARMISTEADS' BRIGADE [SIC]
[UNIT ROSTER]
ARMISTEAD'S BRIGADE, OR
SOME PORTION OF IT, WAS
ENGAGED IN THE FOLLOWING BATTLES:
BIG BETHEL, RICH MOUNTAIN,
FAIR OAKS, SEVEN DAYS' BATTLES
SECOND MANASSAS, HARPER'S
FERRY [SIC], SHARPSBURG, FREDERCKS-
BURG, GETTYSBURG, CHESTER
STATION, DREWRY'S BLUFF, COLD
HARBOR, CLAY HOUSE, FIVE FORKS
AND SAILORS' CREEK.
DEO VINDICE
GLORIOUS IS HIS FATE AND
ENVIED IS HIS LOT WHO
FOR HIS COUNTRY FIGHTS AND
FOR HIS COUNTRY DIES
NOR SHALL THEIR GLORY BE FORGOT
WHILE FAME HER RECORD KEEPS,
OR HONOR POINTS THE HALLOWED SPOT
WHERE VALOR PROUDLY SLEEPS.
NOR WRECK, NOR CHANGE,
NOR WINTER'S BLIGHT
NOR TIME'S REMORESELESS DOOM
CAN DIM ONE RAY OF HOLY LIGHT
THAT GILDS THEIR GLORIOUS TOMB.

—

GARNETT'S BRIGADE
[UNIT ROSTER]
GARNETT'S BRIGADE, OR
SOME PORTION OF IT, WAS

ENGAGED IN THE FOLLOWING BATTLES:
FIRST MANASSAS, BALL'S BLUFF,
FORT DONELSON, WILLIAMSBURG,
DREWERY'S BLUFF 1862,
FAIR OAKS, SEVEN DAYS' BATTLES
SECOND MANASSAS, CHANTILLY,
TURNER'S GAP, SHARPSBURG,
FREDERICKSBURG, GETTYSBURG,
DREWRY'S BLUFF 1864,
COLD HARBOR, CLAY HOUSE,
GRAVELY RUN, SAILORS' CREEK
WHATEVER CHANGES TIME HAS WROUGHT,
HOW WRONG OR RASH THEIR
COURAGE MAY SEEM;
THOUGH ADVERSE DOCTRINES
MAY BE TAUGHT,
THE FUTURE SURELY WILL REDEEM
THE PATRIOT'S CAUSE FOR LIBERTY
AND KEEP THEIR ACT FROM CENSURE FREE,
FOR "ETERNAL RIGHT, THO' ALL ELSE FAIL,
CAN NEVER BE MADE WRONG."

—

THIRTY-EIGHTH
BATTALION OF ARTILLERY
[UNIT ROSTER]
THE THIRTY-EIGHTH BATTALION
OF ARTILLERY, OR SOME PORTION
OF IT, WAS ENGAGED IN THE
FOLLOWING BATTLES: FIRST
MANASSAS, YORKTOWN, WILLIAMS-
BURG, SEVEN PINES, MECHANICS-
VILLE, GAINES' MILL, FRAZIER'S
FARM, MALVERN HILL, CEDAR
MOUNTAIN, RAPPAHANNOCK
BRIDGE, SECOND MANASSAS,
CHANTILLY, BOONESBORO,
CRAMPTON'S GAP, HARPER'S FERRY [SIC],
SHARPSBURG, FREDERICKSBURG,
SUFFOLK, GETTYSBURG, NEW BERN,
N. C., BACHELOR'S CREEK, BEECH
GROVE, N. C., FORT GRAY, FORT WES-
SELS, PLYMOUTH, DREWRY'S BLUFF,
COLD HARBOR, PETERSBURG, THE
CRATER, REAMES' STATION, SIEGE
OF PETERSBURG, FORT HARRISON,
BURGESS' MILLS, ASSAULT ON FORT
STEADMAN, SAILORS' CREEK, CUM-
BERLAND CHURCH, APPOMATTOX
STATION

"YET THOUGH FATE WITH
PITILESS HAND HAS FURLED
THE FLAG THAT ONCE CHALLENGED
THE GAZE OF THE WORLD
"THE FAME OF THEIR STRUGGLE
WILL EVER ABIDE
AND DOWN INTO HISTORY
GRANDLY WILL RIDE
ON A RECORD OF DEEDS THAT
NEVER CAN FADE
FROM FIELDS WHICH THEIR VALOR
IMMORTAL HAVE MADE."

—

CORSE'S BRIGADE
[UNIT ROSTER]
CORSE'S BRIGADE, OR
SOME PORTION OF IT, WAS
ENGAGED IN THE FOLLOWING BATTLES:
BIG BETHEL.
ACQUIA CREEK, BULL RUN,
FIRST MANASSAS, WILLIAMSBURG
SEVEN PINES, FAIR OAKS, SEVEN
DAYS' BATTLES, SECOND MANASSAS
HARPER'S FERRY, TURNER'S GAP,
SHARPSBURG, FREDERICKSBURG
BLOUNTSVILLE, TENN., BEAN
STATION, TENN., DANDRIDGE, TENN.,
NEW BERNE, N. C., DREWRY'S BLUFF,
HOWLETT HOUSE, HATCHER'S RUN,
DINWIDDIE, COURTHOUSE, FIVE
FORKS, SAILOR'S [SIC] CREEK,
APPOMATTOX
"THEY MARCHED THRO' LONG
AND STORMY NIGHTS,
THEY BORE THE BRUNT OF
A SCORE OF FIGHTS;
HUNGER AND COLD AND
THE SUMMER'S HEAT,
ON THE ADVANCE AND IN THE RETREAT,
AND MANY A NOBLE FORM THEY GAVE
TO FILL, ALAS! SOME NAMELESS GRAVE
THEIR DEAD LAY THICK ON
FIELDS THEY WON,
AS WHERE THEY LOST, WERE BEAT, UNDONE,
YET STILL THEY LEFT A DEATHLESS NAME,
A GLORIOUS RECORD OF THEIR FAME
AND MEMORY OF SUCH DEEDS SHALL LIE
'MID TREASURED THOUGHTS
THAT CANNOT DIE."

—

KEMPER'S BRIGADE
[UNIT ROSTER]
KEMPER'S BRIGADE, OR
SOME PORTION OF IT, WAS
ENGAGED IN THE FOLLOWING
BATTLES:
BULL RUN, FIRST MANASSAS,
DRANESVILLE, WILLIAMSBURG,
SEVEN PINES, FAIR OAKS, SEVEN
DAYS' BATTLES, SECOND MANASSAS,
TURNER'S GAP, SHARPSBURG,
FREDERICKSBURG, GETTYSBURG,
PLYMOUTH, N. C., DREWERY'S BLUFF,
HOWLETT HOUSE, MILLFORD
STATION, COLD HARBOR, CLAY
HOUSE, DEEP BOTTOM, DINWIDDIE
COURTHOUSE, FIVE FORKS,
SAILORS' CREEK.
VIRGINIA! MOTHER OF HEROES,
STATESMEN, PATRIOTS!
IN THE LONG LIST OF GLORY—
LIGHT NAMES THAT SLEEP
WITHIN THY BOSOM, NONE SHALL
BRIGHTER SHINE THAN THESE—
WHO, BRAVELY STRIVING TO
BEAR ALOFT THY BANNER,
BATTLING FOR DUTY, GOD AND NATIVE LAND
FELL ON THE FIELD OF HONOR.
THEY DIED FOR THEE!

This granite and bronze octagon serves as a tombstone over Pickett's grave and a unit tribute to Pickett's Division of the Army of Northern Virginia. It was sponsored by the Pickett's Division Association of Virginia and was dedicated October 5, 1888. The monument was originally intended for the Gettysburg battlefield, but its placement there was refused. It would have been one of the few Southern monuments at Gettysburg. As it is, it is the only division monument in Virginia.

The design is in keeping with Gettysburg monuments, with their emphasis on unit rosters and lists of battlefields which the units had fought on. Even by those standards, this octagon is copious with details and poetic flourishes. Separate plaques are dedicated to the brigades of Armistead, Garnett, Corse, Kemper, and the 38th Battalion Artillery.

- Pickett's wife, LaSalle Corbell Pickett (1843–1931), is buried at the base.
- Excerpt from Maj. R. Taylor Scott's "Address at the Unveiling":

Bless, too, O Lord, these men from Pennsylvania, who have come here to participate with us in these services, whom we once met as foes, but now esteem as friends. . . . May our reunions be genuine, and like leaven permeate the whole land. Bless Pennsylvania and Virginia, and all the States of our Union.

And this:

What are monuments? Why are they, and what do they mean? Monuments embody two ideas—the commemoration of the past and admonition to the future. They are landmarks of civilization, and write the history of the nations of the earth, mark their epochs, and hand down to posterity their illustrious dead.

196. Dabney Maury Shaft, U.D.C. of Philadelphia

Monument is a bronze plaque set on a granite shaft and base.
LOCATION: North of pyramid
DATE: October 26, 1902
MEDIA: Bronze, granite

> ERECTED BY THE
> GENERAL DABNEY H. MAURY
> CHAPTER
> DAUGHTERS OF THE CONFEDERACY
> OF PHILADELPHIA
> IN LOVING AND GRATEFUL MEMORY OF

> THE 224 KNOWN AND UNKNOWN
> CONFEDERATE SOLDIERS FROM
> VIRGINIA, NORTH CAROLINA
> SOUTH CAROLINA, GEORGIA AND ALABAMA
> WHO LIE BURIED IN NATIONAL
> CEMETERIES IN PHILADELPHIA.
> UNVEILED OCTOBER, 1902
> —
> FATE DENIED THEM VICTORY BUT GAVE
> THEM A GLORIOUS IMMORTALITY
> [RELIEF OF C.S.A. NATIONAL FLAG,
> VIRGINIA STATE FLAG, BATTLE FLAG]
> FURLED BUT NOT FORGOTTEN

Like the Pickett monument described above, the erection of this memorial in the North was refused, and Hollywood took the monument instead. In this case, the Grand Army of the Republic, a Union veterans organization, denied the effort of the Philadelphia U.D.C. to place this monument in Pittsville Cemetery, Philadelphia (although monuments to Confederate prisoners of war stand in Chicago, Illinois; Elmira, New York; and Sandusky, Ohio). "Fate denied them . . ." is also found at cemeteries or courthouses across Virginia.

197. Jewish Confederates Tablet

Monument is a bronze tablet set in a granite shaft and base.
LOCATION: West of pyramid
DATE: 2006
MEDIA: Bronze, granite

> [STAR OF DAVID]
> 1861–1865
> "Shemeang Yisroel"
> ADONOY ELOHOAINOD, ADONOY ACHOD!
> HEAR, O ISRAEL

IN BLESSED AND ETERNAL MEMORY OF THE
SOUTH'S SONS
AND DAUGHTERS OF ABRAHAM. UPON THE
BATTLEFIELDS AND HOMEFRONT IN
DIXIE'S LAND THEY GAVE ALL TO THE
CAUSE OF THE CONFEDERACY.

This Jewish Confederate monument draws upon the Shema, the great confession of Israel's monotheistic faith, is recited morning and evening by observing Jews, and is taken from Deuteronomy 6:4–9. The traditional translation—with Hebrew (as opposed to Yiddish) transliterates in this fashion:

Shma Israel—Hear O Israel

Adonai Eloheinu—The Lord our God

Adonai Echad—The Lord is One.

Shema Yisrael or Shema

- The two "Richmond" granite blocks that make up the monument were taken from the Marshall/Richmond Theatre, which stood at Seventh and Broad streets in Richmond.
- Stones placed atop the marker follow a tradition of unknown origins in Jewish cemeteries.
- The expression "Daughters of Abraham" is unusual, occurring only once in the New Testament (Lk. 13:10–17) and not at all in the Hebrew Bible.
- Though there can be little doubt of the intention, the word Jewish does not appear.

198. Drewry's Bluff Shaft

Monument is a granite base and shaft.

DATE: May 30, 1927

MEDIUM: Granite

TO 52 OF OUR
CONFEDERATE SOLDIERS
WHO DIED IN SERVICE AT
DREWRYS BLUFF
1861–1865
RE-INTERRED BY
JUNIOR HOLLYWOOD MEMORIAL
ASSOCIATION
THIS STONE PLACED BY
HOLLYWOOD MEMORIAL ASSOCIATION
ON MEMORIAL DAY, MAY 30, 1927.
"ONLY THE FORGOTTEN ARE DEAD."

This monument is typical of the markers for the many reinterment projects surrounding the Pyramid. These men were likely nonbattle casualties from the grounds of the fort at Drewry's Bluff. The fort still stands, seven miles south of Richmond in Chesterfield County. The site rises ninety feet above the James River, commands a sharp bend in the river's course, and withstood several assaults. Fortification of the site began on March 17, 1862, by the men of the Southside Artillery, Captain Augustus Drewry commanding. The fort was held until the fall of Richmond in April 1865, when it was abandoned and its garrison joined the retreat of the Confederate Army to Appomattox. It is now on National Park Service grounds.

199. Arch, Confederate Officers' Section

Monument is a granite arch.

DATE: October 1918
MEDIUM: Granite

1861–1865
CONFEDERATE OFFICERS SECTION
ERECTED BY THE
JR. HOLLYWOOD MEMORIAL ASSO.
OCT. 1918

A two-year fundraising drive by the Junior Hollywood Memorial Association led to this thirteen-and-a-half-foot granite arch with a funeral urn surmounting it. Five Confederate generals are buried here. John C. C. Sanders, the only one killed in action, died at the age of twenty-four in the battle of the Weldon Railroad.

The dedications ceremonies for the monument evidently had a raucous element to them. Members of the association were so rowdy that they were almost unmanageable. They were readily identified: they wore gray caps and waved Confederate flags for the occasion. They were finally herded into buses for the parade because they would not keep in line for marching. Mrs. Sidney Johnson unveiled the arch, and members of the "Grandchildren of the Confederacy" provided music.

Also buried at Hollywood Cemetery are the following generals: Joseph R. Anderson, James J. Archer, Robert H. Chilton, Philip St. George Cocke, Raleigh E. Colston, John R. Cooke, Henry Heth, Eppa Hunton, John D. Imboden, Edward Johnson, David R. Jones, Samuel Jones, Fitzhugh Lee, Thomas M. Logan, John Pegram, William E. Starke, Walter H. Stevens, James Ewell Brown Stuart, Isaac M. St. John, William R. Terry, R. Lindsay Walker, and Henry A. Wise.

South Richmond

200. Wise Street Cemetery Tablet

Monument is a granite shaft behind a chain-link fence.
LOCATION: Wise and 24th streets, 23223
DATE: October 6, 1939
MEDIUM: Granite

HERE REST MORE THAN ONE HUNDRED
SOUTH CAROLINA SOLDIERS WHO DIED
IN THE HOSPITAL IN MANCHESTER VA.
1861–1865
ELLIOTT GRAYS CHAPTER
UNITED DAUGHTERS OF THE CONFEDERACY
ERECTED OCTOBER 6, 1939

Data is incomplete on this monument. The grounds of the Weisiger-Carroll House (circa 1765) at 2408 Bainbridge Street served as a hospital for Confederates, and bones are frequently found on the lot of the house. This monument stands on the next block, behind the house but in front of the Wise Street Station, an Egyptian revival style building of the Richmond Department of Public Utilities, which is directly behind this monument. It is unclear whether this building intrudes on any gravesites.

- A 'South Carolina Hospital' is mentioned in an 1862 list of hospitals as standing near here at Mayo's Bridge in Manchester, probably in one of the buildings of the Manchester Cotton Factories.

201. Maury Cemetery Tablet

Monument is a triangular granite shaft.
LOCATION: 2700 Maury Street, 23224
DATE: 1930
MEDIUM: Granite

[CROSSED C.S.A. BATTLE FLAG
AND VIRGINIA FLAG]
ERECTED BY
ELLIOTT GRAYS CHAPTER
U.D.C.
1930.

The Elliott Grays Chapter of the United Daughters of the Confederacy erected several monuments in Manchester, now South Richmond, in the 1930s. Several wartime hospitals were located in this area, but most of the dead buried in Manchester were reinterred in Maury Cemetery as development occurred.

- This U.D.C. chapter remains active. It has outlived its wartime namesake, the Elliott Grays, a Manchester militia unit that served as Company I, 6th Virginia Infantry.

Fauquier County
Warrenton Cemetery

202. Central Column

Monument is a plinth, base, dado, shaft, and pedestal, surmounted by woman standing, in mourning.
LOCATION: Main Street to Keith Street, 20186
DATE: May 30, 1877
MEDIA: Granite, marble
Front

[RELIEF OF FLAG, MUSKETS, SWORD,
STACKED CANNON BALLS, AND CANNON,
WITH BARREL POINTED DOWN]

CONFEDERATE DEAD
SIX HUNDRED.
VIRGINIA'S DAUGHTERS TO VIRGINIA'S
DEFENDERS.
—
HERE ON THE SOIL OF VIRGINIA
THEY SLEEP, AS
SLEEPS A HERO ON
HIS UNSURRENDERED SHIELD
WILSON & SANDS
RICHMOND VA.
—
GO, TELL THE SOUTHRONS WE LIE HERE
FOR THE RIGHT OF THEIR STATES.
THEY NEVER FAIL WHO DIE
IN A GREAT CAUSE.
—
GOD WILL JUDGE THE RIGHT.

Warrenton's 1877 shaft is grim and funereal, but the claims ascribed to the "600 Dead" are the most provocative in northern Virginia. "Virginia's Daughters" give tribute; Virginia's "Confederate Dead" answer; the passerby is called. The call concludes with a paraphrase of the Confederate motto, "Deo Vindice": "God will Judge the Right."

This monument stands over a mass grave of dead removed from shallow burial graves and reinterred here. Warrenton Hospital opened in 1861, but the majority of its patients were casualties of the battle of Manassas, August 30–31, 1862, with some from the battle of Chantilly on September 1, 1862. The hospital became a collection of appropriated buildings. Casualties were treated in private homes, barns, businesses, churches, a Masons' lodge, an Oddfellows' hall, and a picnic grounds. Wooden headboards identifying the dead were used for firewood by Union troops, but at this writing only eighty of the dead remain unknown, thanks to research in the 1990s that culminated in the wall and roster cited below.

Former Confederate general Wade Hampton gave an unabashedly unapologetic speech at the dedication ceremonies on Decoration Day, May 30, 1877. Hampton justified the war as a veritable Second American Revolution. That stance—a lost cause but a righteous one—gradually gained favor in the South. Hampton declared:

> Why should we admit we are in the wrong? . . . We believe we have truth on our side; let us then assert and maintain our faith, and God will in His own good time make it manifest that we were right. If we were wrong in our struggle, then was the Declaration of Independence in '76 a terrible mistake, and the revolution to which it led a palpable crime; Washington should be stigmatized as traitor and Benedict Arnold canonised as patriot. If the principles which justified the first revolution were true in 1776, they were no less true in that of 1861. The success of the former can add not one jot or tittle to the abstract truth of the principles which gave it birth, nor can the failure of the latter destroy one particle of those ever-living principles. If Washington was a patriot, Lee cannot have been a rebel; if the grand enunciation of the truths of the Declaration of Independence made Jefferson immortal, the observance of them cannot make Davis a traitor.

- The Fauquier Memorial Association sponsored the monument, which was erected at a cost of $2,650.
- John S. Mosby is interred beside his wife near the monument. Also buried here: John Q. Marr, first Southern soldier killed in action, and generals Lunsford Lomax

and William H. F. Payne.
- The statement "They never fail, who die in a great cause" is attributed to Lord Byron and is taken from *Marino Faliero*, act 2, scene 2.

203. Memorial Wall

Monument is a wall two feet high encircling the shaft.
DATE: May 24, 1998
MEDIUM: Granite

THE MEMORIAL WALL TO NAME THE FALLEN
SPONSORED BY
BLACK HORSE CHAPTER #9, UNITED
DAUGHTERS OF THE CONFEDERACY
DEDICATED MAY 24, 1998
BENEFACTORS
[ROSTER]
TRUSTEES
[ROSTER]
IN MEMORIAM

This granite wall is inscribed with the names of 520 of the estimated 600 dead buried here. The roster is based on the research of Robert E. Smith, who undertook this project initially as part of a search for a relative and ancestor. The wall was sponsored by the Black Horse Chapter of the U.D.C. and was dedicated May 24, 1998.

- Memorialized on the wall are Confederate soldiers from ten states: Alabama, Florida, Georgia, Louisiana, Mississippi, North Carolina, South Carolina, Tennessee, Texas, and Virginia.

Warrenton Courthouse

204. Col. John S. Mosby

Monument is a granite plinth, base, dado, and obelisk with bronze plaque and relief of Mosby.
LOCATION: 6 Court Street, 20186
DATE: June 26, 1920
MEDIA: Bronze, granite
Front

[BRONZE PLAQUE]
THIS TRIBUTE IS AFFECTIONATELY
DEDICATED TO
COL. JOHN S. MOSBY,
WHOSE DEEDS OF VALOR AND
HEROIC DEVOTION TO STATE

AND SOUTHERN, [SIC] PRINCIPLES ARE
THE PRIDE AND ADMIRATION
OF HIS SOLDIER COMRADES
AND FELLOW COUNTRYMEN.

—

[BAS-RELIEF OF MOSBY]

—

[BRONZE PLAQUE]
HE HAS LEFT A NAME
THAT WILL LIVE TILL
HONOR, VIRTUE, COURAGE,
ALL, SHALL CEASE TO
CLAIM THE HOMAGE OF
THE HEART.

—

JOHN SINGLETON MOSBY
LAWYER
SOLDIER
PATRIOT
DEC. 3, 1833
MAY 30, 1916

The Mosby obelisk is an early commemorative-era tribute to a local lawyer who established himself in the pantheon of Confederate heroes. His notoriety derives from his service as a partisan, principally in the Piedmont—"Mosby's Confederacy"—from 1863 to 1865, with the 43rd Cavalry Battalion, later the Partisan Rangers.

This is one of only two courthouse monuments to an individual; the other is the J. E. B. Stuart marker at Stuart, Virginia. The monument honors a man who left a singular legacy. The memorial praises Mosby's devotion to "State and Southern Principles" but describes him in dichotomous ways. His primary profession was as a lawyer before and after the war, and, in fact, Mosby argued cases in the Warrenton courthouse. However, the relief shows him in uniform, and it was as a soldier that Mosby won fame. Ultimately he earned admiration on both sides of the Mason-Dixon Line. Like other relatively young veterans such as E. Porter Alexander or, for that matter, the Union soldier Joshua L. Chamberlain, he lived long enough and had the ambition and wherewithal to shape the rhetoric of his reputation and legacy.

Upperville

205. Ivy Hill Cemetery Obelisk, Upperville

Monument is an obelisk surmounting a plinth, base, and dado.
LOCATION: 9194 John S. Mosby Highway, 20184
DATE: 1894
MEDIUM: Granite
Front

> TRUTH, COURAGE & PATRIOTISM
> SHALL ENDURE FOREVER.
> CONFEDERATE DEAD
> RESTORED 1989
> UNITED DAUGHTERS OF THE CONFEDERACY
> DISTRICT OF COLUMBIA AND
> VIRGINIA DIVISIONS
> —
> [7 NAMES]
> —
> [BLANK]
> —
> [7 NAMES, 2 UNKNOWN]
> ERECTED 1894
> UPPERVILLE CONFEDERATE VETERANS

Upperville was the site of cavalry action during the Gettysburg Campaign. Federal troopers under Brig. Gen. Alfred Pleasonton clashed with Maj. Gen. J. E. B. Stuart's Confederate cavalry screen on June 21, 1863. The Confederates blunted the assault, and some four hundred casualties resulted. There are sixteen headstones and sixteen names on the monument, all cavalrymen, presumably from that action. The legible names match, though some are too weathered to read.

Marshall

206. City Cemetery Obelisk
Monument is an obelisk set on a plinth and base.

LOCATION: East on V.R. 55, 20115
DATE: 1928
MEDIUM: Granite

> [SEAL OF THE CONFEDERACY]
> IN MEMORY OF OUR
> CONFEDERATE DEAD.
> ERECTED BY
> PIEDMONT CHAPTER U.D.C.
> NO. 169 1928

Data is limited on this monument. The marker is terse and plain, but cemetery elegies of this type are common in rural Virginia. Perspectives on the past, present and future are brought together: the seal of the Confederacy and Confederate dead representing the past; the U.D.C. Piedmont Chapter representing the present, and the granite medium intended to last to perpetuity.

207. Col. John S. Mosby Obelisk

Monument is a granite obelisk.
LOCATION: Corner of Frost and West Main streets
DATE: 1928
MEDIUM: Granite

> HERE, APRIL 21, 1865
> COL. JOHN S. MOSBY
> DISBANDED HIS
> GALLANT PARTISAN
> RANGERS—THE
> FORTY-THIRD
> BATTALION
> VIRGINIA CAVALRY

Marshall (called Salem during the war) is the site where Mosby disbanded the 43rd Virginia Cavalry on April 21, 1865. The disbanding—Mosby famously chose not to surrender—is distinctive. So too is the dual identity of his men: they are the "gallant partisan rangers" and only secondarily the 43rd Battalion.

- The address:
Soldiers: I have summoned you together for the last time. The vision we have cherished for a free and independent country has vanished and that country is now the spoil of a conqueror. I disband your organization in preference to surrendering it to our enemies. I am no longer your commander. After an association of more than two eventful years I part from you with a just pride in the fame of your achievements and grateful recollections of your generous kindness to myself. And now at this moment of bidding you a final adieu accept the assurance of my unchanging confidence and regard.   Farewell.

- The actual site of the disbanding, now a housing subdivision, was a field about two tenths of a mile to the north.

Rappahannock County

208. Washington, Courthouse Common Soldier

Monument is an obelisk set on a plinth, base, and dado.
LOCATION: Gay Street 22747
DATE: 1900
MEDIA: Granite, marble, sandstone
Front

> THIS MONUMENT
> erected through the efforts

and consecrated devotion
of the local chapter of the
DAUGHTERS OF THE CONFEDERACY
and other votaries
of Southern Chivalry.
a tribute of honor and affectionate
regard for the unwavering patriotism
faultless fealty, and dauntless courage,
of the heroic men from
Rappahannock County,
who so faithfully served their cause and
country in the War Between the States.
WILDERNESS.
DEATHLESS DEAD
CO. B. 49TH VA INFANTRY
CO. G. 49TH VA INFANTRY
[9 NAMES]   [27 NAMES]
—

THE WORLD SHALL YET DECIDE
IN TRUTHS CLEAR FAR OFF LIGHT,
THAT THOSE WHO SERVED
WITH LEE AS GUIDE,
WERE HEROES IN THE RIGHT.
COLD HARBOR.
HALLOWED NAMES
CO. B 7TH VA INFANTRY
CO. G. 7TH VA INFANTRY
[40 NAMES]   [2 NAMES]
—

[BAS-RELIEF OF R. E. LEE]
MANASSAS.
HEROES OF RAPPAHANNOCK
CO. B. 6TH VA CAVALRY.
CO.B. 7TH VA INFANTRY.
CO. G. 13TH VA. "   CO. G. 7TH, VA. "
WITH MOSBY'S MEN 43, BAT.   " B. 49TH, VA. "
WITH WHITE'S BAT.   " G. 49TH, VA. "
CO. C. 4TH VA. CAVALRY   " I. 49TH, VA. "
CO. D. 4TH VA "   D V. M. I.
—

[BAS-RELIEF OF CONFEDERATE SOLDIER]
CHANCELLORSVILLE
SACRED MARTYRS
MOSBY'S MEN 43RD BAT.   CO B ___ CAVALRY
[6 NAMES]   [27 NAMES]
CO. G. 12TH VA. CAVALRY
[9 NAMES]

The marble lettering is weathered and hard to read in this Herbert Barbee design, but the inscription is imposing, with an unabashed claim that the "heroic men from Rappahannock" were "Heroes in the Right."

The four, arguably five battles inscribed—Wilderness (1864), Chancellorsville (1863), Manassas (both 1861 and 1862), Cold Harbor (1864)—were major engagements in the Piedmont area north of Richmond. All of them, with the arguable exception of Wilderness, were Confederate victories.

- Most lists of participants on Confederate monuments are not comprehensive. Of this site a county history notes that "Possibly 800 of our young men—and sometimes old men—fought in the Civil War. This monument lists 116 dead, but the number was far greater, as those who died from disease were not always listed, nor were those who came home to die from wounds, consumption, or typhoid."

- The two mentions of "Mosby's men," are consonant with the renown and "irregular" nature of the service of the Partisan Rangers.

- "With Whites Bat." is White's Battalion, organized in the fall of 1862, first commanded by Elijah White and designated the 35th Cavalry Battalion. What the distinction "with" means is not clear.

- A blank space for the twenty-seven names associated with a "Co B" has no further identification.

- Decorative stacked muskets, cannon balls, a gun belt, and a holster are thought to have been removed from the top of the monument shortly after the dedication date. Some relics are in the keeping of the Rappahannock County Historical Society.

- There has been difficulty dating this monument, but the *Culpeper Exponent* of May 25, 1900, calls it the work of Herbert Barbee and notes that the contract for the statue was to be signed May 25, 1900.

Culpeper County

209. Courthouse Common Soldier

Monument is a private soldier standing at parade rest on a pedestal surmounting a plinth, base, dado, and shaft.

LOCATION: 135 West Cameron Street, 22701
DATE: May 31, 1911
MEDIA: Bronze, granite
Front

> [C.S.A. BATTLE FLAG]
> CULPEPER'S MEMORIAL
> TO HER
> CONFEDERATE SOLDIERS
> 1861–1865
> BY
> A. P. HILL CAMP NO. 2 C. V.
> AND THE CITIZENS OF THIS COUNTY
> 1911
> —
> [MEDALLION: SEAL OF THE CONFEDERACY]
> —
> [MEDALLION: SEAL OF VIRGINIA]

Confederate veterans are the most conspicuous sponsors of this monument. Their affirmation of the secessionist stance is prominent, this in a town that marks the American Revolution with a monument to the Culpeper Minutemen.

Culpeper residents unanimously voted to approve Virginia's Ordinance of Secession on May 23, 1861. Shortly thereafter, the Culpeper Minutemen assembled at the same site where the 1775 Minutemen had organized. They carried the same rattlesnake flag and were eventually mustered in as Company B of the 13th Virginia Infantry. The display of the seal of Virginia might be expected, but the seal of the Confederacy, inscribed fifty years after the war's end, is more provocative.

Culpeper's connection to Confederate Lt. Gen. A. P. Hill, who was born in a house still standing, only a block away, is also noted. The United Daughters of the Confederacy placed a plaque up the block on the corner building. It reads:

> THIS MARKS THE SITE OF
> THE BOYHOOD HOME
> OF
> GEN. A. P. HILL, C.S.A.
> ERECTED BY
> THE CULPEPER CHAPTER, U.D.C.
> 1932

210. Fairview Cemetery Obelisk

Monument is an obelisk surmounting a plinth, base, and dado.
LOCATION: U.S. 522, Sperryville Pike, to Gate Four, 22701
DATE: July 21, 1881
MEDIA: Bronze, granite, marble
Front

[CROSSED C.S.A. BATTLE FLAG AND
SECOND NATIONAL FLAG]
[RELIEF OF FLAGS AND CANNON]
IN MEMORY OF
OUR CONFEDERATE DEAD
VIRGINIA:
[30 NAMES]
LOUISIANA:
[25 NAMES]
MARYLAND:
[1 NAME]
TEXAS:
[1 NAME]
TENNESSEE:
[2 NAMES]
—
SOUTH CAROLINA:
[53 NAMES]
REG'T UNKNOWN:
[26 NAMES]
UNKNOWN: 87
—
GEORGIA:
[57 NAMES]
NORTH CAROLINA:
[17 NAMES]
—
ALABAMA:
[33 NAMES]
MISSISSIPPI:
[34 NAMES]

Fundraising by the local Ladies Memorial Association resulted in this granite shaft about fifteen feet high standing over a mass grave. Ten states and the names of 279 Confederate soldiers are inscribed on four bronze tablets, along with 87 unknown. More than one hundred battles or skirmishes occurred between 1862 and 1864 at or near Culpeper, including Cedar Mountain, Rappahannock Station, Kelly's Ford, and Brandy Station. Both sides camped at various times around Culpeper and along the Orange and Alexandria Railroad.

The town's three churches and the courthouse and courthouse grounds were used as hospitals and were collectively called "Culpeper General Hospital." Most of the dead were initially buried at a site south of Culpeper—the Old Confederate Cemetery on the Jameson Estate near the present day Culpeper United Methodist Church. After the war they were reinterred here. Sectional and national distinctions are preserved to this day: this may be a mass grave, but these are Confederate soldiers, ranked by state. There are exceptions. At least one name is that of a Union soldier, Thomas Needham of Massachusetts, whose name was incorrectly linked to a Mississippi unit. Needham's fellow Union soldiers are buried in the national cemetery across town, at the end of Stevens Street.

211. Rixeyville, Little Fork Church, Shaft

Monument is a plinth, base, dado, and shaft, surmounted by female figure.
LOCATION: 16461 Oak Shade Road, 22737
DATE: May 25, 1904
MEDIA: Granite, marble

Front

1861,
AFFECTIONATELY DEDICATED TO
THE LITTLE FORK RANGERS.
(CO. D. 4, VA. CAVALRY.)
FOR HEROIC DEEDS, AND
PATRIOTIC DEVOTION.
1865.

—

[BAS-RELIEF OF CONFEDERATE SOLDIER]

—

Firm as the firmest where duty led,
They hurried without a falter;
Bold as the boldest, they fought and bled,
The battles were won, but the fields were red.
And the blood of their fresh young hearts was shed.
On their Country's hallowed altar.

Ryan

—

Company D. 4. Va. Cavalry
[126 NAMES IN FOUR COLUMNS, WITH
PERIODS AFTER EACH NAME]

This colonial-era church site dates from 1773–76, the congregation from circa 1731. The brick church grounds served as an assembly place and drill field for the Little Fork Rangers which, as the inscription notes, became Company D, 4th Virginia Cavalry and served until Appomattox.

The marble of the Little Fork monument is weathered, and the scale is modest, but the five-foot figure of a "southern maiden," as a church history calls her, crowning the shaft of this fifteen-foot monument has a languorous, cheerful appearance. She caresses a sheathed sword, wears a crown of eleven stars, and is wrapped in a battle flag. If she seems idealized, one should note that at Amelia Springs, where Robert E. Lee stayed the night of April 4, 1865, during the Appomattox campaign, a young woman refused to let an aide enter until he draped a Confederate flag around her.

The monument was dedicated on the forty-third anniversary of the unit's enrollment for wartime service. In the unit's early days, crowds of people turned out to watch the company drills on the church grounds. Union soldiers, quartered in the area during the winter of 1863–64, tore out most of the wood in the building for fire or winter quarters.

- Herbert Barbee is the sculptor. "Ryan" is Father Abram J. Ryan, who is also excerpted on the Luray monument. The larger context reads:

AND THE DAY WAS WON BUT
THE FIELD WAS RED,
AND THE BLOOD OF HIS FRESH
YOUNG HEART WAS SHED
ON HIS COUNTRY'S HALLOWED ALTAR.
ON THE TRAMPLED BREAST
OF THE BATTLE PLAIN
WHERE THE FOREMOST RANKS
HAD WRESTLED . . .

212. Brandy Station, Battlefield Tablet

Monument is a bronze tablet set on a granite base.
LOCATION: C.R. 685 off U.S. 15/29, 22714
DATE: circa 1927
MEDIA: Bronze, fieldstone

BATTLE OF BRANDY STATION
GREATEST CAVALRY BATTLE
OF THE CIVIL WAR
FOUGHT JUNE 9, 1863
GEN. J. E. B. STUART DEFEATED
GEN. A. PLEASONTON
CONFEDERATES ENGAGED,
10,200. FEDERALS, 10,900
CASUALTIES, CONFEDERATES,
485. FEDERALS, 866
THIS IS FLEETWOOD HILL
THE CRUCIAL POSITION
FINALLY OCCUPIED BY THE CONFEDERATES

Union cavalry crossed the Rappahannock River and surprised the Confederates here, including Maj. Gen. J. E. B. Stuart. That Stuart defeated Brig. Gen. Alfred Pleasonton is a central claim of the memorial: Stuart's troopers held the field after the action, and the claim is justified. Stuart's victory was well earned, however. The tide of battle changed repeatedly, from Union ascendancy to Confederate and back again. That they "Finally Occupied" Fleetwood Hill, where this marker stands, hints at the challenge the Confederate troopers faced in warding off the Federals, who finally withdrew and recrossed the Rappahannock.

The claim that this was the "Greatest Cavalry" action is challenged by the Trevilians battlefield tablet, but Brandy Station was the largest cavalry battle of the war in terms of numbers engaged. It was also the opening engagement of the Gettysburg Campaign. The battle marked a high point of the Confederate cavalry service in the east, but from here on, Federal cavalry would prove to be a formidable, even superior opponent.

- The use of the term "Civil War" is uncommon. "War Between the States" was the preferred expression and remains so from many Southern perspectives.

213. Col. John Pelham Obelisk at U.S. 15/29

Monument is a marble shaft set on a granite pedestal.

LOCATION: Intersection of U.S. 15–29 and Beverly Ford Road (C.R. 685), 22734
DATE: 1926
MEDIA: Bronze, fieldstone, marble

IN MEMORY
OF
MAJOR JOHN PELHAM
BORN SEPT. 7, 1838
IN CALHOUN CO. ALA.
MORTALLY WOUNDED
MARCH 17, 1863
NEAR KELLEY'S FORD VA.

—

BASE STONE
FROM KELLEY'S

FORD BATTLEFIELD
NEAR SPOT WHERE
PELHAM FELL.

—

ERECTED BY
GEO. E.
AND HIS WIFE
LENORA J. DOUGLAS
1926.

—

LIKE MARSHAL NEY
ONE OF THE
BRAVEST OF
THE BRAVE.

The cause Maj. John Pelham fought for is not mentioned, but his courage is praised in this tribute given by George E. Douglas. *Confederate Veteran* called Douglas "a merchant and farmer living near Elkwood, now an elderly man, who [grew] up in the heart of Virginia made historic by the battlefields of the War between the States."

Note the comparison between Pelham and Marshal Ney. Michel Ney (1769–1815), Marshal of France, was called 'the bravest of the brave' by Napoleon. The reference to Ney is unique in Virginia monuments, but American military tactics, vocabulary, and uniforms drew upon the French military, and Civil War–era officers

often imitated Napoleon when they posed for photographs.

- *Confederate Veteran* notes that "The shaft stands on a corner of the grounds of the Douglas home, on the highway, approximately marking the spot where the cavalcade bearing the unconscious form of Maj. Pelham reached the highway on its way to Culpeper the evening after the battle."
- A granite shaft at the base reads:

> DEED OF GIFT TO
> CULPEPER CHAPTER
> UDC #73
> 20 JAN. 1998

- A bronze plaque in front of the monument reads:

> PROPERTY PELHAM
> CHAPTER
> U.D.C.
> BRMINGHAM
> ALA.

214. Col. John Pelham Tablet Near Kelly's Ford

Monument is a granite shaft set on a base.

> [CROSSED CANNON BARRELS]
> MAJOR JOHN PELHAM, C.S.A.,
> COMMANDING
> THE STUART HORSE ARTILLERY,
> WAS MORTALLY WOUNDED
> AT THIS SITE IN
> THE BATTLE OF KELLY'S FORD
> MARCH 17, 1863.
> ERECTED 1981
> BY ADMIRERS OF
> THE GALLANT PELHAM

Here some eight hundred Southern cavalrymen under Brig. Gen. W. H. Fitzhugh Lee repulsed a Union foray of twenty-one hundred troopers under Brig. Gen. William W. Averell. Some two hundred casualties resulted in this action along the Rappahannock River. The action was fierce but tactically indecisive. The battlefield is commemorated only with this shaft in memory of the "Gallant" Pelham, who suffered a mortal head wound when a shell exploded above him.

The marker stands near the extant stone wall in the woods used by Federal cavalry during the battle. The C. F. Phelps Wildlife Management Area owns and maintains the grounds.

215. Cedar Mountain, Battlefield Tablet

Monument is a bronze tablet set on a granite base.

LOCATION: West of intersection of C.R. 657 (General Winder Road) and U.S. 15, south of Culpeper, 22701

DATE: circa 1927

MEDIA: Bronze, fieldstone

> BATTLE OF CEDAR MOUNTAIN
> FOUGHT AUGUST 9. 1862. A
> CONFEDERATE VICTORY.
> COMMANDERS
> CONFEDERATE, GEN. T. J.
> "STONEWALL" JACKSON
> FEDERALS, GEN. JOHN POPE
> CASUALTIES, CONFEDERATE,
> 1369. FEDERAL, 2263
> GEN. C. S. WINDER, C.S.A. FELL HERE
> THIS IS THE ONLY BATTLEFIELD ON WHICH
> GEN. STONEWALL JACKSON DREW HIS SWORD.

Some twenty-five thousand troops under Maj. Gen. Nathaniel P. Banks gave a creditable fight against a force of seventeen thousand men under Maj. Gen. Thomas J. Jackson but were defeated. (Maj. Gen. John Pope had overall command of Union forces but was not on the field.) Fortunes swayed, the outcome was uncertain, Confederate Brig. Gen. Charles S. Winder was killed near this site, but victory was won, and it gave Lee the initiative as the war in Virginia shifted from the peninsula to northern Virginia. Jackson, though, is the focus of the United Daughters of the Confederacy narrative. The humor and notoriety of the scabbard incident alluded to here loom large in the history of the battle, since it was not the sword that was drawn, but the scabbard. Capt. Jedediah Hotchkiss, who rode beside Jackson, described the moment in a letter:

> I recollect well his attempt to draw his long cavalry sabre to help him stop the rout, when he found it so rusted in from non use, that he could not withdraw it . . . so he deliberately unsnapped it from his belt holdings and used it scabbard and all on the heads of the fleeing panic-stricken troops.

Artillery was posted here and across present-day U.S. 15 and dueled with Federal troops to the northeast. Jackson rallied his men near this point after Union attacks shattered the Confederate line.

Madison County

216. Madison, Courthouse Common Soldier

Monument is a private soldier standing at parade rest surmounting a plinth, base, dado, and shaft.

LOCATION: 2 Main Street, 22727

DATE: October 31, 1901

MEDIUM: Granite

> 1861–1865
> MADISON COUNTY
> [SEAL OF VIRGINIA]
> CONFEDERATE DEAD
> PLANT THE FAIR COLUMN
> OVER THE VACANT GRAVE
> A HEROE'S HONORS
> LET A HERO HAVE

The rural setting of this county seat offers a stark contrast to the Confederate memorial's somber subject matter, decorative extravagance, extended shaft, and stolid granite composition. The United Confederate Veteran sponsors may have intended defiance by sponsoring and erecting this monument, but at least one of the local residents accepted it as a benign, placid presence. Nancy Byrd Turner's poem, written shortly after the dedication, imagines the soldier

> Still watching far with tranquil eyes,
>
> The blue Virginia mountains rise
>
> Into the blue Virginia skies
>
> Against the sunset west.

The monument was shipped by train to Orange and arrived in Madison by wagon. Ground was broken at the site September 19, 1900. The United Confederate Veterans presented it to the county on October 31, 1901.

- The expression "Plant the Fair Column" is also inscribed on the courthouse monument at Gloucester and at Petersburg's Blandford Cemetery.
- Madison County makes claims to a second disbanding and farewell by John S. Mosby.

217. Cedar Hill Cemetery Tablet

Monument is a granite shaft set on a base.
LOCATION: Main Street, north of courthouse
DATE: April 26, 1910
MEDIUM: Granite

> [CROSSED C.S.A. BATTLE FLAG
> AND NATIONAL FLAG]
> 1861–1865
> TO THE UNKNOWN
> CONFEDERATE DEAD

At least six stones mark the graves of unknown soldiers where this marker stands: two stones are southwest of the shaft; six stones and a tombstone marking service to the Confederacy are to the west.

The Piedmont Episcopal Church, near the courthouse, served as a hospital for soldiers wounded in engagements in the area, including James City and Jack's Shop.

Greene County

218. Stanardsville, Courthouse Obelisk

Monument is an obelisk set on a plinth, base, and dado.
LOCATION: 85 Stanard Street, 22973
DATE: 1932
MEDIUM: Granite
Front

> IN MEMORY OF OUR
> CONFEDERATE DEAD
> 1861–1865
> "DEAD—YET STILL THEY SPEAK"
> ERECTED BY THE
> BLUE RIDGE GRAYS.
> U.D.C.
> GREENE CO. CHAPTER
> —1932—
> [BLANK]
> —
>
> UNIDENTIFIED

SOLDIERS
FROM GENERAL
EWELL'S ARMY
—
[BLANK]

Stanardsville's obelisk is in front of the Jeffersonian-style courthouse dating from 1838. The monument was erected late in the cycle of county seat monuments. Five other veterans' monuments on the grounds came after it, however, and have the same design features. From left to right, lined up before the courthouse are matching obelisks, respectively, to veterans of Vietnam, Korea, the Civil War, World War I, and World War II.

Like other northern Virginia monuments, this is a dual commemoration: to the community's dead and to those left here—the "Unidentified Solders from Gen. Ewell's Army." Maj. Gen. Richard S. Ewell's troops—a division, not an army—paused here during the Shenandoah Valley campaign near Swift Run Gap in April 1862. Skirmishing also occurred near here February 29, 1864, but no major battles were fought. The Confederate soldiers are the quick and the dead, both living and dead: "Dead—yet still they speak."

Albemarle County and City of Charlottesville

219. Charlottesville, Courthouse Common Soldier

Monument is a private soldier, in bronze, standing with musket held in both hands at waist, the whole surmounting a plinth, base, dado, and pedestal.
LOCATION: 606 East Market Street, 22902
DATE: May 9, 1909
MEDIA: Bronze, granite
Front

1861 VIRGINIA 1865
[C.S.A. BATTLE FLAG, RAISED RELIEF]
[CROSSED CANNON BARRELS]
—
1909
ERECTED BY
THE DAUGHTERS OF
THE CONFEDERACY,
ALBEMARLE COUNTY,
AND THE CITY OF
CHARLOTTESVILLE
TO COMMEMORATE
THE HEROISM OF
THE VOLUNTEERS OF
CHARLOTTESVILLE AND
ALBEMARLE COUNTY
"LOVE MAKES
MEMORY ETERNAL."
[CROSSED MUSKETS]
—
CONFEDERATE SOLDIERS
DEFENDERS
OF THE
RIGHTS OF THE STATES.
[SEAL OF VIRGINIA]
—
WARRIORS:
YOUR VALOR;
YOUR DEVOTION TO DUTY;
YOUR FORTITUDE
UNDER PRIVATIONS:
TEACH US
HOW TO SUFFER
AND GROW STRONG.
"LEST WE FORGET."
[CROSSED SWORDS]

This twelve-foot-high courthouse memorial combines a tribute—"Love makes . . ."—with a declaration that these "Warriors" should "Teach Us How to Suffer and Grow Strong."

The sculpted Confederate soldier by Caspar Buberl is life-sized but may be an idealized conception of how veterans conceived themselves almost fifty years after the war. He is no callow youth: this soldier is in his forties, at least twice as old as the average, as one observer notes, who adds that the soldier is armed and seems ready to fight but has no cartridge box, cap box, or canteen.

Confederate Veteran gave particular attention to the symbolism behind the materials and weightiness of the monument:

> This is of blocks of solid granite, the first two left unhewn to signify strength; next a block highly polished, then a die four feet square. This is surmounted by the main die, which holds the pedestal for the beautiful bronze statue of a Confederate soldier. . . . The entire height of the monument is twenty feet six inches and its weight forty-five tons.

In addition, the monument has a copper box with

> . . . many interesting memorials, Confederate money, roster of soldiers that left Charlottesville, list of the dead, lists of those whose untiring efforts made the monument possible, etc. On this box the twelve thousand-pound stone was laid, and upon this firm foundation the beautiful monument was erected."

Also buried in Charlottesville: Brig. Gen. Thomas L. Rosser at Riverview Cemetery; generals Armistead L. Long and John M. Jones in Maplewood.
- Inscribed on the base of the rear of the sculpture: "CAST BY AMERICAN BRONZE FOUNDRY CO. CHICAGO."

220. Gen. Thomas Jonathan Jackson, Equestrian Statue

Monument is an equestrian statue, in bronze, surmounting a granite plinth, base, and pedestal.

LOCATION: Jackson Park near courthouse, at Jefferson, High, and Fourth streets
DATE: October 19, 1921

MEDIA: Bronze, granite

CHANCELLORSVILLE
THOMAS JONATHAN
JACKSON
1824   1863
—
MANASSAS
VALOR   FAITH
—
THE VALLEY CAMPAIGN
THOMAS JONATHAN
JACKSON
1824   1863
—
1919

The Charlottesville Jackson monument, the work of Charles Keck, has been called one of the finest equestrian statues in the country. Jackson as legend is the focus of this monument; there is no mention of the nom de guerre, "Stonewall." Jackson—bare-headed, mounted on Little Sorrel—is accompanied by two angels. The male bears a Confederate battle flag emblem on his shield—a possible reference to Exodus 33:1–3, a promise (and a condemnation) of the "Chosen People" of Israel. The female angel has her arms clasped in prayer.

Three military actions offer touchstones of Jackson's greatest feats as a commander. The vita is selective of course: the battles of First and Second Manassas—Jackson fought at both—are apparently conflated. The Seven Days campaign—by all accounts an undistinguished aspect of Jackson's service—is not mentioned. Sharpsburg, a Confederate defeat by some assessments, a draw at best, is not mentioned—although Jackson's leadership was manifestly competent. Cedar Mountain and Chantilly—bloody, marginal Confederate victories—are not mentioned either, even though Cedar Mountain was, in Jackson's judgment, his finest battle.

- A bronze plaque at the site states that the monument and Jackson Park were donated by Paul Goodloe McIntire (1860–1952) "For the Pleasure of All Who Pass By."

221. Gen. Robert Edward Lee, Equestrian Statue

Monument is an equestrian statue, in bronze, surmounting a granite plinth, base, and pedestal.
LOCATION: Lee Park: Jeffers between First and East Second streets
DATE: May 21, 1924
MEDIA: Bronze, granite

ROBERT EDWARD LEE
1807   1870
—
ROBERT EDWARD LEE
1807   1870

This statue was a gift of Paul Goodloe McIntire, as was the Jackson statue down the street. It was erected on a city block of buildings purchased by McIntire and torn down for the park, as part of the "City Beautiful" movement of the early twentieth century. It stands just across the street from a federal office building and post office. *Confederate Veteran* enthused that "The statue has been called by critics a masterful depiction of Lee, showing as it does his dignity, nobleness and fighting spirit."

Sculptor Henry M. Schrady died before the project was completed. Leo Lentilli succeeded him. Lee is mounted but not on Traveller.

Virginia's monuments to Robert E. Lee—here and at Richmond—are majestic in appearance and understated in their inscriptions. None, apart from the 1960 monument at Roanoke, offers any testimony to Lee's significance. The Charlottesville depiction of Lee is typical, with an elaborate sculpture and a terse inscription. His importance is self-evident.

University of Virginia

222. Rotunda Tablets

Monument is two bronze plaques.
LOCATION: Rotunda off University Avenue, 22904
DATE: May 23, 1906
MEDIUM: Bronze

First tablet

THE HONOR ROLL
IN MEMORY OF
THE STUDENTS AND ALUMNI OF
THE UNIVERSITY OF VIRGINIA
WHO LOST THEIR LIVES IN THE MILITARY
SERVICE OF THE CONFEDERACY 1861–1865
[255 NAMES IN FOUR COLUMNS]
ERECTED BY THE LADIES CONFEDERATE
MEMORIAL ASSOCIATION
OF ALBEMARLE COUNTY VIRGINIA

Second tablet

THE HONOR ROLL
IN MEMORY OF
THE STUDENTS AND ALUMNI OF
THE UNIVERSITY OF VIRGINIA
WHO LOST THEIR LIVES IN THE MILITARY
SERVICE OF THE CONFEDERACY 1861–1865
[248 NAMES IN FOUR COLUMNS]
ERECTED BY THE LADIES CONFEDERATE
MEMORIAL ASSOCIATION
OF ALBEMARLE COUNTY VIRGINIA

Completed in 1826, Thomas Jefferson modeled the university library, called the Rotunda, after the Pantheon in Rome. These plaques were placed on both sides of the entryway which looks out on the "Academical Village" of the campus. Each displays a relief of a Confederate battle flag emblem on a shield surrounded by laurel branches. Below the emblem are rosters of the dead, 503 in number. Each name is marked with a cross between and the year of death. Of the university's soldiers the Reverend John Lipscomb wrote in 1871 that "Alumni of the University of Virginia [include] representatives of every Southern State, every religious denomination, every arm of the military service, and every grade short of Major-General."

- This may be the most prominent cultural, academic, or architecturally significant site for a Confederate monument. Note the tone of restraint or caution regarding the Confederacy: these are those "Who Lost their Lives in the Military Service of the Confederacy": there is no explicit endorsement of the cause.

- The "Address of Presentation" by Dr. J. William Jones included the following tribute:

[Y]ou threw yourselves unreservedly into the arms of Liberty, and laid down your all—even life itself—into her holy cause. . . . Farewell, brave comrades, beloved friends, fellow students of "Auld lang Syne," farewell, till the tryst of God beyond the river.

223. University Cemetery, Common Soldier

Monument is a private soldier, in bronze, standing, holding a musket with bayonet fixed surmounting a plinth, base, dado, and pedestal. LOCATION: Cemetery Road, near intersection of Alderman and McCormick roads

DATE: June 7, 1893
MEDIA: Bronze, granite
Front

1861 CONFEDERATE DEAD 1865
VIRGINIA
[196 NAMES]
MARYLAND
[4 NAMES]
LOUISIANA
[84 NAMES]
FATE DENIED THEM VICTORY
BUT CROWNED THEM WITH
GLORIOUS IMMORTALITY

—

GEORGIA
[224 NAMES]
MISSISSIPPI
[69 NAMES]

—

SOUTH CAROLINA
[161 NAMES]
TEXAS
[12 NAMES]
FLORIDA
[12 NAMES]
TENNESSEE
[10 NAMES]
UNASSOCIATED
[25 NAMES]
17 UNKNOWN

—

NORTH CAROLINA
[200 NAMES]
ALABAMA
[82 NAMES]

Several city buildings served as large permanent hospitals in Charlottesville during the war. The General Hospital received some 21,450 cases. Listed here are 1,096 names, including seventeen unknowns. The unknowns are recognized—uniquely but fittingly—with straight lines where their names would have been. The Confederate soldier, sculpted by Caspar Buberl, has removed his hat, as if in honor of the dead, but his weapon is ready, the musket is cocked, and his bayonet is fixed.

- The hospital complex included university buildings used as hospitals, with medical school faculty and students serving as staff.
- Also buried in University Cemetery: Gen. Carnot Posey.

Scottsville

224. Moore's Hill Cemetery Obelisk

Monument is a plinth, base, dado, and obelisk.
LOCATION: From intersection of V.R. 6, V.R. 20: north on C.R. 712 to C.R. 795 (Hardware Street) to Confederate Street, 24590
DATE: 1914
MEDIUM: Granite
Front

OUR CONFEDERATE
DEAD WHO DIED IN
THE HOSPITALS
OF SCOTTSVILLE
1861–1865

—

[RELIEF OF CROSSED SWORDS]

—
ERECTED BY THE
SCOTTSVILLE
CHAPTER U.D.C.
1914
—

[C.S.A. BATTLE FLAG]
IN MEMORY OF
COL. HENRY GANTT
MAJ. JAMES C. HILL
AND
THE OFFICERS AND
MEN OF SOUTHERN
ALBEMARLE WHO
FOUGHT UNDER THE
STARS AND BARS OF
THE CONFEDERACY

Scottsville is on the James River, some twenty miles south of Charlottesville, and its railroad access to the battlefields to the east led to the establishment of four hospitals referred to. It was one of several smaller medical facilities dispersed throughout Virginia in communities like Palmyra and Farmville.

The cemetery contains the graves of forty Confederate soldiers who died here between June 1862 and September 1863. The tombstones are arranged in four neat rows of ten. No names are inscribed, but each is marked "C. V."—Confederate Veteran. Records are extant for only ten months of the hospital's operation. According to historian Richard Nicholas, it appears that the headstones were intended to represent the graves of the forty men who died in the Scottsville hospitals during ten months of 1862–1863, not 1861–1865 as stated on the monument. Logistical issues and inadequate facilities led the Confederate Medical Department to close the Scottsville Hospital at the end of September 1863.

Henry Gantt and James Christian Hill were prominent local citizens. Gantt, a native of Scottsville and a Virginia Military Institute graduate, commanded the 19th Virginia Infantry, whose men were drawn largely from Albemarle and Charlottesville. Hill, a resident of Scottsville, was a major in the 46th Virginia Infantry. The "Dead" from Scottsville's hospi-

tals are still claimed by the U.D.C. as "Ours," despite the fact that this is not a monument to local soldiers.

- In 2001, the Scottsville U.D.C. installed a brass plaque at the cemetery with the names and units of forty of the forty-one deceased soldiers.

Orange County

225. Orange, Courthouse Common Soldier

Monument is a private soldier, in white bronze, standing at parade rest surmounting a plinth, pedestal, dado, cap, and shaft.
LOCATION: 110 North Madison Road, 22960
DATE: October 18, 1900
MEDIA: Granite, white bronze

ORANGE COUNTY
[SEAL OF VIRGINIA]
CONFEDERATE DEAD

THEY FOUGHT FOR THE RIGHT.
THEY DIED FOR THEIR COUNTRY,
CHERISH THEIR MEMORY,
IMITATE THEIR EXAMPLE.

—

CO. C. 7TH, VA. INF'TY.
[12 NAMES]
CO. E. 7TH, VA. INF'TY.
[2 NAMES]
CO. I. 6TH, VA. CAV.
[9 NAMES]
ORANGE ARTILLERY.
[13 NAMES]
WISE ARTILLERY.
[9 NAMES]
CO. C. 13TH, VA. INF'TY.
[1 NAME]

[16 NAMES]
ERECTED BY THEIR
FRIENDS AND COMRADES
OCT. 18TH, 1900

—

CO. A. 13TH, VA. INF'TY.
[36 NAMES]
CO. C. 13TH, VA. INF'TY.
[18 NAMES]
CO. F. 13TH, VA. INF'TY.
[20 NAMES]

Confederate veterans laid the cornerstone for this monument on October 18, 1898; it was dedicated and unveiled two years later, on October 18, 1900. The monument faces Main Street and was originally outfitted with an iron railing and Georgian ivy planting; in 1939 the monument was moved to accommodate the right-of-way of U.S. 15. The total cost of the monument was fifteen hundred dollars. Much of the fundraising was credited to Confederate veteran and Presbyterian minister, the Reverend Lin Cave, who was active in veterans' activities across the South.

The wartime Italian villa–style courthouse of 1849 still stands but is considerably altered. Orange served as a frequent rendezvous point for the Army of Northern Virginia. It was also a staging and bivouac area for Jackson's troops during the battle of Cedar Mountain and a base of operations and logistics for Lee's army from mid-1863 to mid-1864. It defined the action along the Rapidan River at Mine Run and the Wilderness, and it defined the heart of the Confederate winter encampment of 1863–64.

The list of the dead is not definitive. There are one hundred and forty names on the monument, but not all of those listed are from Orange County. Some were from other counties who served with Orange County units. Several of the names are veterans who died as late as 1900.

- About five thousand men were killed in Orange County during the war. A full accounting of the wartime dead from the county has never been compiled, and there is no feasible accounting for those who, buried in yards, family cemeteries, fields, or woods, remain there unnoted or unknown.
- A Confederate cemetery is part of Graham Cemetery west of Orange on V.R. 20, where most of the burials of soldiers who died in Orange General Hospital took place.

Gordonsville

226. Exchange Hotel Tablet

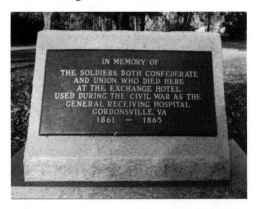

Monument is a bronze tablet set on a granite base and pedestal.
LOCATION: 400 North Main Street, 22942
MEDIA: Bronze, granite
DATE: July 25, 1993

IN MEMORY OF
THE SOLDIERS, BOTH CONFEDERATE
AND UNION, WHO DIED HERE

AT THE EXCHANGE HOTEL
USED DURING THE CIVIL WAR AS THE
GENERAL RECEIVING HOSPITAL
GORDONSVILLE VA
1861–1865

Gordonsville was a key railroad junction in central Virginia before the war. The Exchange Hotel served overnight travelers on the Virginia Central and the Orange and Alexandria railroads. During the war the hotel took in casualties by train from such actions as Second Manassas, Cedar Mountain, Brandy Station, and Trevilian's Station. Its first use as a hospital occurred after First Manassas, when it was given over to the Confederacy for the duration of the war.

As a "Receiving Hospital," it was one of the principal medical facilities in the Confederacy. The system of care that evolved here anticipated the triage methods used to this day. Doctors identified and gave priority levels to each case: patients at Gordonsville were then sent to hospitals at Charlottesville, Lynchburg, or elsewhere, depending on where they might receive the best or most suitable care for their wounds or illness. The Exchange Hotel served as headquarters for a complex so large and extensive that Gordonsville itself eventually became one large hospital. Over six thousand patients were admitted in June 1863; over twenty-three thousand between June 1863 and May 1864. The dead, originally buried here, were eventually reinterred in Maplewood Cemetery.

The building was eventually abandoned and remained so until the late 1980s, when it was converted for use as the Civil War Museum at the Exchange Hotel.

- Note the use of the term "Civil War," in the inscription, rather than "War between States"—another concession to contemporary usage. Note, too, that Union and Confederates are included: this is one of the few monuments to give tribute to both sides.

227. Maplewood Cemetery Tablet

Monument is a bronze tablet set on a granite base.

LOCATION: U.S. 33 west of Gordonsville, 22942

DATE: 1927

MEDIA: Bronze, granite

THE MAPLEWOOD
MEMORIAL ASSOCIATION
HAS ERECTED THIS TABLET
AS A TRIBUTE OF RESPECT TO
SOME SEVEN HUNDRED
CONFEDERATE SOLDIERS
MAINLY FROM NORTH
CAROLINA AND GEORGIA
WHO LAID DOWN THEIR LIVES
FOR THE CAUSE THEY LOVED AND LOST
THEIR NAMES ARE PERISHED
MAY THEIR MEMORY BE IMPERISHABLE!

The Maplewood Memorial Association, a women's group, was organized April 26, 1900. The group sponsored many forms of entertainment to raise money for the cemetery site, including an ice cream festival, movies, concerts, plays, lawn parties, silver teas, colonial teas, and auctions. Their monument was erected in 1925 but was not dedicated until 1927. The tribute includes a rare admission that the war—or at least the cause—was lost.

- The association's membership dwindled to five members by 1947; responsibility for the grounds passed to the local U.D.C. chapter in 1963; today the city of Gordonsville provides upkeep.

Louisa County
Louisa

228. Courthouse Common Soldier, Relief

Monument is a circular granite plinth and base supporting a shaft with bronze relief of private soldier.

LOCATION: 314 West Main Street, 23093
DATE: August 17, 1905
MEDIA: Bronze, granite
Front

[RELIEF, FULL FIGURE OF
CONFEDERATE SOLDIER]

—

IN MEMORY
OF THE
COURAGE, PATRIOTISM AND DEVOTION
OF THE
CONFEDERATE SOLDIERS
OF LOUISA COUNTY
1861–1865
[C.S.A. BATTLE FLAG EMBLEM]
DEO VINDICE

Sponsored by the Louisa Ladies' Confederate Monument Association, the Louisa monument offers an elegant balance of iconography, iconoclasm, affection, and defiance.

The inscription faces south and the 1905 courthouse. Like many monuments, it offers a tribute to Southerners past—"In Memory of"—as well as the present—the 1905 dedication date—and the future: a bronze and granite fixture set for perpetuity.

The bronze high relief of a soldier—idealized, mature in appearance and visage—faces north and is the work of Frederick W. Sievers. The soldier stands with arms at-the-ready, relaxed, mature, alert. The stance is appropriate to a county whose only major wartime engagement, Trevilian's Station, was a Confederate victory.

229. Oakland Cemetery Tablet

Monument is a shaft set on a base and plinth.
LOCATION: C.R. 666 (West Street), 23093
DATE: 1982
MEDIUM: Granite

[U.D.C. SEAL]
"LOVE MAKES MEMORY ETERNAL"
THIS MONUMENT IS DEDICATED
WITH AFFECTION, REVERANCE
AND UNDYING REMEMBRANCE
TO THE MEMORY OF THE MEN
WHO GAVE THEIR LIVES AT
THE BATTLE OF TREVILIANS
JUNE 11–12, 1864
AND WHO LIE BURIED HERE
THE MINERAL CHAPTER
UNITED DAUGHTERS OF THE CONFEDERACY
1982

Small rectangular marble headstones mark the burial site of some sixty Confederates, most of them from the battle of Trevilian's Station, most of whom have not been identified. The three Towles brothers, all of whom served in Company A, 4th Virginia Cavalry, are buried here, as is the commander of the 7th Georgia Cavalry, Lt. Col. Joseph L. McAllister, who was killed in action at Trevilian's Station.

The 1982 monument uses familiar sentiments and phrasing—"Love Makes Memory Eternal"—and is consonant with the postbicentennial revival of interest in Civil War monumentation.

Trevilians

230. Trevilians Battlefield Tablet

Monument is a bronze tablet set on a limestone base.

LOCATION: U.S. 33 near C.R. 613, 23170
DATE: 1926
MEDIA: Bronze, limestone

BATTLE OF TREVILLIANS [*SIC*]
FOUGHT HERE JUNE 11, 12, 1864
CONFEDERATE GENS. WADE
HAMPTON, FITZHUGH LEE
AND THOMAS L. ROSSER, VICTORS OVER
FEDERAL GENS. P. H. SHERIDAN
AND G. A. CUSTER
5000 CONFEDERATES, 8000 FEDERAL
CASUALTIES, CONFEDERATE
612, FEDERAL 1,007
GREATEST ALL-CAVALRY BATTLE OF THE WAR
SIGNAL CONFEDERATE VICTORY.
ERECTED BY THE LOUISA
CHAPTER U.D.C. 1926.
J. ARTHUR LIMERICK FDR'S BALT.

The triumphant tone is unusual in the U.D.C. narrative of this late-war Confederate victory, but it is justified. The use of the superlative "greatest" may be unique, as is the emphasis on the result—"Signal Confederate Victory." The term "Victors," applied to Hampton and Lee, is also unusual. Generals Custer and Sheridan, in turn, merit mention among the defeated Federals. Also of note: Custer and Rosser were brigade commanders mentioned to the exclusion of higher ranking division commanders such as brigadier generals Alfred T. A. Torbert and Wesley Merritt. Their place in the narrative alludes to the drama of the engagement and the dramatic role they played.

Sheridan claimed victory, but his contemporaries and most historians have disputed this. The numbers engaged are reasonably accurate, unlike the arguable exaggerations of tablets at Cedar Creek and Appomattox. Union casualties were 955 men of 9,286 engaged; Confederate casualties: 813 of 6,762 men.

- Historian Eric J. Wittenberg also calls Trevilians the largest all-cavalry battle of the war. Brandy Station, fought June 9, 1863, was larger in numbers engaged, with some 22,000 involved and some 1,090 casualties, and the Brandy Station marker calls that action the "Greatest Cavalry Battle" of the war.

Fluvanna County

231. Palmyra, Courthouse Shaft

Monument is a plinth, base, dado, and shaft surmounted by ball.

LOCATION: 72 Main Street, 22963
DATE: August 31, 1901
MEDIA: Granite, marble
Front

TO THE MEMORY
OF
THE CONFEDERATE
SOLDIERS OF
FLUVANNA COUNTY.
1861–1865.

—

[BLANK]

—

1861–1865.

—

[BLANK]
[ADJACENT SLABS:]
MAJ. D. W. ANDERSON
CO. K. 44 VA. INF.
1861–1865.
IN MEMORY OF
THE PATRIOTIC WOMEN
OF FLUVANA [SIC] CO. VA.
1861
[CROSSED C.S.A. BATTLE FLAGS]
1865.
IN MEMORY OF
FLUVANNA ARTILLERY
NELSONS BATTALION
ARMY OF NORTHERN VA.
1863–65.
C. G. SNEAD CAPTAIN
IN MEMORY OF

Fluvanna is a small town county seat in the foothills of the Blue Ridge. A new courthouse was recently completed. The reconciliation-era obelisk stands on a narrow site in front of the 1830s Greek revival courthouse. The monument is appended with adjacent slabs (apparent later additions) whose subjects are evenly divided between local units of infantry and artillery and the "Patriotic Women" of the county.

- David W. Anderson served as a field officer with the 44th Virginia Infantry, organized June 14, 1861, which served until the surrender at Appomattox. The

Fluvanna Artillery saw action from the battle of First Fredericksburg, December 1862, through the battle of Waynesboro, March 2, 1865. Charles G. Snead served as its captain.

Goochland County

232. Goochland, Courthouse Obelisk

Monument is an obelisk surmounting a plinth, pedestal, and dado.

LOCATION: 2938 River Road West, 23063
DATE: June 22, 1918
MEDIUM: Granite
Front

TO THE GLORIOUS MEMORY
OF

THE CONFEDERATE SOLDIERS
OF
GOOCHLAND COUNTY
1861–1865.

—

ERECTED BY
GOOCHLAND CHAPTER
UNITED DAUGHTERS OF THE
CONFEDERACY
JUNE 22 1918
LEST WE FORGET

This simple obelisk outside the Greek revival courthouse (1826) casts a nostalgic sheen over the county's Confederate soldiers. The World War I–era dedication date may account for the focus on the soldiers and the absence of any apologetic or nationalist sentiments in the memorial. Past—the Second War of Independence—and present—the "World War," as it was called—are joined together. In fact, on the same day as the dedication a large service flag was presented to the county by the Goochland U.D.C. Four children of the members unfurled it, dressed respectively as a Red Cross nurse, as "America," as a U.S. soldier, and as a U.S. sailor. The county history also notes that the occasion was in keeping with wartime activities:

> Thrift stamps were sold at a booth erected for the purpose; there was an executive meeting of the Red Cross Chapter: a band played, and a striking feature of the day was that for the first time in the history of the county the white and colored races met together to celebrate with the same feeling of patriotism the honor done to their soldier boys. All were so united, so peaceful, it was difficult to realize that a terrible war was being waged overseas and that there were few persons present who were not anxious, even sick at heart, over the fate of their absent ones.

The keynote speaker was Robert E. Lee, grandson of General Robert E. Lee. The great-granddaughter of Goochland's Colonel David B. Harris, who served as Gen. P. G. T. Beauregard's chief of staff, unveiled the monument.

233. Pvt. James Pleasants Pyramid

Monument is a granite pyramid set on a fieldstone base.
LOCATION: V.R. 6 to C.R. 670 and 641, 23063
DATE: 1929
MEDIA: Fieldstone, granite

TO COMMEMORATE
THE HEROISM OF
JAMES PLEASANTS
1844–1872.
MEMBER OF GOOCHLAND TROOP
MARCH 1, 1864.
ALONE KILLED ONE FEDERAL
CAPTURED 13 AND 16 HORSES.
ERECTED BY GOOCHLAND CHAPTER 1929.

Near this site, James Pleasants, nineteen-year-old private in Company F, 4th Virginia Cavalry, was on furlough when he reputedly captured thirteen "Federals" and killed another. The Federals seem to have been rounded up easily; and historians are divided about the credibility of the story.

4. The Northern Neck, Middle Peninsula, Eastern Shore, and Eastern Southside

Geographical Outline. Twenty-one counties; independent cities such as Chesapeake, Emporia, Franklin, Hampton, Newport News, Norfolk, Portsmouth, Suffolk, Virginia Beach, and Williamsburg.

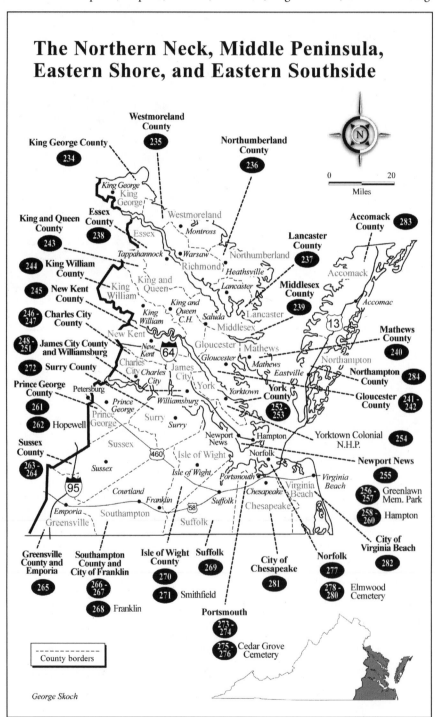

The Northern Neck, Middle Peninsula, Eastern Shore, and Eastern Southside

Westmoreland County 235

King George County 234

Northumberland County 236

Accomack County 283

King and Queen County 243

Essex County 238

Lancaster County 237

King William County 244

New Kent County 245

Middlesex County 239

Charles City County 246 - 247

James City County and Williamsburg 248 - 251

Mathews County 240

Surry County 272

Northampton County 284

Prince George County 261

Gloucester County 241 - 242

262 Hopewell

York County 252 - 253

Sussex County 263 - 264

Yorktown Colonial N.H.P. 254

Newport News 255

Greenlawn Mem. Park 256 - 257

Hampton 258 - 260

City of Virginia Beach 282

Greensville County and Emporia 265

Southampton County and City of Franklin 266 - 267

Isle of Wight County 270

Suffolk 269

City of Chesapeake 281

Norfolk 277

Elmwood Cemetery 278 - 280

268 Franklin

271 Smithfield

Portsmouth 273 - 274

Cedar Grove Cemetery 275 - 276

County borders

George Skoch

192

Campaigns. Actions took place from 1861 to 1865 with engagements and resulting monuments at Big Bethel in 1861; the Peninsula and Seven Days campaigns in 1862, with actions at Williamsburg; the siege of Suffolk in 1863; and the Overland Campaign of 1864. Naval activities include the Union blockade of the coast throughout the war—uncommemorated apart from mentions or statues of sailors—and the battle of the U.S.S. *Monitor* and C.S.S. *Merrimac* in 1862 off Hampton—commemorated with a shaft and monument at Portsmouth.

Terrain. The Southside is primarily agricultural; so, too, is the Eastern Shore and Northern Neck. The Hampton Roads area is densely populated—"quite un-Virginian"—with the best natural seaport between New York and Rio de Janeiro. The Northern Neck peninsula is bounded on the north by the Potomac and the south by the Rappahannock, the Middle Peninsula by the Rappahannock and the James. The Tidewater is a plain that stretches about one hundred miles inland. The country is mostly rural; agriculture and fishing are predominant. In his memoirs of the 1864 Overland Campaign, Grant describes the terrain this way:

> The country over which the army had to operate, from the Rapidan to the crossing of the James River, is rather flat, and is cut by numerous streams which make their way to the Chesapeake Bay. The crossings of these streams by the army were made not far above tide-water, and where they formed a considerable obstacle to the rapid advance of troops even when the enemy did not appear in opposition. The country roads were narrow and poor. Most of the country is covered with a dense forest, in places, like the Wilderness and along the Chickahominy, almost impenetrable even for infantry except along the roads. All bridges were naturally destroyed before the National troops came to them.

The bridges have been repaired or rebuilt, and much of the farmland and forest has been converted to housing, highways and commerce,

but the rivers still run, and the back roads essentially follow the same paths as those in the nineteenth century.

Apart from the Hampton Roads area, Eastern Virginia has smaller populations and, to date, more modest growth than elsewhere. The monuments are relatively modest in size and rhetoric. So, too, are eighteenth century courthouses by comparison to others in Virginia, which date from the nineteenth and twentieth century. The colonial heritage has a strong influence and—especially at Charles City and Mathews—arguably a stronger and more convenient place in public memory than the Civil War.

King George County

234. King George, Courthouse Obelisk

Monument is an obelisk set upon a base, plinth, and dado.

LOCATION: 9483 Kings Highway, 22485
DATE: November 15, 1869
MEDIUM: Granite
Front

TO

THE OFFICERS AND SOLDIERS

OF THE CONFEDERATE ARMY FROM
KING GEORGE,
WHO GAVE THEIR LIVES FOR THE
SOUTH.
A TRIBUTE OF GRATITUDE
AND RESPECT, FROM THE
LADIES MEMORIAL ASSOCIATION
OF THIS COUNTY.
IMPERISHABLE AS GRANITE BE THEIR FAME,
LET HISTORY HONOUR AND
RECORD THEIR DEEDS.
SOLDIERS WHO SURVIVED THE WAR
[41 NAMES]
—
[75 NAMES]
—
[73 NAMES]

King George may be the earliest courthouse monument in Virginia, although the Lancaster monument has the same claim attached to it (1872). Appropriations for the project were made in 1867—very early in the courthouse monument movement, and the structure appears to have been erected by 1869. The King George Historical Society has this description of Ladies Memorial Association activities:

> To carry out the purposes of their organization [they] determined to erect a monument at the Court House with the names of those who had lost their lives in the war engraved thereon. To raise the money for the accomplishment of this object they had a series of entertainments, dinners, tableaux, tournaments, etc. A sufficient amount of money having been obtained the monument was bought and landed at the ... Yard wharf; the pieces of which it was composed were so heavy that there was considerable difficulty hauling them in place. Finally they were gotten in place[,] the monument was erected and on the 15th of November 1869 with appropriate ceremonies unveiled.

The 189 names inscribed on the face of this obelisk are unusually weathered—so much so as to give the marker the appearance of being several centuries older than it is. It is ironic, therefore, that the L.M.A. expresses the hope that the fame of the county's "Officers and Soldiers" would be "imperishable."

- The inscription beginning "Soldiers Who Survived" is a 1912 addition. Ninety-seven King George County men were listed among those killed from King George County in the United Confederate Veterans minutes, but this may be an underestimate.

Westmoreland County

235. Montross, Courthouse Shaft

Monument is a shaft and cap surmounting a base, plinth, and dado.
LOCATION: 111 Polk Street, 22520
DATE: 1876
MEDIUM: Marble
Front

TO THE CONFEDERATE SOLDIERS
OF
WESTMORELAND,
WHO FELL IN DEFENSE OF
VIRGINIA,

AND IN THE CAUSE OF
CONSTITUTIONAL LIBERTY.
THIS MONUMENT
IS ERECTED IN GRATITUDE AND LOVE
BY
THE WOMEN OF WESTMORELAND.
ERECTED
BY THE
LADIES MEMORIAL ASSOCIATION
OF
WESTMORELAND CO. VA.
BEVAN & SONS
BALTO. MD.

—

[1 NAME] 48TH VA.
47TH VA. INFANTRY, CO. G
[29 NAMES]
CO. B., [1 NAME]
30TH VA. [1 NAME]
CO. H. 9TH VA. CAV. [2 NAMES]
CADETS V.M.I. [2 NAMES]

—

1876
9TH VA. CAVALRY, CO. C.
[31 NAMES]
15TH VA. CAVALRY, CO. A.
[27 NAMES]

—

40TH VA. INFANTRY, CO. K.
[28 NAMES]
55TH VA. INFANTRY, CO. E.
[27 NAMES]

The Westmoreland elegists make broad claims for the altruism of their county's soldiers: they "Fell in the Defense of Virginia and in the Cause of Constitutional Liberty." Unabashed, too, is the "Love" espoused by the women of Westmoreland. The funereal roster of the dead is displayed, but this is nevertheless a typical centennial-era monument: the withdrawal of Federal troops from the South and the centennial of the American Revolution gave rise to patriotic justifications of the second war of independence, a Second American Revolution. That stance—a lost cause but a righteous one—gradually gained favor and retains currency to this day. Its beginnings are discernible in monuments like this.

Documentation on this monument is limited. The thirty-foot-high obelisk is topped with an obscure "sculptural element." Speculation varies on what it is; it may be a kind of flame or torch.

- The monument was originally located in a local cemetery across the street from its present position but was moved in July 1930 to make room for construction. Ownership of the monument was conveyed from the local Ladies Memorial Association to Westmoreland County.

Northumberland County

236. Heathsville, Courthouse Shaft

Monument is a shaft surmounted by statue of female, the whole set upon a base, plinth, and dado.

LOCATION: 39 Judicial Place, 22473
DATE: April 26, 1873
MEDIUM: Marble
Front

1873
[RELIEF OF FUNEREAL URN WITH
CLOTH DRAPED OVER IT]
IN MEMORY OF
THE
SOLDIERS OF
NORTHUMBERLAND
WHO GAVE THEIR
LIVES FOR THE
CAUSE OF THEIR
NATIVE STATE
AND THE SOUTH
THIS MONUMENT
IS ERECTED BY THE
LADIES MEMORIAL
ASSOCIATION OF
NORTHUMBERLAND
COUNTY.
[CROSSED SWORDS]
[12 NAMES]

GADDES BROS.
BALTO.

—

[RELIEF OF CROSSED CANNON BARRELS]
[51 NAMES]
—

[RELIEF OF LAUREL WREATH]

[53 NAMES]
—

[RELIEF OF CROSSED STACKED MUSKETS]
[40 NAMES]

Erected only nine months after the Lancaster monument, the twenty-three-foot Heathsville monument, like its counterpart, is conspicuous for making no mention of the Confederacy: here the South is the cause and the dead are the focus. One hundred and fifty-six names are listed. No war years are inscribed: the events were too recent, one presumes, to mention. The marble is weathered after a century's exposure; a draped funereal urn is displayed on the front of the obelisk. The monument is crowned by the figure of a woman holding an anchor, a symbol of redemption and hope cited in He-

brews 6:19 ("Which hope we have as an anchor of the soul, both sure and stedfast, and which entereth into that within the veil").

Lancaster County

237. Lancaster, Courthouse Obelisk

Monument is a marble obelisk surmounting a plinth, base, and dado with bronze plaques.
LOCATION: 8311 Mary Ball Road, 22503
DATE: July 27, 1872
MEDIA: Marble, bronze
Front

[RELIEF OF ANGEL PLACING A WREATH
ON FALLEN SOLDIER/OFFICER]
1872
TO
THE GALLANT SONS
OF LANCASTER.
WHO GAVE THEIR LIVES FOR THE
CAUSE OF THEIR NATIVE STATE
AND THE SOUTH,
THIS MONUMENT IS ERECTED
BY THE
LADIES MEMORIAL ASSOCIATION
OF LANCASTER COUNTY,
VIRGINIA.
[BRONZE PLAQUE]
SURVIVORS OF THE WAR OF 1861–1865
[120 NAMES IN SIX COLUMNS]
—

[39 NAMES, EACH PUNCTUATED

WITH PERIODS]
[BRONZE PLAQUE]
SURVIVORS OF THE WAR OF 1861–1865
[119 NAMES IN SIX COLUMNS]

—

[38 NAMES]

—

[34 NAMES]
[BRONZE PLAQUE]
SURVIVORS OF THE WAR OF 1861–1865
[120 NAMES IN SIX COLUMNS]

Lancaster was one of the first counties in Virginia to erect a courthouse monument. The memorial is similar to later examples at Heathsville, Tappahannock, and Westmoreland. The lists of the dead in orderly rows is a prototype for the eastern Virginia emphasis on individual service and is descended from classical funereal tributes to Greek infantry—citizen-soldiers, Hoplites—who fought together in ranked, phalanx form, shoulder to shoulder. The names here are inscribed in similar fashion, rank on rank, as it were, shoulder to shoulder.

The Confederacy bears no mention, a tendency common to funereal-era monuments. The "Survivors"—over four hundred of them—are inscribed on bronze plaques, which are apparent later additions. The use of the term "Survivors" rather than veterans, soldiers, or heroes is unique. The assertion that they "Gave Their Lives for the Cause" is the final word on their legacy.

Essex County

238. Tappahannock, Courthouse Common Soldier

Monument is a private soldier, in marble, standing at parade rest, surmounting a granite plinth, base, dado, and shaft, with bronze plaques affixed.
LOCATION: 300 Prince Street, 22560
DATE: August 25, 1909
MEDIA: Bronze, granite, marble
Front
[BRONZE RELIEF OF TWO DRAPED
C.S.A. BATTLE FLAGS]
1861–1865

ERECTED
TO SOLDIERS OF ESSEX AND THOSE
WHO FOUGHT WITH THEM
THEY FOUGHT FOR THE PRINCIPLES
OF STATE SOVEREIGNTY
AND IN DEFENSE OF THEIR HOMES.
TO MAINTAIN THESE RIGHTS THE
GALLANT SONS OF THIS
GALLANT COUNTY MARCHED
GLADLY TO THE FRONT AND
DID THEIR DUTY LIKE MEN, FROM
THE OPENING GUNS AT
FIRST MANASSAS TO THE FINAL
CHARGE AT APPOMATTOX.
OFFICERS
COMPANY A, 55TH VA. REGT.
[150 NAMES]

—

COMPANY A, 55TH VA. REGT.
CONTINUED
[30 NAMES]
COMPANY D, 55TH VA. REGT.
[101 NAMES]
COMPANY F, 55TH VA. REGT.
[54 NAMES]

—
[SEAL OF VIRGINIA]
COMPANY F, 55TH VA. REGT.
CONTINUED
[57 NAMES]
COMPANY G, 55TH VA. REGT.
[74 NAMES]
COMPANY K, 55TH VA. REGT.
[61 NAMES]
COMPANY F, 9TH VA. CAVALRY.
[63 NAMES]

—

9TH, VA. CAVALRY
[91 NAMES IN THREE COLUMNS]
[111 OTHER NAMES IN TWO COLUMNS]

No eastern Virginia courthouse monument is as detailed or expressive—almost jubilant—as this. Some eight hundred names are inscribed, among the largest rosters in Virginia. The tone is exuberant: the county itself is "Gallant"; so, too, are its "Gallant Sons": happy warriors who "Marched Gladly to the Front."

The soldier stands in front of the courthouse, facing north, with the Tappahannock River just a short distance away in the same direction. The statue surmounts a thirty-foot, tiered granite pedestal. The bronze plaques contain the names of 772 officers and men, including eleven senior officers. Of these, 496 were with the 55th Virginia Infantry and 154 with the 9th Virginia Cavalry, with 111 names listed with other units. Among the officers is Brig. Gen. Richard B. Garnett, who was killed at Gettysburg. Also listed is his cousin, Brig. Gen. Robert S. Garnett, the first Confederate general killed in the war.

- The cornerstone was laid June 28, 1906. Festivities abounded on August 28, 1909, the day of the dedication:

Amid the boom of cannon, strains of martial music and cheers of nearly four thousand ex-Confederates, their wives, sons and daughters, a monument to the memory of the dead soldiers, sailors and officers of Essex County, who gave their lives for the Lost Cause, was unveiled at Tappahannock. . . . That night the town was filled to its doors with dancers. The Virginia Reel was led by Mrs. T. R. B. Wright. . . . It was a brilliant society occasion."

Middlesex County

239. Saluda, Courthouse Column

Monument is a granite plinth, base, dado, and column, the whole surmounted by a cannon ball.

LOCATION: 73 Bowden Street, 23149
DATE: July 4, 1910
MEDIUM: Granite

[RELIEF OF C.S.A. NATIONAL FLAG]
1865
[CROSSED SWORDS RELIEF]
TO COMMEMORATE THE
VALOR AND PATRIOTISM
OF THE MEN, AND THE
DEVOTION AND SACRIFICE
OF THE WOMEN OF
MIDDLESEX IN DEFENSE
OF THEIR LIBERTIES AND
THEIR HOMES.
ERECTED BY MIDDLESEX CHAPTER
DAUGHTERS OF THE CONFEDERACY
JULY 4, 1910

An elegant series of parallel attributes is presented in this Second War of Independence tribute dedicated on the Fourth of July, which celebrates the county's wartime men and women: "Valor and Patriotism"; "Devotion and Sacrifice" for "Liberties" and "Homes." The United Daughters of the Confederacy elegists make no distinction to the men as soldiers, nor of the women as Confederate women: they are cited as equal partners in the unspecified conflict between 1861 and 1865.

To judge by the tone and content of the memorial, the defense was successful. Like the Tappahannock monument in the adjacent county, references to the war are indirect, even incidental: the Confederacy is mentioned only in the sponsorship. Instead, tributes are offered to the citizens of Middlesex for serving the cause of defending liberty and home.

A stone at the base of the east side of the monument is inscribed:

PRESENTED
TO THE U. D. C.
AND LAID BY
URBANNA LODGE #83 AF&AM

Mathews County

240. Mathews, Courthouse Common Soldier

Monument is a private soldier, in marble, standing at parade rest surmounting a granite plinth, base, dado, and shaft.

LOCATION: 10622 Buckley Hall Road, Liberty Square, 23109
DATE: September 12, 1912
MEDIA: Granite, marble
Front

[C.S.A. BATTLE FLAG RELIEF]
1861 CSA 1865
[CROSSED SWORDS RELIEF]
OUR
CONFEDERATE
SOLDIERS.
—
IN MEMORY OF THE
SOLDIERS AND SAILORS
OF MATHEWS COUNTY VA.
—
[RELIEF OF CROSSED CANNON BARRELS]
—
ERECTED BY THE
LANE DIGGS CAMP C. V.
AND THE SALLIE [SIC] THOMPKINS [SIC]
CHAPTER U.D.C.

The twenty-four-foot Mathews monument stands at the northeast corner of the courthouse square. The lofty shaft of granite and marble was dedicated to "the memory of Confederate soldiers living and dead," according to Confederate Veteran. At the unveiling ceremonies, the magazine observed, "Col. Robert E. Lee, a grandson of General Lee, was the orator of the day, and his eloquence was a memorable feature."

- Sally Louisa Tompkins (1833–1916) opened the Robertson Hospital in Richmond to tend Confederate wounded after the First Battle of Manassas. The hospital remained in service for the rest of the war. President Jefferson Davis awarded Tompkins an officer's commission as a captain in the Confederate States Army. At her death Tompkins was buried with full military honors at nearby Christ Church.
- A metal railing installed in 1913 was later removed.

Gloucester County

241. Gloucester, Courthouse Obelisk

Monument is an obelisk surmounting a plinth, base, and dado.

LOCATION: 7400 Justice Drive, 23061
DATE: 1889
MEDIUM: Granite
Front

[21 NAMES]
TO THE
CONFEDERATE DEAD
OF GLOUCESTER.

—

[42 NAMES]

—

[39 NAMES]
ERECTED BY THEIR SURVIVING COMRADES
AND FRIENDS
"PLANT THE FAIR COLUMN O'ER
THE VACANT GRAVE,
A SOLDIER'S HONOR LET A SOLDIER HAVE"
1889

—

[30 NAMES, 1 UNKNOWN]

This late funereal example stands at the center of the courthouse grounds rather than in a cemetery, reflecting the gradual shift of the focus of local public memory of the war from graveyards to town squares and courthouse sites. In this case, a roster of the dead is inscribed at the heart of the 1766 courthouse square.

The grim sentiment, "Plant the fair column . . ." is also used on courthouse monuments at Gloucester and Madison and at Petersburg's Blandford Cemetery. At Gloucester, however, the concession—"A Soldier's Honor Let a Soldier Have"—is appended with the remembrance of the soldiers' "Surviving Comrades and Friends."

• The ceremonies:

An "immense crowd of ladies and men from Gloucester and adjoining Counties" watched as "Miss Bettie H. Ware, drew the veil from the Monument, which was done and the Monument was seen and admired for the first time . . ."

• From the "Masonic Address":

This occasion is suggestive of only one thought—the martyrdom of the dead heroes whose names are cut upon this towering shaft. The cause—the lost cause—the cause for which, upon their country's altar, they offered up all that in them was mortal, must be the groundswell of every sympathetic heart before me to-day.

242. Abingdon Church Cemetery Tablet

Monument is a granite shaft.

LOCATION: U.S. 17 north of Coleman Bridge, 23183
DATE: 1937
MEDIUM: Granite

IN MEMORY OF
CONFEDERATE SOLDIERS
ABINGDON DISTRICT
GRAVES NOT LOCATED
1861–1865
SALLY TOMPKINS CHAPTER U.D.C.
1937

The Abingdon Church cemetery shaft is on the grounds of a church dating from circa 1750. Like other monuments of the 1930s, it puts a note of nostalgia and decorum on a site that might otherwise have been lost to memory.

King and Queen County

243. King and Queen, Courthouse Obelisk
Monument is an obelisk surmounting a plinth, base, and dado.

LOCATION: 242 Allens Circle, 23085
DATE: August 1913
MEDIUM: Granite

CSA
[FURLED C.S.A. NATIONAL FLAG RELIEF]
TO THE CONFEDERATE SOLDIERS
AND SAILORS OF KING AND QUEEN
COUNTY VIRGINIA 1861–1865
FATE DENIED THEM VICTORY BUT GAVE
THEM THE LOVE AND VENERATION OF
THEIR NATIVE LAND, THE WONDER

AND ADMIRATION OF THE WORLD.
[CROSSED SWORDS]
—
[CANNON RELIEF]
—
[ANCHOR RELIEF]
—
[CROSSED MUSKETS RELIEF]

The flag on the King and Queen obelisk is partially furled—or partially unfurled—but the inscription is especially vivid. The tribute, "Fate Denied Them . . ." is also invoked at the courthouse elegies of Berryville, Bland, and Hillsville, and the university cemetery at Charlottesville. Here, however, it is appended with the sentiment that the county's "Soldiers and Sailors" have the "Wonder and Admiration of the World."

- The courthouse dates from circa 1750. Federal troops burned the edifice March 10, 1864, but it was repaired and is still in service.

King William County

244. King William, Courthouse Common Soldier

Monument is a private soldier, in marble, standing at parade rest surmounting a granite plinth, base, dado, and shaft.

LOCATION: 351 Courthouse Lane, 23086
DATE: July 28, 1904
MEDIA: Granite, marble
Front

1861
1865
[CROSSED C.S.A. BATTLE FLAGS]
CARTER'S BATTERY OF THOMAS H. CARTER
OFFICERS
[27 NAMES]
PRIVATES
[84 NAMES]
TO OUR SOLDIERS
OF THE
CONFEDERACY.
KING WILLIAM CO. VA.

—

LEE RANGERS CO. H 9TH VA.
OFFICERS
[11 NAMES]
PRIVATES
[63 NAMES]
CO. C. 22ND VA.
[1 OFFICER, 33 OTHER NAMES]

—

TAYLOR GRAYS CO. D. 63 VA.
[1 OFFICER, 69 OTHER NAMES]
MATTAPONI GUARDS CO. H. 53 VA.
[1 OFFICER, 42 OTHER NAMES]

—

CONTINUED FROM CO. H. 53, VA.
[15 NAMES]
LIST OF SOLDIERS IN OTHER
THAN THE FIVE COMPANIES
FROM KING WILLIAM CO.
[100 NAMES]

Tidewater monuments are generally modest in scale and adornment. So, too, are its colonial-era courthouses. King Williams's monument, however, is large and lavish, standing about twenty-three feet high, with a roster of some 447 Confederates inscribed: soldiers, veterans—not just the dead. The uncited elegists offer no apologetics or paeans, just the evocation, "To Our Soldiers of the Confederacy,"

but the J. Henry Brown statue has a prominent place at the center of the T-shaped courthouse. There is no comment on what the Confederate soldiers did, there is no list of engagements, but courthouses were intended to be the center of justice and every facet of public life, and this monument arguably connotes a Second War of Independence legitimacy to the Confederate cause. The courthouse, erected circa 1725, may be the oldest public building in continuous use in Virginia, perhaps in the country.

Twenty-five hundred people were in attendance at the dedication. The occasion included a prayer by the Reverend James Power Smith of Fredericksburg, a reunion of veterans, and the singing of "The Bonnie Blue Flag" by a women's chorus. Commonwealth Attorney Herbert L. Lewis served as master of ceremonies; his daughter pulled the cord that unveiled the statue. The *Richmond Times-Dispatch* reported that "As the veil fell from the effigy of the typical Confederate soldier, the old 'rebel yell' went up with thousand-throat volume."

- Excerpt from the dedication address by the honorable Caperton Braxton:

There need be no monuments of stone or tables of bronze to preserve from oblivion the memory of Confederate soldiers, for their sacrifices and achievements will live in song and story as long as virtue and valor shall be esteemed among mankind. In 1861 many Virginians would gladly have seen the Union made irrevocable, but they well knew that as it had not been made so by any agreement by the States and believing, as stated in our immortal Declaration of Independence that the just powers of government can be derived only from the consent of the governed, they were unwilling to see Southern States coerced into a Union without their consent. This alone was the cause of Virginia's separation from that Union which she herself had formed.

- A bronze plaque to Henry Jones, a Virginia Military Institute cadet killed at New Market, is also on this site. Jones is buried under the New Market Battle Monument on the V.M.I. campus in Lexington.

IN MEMORY OF
HENRY JENNER JONES
BORN IN
KING WILLIAM COUNTY
VIRGINIA
ON MARCH 10, 1847
A VMI CADET
PRIVATE D COMPANY
KILLED IN
THE BATTLE OF NEW MARKET
ON MAY 15, 1864
ERECTED BY
WEST POINT CHAPTER
UNITED DAUGHTERS OF
THE CONFEDERACY

New Kent County

245. New Kent, Courthouse Obelisk

Monument is an obelisk set on a plinth, base, and dado.
LOCATION: 12001 Courthouse Circle, 23124
DATE: 1934
MEDIUM: Granite
Front

[LAUREL WREATH, C.S.A. BATTLE FLAG]
TO THE REVERED MEMORY
OF
THE CONFEDERATE
SOLDIERS AND SAILORS

FROM
NEW KENT COUNTY
1861–1865
—
C.S.A.
"LEST WE FORGET"
MILITARY UNITS ORGANIZED IN NEW KENT
PAMUNKEY RIFLES
CO. E. 53, VIRGINIA REGIMENT.
BARHAMSVILLE GRAYS
CO. B. 53, VIRGINIA REGIMENT.
NEW KENT CAVALRY
TROOP F. THIRD VIRGINIA CAVALRY.

The most recent Tidewater courthouse monument is New Kent's elegy, outside the 1909 courthouse. Period notes on the design and sponsorship are not extant, but the tone is nostalgic: the "revered" Confederate soldiers are held in "memory." The unit roster, including the almost quaint prewar designations, is unique to commemorative era monuments of the 1930s and may also reflect retrospective sentiments. A laurel wreath surrounds the battle flag, but the effect is less strident than the 1904 King William memorial in the adjacent county. Neither the Stannardsville obelisk (1932) in the Piedmont nor the Stuart monument (1936), erected in the same decade on the Southside, has a roster of units. All three, erected late in the monument-building era, are more evocative than defiant, and more sentimental than fervent.

Charles City County

246. Charles City, Courthouse Obelisk

Monument is an obelisk set on a plinth, base, and dado.

LOCATION: 10780 Courthouse Road, 23030
DATE: November 21, 1900
MEDIUM: Granite

Front

TO THE

CONFEDERATE SOLDIERS

OF

CHARLES CITY COUNTY.

1861–1865

—

DEFENDERS OF

CONSTITUTIONAL LIBERTY

AND THE RIGHT OF

SELF GOVERNMENT.

—

ERECTED A. D. 1900.

—

PRO ARIS ET FOCIS.

Sponsored by the Harrison-Harwood United Daughters of the Confederacy, this modestly sized obelisk is a "graceful shaft of Virginia Granite, twenty feet high," according to contemporary accounts. Its understated scale and tone set an appropriate tone for a county that continues to resist suburban inroads. Development has spread north, south and west of Richmond and west from Williamsburg, but it has had little effect in this county, even to this day.

No major battles were fought in Charles City County, but extensive troop movements and destruction of property took place, especially during the Peninsula campaign of 1862 and the Overland Campaign of 1864.

- "Pro Aris Et Focis" is translated from the Latin as "For Altars and Firesides."
- Fundraising for the six-hundred-dollar monument by A. J. Wray of Richmond was completed with "promptness and liberality," according to U.D.C. records.
- The dedication:

November 21, 1900. The day came and went, the greatest in the recent history of Charles City, and leaving such memories as will make the hearts throb, until they cease to beat, of those of us to whom the Confederacy was dear, and with whom, though dead, it yet liveth. Fine weather, an unexampled crowd in numbers, in orderliness and in enthusiasm; the presence of the Governor of Virginia and many other visitors; profuse decorations of red, white and red, with Confederate flags fluttering at every turn; a luncheon spread, in its lavish abundance more than upholding the legend of Virginia hospitality . . . splendid speeches from distinguished sons of Charles City. . . . Surely a day never to be forgotten, great and glorious in the annals of this or any other county.

247. John Tyler Tablet

Monument is an inscribed shaft.
DATE: 1961
MEDIUM: Granite

TO COMMEMORATE THE EFFORTS OF
JOHN TYLER, NATIVE SON, PRESIDENT OF
THE UNITED STATES 1841–1845
CHAIRMAN OF THE PEACE CONVENTION, 1861
TO PRESERVE THE UNION AND
TO PREVENT THE WAR BETWEEN THE STATES
ERECTED 1961

Centennial credit is given to Tyler (1790–1862), tenth president of the United States, who chaired the ill-fated Virginia Peace Convention. The movement failed, and Tyler took sides with the Confederacy. He died in 1862, a member of the Confederate House of Representatives.

James City County and Williamsburg City

248. Williamsburg Courthouse Obelisk

Monument is an obelisk set on a plinth, base, and dado.
LOCATION: Bicentennial Park, near the Galt family burial plot at Newport and Court streets
DATE: May 5, 1908
MEDIUM: Granite
Front

1861–1865
[C.S.A. BATTLE FLAGS]
TO THE
CONFEDERATE SOLDIERS AND
SAILORS OF WILLIAMSBURG
AND JAMES CITY COUNTY

—

"LORD GOD OF HOSTS, BE WITH US YET,
LEST WE FORGET—LEST WE FORGET!"

—

[BLANK]

—

ERECTED BY THE DAUGHTERS
OF THE CONFEDERACY AND THE
CITIZENS OF WILLIAMSBURG AND
JAMES CITY COUNTY.

Dedicated on the thirty-sixth anniversary of the battle of Williamsburg, this former court-house monument strikes a discordant note here. The nineteenth century has a relatively low profile in "Colonial Williamsburg," despite the fact that the first major battle of the Peninsula campaign was fought here on May 5, 1862.

The Kipling excerpt, "Lest We Forget," inscribed at so many locations elsewhere, takes on a different meaning in a town that is dominated by its colonial heritage. The obelisk represents neither the Williamsburg of the colonial era that the town has been given over to, nor that of the former courthouse of 1969 near where it stands now. Even in 1940, writer Agnes Rothery concluded that "Colonial Williamsburg is a picture of a town that never existed; a compromise between architects, historians, idealists, and benefactors. . . . But as a historical display and an educational enterprise and a charming objective for tourists, it is genuine and wholly successful.

- The wartime courthouse, erected 1772, was converted to a museum; so too was the 1932 courthouse. The south end of Palace Green was the original location for this monument. The monument was removed in the 1930s with the restoration of the city to its eighteenth-century appearance. It now stands in Bicentennial Park.

249. Bruton Parish Church, Cemetery Obelisk

Monument is an obelisk set on a base and plinth.

LOCATION: 201 Duke of Gloucester Street, 23185

DATE: 1887

MEDIUM: Granite

[WREATH]
LORD KEEP THEIR
MEMORY GREEN.
ERECTED IN MEMORY OF THE
CONFEDERATE SOLDIERS WHO FELL IN THE
BATTLE OF WILLIAMSBURG MAY
5TH 1862, AND LIE BURIED
UNDER AND AROUND THIS MONUMENT.
[9 NAMES]
—
[10 NAMES]
—
[BLANK]
—
[10 NAMES]

Bruton Parish Church has been in use since 1715. The still-active parish is now part of Colonial Williamsburg. Like all public buildings and many private homes, it served as a hospital during the battle of Williamsburg. At least forty Confederate soldiers, most of them from the battle and most of them in unknown graves, are buried in the churchyard and are commemorated with this obelisk. Several soldiers who died in the Williamsburg Baptist Church were eventually interred here as well.

- The phrase "Lord Keep Their Memory Green" may derive from its earlier use in Charles Dickens' *A Christmas Carol* (1843).
- The top of the obelisk is missing and may have been damaged in a storm.
- The cemetery is gated, but access can be had by making a request to the staff.
- The restoration of colonial Williamsburg began here with W. A. R. Goodwin, rector of Bruton Parish, in 1926.

250. Cedar Grove Cemetery Obelisk

Monument is an obelisk set on a base and plinth.

LOCATION: 809 South Henry Street (V.R. 132), 23185

DATE: May 5, 1935

MEDIUM: Granite

1861
[CROSSED C.S.A. BATTLE FLAGS]
1865
OUR CONFEDERATE DEAD

Granite riser with battle flag emblems:

1861 THE CONFEDERACY 1865

More than 250 Confederates from the battle of Williamsburg were interred in a common grave at this site in the northeast section of the cemetery. They were among the fifteen hundred Southern casualties incurred in the battle fought on May 5, 1862, as part of the Peninsula campaign of March–September 1862. Union dead from the battle are buried in the National Cemetery at Yorktown.

251. Fort Magruder Tablet

Monument is an inscribed shaft.
LOCATION: Penniman Road to intersection with Queens Creek (C.R. 641), 23185
DATE: May 4, 1962
MEDIUM: Granite

> FORT MAGRUDER
> THIS LARGE REDOUBT WAS THE
> CENTER OF A DEFENSIVE
> LINE CROSSING THE PENINSULA.
> THESE EARTHWORKS,
> CONSTRUCTED BY THE COMMAND
> OF GENERAL JOHN B.
> MAGRUDER, WERE A PART OF
> THE SUSTEM OF FORTIFI-
> CATIONS DESIGNED TO PROTECT RICHMOND.
> HERE ON MAY 5, 1862, THE
> BATTLE OF WILLIAMSBURG
> DELAYED THE ADVANCE OF
> THE FEDERAL ARMY AND
> MADE POSSIBLE THE CONTINUED
> DEFENSE OF RICHMOND.
> THIS SITE PRESERVED BY
> THE UNITED DAUGHTERS OF
> THE CONFEDERACY
> THIS MARKER ERECTED BY
> THE CITIZENS OF WILLIAMSBURG ON THE
> OCCASION OF THE HUNDRETH ANNIVERSARY
> OF
> THE BATTLE OF WILLIAMSBURG
> MAY 4, 1862

This vestige of the Williamsburg Line fortifications stands in a residential neighborhood east of Williamsburg. The site is now a park maintained by the United Daughters of the Confederacy. It bears no resemblance to a battlefield: the works are wooded and overgrown, and the site is fenced, gated, and locked. Still, it remains as a reminder of the battle that was fought here. The original line consisted of fourteen redoubts, actually redans of various sizes and shapes.

The memorial emphasizes the apparent importance of this site and the success of the defense of this ground. Although the National Park Service narrative calls the outcome of the battle inconclusive, the United Daughters of the Confederacy observes that the battle ensured the "defense of Richmond." The record shows that Federal troops under Maj. Gen Joseph Hooker assaulted Fort Magruder but were repulsed. Confederate counterattacks, directed by Maj. Gen. James Longstreet, threatened the Union left flank, but troops commanded by Brig. Gen. Philip Kearny interposed to stabilize the Federal lines. The battle essentially ended as a draw, but Confederate troops withdrew from the field that night.

• A bronze plaque on a cement base reads:

> THIS LAND WAS DONATED
> TO THE WILLIAMSBURG CHAPTER
> OF THE
> UNITED DAUGHTERS
> OF THE
> CONFEDERACY
> BY THE BENEL
> CORPORATION
> BEN G. LEVINSON
> PRESIDENT

York County
252. Big Bethel Battlefield Obelisk

Monument is an obelisk surmounting a plinth, base, and dado.

LOCATION: Big Bethel Road at Big Bethel Reservoir, 23666

DATE: 1905

MEDIUM: Granite

Front

> TO COMMEMORATE
> THE BATTLE OF BETHEL JUNE
> 10, 1861, THE FIRST CONFLICT
> BETWEEN THE CONFEDERATE
> AND FEDERAL LAND FORCES:
> AND IN MEMORY OF HENRY A.
> WYATT, PRIVATE, CO. A 1ST REGI-
> MENT NORTH CAROLINA VOL-
> UNTEERS, THE FIRST CONFED-
> ERATE SOLDIER TO FALL IN
> ACTUAL BATTLE
>
> —
>
> BETHEL
> 1861
>
> —
>
> ERECTED
> BY THE BETHEL MONUMENT
> ASSOCIATIONS OF VIRGINIA
> AND NORTH CAROLINA.
> JUNE 10, 1905.
>
> —
>
> BETHEL
> [C.S.A. BATTLE FLAG]
> 1905

Much of the battlefield around Big Bethel Church and Cemetery was flooded early in the twentieth century. Part of the grounds is also on the property of Langley Air Force Base. The whole of the monument site is behind a chain link fence, although a gate, installed several years ago, permits access.

Within a one-half-mile radius of this site, some thirty-five hundred Federals under Brig. Gen. Ebenezer W. Pierce clashed with twelve hundred Confederates under colonels John B. Magruder and D. H. Hill in the first land battle in Virginia. Several hours of confused fighting took place. The Confederates won the victory, although no such claim is made in the memorial. The action had no military significance other than being the first organized battle of the war. By declaring this to be the "First Conflict" and the "First Actual Battle," the elegists justly discount Philippi, June 3, 1861—more of a retreat than an engagement—and the Fairfax skirmish of June 1.

- The monument stands on the site of the Third Bethel Church edifice, which was destroyed during the war. The Fourth Bethel Church stood until 1926.

253. Pvt. Henry L. Wyatt Tablet

Monument is a granite shaft set on a base and plinth.

DATE: June 10, 1905

MEDIA: Concrete, granite

> ON THIS SPOT JUNE 10, 1861 FELL
> HENRY LAWSON WYATT
> PRIVATE COMPANY A.
> 1ST NORTH CAROLINA REGIMENT
> THIS STONE PLACED HERE
> BY THE COURTESY OF
> VIRGINIA, IS ERECTED BY
> AUTHORITY OF THE STATE
> OF NORTH CAROLINA.
> JUNE 10, 1905
> [5 NAMES]
> COMMISSIONERS

Nineteen-year-old Henry L. Wyatt was shot and killed during an advance on Union troops. Wyatt was born in Richmond but was raised in North Carolina. This may account for the "courtesy" exchanged between the two states in the inscription.

Wyatt fell near the close of the battle. His body was taken to Richmond and was buried in Hollywood Cemetery—one of the first; eighteen thousand more burials would follow. He was the first Confederate soldier killed in action.

Yorktown, Colonial National Historical Park—Yorktown Battlefield

254. Confederate Cemetery Tablet

Monument is a tablet set on a base.
LOCATION: South of the Second Allied Siege Line, 23690
DATE: 1954
MEDIA: Cement, granite

> IN MEMORY OF UNKNOWN
> CONFEDERATE SOLDIERS BELIEVED
> TO BE BURIED HERE IN 1861–1865
> PLACED BY OLD DOMINION
> DRAGOONS CHAPTER U.D.C.
> HAMPTON, VA. 1954.

Ten Confederates buried here are well outside the walls of Yorktown National Cemetery. This low granite shaft stands in an open field several hundred yards to the east of the national cemetery; access can be made only on foot, and it is obscured by the reconstructed Second Allied Siege Line. The Civil War is of secondary importance to the American Revolution at Yorktown as well as Williamsburg, but this stolid anomaly remains.

City of Newport News

255. Warwick Courthouse Common Soldier

Monument is a private soldier, in granite, standing at parade rest surmounting a plinth, base, dado, and shaft.
LOCATION: 14421 Old Courthouse Way, 23607
DATE: May 27, 1909
MEDIA: Granite, marble

> 1861 VIRGINIA 1865
> [RELIEF OF C.S.A. BATTLE FLAGS]
> UNVAILED [SIC] MAY 27, 1909
> TO OUR
> GALLANT SOLDIERS
> OF THE
> CONFEDERACY
> WARWICK COUNTY
> —
> [RELIEF OF ANCHOR]

The superlative "Gallant" dominates this ardent Lost Cause display, with a soldier sculpted by Charles Walsh. The monument is thirty feet tall and was built at a cost of $2,036. Over a thousand people attended the dedication ceremonies on a rainy May 27, 1909. Some documents state that it was dedicated to a local company, the Warwick Beauregards (Co. H, 32nd Virginia Infantry), but the memorial does not mention them, although the Warwick Beauregard Chapter, United Daughters of the

Confederacy, was present at the dedication. Only a few veterans were present. The "most touching moment" of the day occurred when "Major Stubbs"

> read the roll of the more than 200 men from Warwick County who had served the Confederacy. The crowd listened in reverent silence, applauding only when a veteran answered, "Here," as his name was called. Only eight responses were heard, spoken by the last county representatives of the thin gray line.

- Warwick County was dissolved in 1952 when it became the city of Warwick. The courthouse dates from 1884 and served as such until 1958, when the city became part of Newport News.

Greenlawn Memorial Park

256. Confederate Prisoners of War Tablet

Monument is an obelisk set on a plinth, base, and dado.

LOCATION: 2700 Parish Avenue, 23607
DATE: circa 1900
MEDIUM: Marble
Front

CONFEDERATE

DEAD

—

TO OUR SOLDIER DEAD

ERECTED BY LEE CAMP NO. 3

CONFEDERATE VETERANS

OF HAMPTON VA.

A TRIBUTE FROM THE HEARTS

OF SURVIVING COMRADES

—

REMAINS OF 154

CONFEDERATE SOLDIERS

DIED AT

NEWPORT NEWS, VA.

1861.

1865.

Adjacent granite slab at base

[CROSSED C.S.A. BATTLE FLAGS WITH SEAL

OF THE CONFEDERACY AT CENTER]

[163 NAMES]

THIS MEMORIAL WAS DONATED BY

[2 NAMES]

The story behind the "Soldier Dead" commemorated here is a little known epilogue to the war's end. These Confederates were taken prisoner before Appomattox and died in Federal prison in Newport News between April and July 1865. Ironically, Southerners who surrendered after them at Appomattox were paroled; these men were kept after the war. Lincoln's assassination on April 14 halted paroles, although the Confederates in North Carolina who surrendered on April 26 were paroled as well. The site held 3,490 men. In August 1865, the camp finally closed. In June 1900, the Magruder Camp No. 36, United Confederate Veterans, arranged with Greenlawn Cemetery for a plot in which to reinter the bodies of the 163 Confederate soldiers who died while imprisoned. The names of 154 soldiers, not 163, are inscribed.

257. Entry Tablet

Monument is a shaft set on a base.
LOCATION: 2700 Parish Avenue, 23607
DATE: December 8, 1941
MEDIUM: Granite

> C.S.A.
> [C.S.A. BATTLE FLAG]
> 1861–1865
> IN MEMORY OF ALL
> CONFEDERATE SOLDIERS
> BURIED IN GREENLAWN.
> ERECTED BY
> BETHEL CHAPTER
> UNITED DAUGHTERS
> OF THE
> CONFEDERACY.
> DEC. 8, 1941.

Nostalgia is evident in this cemetery memorial. The Confederacy is referred to in three places. The tribute is dedicated to "All Confederates"—however defined, whatever their contributions. The monument has the lasting, anticlimactic irony of having been dedicated on December 8, 1941, a Monday, the day after the Japanese attack on Pearl Harbor, and the same day that Congress met to declare war on Japan.

City of Hampton

258. St. John's Church Cemetery, Soldier

Monument is a private soldier standing at parade rest surmounting a plinth, base, dado, and shaft.
LOCATION: 100 West Queens Way, 23669
DATE: October 29, 1901
MEDIA: Granite, marble
Front

> CSA
> 1861–1865
> [C.S.A. BATTLE FLAG]
> OUR
> CONFEDERATE
> DEAD
> —
> [BLANK]
> —
> ERECTED BY
> HAMPTON CHAPTER NO. 19
> DAUGHTERS OF THE
> CONFEDERACY
> UNVEILED OCT. 29, 1901
> —
> [BLANK]

St. John's, established in 1610, is the oldest Anglican parish in continuous existence in

America; the church building was erected in 1728. The fourteen-foot monument—tall, lavish, and prominent—stands near the front door of the church. The sculptor of the six-foot figure is unknown. The building, along with much of the town, was burned on August 7, 1861, to keep Hampton out of Federal hands. Only the blackened walls remained by the time Union troops arrived and camped on the grounds. Church tour literature does not mention the monument. However, it takes ample note of the damage done to the church edifice during the war and the extensive repairs afterwards.

259. Oakland Cemetery Tablet

Monument is a granite shaft set on a base.
LOCATION: East Pembroke Avenue and Calhoun Street 23669
DATE: Mid-twentieth century (estimated)
MEDIUM: Granite

OUR CONFEDERATE DEAD
1861–1865

Located in a modest working class neighborhood, Oakland Cemetery, established in 1880, has a late commemorative-era monument that is both mundane and mysterious. There is no sponsorship and nothing stylistically distinctive about it. No major research source mentions it, and local sources have no documentation on it. One wonders who the "Our" is, and why they placed the monument here, since only a few Confederate graves mark this site.

260. Tablets at Hampton National Cemetery, Hampton University

Monument is two granite tablets with inscriptions facing up.
LOCATION: Tyler Street to Hampton University to Cemetery Road, left (through a University security check point) to cemetery grounds.
CEMETERY Road and Marshall Avenue, 23669
MEDIUM: Granite
First tablet

TO OUR
CONFEDERATE DEAD

Second tablet

TO OUR
CONFEDERATE DEAD

These stout tablets stand in Sections D and E of this national cemetery over the graves of 272 Confederate soldiers. The site of this cemetery—a historically black college—is unique in Virginia: on the same grounds an enormous obelisk offers a tribute to Union troops. Also here are the remains of United States Colored Troops, German sailors of World War II, and service personnel—to date—from the Spanish-American War, World War I, World War II, Korea, and Vietnam.

- Hampton National Cemetery has two locations. The Confederate monuments are at Hampton University.

Prince George County

261. Prince George, Courthouse Obelisk

Monument is an obelisk set on a base and plinth.

LOCATION: 6601 Courts Drive, 23875
DATE: October 21, 1916
MEDIUM: Granite

> 1861–1865
> ERECTED BY THE PRINCE
> GEORGE CHAPTER U.D.C.
> TO THE MEMORY OF THE
> CONFEDERATE SOLDIERS
> OF PRINCE GEORGE CO.
> THAT THEIR HEROIC DEEDS,
> SUBLIME SELF-SACRIFICE
> AND UNDYING DEVOTION
> TO DUTY AND COUNTRY MAY
> NEVER BE FORGOTTEN.

The warfare in Prince George County and environs, especially the ten-month Siege of Petersburg 1864–65, may account for the relatively late date of this large, stolid obelisk standing in front of the former courthouse. Formal commemoration seems redundant in a region where reminders of the conflict were—and in some ways still are—pervasive.

Data on this monument is limited, but the tone of the memorial is unusual: United Daughters of the Confederacy texts are apt to be more sentimental, less acrid than their Sons of Confederate Veteran counterparts, for example, but this is not. The legacy of the siege—the valiant, Trojan, to-the-death stubbornness of the defense—may account for the defiant words, which are similar to the wording on the Dinwiddie courthouse monument (1909) in the adjacent county. The firm of Burns and Campbell, which also did the work for many Petersburg monuments, erected a solemn, fortress-like bulwark here. Its stalwartness perpetually evokes the state of siege that once dominated this country.

City of Hopewell

262. Hopewell Shaft

Monument is a shaft set on a base with extensions.

LOCATION: Corner of North Second Avenue and West Cawson Street, 23860
DATE: 1949
MEDIUM: Granite

> [CROSSED C.S.A. BATTLE FLAGS]
> DEDICATED TO THE
> GLORY OF GOD IN
> MEMORY OF OUR
> CONFEDERATE
> SOLDIERS WHO
> FOUGHT IN THE WAR

BETWEEN THE STATES
1861–1865
[U.D.C. SEAL]
ERECTED BY THE CITY POINT CHAPTER
UNITED DAUGHTERS OF THE CONFEDERACY
1949
STANDING HAND TO HAND
AND CLASPING HANDS
WE SHALL REMAIN UNITED
—CITIZENS OF THE SAME COUNTRY—
MEMBERS OF THE SAME GOVERNMENT—
ALL UNITED NOW AND FOREVER

The initiative for the erection of this monument began before World War II, but the war delayed progress, and it was not completed until some years after the conflict. The 1949 Hopewell monument offers a final word on Confederate monuments of the first half of the twentieth century. The acclaim for "Our Confederate Soldiers" is traditional, as is the name of the conflict, but the Cold War–era context may have motivated the blunt, countervailing conclusion that an imagined "We" will clasp hands and remain united in future decades. No such desire is expressed in any other Virginia monument.

In 1864–65, General Ulysses S. Grant directed the ten-month Siege of Petersburg near here, on the site of what is now the City Point Unit of Petersburg National Battlefield. City Point, today part of Hopewell, was one of the busiest ports in the world during the siege. It retains a strong industrial presence.

Sussex County

263. Sussex, Courthouse Common Soldier
Monument is a private soldier standing at parade rest surmounting a plinth, base, dado, and shaft.
LOCATION: 15098 Courthouse Road, 23884
DATE: November 1912
MEDIUM: Marble
Front

CSA
"THE PRINCIPLES FOR
WHICH THEY FOUGHT
LIVE ETERNALLY."
OUR

CONFEDERATE
SOLDIERS
—
[RELIEF OF CROSSED SWORDS, SHEATHED]
—
LIST OF COMPANIES ORGANIZED IN
AND SENT OUT FROM SUSSEX COUNTY:
CO. A, 41ST VA. REG'T, INFANTRY,
"SUSSEX SHARP SHOOTERS;"
CO. D, 13TH VA. REG'T, CAVALRY;
CO. E, 16TH VA. REG'T, INFANTRY;
CO. F, 41ST VA. REG'T, ARTILLERY,
WISE'S LEGION;
CO. H, 13TH VA. REG'T, CAVALRY;
"SUSSEX LIGHT DRAGOONS,"
FOR ROLL OF MEMBERS SEE RECORDS
IN THE COUNTY CLERK'S OFFICE.
ERECTED BY
SUSSEX CHAPTER
U.D.C.
NOV.-1912
CHAPTER ORGANIZED
SEPT. 29, 1909
—
1861–1865
[CROSSED C.S.A. BATTLE FLAG
AND NATIONAL FLAG]

This semicentennial monument, the work of McNeel Marble, is more celebratory in tone and content than the nearby county examples at Dinwiddie (1909) or Prince George (1916). The monument faces south, toward the courthouse, an impressive Jeffersonian structure erected in 1828.

Sussex was described as a small village by Union troops marching through during the "Applejack Raid" of December 7–12, 1864. It is still small, and it remains isolated from major highways in the area: U.S. 460 is some fifteen miles to the east; Interstate 95 is seven miles to the west.

- Four marble cannon balls originally at the corners of the base have been removed.
- "Co. D, 13th Va. Reg't, Cavalry" was dubbed "Jackson's Avengers," but that name is not inscribed.

264. Stony Creek, Cannon

Monument is a cannon on cement base with plaque.
LOCATION: North of B.R. V.R. 40 in Stony Creek, to corner of Main and Flatfoot roads, C.R. 657 and 658 near railroad bridge, 23882
MEDIA: Concrete, iron

> THIS CONFEDERATE CANNON
> WAS FOUND, REMOVED FROM STONY
> CREEK, AND SET UPON THIS BASE
> BY CHARLES RICHARD WILLIAMS,
> ENGINEER AND CONTRACTOR WHO
> BUILT THE FIRST DOUBLE TRACK
> RAILROAD BRIDGE DURING 1911
> AND 1912.

Stony Creek Station, where this cannon is emplaced, was a strategically important railhead for the Army of Northern Virginia during the Siege of Petersburg. After Federal troops severed the Weldon Railroad near Globe Tavern in August 1864, the Confederates established this site to off-load military supplies from rail cars for a thirty-mile wagon haul up the Boydton Plank Road to Petersburg. Its usefulness ended when the Petersburg siege lines were broken in April 1865.

Several skirmishes occurred in this area in the latter days of the war. Near here, at Sappony Church on June 28, 1864, retreating Union cavalry under Brig. Gen. James H. Wilson and Brig. Gen. August V. Kautz fought off Southern cavalry under Maj. Gen. Wade Hampton and Maj. Gen. William H. F. "Rooney" Lee during the Wilson-Kautz raid.

Greensville County and City of Emporia

265. Emporia, Courthouse Common Soldier

Monument is a private soldier standing at parade rest surmounting a plinth, base, dado, and shaft.
LOCATION: I-95, Exit 11 (U.S. 58); south of intersection of B.R. U.S. 58 (Atlantic Street) and B.R. U.S. 301 (Main Street), 315 South Main Street, 23847
DATE: 1910
MEDIA: Granite, marble

> CSA
> TO THE
> CONFEDERATE SOLDIERS
> OF GREENSVILLE COUNTY
> 1861.–1865.

WHO, IN DEFENSE OF RIGHTS
THEY BELIEVED SACRED,
TOOK UP ARMS AGAINST
THE INVADERS OF VIRGINIA.
"THE GLORY DIES NOT, AND
THE GRIEF IS PAST."

—

ERECTED BY THE DAUGHTERS
OF THE CONFEDERACY,
OF GREENSVILLE COUNTY,
VIRGINIA, 1910.

The Greensville County tribute stands in front of the Jeffersonian-style courthouse of 1831. The sculptor is unknown. It may be the most militant county monument in Virginia and is appropriate for a county where secessionist sentiment was especially strong. The elegists do not claim the same legacy as the Greensville County Confederates: the men who went to war are sanctified as those who acted in defense of rights "They Believed Sacred." But Greensville County is mentioned twice, and it is the county which defines the war's legacy: these men justly "Took Up Arms Against the Invaders of Virginia."

- The expression "The glory dies not, and the grief is past" is attributed to Sir Samuel Egerton Brydges on the death of Sir Walter Scott.

Southampton County and City of Franklin

266. Courtland, Courthouse Common Soldier

Monument is a private soldier standing at parade rest surmounting a plinth, base, dado, and shaft.

LOCATION: V.R. 35 and B.R. 58 (22350 Main Street), 23837
DATE: September 17, 1902
MEDIUM: Granite
Front

1861 CSA 1865
[SEAL OF VIRGINIA]
OUR
CONFEDERATE DEAD
A TRIBUTE TO LOYALTY
BY COMRADES AND FRIENDS
DEDICATED 1902

—

COMPANIES
D. 3RD VA. INFANTRY,
G. 3RD VA. INFANTRY,
A. 13TH VA. CAVALRY,
B. 9TH VA. INFANTRY.
A. 18TH VA. BATTALLION ARTILLERY.
H. 41ST VA. INFANTRY.
"WITH SHOUTS ABOVE THE CANNON'S ROAR
THEY JOINED THE LEGIONS GONE BEFORE;
THEY BRAVELY FOUGHT, THEY BRAVELY FELL,
THEY WORE THE GRAY, AND WORE IT WELL."

—

[C.S.A. BATTLE FLAG]

—

"THIS SHAFT ON WHICH WE CARVE NO NAME,
SHALL GUIDE VIRGINIA'S YOUTH—
A SIGN-POST ON THE ROAD TO FAME,
TO HONOR AND TO TRUTH
A SILENT SENTRY, IT SHALL STAND
TO GUARD THRO' COMING TIME
THEIR GRAVES WHO DIED FOR NATIVE LAND
AND DUTY MOST SUBLIME."

The Courtland monument is the first of three markers at this site. Sponsored by the Southampton Monument Association, it has the vernacular, down-to-earth affections common to the Southside. There are no Latin proverbs. The paean, "Wore the Gray," is also inscribed on the 1889 cemetery monument at Suffolk.

The dedication date, September 17, 1902, was the fortieth anniversary of the battle of Antietam. John Warwick Daniel was the featured speaker at the ceremonies.

The Greek revival courthouse was completed in 1834. The town was formerly known as Jerusalem; the name was changed in 1883. It was the site of the trial and hanging of Nat Turner, who led the slave uprising in the Southampton Insurrection of 1831.

Courthouse renovations led to the monument's being moved from the front of the courthouse to its present site with the Nottoway River behind it and the courthouse parking lot before it. The monument's sculptor is unknown. A plaque near the base commemorates the rededication and testifies to commemorative interest in the war and its legacy at the turn of the twenty-first century:

ORIGINALLY DEDICATED SEPTEMBER 17, 1902
MOVED TO PRESENT SITE AND REDEDICATED
SEPTEMBER 17, 1992
URQUHART-GILLETTE CAMP #1471
SONS OF CONFEDERATE VETERANS
[S.C.V. SEAL]

Another plaque, of bronze and granite, sponsored by the Urquhart-Gillette Camp #1471, S.C.V. was erected circa 2008:

Not Forgotten

The two hundred and nineteen names that are engraved on the bricks before you are the men from Southampton County who gave their lives defending their family, friends and their homes from the Northern Invaders. They were killed in action or died from wounds or disease in the War of Northern Aggression 1861–1865. We honor their bravery and ultimate sacrifice. We will not forget their struggle to preserve the principles on which our country was founded.

This provocative tablet stands directly in front of the monument. No sponsor is cited. The phrase, the "War of Northern Aggression," is used nowhere else in Virginia; neither is the phrase "Northern Invaders" used elsewhere in Virginia.

267. Courtland Church Cemetery, Texas Confederates Tablet

Monument is a granite shaft.
LOCATION: B.R. 58 (22264 Main Street), 23837
DATE: 1924
MEDIUM: Granite

TEXAS
CONFEDERATE SOLDIERS
HOOD'S BRIGADE
1861–1865
ERECTED BY TEX. DIV.
UNITED DAUGHTERS
OF THE
CONFEDERACY

This sober shaft stands on the grounds of the Courtland Baptist Church, near a playground as well as the banks of the Nottoway River. The church dates from 1845 and was formerly named Jerusalem Baptist Church.

Lt. Gen. James Longstreet's First Corps was stationed here and engaged Federal troops under Maj. Gen. John Peck during the Siege of Suffolk, February–May 1863. Many men were stricken with fever; others were wounded in skirmishes on the east side of the Blackwater River. A Sons of Confederate Veterans plaque on the wall of the church provides notes on this site and a partial listing—twenty-five names—of the dead from Texas, North Carolina, Georgia, South Carolina, and Virginia.

- Two footers to the left and right forefront of the monument are inscribed "C.S.A."

Franklin

268. Memorial Park, Common Soldier

Monument is a private soldier, in marble, standing at parade rest surmounting a granite plinth, base, dado, and shaft.
LOCATION: Franklin Memorial Park: off Clay Street (B.R. 58) and Meadow Lane, 23851
DATE: June 3, 1911
MEDIA: Granite, marble
Front

1911
ERECTED BY
AGNES LEE CHAPTER,
U.D.C.
"LOVE MAKES MEMORY
ETERNAL."
TO OUR
CONFEDERATE
DEAD.
—

[BLANK]
—

1861
[C.S.A. BATTLE FLAG]
1865
—

[BLANK]

This semicentennial monument to the dead was moved several times before it was placed here, after the grounds were given to the city as Franklin Memorial Park in 1946. No other monuments have been added to this memorial park, and this monument dominates the site.

Dedicated on the anniversary of Jefferson Davis's birthday, it is similar to other city monuments such as Bristol or Lynchburg. The monument was originally erected at Second Avenue and High Street.

- An unfurled C.S.A. battle flag is displayed in high relief. The staff of the battle flag is snapped in two.

Suffolk

269. Cedar Hill Cemetery, Common Soldier

Monument is a private soldier, in white bronze, standing at parade rest surmounting a granite plinth, base, dado, and shaft.

LOCATION: B.R. 460/U.S. 58 (Main Street), near Constance Road
326 North Main Street, 23434
DATE: 1889
MEDIA: Granite, white bronze
Front

ERECTED BY
THOS [SIC] W. SMITH
IN MEMORY OF
HIS COMRADES.
CONFEDERATE DEAD

—

This shaft on which we carve
no name
Shall guide Virginia's youth—
A sign-post on the road to
fame,
To honor and to truth.
A silent sentry, it shall stand
To guard thro' coming time
Their graves who died for
native land
And duty most sublime.

—

1861–1889.

—

With shouts above the battle's
roar,
They join the legions gone
before;
They bravely fought, they
bravely fell,
They wore the Gray and wore
it well.

There is no courthouse monument in Suffolk (Nansemond County was dissolved in 1974 when it merged with the city of Suffolk), but the former courthouse is adjacent to Cedar Hill Cemetery, where this monument was erected in 1889. It is unusual for sponsorship to be credited to one person, but in this case Thomas Washington Smith was evidently the sole sponsor. Smith served as a lieutenant throughout the war, refused promotion in order to stay with his men, was wounded three times, and surrendered the remnants of the two companies of the 16th Virginia Infantry he commanded at Appomattox. Smith's grave and that of his wife are adjacent to this site.

Confederate Veteran notes that it "stands in Cedar Hill Cemetery at that place, guarding the dust of those gathered there to await the grand reveille of the resurrection, and it also stands as a symbol of the great love of one man for those who fought with him the battles of the South."

- Of this site Mrs. Ida Lewis Harper wrote in *Historic Southern Monuments*: "It was erected by Colonel Smith solely at his own expense, and no one knows the cost; I have heard it estimated at not less than two thousand dollars. . . . It was [Smith's] memorable words 'I am one of the men whose proudest boast is: 'I followed Lee.'"
- The inscription was written by Dr. Beverly Tucker. The poetic excerpt beginning "With Shouts above . . ." is taken from "Private Tucker's Poem," by Confederate soldier Henry Tucker, and is also excerpted at Courtland.
- Also buried in Cedar Hill: Gen. Laurence S. Baker.
- Renovations to the site, sponsored by the Sons of Confederate Veterans, were completed in 2001.

Granite post, bronze plaque, to the right, facing the monument

THIS CORNERSTONE WAS
PLACED BY
THE SUFFOLK CHAPTER NO. 173
UNITED DAUGHTERS OF THE
CONFEDERACY
2000
CSA

On the post, to the left, facing the monument

SONS OF CONFEDERATE VETERANS
1896
[S.C.V. EMBLEM]
THE TOM SMITH CAMP NO. 1702
SONS OF CONFEDERATE VETERANS
SUFFOLK, VIRGINIA
IS PROUD TO HAVE MADE THE
RESTORATION OF THIS SITE POSSIBLE.
1997–2001
THE EFFORTS OF MANY HAVE ENSURED
THAT THIS HALLOWED GROUND REMAINS

PRESERVED IN PERPETUITY, HONORING
OUR CONFEDERATE VETERANS.
FUTURE GENERATIONS MUST
NEVER FORGET THE VALOR OF
THE SOUTHERN SOLDIERS,
THE PRINCIPLES FOR WHICH THEY FOUGHT,
THEIR LOYALTY TO STATE,
DEVOTION TO DUTY,
AND THEIR PERSONAL SACRIFICES.
DEO VINDICE
CSA

Isle of Wight County

270. Isle of Wight, Courthouse Common Soldier

Monument is a private soldier standing at pa-
rade rest surmounting a plinth, base, six-sided
dado, and shaft.
LOCATION: 17110 Monument Circle, 23397
DATE: May 30, 1905
MEDIUM: Granite

1861 CSA 1865
ISLE OF WIGHT'S LOVING
TRIBUTE,
TO HER HEROES OF
1861 TO 1865.
"THEY BRAVELY FOUGHT,
THEY BRAVELY FELL,
THEY WORE THE GRAY
THEY WORE IT WELL."
CONFEDERATE DEAD
[SEAL OF VIRGINIA]
—

"BRIGHT WERE THE LIVES
THEY GAVE FOR US
THE LAND THEY STRUG-
GLED TO SAVE FOR US
WILL NOT FORGET
ITS WARRIORS YET
WHO SLEEP IN SO MANY
GRAVES FOR US."
—

"THEY BLEED, WE WEEP,
WE LIVE, THEY SLEEP"
—

[CROSSED C.S.A. NATIONAL
AND BATTLE FLAGS]
DEDICATED MAY 30, 1905
—

"GLORIOUS IS HIS FATE,
AND ENVIED IS HIS LOT,
WHO FOR HIS COUNTRY
FIGHTS AND FOR IT DIES."
—

"THERE IS A TRUE GLORY
AND A TRUE HONOR;
THE GLORY OF DUTY DONE
THE HONOR OF THE INTEGRITY
OF PRINCIPLE"

The only Virginia courthouse monument
with a six-sided dado stands in front of a colo-
nial-style 1750 edifice. The memorial is effusive,
with "Loving," turn-of-the-century sentiments
for what was by then a senior generation. There
are no Latin or Greek neoclassical references.
The quotation beginning "True Glory . . ." is
attributed to Robert E. Lee and is also invoked
at Thornrose Cemetery, Staunton. The rhymed
couplets, "Bright were . . ." and "They Bleed . . ."

are taken from the poem "C.S.A. Heroes," by Father Abram J. Ryan.

- The use of the word "love" on a monument is uncommon. Other examples are at Alleghany, Low Moor, Hanover, Oakwood, Westmoreland, King and Queen, and Surry.

Smithfield

271. Ivy Hill Cemetery Tablet and Podium

Monument is a granite shaft set on a base.
LOCATION: West of North Church Street, off V.R. 10, 23431
DATE: 1916
MEDIUM: Granite

> TO OUR CONFEDERATE DEAD
> 1861–1865
> ERECTED BY
> ISLE OF WIGHT CHAPTER U.D.C.

Established in 1886, Ivy Hill Cemetery is set in a landscape planted in oaks, hollies, magnolias, and boxwood. It stands on a bluff overlooking the Pagan River and surrounding wetlands. The only war monument is dedicated to the Confederate dead.

Prior to World War I, Memorial Day services at Ivy Hill were held in early June instead of the traditional May 30, because of the day's association with the commemoration of Union dead.

- The accompanying podium is a centennial addition.

> ERECTED BY
> ISLE OF WIGHT CHAPTER
> U.D.C.
> 1961

Surry County

272. Surry, Courthouse Common Soldier

Monument is a private soldier, in bronze, standing at parade rest surmounting a granite plinth, base, dado, and shaft.
LOCATION: V.R. 10 and 31, 23883
DATE: 1909
MEDIA: Granite, bronze, steel
Front

> [C.S.A. BATTLE FLAG]
> OUR HEROES
> 1861–1865
> —
> TO
> THE CONFEDERATE SOLDIERS
> OF SURRY COUNTY.
> —
> "THAT WE THROUGH LIFE MAY NOT FORGET
> TO LOVE THE THIN GRAY LINE."
> —
> ·ERECTED BY THE CONFEDERATE
> MEMORIAL ASSOCIATION OF SURRY
> COUNTY A. D. 1909.

The Surry County courthouse was erected 1923, and its six-column Roman Ionic portico is imposing. However, the twenty-one-foot monument dominates the grounds before it. *Confederate Veteran* notes that the pedestal is of "Confederate gray granite," most of which was quarried near Petersburg; the largest stone, the die, was quarried in South Carolina. The bronze figure is a cavalryman at parade rest with hands clasped on the hilt of a drawn steel saber. The soldier has the slack, relaxed stance of many Confederate soldier/statues; the cavalryman is one of only two in Virginia; the other is at Portsmouth. The phrase beginning "That We Through Life" is excerpted from a poem by Armistead Gordon (1855–1931), Virginia attorney and writer. The monument is dated 1909, but it was not unveiled until August 2, 1910.

City of Portsmouth

273. Portsmouth Courthouse Soldiers and Sailor

Monument is a plinth, base, and obelisk, with four extensions at the base, each surmounted by a Confederate serviceman, in white bronze, standing at parade rest.

LOCATION: From I-264: Exit 7B to Crawford Street, north to Court and High streets, 23705

DATE: June 15, 1893

MEDIA: Bronze, granite, marble, white bronze

Front

1861
1865
TO OUR
CONFEDERATE
DEAD
—
1862

—
1863
—
1864

This lofty, early reconciliation example stands at what was once the center of community life in Portsmouth: the corner of High and Court streets, beside the Greek revival 1849 structure that was formerly the Norfolk County/Portsmouth courthouse.

Construction of the monument began in 1876 and was completed in 1884. The obelisk is of North Carolina granite and stands thirty-five feet, six inches high. The monument is unique in having four white bronze statues of three Confederate soldiers—representing infantry, cavalry, and artillery—and a sailor, one of only three statues of Confederate sailors in the South and the only statue of a Confederate sailor in Virginia. The four figures surround a central obelisk.

Contemporary records take particular note that the statues are not generic: four local men posed for the figures. The statue of the sailor faces the Elizabeth River, the route taken by the C.S.S. Virginia in her engagement with the U.S.S. Monitor on March 8–9, 1862, during the battle of Hampton Roads. The word "Merrimac" is inscribed along the headband of the sailor's flat hat. Portsmouth men served on the crew of the C.S.S. Virginia.

• The inscription at the base of the rear of the monument—an utterly modest sponsorship—is an apparent addition. It is so weathered that a 1992 bronze plaque addition was installed to clarify the wording.

Bronze plaque

THE WEATHERED STONE READS
THIS TABLET
IS PLACED HERE BY
STONEWALL CAMP C.V.
IN MEMORY OF
MAJ. F. W. JETT C.S.A.
TO WHOSE LABOR AND DEVOTION
THE ERECTION OF THIS MONUMENT
IS PRINCIPALLY DUE
JUNE 19, 1992
PORTSMOUTH CIVIL WAR ROUND TABLE

274. City Park, Grimes Battery Obelisk

Monument is an obelisk surmounting a base and plinth.
LOCATION: 140 City Park Avenue, 23701
DATE: June 8, 1906
MEDIUM: Granite

[CROSSED U.S. AND C.S.A. NATIONAL FLAGS]
To Commemorate the
Organization of the
PORTSMOUTH
LIGHT ARTILLERY
August 14, 1809.
And to perpetuate its war
Roster under two flags.
Roll in the U.S. Service at
CRANEY ISLAND
June 22, 1813.
[41 names]
[relief of cannon]
CRANEY ISLAND
—

[CROSSED U.S. AND C.S.A. NATIONAL FLAGS]
[38 NAMES]
SHARPSBURG
—

[CROSSED U.S. AND C.S.A. NATIONAL FLAGS]
[48 NAMES]
2ND MANASSAS
—

[CROSSED U.S. AND C.S.A. NATIONAL FLAGS]
[45 NAMES]
MALVERN HILL

Three sides of the Portsmouth Light Artillery obelisk give tribute to Confederate soldiers, the fourth to a War of 1812 engagement at Craney Island, fought near here on June 22, 1813. Like other monuments to standing units, especially artillery, credit is given for the unit's willingness to fight when called upon, whatever the cause, and in this case with pride in doing so. The *Portsmouth Star* notes that "the old battery fought as loyally [for the Union] as it did for the South, and . . . stands ready to fight again."

From early on, the eighteen-foot-high Virginia granite shaft was called "the first monument in the United States containing both the Stars and Stripes and the Confederate flags." The *Star* also noted in its report on the dedication that "It will stand, although small in proportions, as a great peace monument between the sections, exemplifying the beautiful sentiment which has united the country in spirit as well as in lay" [sic].

- The monument faces north. The *Star* gave special attention to the fact that funding was completed without government support and cost only $554, raised entirely by the Portsmouth Light Artillery Monument Association.

Cedar Grove Cemetery

275. Cedar Grove Cemetery Tablet

Monument is a shaft set on a base.
LOCATION: Effingham and North streets, 23705
DATE: 1903
MEDIUM: Granite
Front

TO OUR
CONFEDERATE
DEAD
1861–1865

—

[C.S.A. BATTLE FLAG]

—

ERECTED 1903
BY
LADIES
MEMORIAL
AID ASSOCIATION

—

[C.S.A. BATTLE FLAG]

The stolid, suggestive 1903 shaft stands in contrast to the profusion of detailed informational plaques installed by the Stonewall Camp #380 of the Sons of Confederate Veterans in the 1990s.

Many Virginia Confederate cemeteries are larger and more prominent than Cedar Grove, but this site is particularly well tended. The larger city cemetery was established in 1832. Local veterans in Portsmouth and Norfolk formed the Stonewall Camp, United Confederate Veterans, and founded the Confederate section. The Camp, one plaque notes, remained active until 1929, when the last three members bequeathed their assets to the Sons and Daughters of Confederate Veterans. The Portsmouth Ladies Memorial Association placed the granite headstones here and at Oak Grove Cemetery nearby. In recent years, the Sons of Confederate Veterans has succeeded them. In addition to the plaques, the S.C.V. reinscribed each headstone on the rear and reversed the stone.

276. C.S.S. *Virginia* Tablet
Monument is a base and shaft.
DATE: 1996
MEDIUM: Granite

IN MEMORY OF THE MEN
who built and manned the
CSS VIRGINIA
1861–1862
Original Granite Dry Dock #1
Gosport Navy Yard
Stonewall Camp #380
SCV 1996

There is no mention of the war and no apologetic in this shaft dedicated on Memorial Day, 1996; its focus is on naval affairs, which bear only scant mention in Virginia monuments. An informational plaque notes that the marker "is of the same granite and is carved in the same shape as it formed a part of the first dry dock built in 1832." The commemorated are not just Confederate sailors, but "men"—since the builders included civilians.

It was here that the abandoned frigate U.S.S. *Merrimac* was converted into the ironclad C.S.S. *Virginia*. In March 1862, the *Virginia* fought the ironclad U.S.S. *Monitor* in the first battle involving ironclad ships.

- The Hampton Roads area has the largest naval base in the world. Gosport Shipyard was established in 1767. Dry Dock 1, now a national historic landmark, is still in use.

City of Norfolk

277. Common Soldier

Monument is a granite plinth, base, dado, and column, surmounted by a private soldier, in bronze, standing with flag, bearing a sword.
LOCATION: Commercial Place, Main Street, 23510
DATE: May 16, 1907
MEDIA: Bronze, granite
Front

CSA
OUR CONFEDERATE DEAD
1861–1865

—

61ST AND FINAL
REUNION
UCV
NORFOLK
MAY 30–JUNE 3,
1951

—

[SEAL OF VIRGINIA]

—

VETERANS ATTENDING
FINAL REUNION
[4 NAMES]

The neighborhood surrounding this fifty-foot shaft and sculpture monument reflects the many changes that have occurred in the Norfolk area. The cornerstone was laid on February 22, 1899, thirty-two years after Jefferson Davis's inauguration as president of the Confederacy. The Couper Marble Works of Norfolk designed it; the fifteen-foot bronze statue is by Norfolk-born sculptor William Couper. It was unveiled on May 16, 1907, during the tricentennial of the Jamestown Exposition.

The original inscription—"Our Confederate Dead"—was appended with a United Confederate Veterans inscription about the last Confederate veterans reunion in 1951. The city was decorated with Confederate flags for the occasion, a commemorative U.S. postage stamp was issued, and numerous commemorative events led up to a climactic parade. The Pickett-Buchanan Camp, Sons of Confederate Veterans, who had originally sponsored the monument, led the procession dressed in Confederate uniforms.

The monument was dismantled and placed in storage in 1964–65 for the construction of an office building, and there was some question about when or whether the monument should be reerected, but it was, in 1971. Standing over fifty feet high, it is one of the tallest monuments in Virginia, but today, surrounded by steel and glass office buildings, it seems anachronistic and outsized.

- A more ambitious design called for the column to be topped with a heroic bronze figure of Peace, while four life-sized bronze figures representing a Confederate sailor, infantryman, cavalryman, and artilleryman would adorn the base.
- The records cannot confirm with certainty that any of the four names on the roster is that of a veteran. John Salling of Virginia almost certainly was not a vet-

eran. William J. Bush of Georgia probably was; William D. Townsend and Arnold Murray may have been.

Elmwood Cemetery

278. Common Soldier

Monument is a private soldier standing at parade rest surmounting a plinth, base, and shaft with bronze plaques; extensions support four cannon balls.
DATE: November 7, 1912
MEDIA: Bronze, granite

—

TO OUR
CONFEDERATE DEAD
—
1861
1865
—
[BLANK]
—

ERECTED NOVEMBER 7, 1912 BY
NEIMEYER-SHAW CHAPTER 595
SOLDIER STATUE DONATED MAY 6, 2007
BY PICKETT-BUCHANNAN CHAPTER 21
UNITED DAUGHTERS OF THE CONFEDERACY
LEST WE FORGET

The recent addition of a statue of a Confederate soldier to this monument dramatically changed its appearance and presentation. Before the statue this was something of a grim shaft with a terse inscription, which stood in contrast to the other more defiant and celebratory tributes erected in the semicentennial era. It remains distinctive: Who the "Our" in "Our Confederate Dead" was is a particularly provocative issue, given the fact that the cornerstone of the West Point monument to "Colored soldiers and sailors" had been laid in 1909 in the adjacent, once-segregated grounds within sight of this monument.

The monument was moved to the Elmwood Cemetery in 1987 because of road construction. The Pickett-Buchanan Chapter 21 of the United Daughters of the Confederacy assumed responsibility for the monument. It was originally designed to have a statue of a Confederate soldier atop the pedestal, but this was not installed until nearly ninety-five years after the dedication ceremonies, when a thousand-pound statue of a Confederate soldier, carved at a granite quarry in China, was shipped to Norfolk and was erected here on February 1, 2007.

279. Elmwood Obelisk

MONUMENT is an obelisk set on a plinth and base.
MEDIUM: Granite

OUR
CONFEDERATE DEAD

ERECTED BY THE
DAUGHTERS OF THE CONFEDERACY
AND SONS OF VETERANS
OF PICKETT BUCHANAN CAMP.
"TIRED SOLDIER REST!
VIRGINIA'S BREAST
NO NOBLER DUST ENCLOSES."

Granite riser:

PICKETT BUCHANAN CAMP. C.V.

This is one of the few mentions of Maj. Gen. George E. Pickett other than at Hollywood Cemetery, the Five Forks battlefield, and the Chatham courthouse. Born in Richmond, Pickett was an insurance agent in Norfolk after the war. He was originally buried in Norfolk but was reinterred at Hollywood Cemetery in Richmond in October 1875.

The eulogy, "Tired Soldier Rest," is a theme common to Northern and Southern epitaphs. The genteel oxymoron, "Noble Dust," may be a reference to Genesis 3:19 ("Dust thou art and unto thou shalt return").

280. The Anchor

Monument is an anchor and capstan.
DATE: 1900
MEDIUM: Iron

A large ship's anchor and capstan with no inscription is the presiding monument over the Confederate cemetery's approximately 224 headstones. The anchor is the only such example in Virginia. The maritime intention is obvious, although the anchor is also a symbol of hope in the Christian tradition. The headstones are blank: no epitaphs are inscribed.

- Also buried in Elmwood: Brig. Gen. Richard L. Page; Col. Walter H. Taylor, who served as Robert E. Lee's aide-de-camp; and Father Abram J. Ryan, poet and priest.

City of Chesapeake

281. Pleasant Grove Cemetery/Jackson Greys Obelisk

Monument is an obelisk set on a plinth and base.
LOCATION: Southwest of present-day Pleasant Grove Baptist Church, 23322; THREE miles west of V.R. 168 on St. Brides Road
DATE: July 11, 1905
MEDIUM: Granite

TO
Commemorate the
organization of the
JACKSON GREYS,
Co A, 61st Va. Regt. at
this place June 1st, 1861,
and to perpetuate the
roll of its members.
Mustered into the Confederate States Army, July
11 and surrendered at Appomattox.
[14 NAMES]
—
[30 NAMES]

—

—

[30 NAMES]

This rough granite shaft with polished faces stands on the former site of Pleasant Grove Baptist Church. The church building burned down in subsequent years; the congregation built a new building, still standing, relocated several miles to the northeast. *Confederate Veteran* notes that the monument was erected "to commemorate the organization of the Jackson Grays [sic], Company A, 61st Virginia Infantry Regiment, Mahone's brigade, A. N. V., at that place on July 11, 1861."

The Jackson Greys were recruited from St. Bride Parish of Norfolk County and named for James W. Jackson. Jackson shot and killed Col. Elmer Ellsworth on May 24, 1861, when Ellsworth removed the Confederate flag from his Alexandria hotel, the Marshall House Inn. Ellsworth was the Union's first casualty of the war. Jackson was killed in the melee that followed.

City of Virginia Beach

282. Princess Anne Courthouse Common Soldier

Monument is a private soldier standing at parade rest surmounting a plinth, base, dado, and shaft.

LOCATION: Corner of Princess Anne and North Landing, 23456
DATE: November 15, 1905
MEDIUM: Granite
Front

1861 VIRGINIA 1865
[SEAL OF VIRGINIA]
PRINCESS ANNE COUNTY
CONFEDERATE
HEROES

—

YOUR ARMS ARE STACKED,
YOUR SPLENDID COLORS FURLED,
YOUR DRUMS ARE STILL,
ASIDE YOUR TRUMPETS LAID.

—

[CROSSED C.S.A. NATIONAL
AND BATTLE FLAGS]

—

Charles M. Walsh was the sculptor of the six-foot-tall granite soldier. Triumphant closure is the theme of this reconciliation-era monument. Note the direct address to the county's "Confederate Heroes": "Your arms . . . Your Splendid Colors . . ." While funereal monuments mourned the dead, reconciliation monuments like this conspicuously consigned the wartime generation to history. The "Heroes" are praised, but their instruments of war, though prominent, are stilled and quiet, and their flags are promenaded but fixed in place. The whole of the monument stands twenty-one feet high, of granite. The base is Virginia granite.

- Historic Southern Monuments approved of the monument, concluding that it "displays fine artistic taste on the part of the artist."
- Princess Anne County no longer exists, and the courthouse is no longer in service as such. In 1963, Virginia Beach and the county were consolidated and the county was dissolved.

Accomack County

283. Parksley, County Memorial, Common Soldier

Monument is a private soldier standing at parade rest surmounting a plinth, base, dado, and shaft.

LOCATION: Mary Street and Cassatt Avenue off V.R. 176 and 316, 23301
DATE: October 20, 1899
MEDIA: Bronze, copper, granite
Front

1861
1865
[SEAL OF VIRGINIA]
ERECTED BY
HARMANSON-WEST CAMP
CONFEDERATE VOLUNTEERS
IN MEMORY OF
THEIR DEAD COMRADES
FROM
ACCOMACK AND NORTHAMPTON
COUNTIES
[BRONZE PLAQUE]

UNVEILED
OCTOBER 20, 1899
—
1861
1865
THEY DIED FOR THE PRINCIPLES
UPON WHICH ALL TRUE
REPUBLICS ARE FOUNDED
—
1861
1865
[C.S.A. BATTLE FLAG]
THEY FOUGHT FOR CONSCIENCE
SAKE AND DIED FOR RIGHT
—
1861
1865
AT THE CALL OF PATRIOTISM
AND DUTY, THEY ENCOUNTERED
THE PERILS OF THE FIELD
AND WERE FAITHFUL
EVEN UNTO DEATH

Accomack County's monument stands in a town founded by Northerners two decades after the war. The campaign for this thirty-foot-high edifice, built of Vermont gray granite, began on November 19, 1898, when a local newspaper called for a Confederate monument to be erected at Accomac, the county seat. Parksley responded with an aggressive effort to secure the monument instead. Both communities offered a location and money for the project, but in May 1899 the project was awarded to Parksley.

The Confederates are praised as "Volunteers" in the 1899 Parksley monument, but more venerable as "Veterans" in the Eastville monument of 1913, which was erected fourteen years later.

Parksely is a railroad town; tracks laid in 1884 bypassed Accomac and were an evident factor in the monument's coming to Parksely. Other veterans' memorials are, however, located at Accomac. Another story avers that a Mr. Henry Bennett lobbied to move the county seat from Accomac to Parksley, but a referendum defeated his efforts. The monument is the town's consolation prize.

Northampton County

284. Eastville, Courthouse Common Soldier

Monument is a private soldier standing at parade rest surmounting a plinth, base, dado, and column.

LOCATION: Courthouse Road, B.R. U.S. 13, 23347

DATE: 1913

MEDIA: Bronze, granite

Front

1861 CSA 1865
[SEAL OF THE CONFEDERACY]
—
ERECTED BY THE HARMANSON-WEST
CAMP CONFEDERATE VETERANS,
THE DAUGHTERS OF
THE CONFEDERACY, AND
THE CITIZENS OF THE
EASTERN SHORE OF VIRGINIA; TO THE
SOLDIERS OF THE CONFEDERACY FROM
NORTHAMPTON AND ACCOMACK
COUNTIES. THEY DIED BRAVELY IN WAR,
OR IN PEACE LIVED NOBLY TO
REHABILITATE THEIR COUNTRY
A. D.
ONE THOUSAND NINE HUNDRED
AND THIRTEEN

This is the second and final courthouse monument erected on the Eastern Shore. Dedicated in 1913 with the seal of the Confederacy displayed, it is also the newest structure on the "Green" at Eastville (population 185). The present courthouse dates from 1899; the old courthouse from 1732; and the Old Clerk's office from the 1830s. The 1731 courthouse was dismantled, moved, and reconstructed in 1913 in order to make room for the monument.

The Parksley and Eastville monuments have the same sponsors and give tribute to Confederate soldiers of both counties; Eastville, however, includes those who "in Peace Lived Nobly to Rehabilitate Their Country."

- The sculptor is unknown. The figure is of Westerly granite, the column and base of Mt. Airy granite. The monument stands approximately twenty-six feet high.

5. PETERSBURG, THE SOUTHSIDE WEST OF PETERSBURG, AND CENTRAL VIRGINIA WEST OF RICHMOND

Geographical Outline. Twenty-one counties, independent cities at Bedford, Danville, Lynchburg, and Petersburg: Interstate 85 on the east, Interstate 64 or James River to the north, North Carolina to the south, and the Blue Ridge Mountains to the west.

Campaigns. Siege of Petersburg, 1864–65, including battles and monuments or markers at the Crater, Hatchers Run, and Reams Station, along with the action at Staunton River; and the Appomattox campaign, 1865, including battles and monuments at Dinwiddie, Five Forks, Sutherland Station, Amelia Springs, Sailor's Creek, Appomattox Station, and Appomattox Court House. The 1864 Valley campaign of Hunter's army culminated in the battle of Lynchburg, also commemorated with several monuments.

Commentary. As a rule, Southside county monuments are more terse and taciturn than in other areas such as the Northern Neck or eastern Virginia, but they also tend to be larger. The prominent place they still have in rural county seats brings to mind historian Thomas Beer's assertion that the war "ceased physically in 1865[, yet] its political end may be reasonably expected about the year 3000." One Southside preservationist asserted to the author that people in Richmond have "forgotten their history" regarding the war. That may or may not be true, but sites at Appomattox and Lynchburg's Old City Cemetery are particularly well cared for by local community groups.

The Southside retains much of the character of the nineteenth century. The Piedmont foothills are the dominant physical feature;

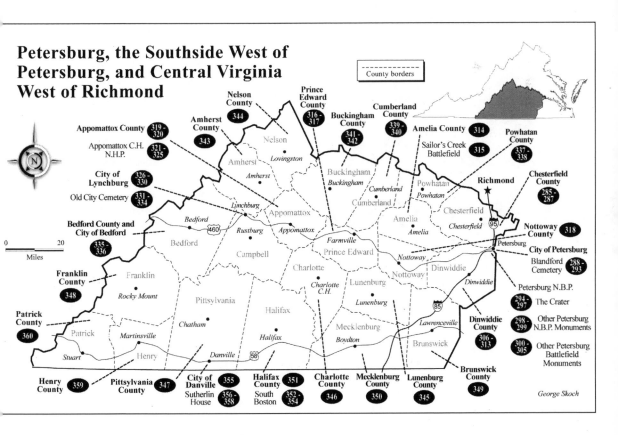

Petersburg, the Southside West of Petersburg, and Central Virginia West of Richmond

George Skoch

farming and lumber are common industries. Small towns predominate; Lynchburg is the largest city. No interstate highways cross the Southside west of Interstate 85. Some of the highways that do—U.S. 15, 58, 360, 460—are not heavily traveled. That relative isolation sometimes provides a dramatic context to a landscape that includes the site of the 1864–65 Siege of Petersburg; Blandford Cemetery, with its thirty thousand Confederate dead, most of them unknown; Danville, last capital of the Confederacy; and Lee's army's line of retreat to the "surrender grounds," as they are locally known, at Appomattox.

Chesterfield County

285. Chesterfield, Courthouse Common Soldier

Monument is a private soldier, in white bronze, standing at parade rest surmounting a base, plinth, and extended granite block shaft.
LOCATION: 9500 Courthouse Road, 23832
DATE: September 2, 1903
MEDIA: Granite, white bronze
Front

VIRTUS
1861
IN MEMORY OF THE
CONFEDERATE SOLDIERS OF

CHESTERFIELD AND MANCHESTER
1865
—

VERITAS
DULCE ET. DECORUM EST.
PRO PATRIA MORI

Authorized by the county's board of supervisors and sponsored in part by Confederate veterans, this is one of the tallest courthouse monuments in Virginia. Initially granite from a dismantled debtors jail, in which Baptist preachers were imprisoned for preaching without a license, was used, but it was "deemed inadequate" and was supplemented by new granite from a local source. The statue stands almost thirty feet high and was placed off-center on the courthouse grounds. It looms over the site but is not intrusive. The Latin inscriptions—"Virtus"—add neoclassical flourishes, but the white bronze statue is a factory-model Confederate soldier.

A thousand people attended the dedication ceremonies on September 2, 1903. One speaker, the Honorable Philip V. Cogsbill, declared to the crowd that the monument would serve to "teach the children and grandchildren of those present that the forefathers and kinsfolk of the Confederate War, instead of being traitors, were noblemen and patriots deserving the highest fame."

- Manchester, cited on the inscription, was once part of Chesterfield County; it was annexed by Richmond in 1910.
- The Latin expression "Virtus" is translated as "valor, manly excellence, virtue."
- Judge John Henry Ingram, orator of the day, was quoted in the *Richmond Times-Dispatch* of September 6, 1903:

This occasion would be incomplete if those of us of this generation who came after the heroes, to whose memory is dedicated, did not take its lessons to heart. Issues of a different character confront us to-day, but as serious as those which confronted previous generations. We do not have to seek them; they are knocking at every man's door. They are social, economic and political, and are to be met by the same spirit which characterized our fathers and our father's fathers.

286. Parker's Battery Tablet

Monument is a granite shaft.

LOCATION: 1801 Ware Bottom Spring Road, 23836

DATE: 1921

MEDIUM: Granite

> PARKER'S BATTERY
> C.S.A.
> POSITION
> JULY 1864
> TO
> APRIL 1865

This is another memorial marking Confederate siege lines: Parker's Battery (Capt., later Maj. William W. Parker) of four guns was stationed here, on the Howlett Line, from mid-June 1864 until near the end of the war. The unit, which originally organized in Richmond, saw little action—occasional shelling, pickets exchanging fire—during the nearly ten months it was stationed there, but the site was evidently so memorable that Lt. J. Thompson Brown, veteran of the battery, purchased and preserved the area and the earthworks after

the war. The monument was erected in 1921, by surviving members of the battery.

The battery served on numerous battlefields, and its place at Fredericksburg is also marked with a monument. Its time at this site ended with the fall of Petersburg, when the battery retreated with the Army of Northern Virginia to Appomattox. The site is now on National Park Service grounds.

287. Winterpock Church Tablet

Monument is a triangular granite shaft.

LOCATION: From Richmond, U.S. 360 to C.R. 621 (Winterpock Road) to C.R. 603 (Beaver Bridge Road), 23838

DATE: 1947

MEDIUM: Granite

> [CROSSED VIRGINIA AND
> C.S.A. BATTLE FLAGS]
> IN MEMORY OF
> CONFEDERATE DEAD OF
> WINTERPOCK.
> ERECTED BY CHESTERFIELD CHAPTER, U.D.C.
> 1947.

This modest shaft is one of the last monuments sponsored by the first generation of wartime descendents. It may also be the last for the "Confederate Dead" and the last churchyard monument.

Among other post–World War II monuments, the 1949 Hopewell elegy takes a more hopeful tone of closure, while the 1952 Halifax cemetery monument adds a note of familiarity, referring to its Confederates as "Veterans," as if they were contemporaries.

City of Petersburg

Rochelle Lane, 23803
Blandford Cemetery

288. Washington Artillery Tablet

Monument is a granite shaft set on a base and plinth.
LOCATION: Just south of churchyard wall
DATE: 1912
MEDIUM: Granite

> ERECTED BY THE
> WASHINGTON ARTILLERY
> OF NEW ORLEANS, LA.,
> IN MEMORY OF THEIR
> COMRADES KILLED DURING
> THE SIEGE OF PETERSBURG,
> 1864.–1865.
> [31 NAMES]

The Washington Artillery was organized in 1838. Its various sections and batteries fought in over sixty battles during the war, from First Manassas to Appomattox and from Shiloh to Nashville. It exists to this day as a unit of the Louisiana National Guard. Like other monuments to standing units, such as the Richmond Howitzers and Portsmouth Artillery, the war is taken in a veritable nonpartisan context: no cause is cited, as if the men were called to service to do a duty without reference to political or moral justifications.

This monument stands just south of Blandford Church, erected circa 1735–37. The building was abandoned and in ruins at the time of the war, but it served as a hospital during the siege. Blandford stood behind the sites of Gracie's, Colquitt's and Elliot's salients in the Confederate siege line. The church was restored early in the twentieth century and now serves as a Confederate shrine decorated with stained glass windows from former Confederate states. A 1935 marble tablet on the church building notes that the Ladies Memorial Association was given care of the chapel in 1901. It was through their efforts that the structure was restored as a memorial to Confederate soldiers.

289. Fort Steadman Tablet

Monument is a granite shaft.
LOCATION: North side of Blandford Church, outside of churchyard
DATE: circa 1917–19
MEDIUM: Granite

> FORT STEADMAN [*SIC*]
> HEROES

This Burns and Campbell shaft, sponsored by the Ladies Memorial Association, marks the site where the bodies of twelve soldiers killed in the assault on Fort Steadman were buried after the war. It was the last major assault by the Army of Northern Virginia and an ill-fated one, which may explain why the monument distinguishes these "Heroes" from the state monument inscriptions in the Confederate cemetery.

Blandford Cemetery, Confederate Section

290. The Arch and Adjacent Tablets

Monument is a series of three stone arches over a central roadway and two pedestrian entryways.

DATE: 1913
MEDIUM: Granite
Across the arch facing west

> OUR CONFEDERATE HEROES
> 1861–1865   1866–1913

Plaque at left base

> "THERE COMES A VOICE THAT
> AWAKES MY SOUL,
> IT IS THE VOICE OF YEARS
> THAT ARE GONE;
> THEY ROLL BEFORE ME
> WITH ALL THEIR DEEDS."
> LADIES MEMORIAL ASSOC.
> PETERSBURG VA

Plaque at right base

> THIS ARCH
> REPLACES ONE
> DESIGNED BY
> WILLIAM S. SIMPSON
> AND ERECTED BY THE
> L.M.A. OF PETERSBURG VA.
> IN 1884.

Reverse side, facing east, crest of arch

> AWAITING THE REVEILLE
> 1866–1913   1861–1865

Behind this arch is the largest mass gravesite in Virginia. Some twenty-eight thousand Confederate soldiers are interred in thirteen acres that are, appropriately enough, between the former Union siege lines and Petersburg. Many of the men buried here died during the Siege of Petersburg, June 1864–April 1865, but not all. Some were former prisoners whose bodies were returned from the North until exchanges were stopped on May 25, 1863. Others came from as far away as Richmond and Lynchburg.

Approximately one in five of the wartime dead is buried here. The Petersburg Ladies Memorial Association, organized May 6, 1866, took as its mission the recovery and reburial of the Confederate dead from battlefields, military hospitals, and other sites in the area. Ultimately they oversaw the removal and reinterment the bodies of some twenty-four thousand Confederate dead. Another two thousand soldiers are buried elsewhere in the cemetery.

- The dead are simply "Awaiting the Reveille," to judge by the inscription—taken from the New Testament book of I Corinthians 15:52 ("In a moment, in the twinkling of an eye, at the last trump: for the trumpet shall sound, and the dead raised incorruptible"). The phrase may also be a reference to the field of bones described in Ezekiel 37 and prophesied to live again ("Can these bones live?")
- A gothic-style arch destroyed in a storm preceded the present-day structure.
- "There comes a voice . . ." is taken from a cycle of poems said to have been translated from ancient Gaelic or Erse language sources by eighteenth-century Scottish poet James McPherson
- Also buried here: Confederate generals Cullen A. Battle, David A. Weisiger, and William Mahone, the latter in an Egyptian-style mausoleum with only the letter "M" for an epitaph.

SITE: Granite shafts, various across the Confederate section

DATE: circa 1917–19
MEDIUM: Granite

UNKNOWN
1861–1865

Granite shafts were erected across the large breadth of the Confederate cemetery under the direction of the Ladies Memorial Association circa 1917–19. The markers are the work of Burns and Campbell. Three shafts north of Arch Avenue and east of the dry streambed are inscribed to Virginia, as are three from North Carolina. North of the arch and west of the streambed are seven shafts, six inscribed, "CONFEDERATE DEAD. 1861–1865," with one inscribed to Georgia. Three granite shafts south of Arch Avenue stand for Virginia soldiers, and one each is to Arkansas, Texas, Tennessee, South Carolina, Alabama, Georgia, and Florida; four shafts are inscribed "UNKNOWN." Nearby are shafts, one each, for Mississippi, Missouri, and Louisiana.

291. Blandford, Common Soldier

Monument is a plinth, base, and shaft surmounted by Confederate private soldier, in white bronze, standing at parade rest.
DATE: June 1890
MEDIA: Granite, white bronze

Front

GLORIA VICTIS
1861–1865
"Plant the fair column o'er the vacant grave
A hero's honor let a hero have."
[SEAL OF VIRGINIA]
CONFEDERATE DEAD
—
CITIZENS KILLED JUNE 9, 1864
[13 NAMES]
JUNE 18
[4 NAMES]
UNKNOWN
—
VIRGINIA
N. CAROLINA
S. CARLINA
GEORGIA
FLORIDA
TENNESSEE
ALABAMA
MISSISSIPPI
LOUISIANA
TEXAS
ARKANSAS
MISSOURI
KENTUCKY
ERECTED BY THE
"PETERSBURG LADIES MEMORIAL
ASSOCIATION"
JUNE, 1890.
—
CRATER
JULY 30.
1864

This monument stands at the crest of Memorial Hill and overlooks the mass gravesite. The white bronze soldier faces north. The site was the objective point of assaulting Federal columns on the morning of June 30, 1864. The assault was unsuccessful, and the siege began thereafter. The monument is of Virginia granite taken from a local quarry.

• The dedication:

It was fully half-past six o'clock before the ceremonies commenced in the cemetery, where fully 10,000 people had assembled around the monument and the stand. The scene was an inspiring one. The first to ascend the stand were thirteen beautiful little girls dressed in white, representing the thirteen Confederate States. On the stand were also seated the ladies of the Memorial Association, Miss Lucy Lee Hill [daughter of A. P. Hill], ministers of the gospel, and Mayor Collier. Prayer was offered by the Reverend C.R. Haines, D. D., after which Mayor Collier introduced Captain W. Gordon McCabe as the orator of the day . . .

- The "Crater July 30. 1864," refers to the battle nearby. "Citizens killed June 9," marks the first attack on Petersburg by Federal troops and the calling out of the home guard in response. The Latin expression "Gloria Victis" is translated "Glory to the Defeated."
- The gothic font of "Plant the fair column . . ." is unusual. The tribute, however, also appears on the monuments at Madison and Gloucester.

Two granite shafts ranged about the above monument are inscribed:

CONFEDERATE
DEAD
18
61–65

292. Sons of Confederate Veterans Tablet
Monument is a granite tablet.

DATE: May 27, 2002
MEDIUM: Granite

[S.C.V. EMBLEM]
THIS FLAGPOLE ERECTED BY
SONS OF CONFEDERATE VETERANS
DEARING-BEAUREGARD CAMP #1813
MAY 27, 2002

This is another of the Sons of Confederate Veterans camps' contributions to the revivalist trend of monuments in recent years. Other S.C.V. markers stand at Suffolk and Courtland.
- Among Virginia monuments, where Robert E. Lee and Stonewall Jackson's names dominate, Beauregard's name only appears here and on the First Manassas monument (1927). Pierre Gustave Toutant Beauregard (1818–1893) commanded Confederate forces in that victory as well as outnumbered troops who staved off Union forces at Petersburg in 1864.

293. "Covered Way" Tablet

Monument is a granite shaft and base.
LOCATION: Crater Road near Brith Achim and Blandford cemeteries
DATE: 1917
MEDIUM: Granite

AT THIS PLACE, LOCATED BY
PARTICIPANTS IN THE BATTLE OF THE
CRATER, THIS ROAD, KNOWN AS THE
JERUSALEM PLANK ROAD, WAS CROSSED
BY A COVERED WAY LEADING EAST-
WARDLY TO THE RAVINE IN REAR OF THE
CONFEDERATE BREASTWORKS, WHICH
RUN NORTHWARDLY FROM THE CRATER.
BY THIS COVERED WAY, ABOUT 8 O'CLOCK
ON THE MORNING OF JULY 30TH 1864,
NEARLY 4 HOURS AFTER THE EXPLO-
SION, THE CONFEDERATE TROOPS UNDER
GEN. WM. MAHONE APPROACHED THE
RAVINE FROM WHICH THEY CHARGED

AND RECAPTURED THE BREASTWORKS.
THIS REPLACES A WOODEN MARKER
ERECTED BY A. P. HILL CAMP CONFEDERATE
VETERANS.

—

PRESENTED TO THE
A. P. HILL CAMP S.C.V.
IN MEMORY OF
WILLIAM R. MCKENNEY
OF PETERSBURG, VA.
1851–1916

Prompt movements of Confederate troops to block Union forces from gaining control of Petersburg led to this commemoration. The covered way—or defilade—refers to the path followed by reinforcements that led eastward from the town into the ravine below this marker and vicinity and then branched north and west of the Crater.

Note the drama implicit in the narrative: the attention to timing—"8 o'clock . . . 4 hours after the explosion"—as well as the sense of stealth followed by the climactic action: " . . . approached the ravine from which they charged and recaptured . . ."

Petersburg National Battlefield
1539 Hickory Hill Road, 23803
The Crater

294. South Carolina Tablet

Monument is a bronze tablet set in a granite shaft.
DATE: 1923
MEDIA: Bronze, granite

ON THIS HILL FOR ONE MONTH
SOUTH CAROLINA TROOPS

GUARDED THE ENTRANCE
TO PETERSBURG AND HERE JULY 30, 1864,
SUFFERED DEATH FROM A MINE
EXPLODED BY THE FEDERALS.
HERE THE SURVIVING CAROLINIANS
UNDER THE COMMAND OF
STEPHEN ELLIOTT
BY THEIR VALOR
TURNED A DREADFUL DISASTER
INTO A GLORIOUS VICTORY.
ERECTED BY
THE SOUTH CAROLINA DIVISION
UNITED DAUGHTERS OF THE CONFEDERACY
1923
[U.D.C. EMBLEM]

Vicious fighting occurred at this famous site. In a surprise attack, Union troops of the Ninth Corps ignited four tons of black powder in a mineshaft underneath "Elliott's salient"; some 278 Confederates were killed in the initial explosion. A well-planned but poorly led, bloody, and unsuccessful assault followed. The defense was valiant. Credit is justly given to Elliot's South Carolinians for rallying, but "Glorious Victory" may be an overstatement. Historian Douglas Southall Freeman concludes that it was "a desperate day in a cause daily more desperate."

- Brig. Gen. Stephen Elliott Jr. (1832–1866) led the South Carolina Brigade. He was wounded here and at the battle of Bentonville and died of his wounds shortly after the war.

295. Mahone's Brigade Tablet

Monument is a granite shaft.
DATE: November 1910

MEDIUM: Granite

> THIS STONE MARKS
> APPROXIMATELY THE EXTREME
> RIGHT OF MAHONE'S BRIGADE
> VIRGINIA VOLUNTEERS
> WHEN IT RE-CAPTURED THE
> CONFEDERATE BREASTWORKS
> ON THE 30TH. OF JULY 1864.
> PLACED BY THE PETERSBURG
> CHAPTER U.D.C. NOVEMBER 1910.

This United Daughters of the Confederacy shaft was the first Southern marker at the Crater and the first at what would become the Petersburg National Military Park. Monuments to the 2nd Pennsylvania Heavy Artillery, circa 1905, preceded them.

- The ceremonies: excerpt from the address by Col. William H. Stewart, 61st Virginia Infantry:

> [T]he Confederate veterans recognize with lofty pride and deepest gratitude the noble work of the Petersburg Chapter, United Daughters of the Confederacy. . . . And now in the name of and for the true daughters of the noble mothers of the Confederacy, I dedicate this monument to the memory of the men of Mahone's Brigade, who recaptured the breastworks on this line on July 30, 1864.

296. Maj. Gen. William Mahone Obelisk

Monument is an obelisk surmounting a plinth, base, and dado.

DATE: 1917
MEDIUM: Granite

> MAHONE
> TO THE MEMORY OF
> WILLIAM MAHONE
> MAJOR GENERAL C.S.A.
> A DISTINGUISHED CONFEDERATE
> COMMANDER, WHOSE VALOR AND
> STRATEGY AT THE BATTLE OF THE
> CRATER JULY 30, 1864 WON FOR
> HIMSELF AND HIS GALLANT
> BRIGADE UNDYING FAME.
> A CITIZEN OF PETERSBURG, VIRGINIA,

> BORN DEC. 1, 1826,
> DIED OCT. 8, 1895.
> ERECTED BY PETERSBURG CHAPTER
> U.D.C.
>
> BURNS &
> CAMPBELL

This late reconciliation monument was erected some fifty-three years after the battle. Mahone earned no special distinction when he served as a brigade commander in the early war years, but by war's end he was the most effective combat leader in the Army of Northern Virginia. Mahone lived in Petersburg in the postwar era and had a career in railroads and as a U.S. senator.

The memorial justifiably praises Mahone for his service at the Crater when, for several crucial minutes, the road to Petersburg was open, and thousands of Union troops stood poised to travel that road. The defense and counterattack he led was prompt, effective, and successful.

297. Centennial Tablet

Monument is a granite shaft set on a base.
DATE: July 30, 1964
MEDIUM: Granite

[CROSSED U.S. FLAG AND C.S.A. BATTLE FLAG]
COMMEMORATING THE 100TH ANNIVERSARY
OF
THE BATTLE OF THE CRATER
JULY 30, 1864
ERECTED BY THE CITIZENS OF PETERSBURG
JULY 30, 1964

This centennial monument offers an arguably simple commemoration to both sides by dint of a display of a U.S. flag and the battle flag. Union and Confederate monuments stand together here, unlike those at the Gettysburg National Military Park, where stipulations segregated the monuments of the opposing sides.

Other Petersburg Battlefield Monuments

298. Colquitt's Salient Tablet
Monument is a granite shaft.
LOCATION: Poor Creek Trail, near Fort Stedman
DATE: circa 1914
MEDIUM: Granite

COLQUITT'S SALIENT
ON JUNE 18 1864 THE
CONFEDERATES ON THIS
HILL REPULSED THE
CHARGE OF THE FIRST
MAINE REGIMENT
ON MARCH 25 1865 FROM
THIS SALIENT GENERAL
JOHN B. GORDON LED A
BODY OF PICKED MEN
TO SURPRISE AND
CAPTURE FORT STEDMAN

The A. P. Hill Chapter of the Sons of Confederate Veterans sponsored this monument. It takes particular note of two actions that span the length of the siege. Both events are well noted in histories of the Siege of Petersburg. The first was a bloody, one-sided victory for the Confederates, the second a defeat and repulse. In the first, June 1864, of 850 men in the 1st Maine Heavy Artillery, 614 were killed or wounded in the assault on Confederate lines. Of the second—March 25, 1864—it is true that Gordon's assault was initially "successful," as the marker notes, and Union lines were breached at Fort Stedman—nearby, still standing—but the Confederates fell victim to a heavy counter-crossfire, and many Southern troops were cut off and captured, while the survivors were forced back to their lines. Both accounts are focused on unit actions without reference to the larger outcome of the battle, the siege, or the war.

299. Gracie's Salient Tablet

Monument is a granite shaft.
LOCATION: Poor Creek Trail, opposite Fort Stedman, south of Colquitt's Salient
DATE: circa 1914
MEDIUM: Granite

> GRACIE'S SALIENT.
> THIS SALIENT, NAMED FOR
> BRIG.-GENL. ARCHIBALD
> GRACIE OF ALABAMA,
> FACED THE FEDERAL FORTS
> STEDMAN AND HASKELL
> AND WAS SUCCESSFULLY
> HELD BY THE CONFEDERATES
> DURING THE ENTIRE SIEGE
> OF PETERSBURG.

Gracie's Salient did not fall during the siege; it retains much of its physical integrity and is representative of Petersburg's fortifications during the war. Stolidity and success, even victory are themes of the memorial: the salient "Was Successfully Held By The Confederates During The Entire Siege."

300. Jack Hare Tablet

Monument is a granite tablet.
LOCATION: 1318 E. Washington Street 23803
DATE: circa 1914
MEDIUM: Granite

> CONFEDERATE BATTERY
> FROM THIS REDOUBT
> JACK HARE A MEMBER
> OF THIS BATTERY
> SHELLED AND DESTROYED
> HIS OWN HOME OPPOSITE
> HERE BECAUSE IT WAS
> BEING USED BY THE
> FEDERAL ARMY
> JULY 1864

In July 1864, John W. "Jack" Hare, as a member of Sturdivant's Battery (also called the Albermarle Artillery, Capt. Nathaniel A. Sturdivant, commanding), was called upon to shell his home, which was being used by Union soldiers. He did so and earned this monument. His was the Hare house at New Market, near the site where the Union army erected Fort Stedman.

The marker, believed to have been sponsored by the A. P. Hill Camp of the Sons of Confederate Veterans, was placed circa 1914, at or in the vicinity of the site occupied by Sturdivant's battery. Today it stands at the foot of an office building located about one quarter mile east of a railroad bridge which crosses Washington Street (V.R. 36).

301. Citizen Soldiers Monument
Monument is a shaft set on a plinth and base.

LOCATION: Crater Road near Sycamore, north of the Gowan monument
DATE: May 1909
MEDIUM: Granite

> THIS STONE MARKS THE SPOT WHERE
> THE OLD MEN AND BOYS OF PETERS-
> BURG UNDER GEN. R. E. COLSTON AND
> COL. F. H. ARCHER
> 125 STRONG
> ON JUNE 9TH, 1864
> DISTINGUISHED THEMSELVES IN A
> FIGHT WITH 1300 FEDERAL CAVALRY
> UNDER GEN. KAUTZ, GAINING TIME FOR
> THE DEFEAT OF THE EXPEDITION.
> PLACED BY THE PETERSBURG CHAPTER
> U.D.C. MAY 1909.

The site of the first battle of Petersburg is marked with a tribute to the "Home Guards"—the "old men and boys of Petersburg [who] distinguished themselves" in a fight with Federal cavalry under Brig. Gen. August V. Kautz. The odds are emphasized: 125 "old men and boys"

versus 1,300 Federal cavalry. So too is their courage: 125 "Strong." The south side of Petersburg was virtually unguarded when these few citizen/soldiers interposed themselves to delay the Union troopers. The Federals attacked near here, along the Dimmock Line of defenses at the Jerusalem Plank Road (present-day Crater Road). Major Fletcher H. Archer led the defense, along with Brig. Gen. Raleigh E. Colston, who happened to be in Petersburg at the time.

The tribute is just: the men took heavy losses, but the disruption they imposed gave time for regular troops to intervene and repulse a second assault. Casualties were about eighty killed, wounded, or captured, with the Federals taking about forty casualties. (A roster of the dead from Petersburg is inscribed on the monument at Blandford Cemetery.)

- The shaft stands on an unobtrusive mound near the sites of the Confederate Fort Mahone and the Union Fort Sedgwick; both were demolished for commercial and residential development, which is extensive in this neighborhood. Two Union monuments stand in the area, but this is the only Confederate monument.

302. Weldon Railroad Battlefield, South Carolina Brigade
Monument is an obelisk set on a plinth and base.

LOCATION: Flank and Halifax roads, Petersburg National Battlefield
DATE: 1908
MEDIA: Bronze, granite
Front

HERE
A BRIGADE
COMPOSED OF THE
7TH BATTALION,
THE 11TH, 21ST, 25TH
AND 27TH REGIMENTS
SOUTH CAROLINA
VOLUNTEERS,
COMMANDED BY
BRIG. GEN. JOHNSON
HAGOOD,
CHARGED WARREN'S
FEDERAL ARMY CORPS,
ON THE 21ST DAY OF
AUGUST 1864,
TAKING INTO THE FIGHT
740 MEN,
RETIRING WITH 273.
NO PROUDER FATE THAN
THEIRS WHO GAVE
THEIR LIVES TO
LIBERTY.
HAGOOD'S BRIGADE

—

A. N. V.

—

[SOUTH CAROLINA SEAL]
MARCH 26 JULY 4
QUIS SEPARABIT
ANIMUS OPIBUSQUE PARATI]
PLACED HERE BY WM. V. IZLAR, A
SURVIVOR OF THE CHARGE, AIDED
BY OTHER SOUTH CAROLINIANS.

—

C.S.A.

The Izlar monument commemorates a counterattack during the battle of the Weldon Railroad, August 18–21, 1864. The assault of Brig. Gen. Johnson Hagood's Brigade took them inside an angle of the Union lines, and the South Carolinians were outnumbered and surrounded. In the confusion some Confederates surrendered, but others refused, and Hagood, future governor of South Carolina, led these survivors out.

The narrative faces east, the same direction the Confederates faced as they charged. "Warren's Federal Army Corps" refers to Maj. Gen. Gouverneur K. Warren and the Fifth Corps. Unmentioned is the title of the engagement and the outcome as a Union victory. The Federals, who seized the Weldon Railroad at this site on August 18, never yielded the ground and eventually erected Fort Wadsworth here—still standing, now on Park Service grounds just outside Petersburg.

- Historian Chris Calkins writes that the attack was misconceived: through some misunderstanding between generals Hill and Mahone, Harris's Mississippi Brigade and Hagood's men assailed strongly held earthworks against superior numbers.
- William Valmore Izlar was a sergeant with the 25th South Carolina Infantry.
- "Animus opibusque parati" on the South Carolina seal is translated as "Prepared in mind and resources." "Quis separabit" is translated as "Who will separate?"

303. Fort Gregg Tablet
Monument is a granite shaft.

LOCATION: Boydton Plank Road and 7th Avenue, 23803
DATE: April 2, 1914
MEDIUM: Granite

FORT GREGG
CONFEDERATE DEFENSE LINE
APR. 2, 1865.
ERECTED APR. 2, 1914.
BY A. P. HILL CAMP S.C.V.

On April 2, 1865, this fort just outside Petersburg was held by Brig. Gen. Nathaniel H. Harris's Mississippi Brigade of about two hundred and fifty men and sections of the Washington Artillery (about twenty-five men). Some five thousand Federals—elements of Gen. John Gibbon's 25th Corps—attacked them. Historian A. Wilson Greene called it "one of the most dramatic combat episodes of the entire war." Although the Federals prevailed, the seven hundred casualties they incurred exceeded the combined garrisons of Fort Gregg and the adjacent Fort Whitworth. The defense lasted long enough for Lee to reform along Petersburg's inner defense lines and prevent the fall of the city before the Army of Northern Virginia could evacuate.

- April 2 commemorates the day of the breaking of the Siege of Petersburg in 1865 and the death of A. P. Hill.
- The grounds, now part of Petersburg National Battlefield, retain much of their integrity; it offers an impressive, if stark landscape, notwithstanding the adjacent interstate highway.
- The adjacent Fort Whitworth still stands and is accessible across I-85/U.S. 460 on the grounds of Central State Hospital.

304. Rohoic Creek Dam Tablet

Monument is a granite shaft.
LOCATION: Boydton Plank and Dupuy roads, 23803
DATE: April 2, 1914
MEDIUM: Granite

ROHOIC DAM
ERECTED BY GENL. R. E. LEE.
AUG. 1864.
ERECTED APR 2, 1914.
BY A. P. HILL CAMP S.C.V.

The impressive remains of this earthen structure on Rohoic Creek stand in woods northwest of Dupuy and Boydton Plank roads. Rohoic Dam shortened the Confederate lines that needed to be manned and prevented or diverted surprise attacks. The dam created the largest of several such bodies of water that confronted Federal troops along the siege lines. Col. Thomas M. R. Talcott of Lee's staff superintended the construction. The project was three hundred feet long, fifty feet tall, one foot thick at the top, and thirty feet wide at the base. The resulting water obstacle stretched half a mile and was thirty feet deep in places.

- Direct access by visitors is challenging, and there is no parking, but the marker stands on the west side of Dupuy Road just north of Boydton Plank Road.

305. Battery 45/Fort Lee Tablet

Monument is a granite shaft.
LOCATION: Boydton Plank and Fort Lee roads, 23803
DATE: April 2, 1914
MEDIUM: Granite

BATTERY 45
SALIENT OF CONFEDERATE LINE
SIEGE OF PETERSBURG.
ERECTED APR. 2, 1914.
BY A. P. HILL CAMP S.C.V.

This shaft stands at the southwest corner of the original Confederate defense line laid out by Capt. Charles H. Dimmock in 1862–63. Battery 45 is also known as Fort Lee. It was a point of action in the final stage of the siege. Trees and undergrowth dominate the landscape of this site, but extensive works remain in a surprisingly evocative state. The monument stands along Boydton Plank Road, facing south toward Federal lines.

Dinwiddie County

306. Lt. Gen. A. P. Hill Tablet at U.S. 1

Monument is a granite shaft.
LOCATION: Northwest corner of Boydton Plank (U.S. 1) and Duncan roads 23803
DATE: circa 1914
MEDIUM: Granite

TO THE MEMORY OF
A. P. HILL, LT-GEN. C.S.A.

HE WAS KILLED ABOUT 600 YARDS
NORTHWARDLY FROM THIS MARKER,
BEING SHOT BY A SMALL BAND OF
STRAGGLERS FROM THE FEDERAL LINES
ON THE MORNING OF APRIL 2ND, 1865.
ERECTED BY A. P. HILL CAMP SONS OF
CONFEDERATE VETERANS PETERSBURG, VA.

Hill was shot out of his saddle near here in the closing hours of the Siege of Petersburg. Hill's death is described as taking place on a spring morning, a time traditionally associated with hope, and he is shot—not by soldiers, as they might be called—but a "band of stragglers." In fact, in the wake of the breaking of Confederate lines, Hill and Sgt. George Tucker were riding to Maj. Gen. Henry Heth's division headquarters at the Pickrell House, which stood across the road from the present-day entrance to Pamplin Park. En route they encountered Pvt. Daniel Wolford and Cpl. William Mauk of the 138th Pennsylvania Infantry, soldiers of one of the regiments that had broken the siege lines earlier in the morning. Both men fired their weapons at the Confederates; it was Mauk's .58-caliber bullet that struck Hill and killed him.

- Pamplin Historical Park and the National Museum of the Civil War Soldier are located just south of this site, off U.S. 1.

307. Lt. Gen. A. P. Hill Tablet, Site of Death
Monument is a granite shaft.

LOCATION: Off Boydton Plank Road (U.S. 1): A. P. Hill Drive, approximately seventy-five yards from the road, 23803
DATE: 1912
MEDIUM: Granite

> SPOT WHERE
> A. P. HILL
> WAS KILLED

This simple shaft is located in a quiet wooded lot behind a residential neighborhood. It stands in tandem with the marker on U.S. 1. There is no glory here, just an ending. The date, April 2, 1865, is omitted, and Hill is killed: stark terms for a tragic death.

308. Dinwiddie, Courthouse Common Soldier

Monument is a private soldier standing at parade rest surmounting a plinth, base, shaft, and pedestal.

LOCATION: U.S. 1 (Boydton Plank Road) and Sycamore Drive, 23841
DATE: November 27, 1909
MEDIA: Granite, limestone
Front

> CSA
> 1861.–1865.
> [RELIEF OF UNFURLED C.S.A. NATIONAL FLAG]
> IN
> MEMORY OF
> DINWIDDIE'S CONFEDERATE
> SOLDIERS, THAT THEIR HEROIC
> DEEDS SUBLIME, SELF-SACRIFICE AND
> UNDYING DEVOTION TO DUTY AND
> COUNTRY MAY NEVER BE FORGOTTEN.
> NOV. 27, 1909

This twenty-four-foot Dinwiddie granite monument stands at the former courthouse, a Greek revival structure dating from 1851. Three sides of the dado are blank, but "Undying Devotion" is ascribed to Dinwiddie's Confederate soldiers on the front. The hope that "They May Never Be Forgotten" may be a paraphrase of the Kipling line, "Lest We Forget."

The granite soldier has been described as looking aloof, but Dinwiddie's Confederate soldier has reason to be wary of what may be on the horizon. The soldier is posed in front of the courthouse for practical reasons, but he also faces northwest, toward the battlefields at Five Forks, Sailor's Creek, and Appomattox.

The monument cost two thousand dollars. Governor Claude A. Swanson was the principle speaker at the dedication ceremonies. Dinwiddie still struggled with the memory of Sheridan's wartime "visit" at the time. A newspaper account described the crowd as the largest "since 1865 when Gen. Philip H. Sheridan and his 13,000 Yankees had been pillaging, pilfering, and plundering on those very grounds before the ill-fated battle of Five Forks." To them, the Dinwiddie monument stood in perpetual vigilance against Sheridan and his "Yankees."

- This is no longer an active courthouse site. New courthouse facilities were completed in 1996.

309. Courthouse, Battlefields Memorial

Monument is a granite shaft.
LOCATION: Former courthouse grounds
DATE: July 31, 1972
MEDIUM: Granite

Front

[CROSSED U.S. FLAG AND C.S.A. BATTLE FLAG]
IN MEMORIAM
BATTLE OF
DINWIDDIE COURT HOUSE
DEDICATED TO THE CONFEDERATE
AND UNION SOLDIERS
WHO GAVE THEIR LIVES IN THE
BATTLE OF DINWIDDIE
COURT HOUSE, SOMETIMES CALLED
CHAMBERLAIN'S BED.
IN THE LAST BRIEF VICTORY
OF THE NORTHERN
VIRGINIA, MARCH 31, 1865,
GENERAL SHERIDAN'S TROOPS
WERE DEFEATED AND FORCED
BACK TO DINWIDDIE'S COURT
HOUSE BY THE CONFEDERATES
LED BY GENERAL PICKETT,
W. H. F. LEE AND FITZHUGH LEE.
THE LAST REBEL YELLS WERE
HEARD HERE. GENERAL

SHERIDAN RALLIED WITH
REINFORCEMENTS THE NEXT DAY,
APRIL 1ST, TO PRACTICALLY END
THE WAR WHEN THE UNION
WON OVERWHELMINGLY AT NEARBY
FIVE FORKS, SOMETIMES
CALLED THE WATERLOO OF THE
CONFEDERACY. THIS LED
TO THE EVACUATION OF PETERSBURG
AND RICHMOND ON
APRIL 2, 1865, WITH THE SURRENDER
COMING A FEW DAYS
LATER AT APPOMATTOX ON APRIL 9, 1865.
ERECTED BY THE CONFEDERATE
MEMORIAL ASSOCIATION
OF DINWIDDIE COUNTY ON JULY 31, 1972.

—

[CROSSED U.S. FLAG AND C.S.A. BATTLE FLAG]
MAIN BATTLES AND DATES OF CIVIL
WAR FOUGHT IN DINWIDDIE
COUNTY 1861–1865
I REAMS—JUNE 29, 1864
I WELDON RAILROAD—AUGUST 18–21, 1864
II. WELDON RAILROAD (GLOBE TAVERN)
AUGUST 18–21, 1864
II. REAMS—AUGUST 25, 1864
PEEBLES FARM, POPLAR SPRINGS CHURCH,
PEGRAM FARM WYATT FARM
SEPTEMBER 29–OCTOBER 1, 1864
SEPTEMBER 30–OCTOBER 2, 1864
BURGESS MILL–OCTOBER 27, 1864
HATCHERS RUN—DECEMBER
8, 1864 (SKIRMISH)
FEBRUARY 5–7, 1865 (BATTLE)
GRAVELLY RUN (QUAKER ROAD, MONK'S NECK
BRIDGE)—MARCH 29, 1865
DINWIDDIE COURT HOUSE
OR CHAMBERLAIN'S
BED—MARCH 31, 1865
WHITE OAK ROAD—MARCH 31, 1865
FIVE FORKS—APRIL 1, 1865
SUTHERLAND—APRIL 7, 1865
FT. GREGG AND FT. BALDWIN—APRIL 2, 1865
DINWIDDIE COUNTY
SCENE OF FORTY-NINE BATTLES,
ENGAGEMENTS,
AND SKIRMISHES, WITH OVER FIFTY MILES OF
FORTIFICATIONS AND SIXTY
FORTS AND BATTERIES.

The front of this copious, Vietnam-era narrative offers a dramatic account of one of the closing battles of the war. The reverse side displays a list of actions that took place in Dinwiddie County. One of the few monuments erected in the 1970s, it is also distinctive for conveying a sense of the bloodshed and destruction that took place in the county. The "Main Battles" inscription is evenhanded—non-partisan—and arguably a reflection of the attitude toward the war in progress at the time: there are no victors, no outcomes, only a bludgeoning of opposing sides.

- "Chamberlain's Bed" refers to a stream that flows into Stony Creek. Troops under generals Pickett and W. H. Fitzhugh Lee, coming from Five Forks, forced a crossing of Chamberlain's Bed against Sheridan's troops, who were driven back to Dinwiddie Courthouse.

310. Ream's Station, North Carolina Battlefield Tablet

Monument is a bronze tablet set on a plinth, granite base, and pedestal.
LOCATION: Halifax (C.R. 604) and Depot (C.R. 606) roads, 23805
DATE: circa 2003
MEDIA: Bronze, granite

[CROSSED NORTH CAROLINA STATE
FLAG AND C.S.A. BATTLE FLAG]

The following North Carolina units
honorable and gallantly
Participated in the action at Reams
Station on August 25, 1864
Infantry
Lane's Brigade
Seventh, Eighteenth, Twenty-Eighth,
Thirty-Third, Thirty-Seventh
Scales's Brigade
Thirteenth, Sixteenth, Twenty-Second,
Thirty-Fourth, Thirty-Eighth
Cooke's Brigade
Fifteenth, Twenty-Seventh, Forty-
Sixth, Forty-Eighth
Kirkland's—McRae's Brigade
Eleventh, Twenty-Sixth, Forty-Fourth,
Forty-Seventh, Fifty-Second
Cavalry
GORDEN'S [SIC]—BARRINGER'S BRIGADE
First, Second, Third, Fifth
"If the men who remain in North Carolina share
the same spirit of those they have sent to the/
field, as I do not doubt they do, her defense
may [be] securely trusted to their hands."
R. E. Lee General
NORTH CAROLINA
ERECTED BY THE N. C. DIVISION, SONS
OF CONFEDERATE VETERANS
—
[LAUREL LEAF]
DEO VINDICE

This is the only monument on the Ream's Station battlefield, site of an Army of Northern Virginia victory during the 1864 Siege of Petersburg and one of two preserves established by the Civil War Preservation Trust in this area in 2003 (the other is at Hatcher's Run). The monument bears comparison to other North Carolina monuments in Virginia—at Appomattox (erected 1905) and Spotsylvania (Ramseur's Brigade, erected 2001)—in advocating a place of prominence for North Carolina troops.

On August 24, 1864, Union Maj. Gen. Winfield S. Hancock's Second Corps, preceded by cavalry under Brig. Gen. David M. Gregg, moved south from Petersburg along the Weldon Railroad (present-day Halifax Road), tearing up track. Troops under Maj. Gen. Henry Heth attacked on the following day, overran the faulty Union position, and drove back the Federals in disorder.

- Ream's Station was a Southern tactical victory, but from a strategic perspective, the Federals held the Weldon Railroad, and they were destined never to yield it.
- Ream's Station is also spelled as Reams or Reams's.
- The North Carolina state flag displayed was the type in use during the Civil War.

311. Brig. Gen. John Pegram Tablet

Monument is a granite shaft set on a base.
LOCATION: Dabney Mill Road (C.R. 613) west of Duncan Road (C.R. 670), 23803
DATE: circa 2003
MEDIUM: Granite

> NEAR THIS SITE
> BRIGADIER GENERAL
> JOHN PEGRAM
> WAS KILLED IN THE
> BATTLE OF HATCHER'S RUN
> ON FEBRUARY 6, 1865

Nearly fifty thousand men were involved in this late war action in which Union troops attempted to break Confederate supply lines. The Union advance was stopped, but the Federals succeeded in extending their siege lines.

Some twenty-seven hundred men became casualties, but the monument marks the site of John Pegram's death. Pegram was killed late in the action by a sharpshooter while leading his division.

Pegram (1832–1865) was born in Petersburg and had been married only seventeen days before his death. His younger brother William was killed at the battle of Five Forks in April.

312. Five Forks, Battlefield Tablet

Monument is a granite shaft set on a plinth and base.
LOCATION: From Dinwiddie, north on C.R. 627 to intersection with C.R. 613
WHITE Oak Road Church Road, 23833
DATE: April 1, 1965
MEDIUM: Granite

> [CROSSED U.S. FLAG AND C.S.A. BATTLE FLAG]
> BATTLE OF FIVE FORKS
> HERE AT FIVE FORKS ON APRIL 1, 1865
> 10,000 CONFEDERATES, COMMANDED BY
> BY GENERAL PICKETT, WERE OVERWHELMED
> BY ABOUT 50,000 FEDERAL TROOPS,
> LED BY GENERAL SHERIDAN, THEREBY
> OPENING THE WAY TO THE SOUTHSIDE

RAILROAD MAKING FURTHER DEFENSE
OF PETERSBURG AND RICHMOND
IMPOSSIBLE. WITHDRAWAL TO
APPOMATTOX FOLLOWED.
DEDICATED TO THE MEMORY OF THE
VALIANT DINWIDDIE SOLDIERS, AS
WELL AS TO ALL SOLDIERS OF THE
SOUTH AND NORTH, TAKING PART IN
THIS ENCOUNTER.
PRESENTED BY THE DINWIDDIE
CONFEDERATE
MEMORIAL ASSOCIATION
AND ERECTED BY THE
DINWIDDIE CIVIL WAR
CENTENNIAL COMMISSION
APRIL 1, 1965.

This monument stands at the Five Forks intersection at the center of the battlefield. The inscription of this 1965 battlefield tablet is in keeping with the bipartisan tone of the centennial era: U.S. and C.S.A. flags are inscribed, and credit is given to "All Soldiers of the South and North." This is still a Virginia monument, however: the first tribute is given to "Valiant Dinwiddie Soldiers," and it was erected under local county auspices. The county, to judge by this marker, claims the field and the right to interpret it.

Command responsibility is placed squarely on Maj. Gen. George E. Pickett. To the lasting embarrassment of his reputation, he was off the field when Federal forces attacked here and forced a decisive breach in the Petersburg-Richmond defense line. No censure of Pickett is intimated. "Withdrawal" rather than retreat followed. To judge by the narrative, no tactics or vigilance on the Confederate side could have stopped the Union forces, who outnumbered the Confederates five to one. That assessment is questionable. It is true that Pickett's force was "Overwhelmed," and that the Southerners were outnumbered. However, "50,000 Federal Troops would have to include all Federals in the area. About thirty thousand Federals were on the field by most accounts, but at a relatively low cost of 634 casualties, the Union troops outflanked the Southerners, drove them from the field, and took some five thousand prisoners.

313. Sutherland, Battlefield Tablet

Monument is a granite shaft set on a plinth and base.
LOCATION: U.S. 460 and C.R. 708, west of Petersburg, 23885
DATE: April 12, 1981
MEDIUM: Granite

[CROSSED SWORDS]
THE BATTLE OF
SUTHERLAND
APRIL 2, 1865
[C.S.A. BATTLE FLAG]
DEDICATED IN SACRED MEMORY TO THOSE
VALIANT CONFEDERATES WHO REMAINED
STEADFAST TO THE END, AND
WHO GAVE THEIR
LAST FULL MEASURE OF
DEVOTION IN DEFENSE
OF THEIR HOMELAND. HERE
THE CONFEDERATES,
UNDER THE GENERALS WILCOX AND HETH,
MADE A GALLANT STAND,
ONLY TO BE OVERCOME
BY OVERWHELMING NUMBERS.
DEDICATED APRIL 12, 1981

This is one of the few monuments erected in the early 1980s, but it was part of a revivalist trend that would continue into the twenty-first century. The battlefield shaft faces south, as the Confederates did, toward the Union battle line.

Union columns converged here on April 2, heading north, ironically, making for the railroad tracks leading into Petersburg after the Confederate defeat at Five Forks on April 1. Elements of four Confederate brigades (Cooke, Scales, MacRae, McGowan) under major generals Cadmus M. Wilcox and Henry Heth stood here, just south of the South Side Railroad and about five miles northeast of Five Forks. They were the final barrier to the South Side Railroad—the last rail line into Petersburg and Richmond. Estimates are that six hundred Confederates confronted twelve hundred Union soldiers—three Union brigades commanded by Maj. Gen. Nelson A. Miles. The Southern stand was successful for a time against these "Overwhelming Numbers," but under sustained pressure the left flank gave way. Half of the Southerners were taken prisoner; the other half, with the Confederacy considered "gone up," withdrew in disorder. The whole of the effort bought additional time for the Army of Northern Virginia to draw away from Petersburg and Richmond.

- Ironically, the tribute "Who Gave Their Last Full Measure of Devotion" bears a resemblance to the Gettysburg Address—"that from these honored dead we take increased devotion to that cause for which they gave the last full measure of devotion."

Amelia County

314. Amelia, Courthouse Common Soldier Monument is a private soldier, in bronze, standing at parade rest surmounting a granite plinth, base, dado, and pedestal.
LOCATION: 16441 Court Street, 23002
DATE: July 15, 1905
MEDIA: Bronze, granite
Front

1861 VIRGINIA 1865
[SEAL OF VIRGINIA]
O COMRADES, WHERESOE'ER
YE REST APART.
AMELIA SHRINES YOU HERE
WITHIN HER HEART
"FATHER" JOHN B. TABB
CONFEDERATE DEAD

—
DEDICATED JULY 15. 1905.
—

DEO VINDICE.
—

AMELIA'S LOVING TRIBUTE
TO HER HEROES OF 1861 TO 1865.

The cornerstone of this unusually sentimental elegy was laid September 20, 1904. Confederate veterans who initiated the project were unsuccessful in raising the necessary money, and responsibility passed to the Amelia Chapter of the United Daughters of the Confederacy, organized in 1901. The latter successfully raised over three thousand dollars for the project. The monument, made of Virginia granite, is twenty-eight feet high. The soldier is the work of Charles M. Walsh. "No prettier monument to the brave Confederate soldier stands anywhere in Virginia," according to the county history.

The flourish and grandeur of the dedication ceremonies were typical of the time. Some three thousand people attended. A memorial box was placed in the base with the names of 640 Confederate soldiers from Amelia County and a history of the Amelia U.D.C. Then, the county history continues, the band played "Dixie" and

six Amelia girls, with Confederate battle flags in their hands, grouped about the monument, and at a signal, and while waving the flags, they pulled the cords which held the veiling over the bronze statue at the top of the magnificent pile of granite, the veiling gracefully fell, and Amelia's tribute to her noble soldiers was no longer a dream but a reality. The two companies of the Seventieth Regiment fired a salute, the good women waved the flags, the men just bellowed themselves hoarse, and it was hard to tell in which direction was to be found the most enthusiasm.

- The direct reference to those who never returned—"Who Rest Apart"—is unusual: courthouse memorials are usually more positive. The U.D.C. claims no credit as a sponsor, but the poetry of Father John Bannister Tabb (1845–1909) has a prominent place. Tabb, whose family estate, "The Forest," is near Amelia, served in the Confederate navy. He converted to Catholicism after the war and entered the priesthood. Ultimately he published five volumes of poetry. He is, says the county history, "Amelia's priest poet."

315. Sailor's Creek Battlefield, Lockett House Tablet

Monument is a granite shaft set on a base.
LOCATION: Sailor's Creek battlefield north of Double Bridge at the Lockett House on C.R. 619, northwest of Holt's Corner (C.R. 618 and C.R. 617), 23966

DATE: 1928

MEDIUM: Granite

> SAILOR'S CREEK
> HERE LEE FOUGHT
> HIS LAST BATTLE,
> APRIL 6, 1865.
> EWELL ALMOST
> WON A GREAT VIC-
> TORY BUT WAS
> OVERWHELMED BY
> SHERIDAN.

NOTTOWAY CHAPTER
U.D.C. 1928.
—
FAITHFUL
UNTO DEATH
CONFEDERATE
HEROES
1861–1865

Gen. Robert E. Lee did not direct this battle, contrary to what this monument indicates. Maj. Gen. Richard S. Ewell bears prominent mention at the site of the Double Bridges action down the hill from this monument, but his performance here was undistinguished. His troops held off the Federals with an initial vigor and success that led to comparisons with the Southern victory at First Fredericksburg, but at length they were overwhelmed and most were taken prisoner.

The Lockett house, known as "Piney Grove," was the home of James Lockett during the war. The house served as a Federal hospital during the battle. Casualties were placed on the grounds surrounding the house as well as the front porch. The dead were temporarily interred across the road. The weatherboarding and chimney of the Lockett house still bear bullet holes from the fighting.

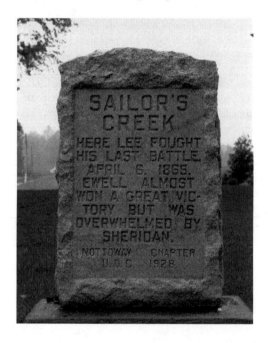

Prince Edward County

316. Sailor's Creek Battlefield, Hillsman's Farm Tablet

Monument is a granite shaft set on a base.
LOCATION: From V.R. 307 north on C.R. 617 to hillside south of Little Sayler's Creek, 23966
DATE: April 2000
MEDIUM: Granite

BATTLES OF SAILOR'S CREEK
APRIL 6, 1865
"MY GOD!
HAS THE ARMY BEEN DISSOLVED?"
GENERAL R. E. LEE
HILLSMAN'S FARM
US: 442 CS: 3,400
MARSHALL'S CROSSROADS
US: 172 CS: 2,600
LOCKETT'S FARM (DOUBLE BRIDGES)
US: 536 CS: 1,700
TOTALS INCLUDE KILLED, WOUNDED,
MISSING AND CAPTURED.
—

IN REMEMBRANCE OF THE
CONFEDERATE AND UNION
SOLDIERS WHO FOUGHT IN
THE SURROUNDING HILLS WITH
GREAT HONOR AND PERSEVERANCE
ON APRIL 6, 1865.
DURING THE THREE ENGAGEMENTS
EACH REGIMENT PARTICIPATED
WITH VALOR AND FRATERNITY,
IN WHAT WAS THE LAST
MAJOR BATTLE OF THE CIVIL WAR

IN VIRGINIA.
DEDICATED BY THE
SAYLER'S CREEK REENACTMENT
AND PRESERVATION COMMITTEE
APRIL 2000

The battle of Sailor's Creek took place at three different sites; the actions are summarized on this hillside shaft. Union cavalry and elements of the Federal Second and Sixth Corps cut off and destroyed nearly one quarter of the Army of Northern Virginia. The losses: an estimated ten thousand men, with many prisoners on the Southern side, including generals Richard S. Ewell, Seth M. Barton, James P. Simms, Meriwether L. Clark, Joseph B. Kershaw, George W. "Custis" Lee, Dudley Dubose, Eppa Hunton, and Montgomery D. Corse. This action was considered a fatal blow to the life of the Army of Northern Virginia.

The outcome of the battle is not mentioned; Robert E. Lee is the only individual cited. Seeing Confederate troops in full retreat, Lee exclaimed, "My God, has the army dissolved?" Maj. Gen. William Mahone, whose division was approaching the field, answered the question. "No, General. Here are troops ready to do their duty."

- Two spellings are used for the battle. To this day, the creek is called Saylers Creek and the state park is called Sailor's Creek Battlefield State Park.

317. Farmville, Courthouse Common Soldier

Monument is a private soldier, in bronze, surmounting a circular plinth, base, dado enclosed by four columns, and pedestal.

LOCATION: Off B.R. 15 (Main Street), to High and Randolph streets, 23909

DATE: October 11, 1900

MEDIA: Bronze, granite

Front

1861 VIRGINIA 1865
DEFENDERS OF STATE "SOVEREIGNTY"
[SEAL OF VIRGINIA]
CONFEDERATE
HEROES
—

ERECTED BY
THE CONFEDERATE VETERANS
AND THE DAUGHTERS
OF THE CONFEDERACY,
OCT. 11, 1900.
—

LIST OF COMPANIES ORGANIZED
IN THE COUNTY 1861.
COMPANY F 18TH. VA INF'TY
"   "   D 18TH.   "   "
"   "   I 23RD.   "   "
"   "   K 21ST.   "   "
"   "   G 53RD.   "   "
"   "   G 20TH.   "   "
"   "   G 44TH.   "   "
"   "   K 3RD. VA CAVALRY.
—

[C.S.A. BATTLE FLAG]

States rights is a theme of this monument. Located across the street from Longwood University and around the corner from the 1939 courthouse. Farmville's nineteen-foot shrine declares that the Confederate soldiers were "Defenders of State 'Sovereignty.'" The seven-foot-tall soldier—mature, watchful, with musket held across waist and chest and wearing a slouch hat and blanket roll—was designed by Charles M. Walsh and fabricated by the Petersburg Marble Works. Walsh is also credited with the Amelia, Warwick, and Princess Anne courthouse monuments. The design is similar to the bronze statue at Boydton—sculptor unknown—and the Charlottesville soldier by Caspar Buberl.

Nottoway County

318. Nottoway, Courthouse Common Soldier

Monument is a private soldier standing at parade rest surmounting a plinth, base, dado, and shaft.

LOCATION: U.S. 460 and C.R. 625 328 West Courthouse Road, 23955

DATE: July 20, 1893

MEDIUM: Marble

JEFFRESS ARTILLERY C.S.A.
[80 NAMES]
ERECTED BY THE LADIES
MEMORIAL
ASSOCIATION OF NOTTOWAY
JULY 20, A. D. 1893.
J. H. BROWN
RICHMOND VA.
BUILDER
—

CO. G. 18. VA. REGT. A. N. V.
[97 NAMES]
CO. "G." 18 VA. REGT. A. N. V.
[40 NAMES]
OTHER COMMANDS
[32 NAMES]
—

CO. C. 18. VA. REGT. A. N. V.
[106 NAMES]
CO. "C." 18 VA. REGT. A. N. V.
[27 NAMES]
NOTTOWAY RESERVES C.S.A.

[52 NAMES]
—

CO. E. 3 VA. CAVALRY
[89 NAMES]
CO E. CONTINUED
[19 NAMES]
JEFFRESS BATTERY CONTINUED
[7 NAMES]
CO C. CONTINUED
[6 NAMES]
CO G. CONTINUED
[5 NAMES]

Although it is a myth that sculptures of Southern soldiers are interchangeable with their Northern counterparts, Nottoway seems to be an exception. The J. H. Brown Company of Richmond sculpted the soldier and the local Ladies Memorial Association sponsored it, but from a distance, in his greatcoat and kepi, "he" has no obvious distinguishing features from a Union soldier, and no Confederate or Union insignia is evident.

The twenty-foot white marble "shrine," as it was called, stands in front of the 1843 Roman revival courthouse. W. H. Fitzhugh Lee was among the speakers at the dedication ceremonies. The county history notes that John L. Irby, a courier for Robert E. Lee during the war, provided the former governor and Confederate general with a beautiful spotted horse to ride for the occasion. The county history further observes that the "imposing white marble monument" faces north, "[a]dorning the court yard, a few paces in front of the courthouse," and declares that it "represents the people of Nottoway County at their best—their very best."

Nottoway has the largest roster of Confederate soldiers on the South Side, although the inscriptions in the soft marble are weathered and unclear. (A typed roster at the Virginia Historical Society dated 1952 lists 532 names.) The sponsors are prominent, the roster profuse. A wrought iron fence and walkway surround the memorial, and spotlights are directed on the site. Its most distinctive feature, though, may be that there is no clear declaration of what the monument testifies to: there is no direct reference to the war years, no direct mention of the Confederacy, and no apologetic or tribute.

- The Nottoway Grays infantry and a cavalry unit mustered on the lawn in 1861. Federal troops passed through in 1865, during the Appomattox campaign.

Appomattox County

319. Appomattox, Courthouse Common Soldier

MONUMENT is a private soldier, in marble, surmounting a granite plinth, base, dado, and shaft.
LOCATION: 297 Court Street, 24522
DATE: June 9, 1906
MEDIA: Granite, marble

1861 1865
APPOMATTOX COUNTY
TO OUR
SOLDIERS
OF THE
CONFEDERACY.

Appomattox has significance as the place where Lee's army surrendered, but that site is up the road from this courthouse monument. The wartime courthouse burned down in 1892. The present courthouse was erected near the railroad, south of the former site, and the town developed here.

This courthouse monument, a standard model by J. Henry Brown of Richmond erected at a cost of fifteen hundred dollars, is a reminder of local, cumulative contributions to history and is dramatically understated.

The unveiling date is coincident with the forty-second anniversary of the beginning of the Siege of Petersburg. *Confederate Veteran* observed at the time that the

> monument is of polished granite, is about thirty feet high, and was made in Richmond, with the exception of the figure on the shaft, which is of marble and was made in Italy. To Mrs. John Randolph Atwood, of West Appomattox, is due credit for the idea of erecting this monument. [S]ome five years ago she took up the self-imposed task of securing subscriptions to [fund the monument]. More than two thousand people attended the ceremonies, which were noted for enthusiasm and good behavior.

- The six-foot, two-thousand-pound, Italian marble statue was knocked from its pedestal by a wind-blown tree during Hurricane Hazel in 1954. The statue broke into hundreds of pieces. It was partially restored and reerected in 1957. A new statue, also of Italian marble, was erected at a cost of $11,500, and the monument was rededicated Memorial Day 2000.

320. Courthouse Tablet

Monument is a granite tablet.
LOCATION: Courthouse grounds
DATE: May 28, 2000
MEDIUM: Granite

APPOMATTOX COUNTY UNITS THAT SERVED
IN THE CONFEDERATE STATES ARMY
APPOMATTOX INVINCIBLES

COMPANY A. 20TH BATTALION
VIRGINIA HEAVY ARTILLERY
FORMERLY COMPANY A. 44TH
VIRGINIA INFANTRY
APPOMATTOX GREYS
COMPANY H. 18TH VIRGINIA INFANTRY
APPOMATTOX RANGERS
COMPANY H. 2ND VIRGINIA CAVALRY
LIBERTY GUARDS
COMPANY B. 46TH VIRGINIA INANTRY
KYLE'S COMPANY HEAVY ARTILLERY
JONES' COMPANY
COMPANY I. 3RD VIRGINIA ARTILLERY
LOCAL DEFENSE TROOPS
APPOMATTOX COUNTY HOME GUARDS
APPOMATTOX RESERVES
COMPANY I. 3RD VIRGINIA RESERVES
PRESENTED BY
APPOMATTOX RANGERS COURTHOUSE SONS
OF CONFEDERATE VETERANS CAMP 1733
MAY 28 2000

This twenty-first-century shaft supplements the text of the larger monument it stands behind and is similar to other contemporary appendices at the Mount Jackson and Warrenton cemeteries. Unit rosters are not uncommon in earlier monuments, but they are a theme of recent memorials.

Appomattox Court House National Historical Park

321. Confederate Cemetery Tablet and Lectern

Monuments are a shaft set on a base and a lectern with plaque
LOCATION: Off V.R. 24, 24522
DATE: May 28, 1972
MEDIUM: Granite

[U.D.C. SEAL]
DEDICATED TO THE MEMORY
OF THOSE WHO SERVED IN
THE DEFENSE OF THE
CONFEDERATE STATES OF AMERICA

Eighteen Confederates—eight known, ten unknown—are buried here, along with one unknown Union soldier. The presiding lectern is one of the few memorials erected in the 1970s. The book is open but unidentified, and the pages are blank.

322. Appomattox Battlefield Tablet

Monument is a bronze tablet set on a granite base.
DATE: June 11, 1926
MEDIA: Bronze, granite

APPOMATTOX
HERE ON SUNDAY APRIL 9, 1865
AFTER FOUR YEARS OF HEROIC STRUGGLE
IN DEFENSE OF PRINCIPLES
BELIEVED FUNDAMENTAL
TO THE EXISTENCE OF OUR GOVERNMENT

LEE SURRENDERED 9000 MEN THE REMNANT
OF AN ARMY STILL UNCONQUERED IN SPIRIT
TO 118000 MEN UNDER GRANT
—
·ERECTED·JUNE 11·1926·
BY
·APPOMATTOX·CHAPTER·
·UNITED·DAUGHTERS·OF·CONFEDERACY.

This marker stands along the old Richmond-Lynchburg Stage Road on a rise above the restored village of Appomattox. The location is on National Park Service grounds.

It was here that the Army of Northern Virginia fought its last battle. The Confederates were surrounded on three sides by Federal troops when elements of Maj. Gen. John B. Gordon's Second Corps and Maj. Gen. W. H. Fitzhugh Lee's cavalry mounted a breakout effort. Attacking at dawn, they initially drove a Union cavalry screen under Maj. Gen. Philip Sheridan—their last success. Union infantry—elements of the Army of the James—stopped the advance. General Lee surrendered the Army of Northern Virginia to General Grant that afternoon. The surrender overshadowed everything else that occurred that day, but the events leading up to it were not bloodless: estimated casualties were about 700 on both sides.

The number 118,000 may be an implicit reference to the "overwhelming numbers" that Lee cited as the cause of the Army of Northern Virginia's surrender in his farewell tribute to his men. It is true that the Confederates were outnumbered, but 118,000 overstates the case by a factor of about two. The Army of the Potomac's Second, Fifth, and Sixth Corps (Maj. Gen. George G. Meade) fielded about 44,000 men at Appomattox. Adding the cavalry under Maj. Philip H. Sheridan and elements of the Army of the James (Maj. Gen. James Ord) brings the total to about 63,000. Lee, in turn, listed 7,892 organized infantry under arms—similar to the number cited by the elegists. Some twenty-one hundred cavalry were also present—many of whom escaped, some to Lynchburg under Col. Thomas Munford. About thirty thousand men, armed or unarmed, were on the field; of these 28,231 were paroled.

323. North Carolina Tablet

Monument is a tablet set on a base and flanked by two adjoining columns.

DATE: April 9, 1905
MEDIUM: Granite
Front

LAST AT APPOMATTOX
AT THIS PLACE THE NORTH CAROLINA
BRIGADE OF BRIGADIER-GENERAL
W. R. COX OF GRIMES DIVISION FIRED
THE LAST VOLLEY 9 APRIL 1865.
MAJOR GENERAL BRYAN GRIMES OF NORTH
CAROLINA PLANNED THE LAST BATTLE
FOUGHT BY THE ARMY OF NORTHERN
VIRGINIA AND COMMANDED THE INFANTRY
ENGAGED THEREIN, THE GREATER PART
OF WHOM WERE NORTH CAROLINIANS.
THIS STONE IS ERECTED BY
THE AUTHORITY OF
THE GENERAL ASSEMBLY
OF
NORTH CAROLINA
IN GRATEFUL AND PERPETUAL
MEMORY OF THE
VALOR ENDURANCE AND PATRIOTISM
OF HER SONS
WHO FOLLOWED WITH
UNSHAKEN FIDELITY THE
FORTUNES OF THE CONFEDERACY
TO THIS CLOSING SCENE.
FAITHFUL TO THE END.
ERECTED 9 APRIL 1905.
NORTH CAROLINA APPOMATTOX
COMMISSION:
[5 NAMES]

—

ESSE QUAM VIDERI.
FIRST AT BETHEL
FARTHEST TO THE FRONT

AT
GETTYSBURG
AND
CHICKAMAUGA
LAST AT APPOMATTOX

—

NORTH CAROLINA TROOPS PAROLED
AT
APPOMATTOX
BRIGADES

COX'S	572	LANE'S	570
GRIMES	530	SCALES'	719
JOHNSTON'S	463	RANSOM'S	435
LEWIS	447	BARRINGERS	23
COOKE'S	560	ROBERTS	93
MACRAE'S	442		

MAJOR GENERAL GRIMES AND STAFF   8
CUMMING'S, MILLER'S, WILLIAMS, FLANNER'S
AND RAMSAY'S BATTERIES   150
TOTAL NORTH CAROLINIANS PAROLED   5,012

—

NORTH CAROLINA
1860
WHITE POPULATION 629,942
MILITARY POPULATION 115,369
1861–5
TROOPS FURNISHED 127,000
KILLED IN BATTLE   14,522
DIED FROM WOUNDS 5,151
DIED FROM DISEASE   20,602

This stout granite shaft, standing near where the last charge of the Army of Northern Virginia took place, is dense with numerical aggregates—uniquely so among Virginia monuments. (The numbers, unlike the 1927 U.D.C. plaque nearby, are consistent with contemporary estimates.) The installation date is forty years to the day after the Army of Northern Virginia's surrender. The location is off V.R. 24, surrounded by trees, near the site of the last attack by North Carolina Confederate troops during a failed attempt to break through Union lines.

Vigorous claims are made for North Carolina's role, and some tension between Virginia and North Carolina was present at the dedication ceremonies on April 9, 1905. Civilities prevailed, but Maj. Henry A. London, chairman of the monument commission, averred that "Without disparaging the bravery of any other Confederate soldiers (for they were all brave), North Carolina proudly boasts that she was the 'last at Appomattox.'" Governor Robert B. Glenn of North Carolina concluded the speeches with this public profession to Governor Andrew Jackson Montague of Virginia:

> Whenever you wish to place a monument over their dust [in North Carolina], we will welcome you with wide open arms; you may write anything you please on the stone to their honor and glory, and all the power of North Carolina will be exerted to protect and defend your tablets. I leave the monument we today unveil on your soil in your keeping, and pray you to protect and defend it.

A "loud whoop was raised," and the ceremonies closed.

- "Faithful to the End," is a paraphrase of the New Testament book of Revelation 2:10.
- The Latin expression "Esse Quam Videri," meaning "To be rather than to seem," was adopted as the North Carolina state motto in 1893.

324. Last Skirmish, North Carolina, Slab

Monument is a marble slab laid face-up.
LOCATION: Roadbed of the old Richmond-Lynchburg Turnpike, off V.R. 24
DATE: circa 1904–5
MEDIUM: Marble

NORTH CAROLINA.
AT THIS PLACE WAS FOUGHT THE LAST
SKIRMISH BY CAPTAIN WILSON T. JENKINS
OF THE FOURTEENTH NORTH CAROLINA
REGIMENT, COMMANDING TWENTY-FIVE
MEN OF THE FOURTH AND FOURTEENTH
NORTH CAROLINA REGIMENTS.

This is one of two granite tablets standing along the roadbed of the old Richmond-Lynchburg Turnpike, testifying to exploits of North Carolina troops on the last day of fighting. A detachment of North Carolina troops stood near here—the site is approximate—to ward off Union troops. Wilson T. Jenkins placed the monument some forty years after the battle, but with many of the landmarks of 1865 vanished at the time, he mistook the site by about three hundred yards.

325. Last Battery Captured, North Carolina, Slab

Monument is a marble slab laid face-up.
LOCATION: Roadbed of the old Richmond-Lynchburg Turnpike
DATE: circa 1904–5
MEDIUM: Marble

NORTH CAROLINA.
THE LAST FEDERAL BATTERY TAKEN BY THE
CONFEDERATES WAS CAPTURED BY THE
NORTH CAROLINA CAVALRY BRIGADE OF
BRIG.-GEN. W. P. ROBERTS AT THIS PLACE.

Two Federal three-inch rifles were taken by Confederate troops, including North Carolina cavalry, near this site. The victory was temporary, the guns were soon yielded, but it was a last flourish on the part of the North Carolina soldiers of the Army of Northern Virginia.

Lynchburg

326. Courthouse Common Soldier

Monument is a private soldier, in bronze, standing with musket held at waist and poised with bayonet fixed, surmounting a plinth, base, dado, and pedestal.

LOCATION: Ninth Street between Church and Court streets, 24504

DATE: 1899

MEDIA: Bronze, granite

Front

1861–1865

CSA

[C.S.A. NATIONAL FLAG, HIGH RELIEF]

OUR CONFEDERATE SOLDIERS

—

OLD DOMINION CHAPTER U.D.C.

—

ERECTED, BY THE

DAUGHTERS OF THE CONFEDERACY OF

LYNCHBURG, VIRGINIA

IN 1899.

To commemorate the heroism

OF

OUR CONFEDERATE SOLDIERS.

—

KIRK WOOD OTEY CHAPTER U.D.C.

The Confederate monument stands at the top of Monument Terrace in downtown Lynchburg. Veterans memorials of other wars stand below it on the 139 steps leading to the James River. The bronze infantryman was sculpted by James O. Scott of Lynchburg—not altogether accurately. The soldier's canteen, one observer notes, is on the wrong side; he does not have a cartridge box; and he is wearing a type of lace-up gaiters that were not in use during the war. Unlike most statues of soldiers, this youngish-looking figure is not standing at parade rest. The monument faces south, toward the courthouse across the street—a Greek revival structure from 1853–55, now a museum—but the soldier's eyes are directed to the east, in the direction of the battlefields of Appomattox, Richmond, and Petersburg. His musket, with fixed bayonet, is raised.

- *Historic Southern Monuments* calls the figure "striking in its vigor and life—a young Confederate infantryman on the qui vive to guard and protect fair Virginia and repel the assaults of the invader." It stands twenty feet high. It cost approximately three thousand dollars. Most of the funding was raised by the United Daughters of the Confederacy chapters; the remainder was contributed by the city of Lynchburg. The project took some twenty years to complete. The Lynchburg Memorial Association formed a "Monumental Society" on May 1, 1883, and collected donations over the next few years, but local chapters of the United Daughters of the Confederacy completed the task with the aid of the city.

- The dual sponsorship by U.D.C. chapters is uncommon. Kirkwood Otey was colonel of the 11th Virginia Infantry. (The spelling of Kirkwood as two words is an error.)

327. Pvt. George M. Jones Statue, Randolph College

Monument is a bronze statue surmounting a granite base, plinth, and pedestal.
LOCATION: Moore Hall, 24503
DATE: 1911
MEDIA: Bronze, granite

IN HONOR OF
GEORGE MORGAN JONES
WHOSE SUGGESTION AND
INFLUENTIAL SUPPORT
WAS THE FIRST FACTOR
IN CREATING
RANDOLPH-MACON
WOMEN'S COLLEGE

In terms of monuments, George Morgan Jones (1824–1903) may be the most celebrated private soldier in Virginia. A successful businessman and philanthropist after the war, Jones served as a private and cook in the 2nd Virginia Cavalry. He was, according to a unit history, a steadfast if 'modest, unpretending soldier.' Jones's wife, Mary Francis Jones, commissioned two identical statues of Jones after his death. The face is that of Jones, but the visage looks much older than he was during the war. He wears a cavalry hat and a sword. He is dressed as a general but wears no stars, no shoulder boards, and no insignia. The two statues, unveiled in 1911, were sculpted by Solon

Borglum (1868–1922), younger brother of Gutzon Borglum, sculptor of the Mount Rushmore monuments. The other Jones statue stands at the Hanging Rock battlefield (chapter 2).

328. Lt. Gen. Jubal A. Early Obelisk, Fort Early

Monument is an obelisk surmounting a base, plinth, and dado.
LOCATION: Memorial and Fort avenues (B.R. U.S. 460 and V.R. 163), 24502
DATE: 1920
MEDIUM: Granite

MEMORIAL TO
JUBAL ANDERSON EARLY
LIEUTENANT GENERAL C.S.A.
AND TO THE BRAVE CONFEDERATE
SOLDIERS UNDER HIM WHO CAME
TO THE RESCUE OF LYNCHBURG
WHEN IT WAS THREATENED BY AN INVASION
OF FEDERAL FORCES AND ERECTED
THESE EARTHWORKS BEHIND WHICH THEY
INTRENCHED THEMSELVES IN THEIR DEFENSE
OF THE CITY ON JUNE 18, 1864

The seventeen-foot obelisk stands on the grounds of the outer defenses of Lynchburg erected by troops under Lt. Gen. Jubal A. Early's command. Union forces under Brig. Gen. David Hunter advanced against the city on

June 17, 1864. Some seven hundred men of the "Crippled Corps" collected from Lynchburg hospitals and two hundred Virginia Military Institute cadets deterred the Union advance; the arrival of Early's Second Corps warded them off.

- As president of the Southern Historical Society, Early came to exert enormous influence on the way history would treat the war, especially the Lost Cause dimension. Historian Douglas Southall Freeman's judgment of him as a general during the war: "unmarried, snarling and stooped, respected as a soldier but never wildly popular as a man."
- Other monuments: The wartime Fort Early is across the street, at Fort and Memorial avenues. An arch entryway is at the fore. A granite shaft reads in part that the grounds were "Parceled . . . in the Charge of Fort Hill Club For Preservation."

An adjacent granite shaft inscription reads, in part:

MEMORIAL ARCH ERECTED JUNE 1924 BY
THE OLD DOMINION CHAPTER
UDC COMMEMORATING THE
BATTLE OF LYNCHBURG WHICH TOOK
PLACE JUNE 18, 1864 AT THIS
POINT ON THE LINE OF
DEFENCES FACING THE OLD SALEM
TURNPIKE

329. Miller Park, 2nd Virginia Cavalry Tablet
Monument is a bronze tablet set in a granite shaft.
LOCATION: 2100 Park Avenue, 24501
DATE: 1913
MEDIA: Bronze, granite
Front

[SEAL OF VIRGINIA]
HERE, ON THE 10TH OF MAY, 1861 THE
2ND VIRGINIA CAVALRY, C.S.A., WAS
ORGANIZED.
HERE, ON THE 10TH OF APRIL, 1865, THE
SAME COMMAND, AFTER YEARS OF VAL-
IANT SERVICE WITH THE ARMY OF NORTH-
ERN VIRGINIA, AND AFTER CUTTING ITS

WAY THROUGH THE ENEMY'S LINES AT AP-
POMATTOX; WAS REGULARLY DISBANDED.
DESIROUS OF COMMEMORATING THESE
MEMORABLE EVENTS, I HAVE DIRECTED
THIS TABLET TO BE PLACED HERE.
CLAUDE A. SWANSON
GOVERNOR OF VIRGINIA
ERECTED BY THE CITY OF LYNCHBURG
1913
—
1861–1865

Miller Park was a fairground before the war. During the war it served as a "Camp of Instruction," a prison for Union soldiers, and as an assembly point for Confederate troops from other states. This monument commemorates a final chapter in its wartime history, when about 150 men of the 2nd Virginia Cavalry gathered here in 1865.

Seven hundred men left Lynchburg with the 2nd Virginia Cavalry at this site on June 1, 1861; a total of 2,225 had served by 1865. Lee surrendered most of the army at Appomattox, but these troopers were said to have made

their escape before the surrender took formal effect, thus not violating the armistice. They were led by Col. Thomas Munford, who rallied them with the declaration "All you men who do not wish to surrender, follow me; I am going to Lynchburg." They disbanded here, "subject to reassemble for the continuance of the struggle," as Munford put it. That reassembly never took place.

- Munford (1831–1918) was paroled May 20, 1865; his remains were buried in Spring Hill.
- Claude A. Swanson (1862–1939) served as governor of Virginia, 1906–10, and as a U.S. senator, 1910–33. He spoke at numerous dedication ceremonies. This is the only Confederate monument where his name is inscribed.

330. John Warwick Daniel Statue

Monument is a bronze figure, seated, surmounting a granite base and pedestal. Location: Park Avenue between Floyd and Ninth streets

DATE: May 16, 1915

MEDIA: Bronze, granite

JOHN·WARWICK·DANIEL
BORN·IN·LYNCHBURG
SEPTEMBER·5,·1842
DIED·IN·LYNCHBURG
JUNE·29·1910
FOREMOST·AND
·BELOVED
VIRGINIAN
OF·HIS·TIME
M. EZEKIEL
ROME 1912
—
ERECTED·BY
THE·MUNICIPALITY
AND·CITIZENS
OF·LYNCHBURG
AND·OTHER·ADMIRERS
1913
—
·SOLDIER·
·JURIST·
·STATESMAN·
—
MAJOR·IN·THE·ARMY
OF·NORTHERN·VIRGINIA
AND·FOR
TWENTY-FOUR·YEARS
A·SENATOR·OF
THE·UNITED·STATES
FROM·VIRGINIA

Along with Claude A. Swanson and Robert E. Lee Jr., John Warwick Daniel was among the most popular and frequently called-upon speakers at monument dedication ceremonies in Virginia. Daniel served in the Confederate army 1861–64 and rose to the rank of major. Called the "Lame Lion of Lynchburg," he was wounded and permanently disabled in the battle of the Wilderness in May 1864 but went on to serve as a congressman and attorney after the war.

His primary identification on this memorial is as a soldier. The monument—the work of Moses Ezekiel—depicts Daniel as seated, with a document, holding a crutch, looking to the southwest toward the mountains in the distance.

Old City Cemetery

331. Archway

Monument is a granite archway entry to Confederate cemetery.
LOCATION: 401 Taylor Street, 24501
DATE: 1926
MEDIUM: Granite

> IN MEMORY OF
> THE CONFEDERATE DEAD
> WHO ARE BURIED HERE
> 1861 1865

Lynchburg's Confederate cemetery is exceptionally well tended. The city's care for soldiers reflects a local tradition of service to military men traveling by rail through Lynchburg that would continue through World Wars I and II.

The Southern Memorial Association, founded in 1866 as the Ladies Memorial Association, sponsored every monument here. This "greenstone arch" was designed by Robert Edley Craighill and erected by the Marsteller Marble and Granite Works. The arch was completed in 1926; the urns on top of the arch were added in 1927; the inscription was carved in 1928.

332. Central Obelisk

Monument is a tapered marble plinth and obelisk surmounting a granite base.
DATE: May 10, 1868
MEDIA: Granite, marble

> MARYLAND
> TEXAS
> FLORIDA
> ARKANSAS
> MISSOURI
> KENTUCKY
> GEORGIA
> ALABAMA
> TENNESSEE
> LOUISIANA
> MISSISSIPPI
> SOUTH CAROLINA
> NORTH CAROLINA
> AND
> VIRGINIA
> SOLDIERS
> SLEEP HERE.

This grim obelisk, whose cornerstone was dedicated May 10, 1868, may be the oldest cemetery monument in Virginia. It stands over the graves of some 2,207 soldiers. Postwar plans for the site began on April 26, 1866, when women of a local Methodist church decided to enclose the area around the soldiers' graves, erect a monument, and plan for an annual service.

Lynchburg was the Confederacy's largest outpost medical center. Several tobacco warehouses and other public buildings were converted for hospital use, along with private homes. Thirty-two hospital sites treated up to four thousand patients at a time, more after major battles. Some twenty thousand patients were admitted to Lynchburg hospitals during the war; of these nearly three thousand died. The firm of W. D. Diuguid was responsible for all burials and kept detailed records of their work.

- The reason for the order in which the states are inscribed is not known. The inscription is repeated on the reverse side.
- A draped urn atop the obelisk was struck by lightning and destroyed some years ago. It was not replaced.

333. Smallpox, Tablet

Monument is a granite shaft.
DATE: 1923–24

IN MEMORY OF
THE CONFEDERATE
SOLDIERS
WHO DIED OF
SMALLPOX
IN THE HOSPITALS
OF LYNCHBURG
DURING THE WAR
BETWEEN THE
STATES

Smallpox was common during the war, and thousands of soldiers eventually died of it. The disease made its first appearance in the Army of Northern Virginia in 1862, shortly after the Maryland campaign. Several thousand men were treated for smallpox in the general hospitals of the Army of Northern Virginia in 1862 and 1863, and the mortality rates were high. Smallpox was so severe at the time of the battle of Chancellorsville that five thousand men were reported unfit for duty because of it.

At least one hundred soldiers died of smallpox in Lynchburg during the war. The Southern Memorial Association erected this collective monument to their memory.

334. Fifty Confederate Graves, Tablet

Monument is a granite shaft.
DATE: 1918
Front

[12 NAMES]
ERECTED TO THE MEMORY OF THE FIFTY

CONFEDERATE SOLDIERS
WHO SLEEP IN THIS PLOT
—
[13 NAMES]
—
[12 NAMES]
—
[13 NAMES]

This shaft, erected in 1918, is a credit to the fidelity of the Southern Memorial Association but also illustrates the practical difficulties of caring for some two thousand graves within a confined space. The fifty soldiers buried in Lot 178 were interred in individual graves and rows, like the other forty-seven lots in the Confederate section, but because that area had been landscaped with walkways and flowers, the women of the S.M.A. did not want to disturb it by installing fifty individual headstones. Their solution was a single marker in the center, inscribed with all fifty names.

Other interments in Lynchburg: Spring Hill Cemetery: generals Jubal A. Early, James Dearing; colonels Thomas Munford, Kirkwood Otey; majors Lucy Otey, John W. Daniel. Presbyterian Cemetery: generals Samuel Garland, Robert E. Rodes.

City of Bedford

335. Bedford, Courthouse Obelisk

Monument is an obelisk surmounting a plinth, base, and dado.
LOCATION: 123 East Main Street, U.S. 460 and V.R. 43, South and Main streets, 24523
DATE: July 16, 1909
MEDIUM: Granite
Front

[C.S.A. BATTLE FLAG]
DEO VINDICE
TO THE CONFEDERATE
SOLDIERS AND SAILORS OF
BEDFORD COUNTY·1861–1865
BEDFORD HONORS HER HEROES;
PROUDLY REJOICING WITH THE LIVING;
SINCERELY MOURNING THE DEAD.
THEIR HISTORY IS IT'S [SIC] BRIGHTEST PAGE,
EXHIBITING THE HIGHEST QUALITIES OF
PATRIOTISM, COURAGE,
FORTITUDE AND VIRTUE.
THIS STONE IS ERECTED TO KEEP
FRESH IN MEMORY THE NOBLE DEEDS
OF THESE DEVOTED SONS.
[CROSSED SWORDS, SHEATHED, HIGH RELIEF]
—
[LIGHT ARTILLERY PIECE, HIGH RELIEF]
—
[STACKED MUSKETS, HIGH RELIEF]
—
[ANCHOR, HIGH RELIEF]

The forty-foot Barre granite obelisk adjacent to the 1930 courthouse was sponsored by the Joseph E. Johnston Camp, Confederate Veterans, and William R. Terry Chapter, United Confederate Veterans. Today Bedford's enormous National D-Day Memorial, located south of the downtown, justifiably attracts attention, and a granite memorial to the "Bedford Boys" of World War II is nearby on the courthouse grounds. This lofty obelisk has its own majesty, however. The *Bedford Democrat* declared that in "symmetrical beauty this tall granite shaft is not excelled by any like monument in the state."

The inscription is broad and conciliatory. Some of the remarks at the dedication ceremonies in 1911 took a different tone, however, and included an unabashedly "unreconstructed" speech given by William Fountain Graves

(1832–1923), veteran of the 2nd Virginia Cavalry, who took the occasion to declare that by war's end the Confederate army was outnumbered one million to eight thousand—a gross distortion. Graves also invoked Lincoln's Second Inaugural in defense of the Lost Cause—"malice for none and charity for all." His speech reads, in part, that only a

> remnant of rugged, starving, worn-out soldiers . . . surrendered to Grant at Appomattox Court House, who was backed by a million fully equipped soldiers. . . . Since we furled our flags and stacked our arms, there have been no more peaceful, law-abiding citizens . . . than the Southern Confederate soldier; but . . . let it be distinctly understood that we have not been going around with our fingers in our mouths whimpering and whining, and asking pardon and promising to do so no more, but with heads erect, we look the world squarely in the eyes, and say that we believe we were right in the brave old days when to do battle was sacred duty; and now, in the light of subsequent events, we know that we were right and, with malice for none and charity for all, we are asking pardon of no living man.

336. Longwood Cemetery Obelisk

Monument is a marble dado and obelisk surmounting a granite base and plinth.

LOCATION: Bus. V.R. 122 and U.S. 221, corner of Longwood Avenue and Oakwood Street, 24523
DATE: 1875
MEDIA: Granite, marble
Front

[AX, WITH CONFEDERATE
NATIONAL FLAG WAVING,
OVER A TENT WITH "CS" INSCRIBED]
OUR
CONFEDERATE
DEAD.
1861–1865
—
[TWO CROSSED SHEATHED SWORDS]
GADDESS
LYNCHBURG
—
[TWO CROSSED CANNON BARRELS]
—
[TWO CROSSED MUSKETS]
[BRONZE PLAQUE ADDITION:]
PLACED IN MEMORY AND HONOR
OF THE FIVE HUNDRED
BRAVE SOLDIERS OF THE
CONFEDERACY INTERRED
BELOW THIS MONUMENT. SOME ARE KNOWN
BY NAME, ALL ARE KNOWN TO GOD.
MAY THEIR MEMORY BE
FOREVER ETCHED IN THE
MINDS AND HEARTS OF THE
SONS AND DAUGHTERS
OF THE CONFEDERACY. THIS
MONUMENT WAS ERECTED AND
DEDICATED BY THE BEDFORD LADIES
MEMORIAL ASSOCIATION,
JOSEPH E. JOHNSTON UNITED
CONFEDERATE VETERANS CAMP, AND
THE GENERAL WILLIAM R. TERRY CHAPTER
UNITED DAUGHTERS OF THE CONFEDERACY.

The Ladies Memorial Association, formed in 1866, originally erected this monument on Piedmont Hill in 1875: a shaft six feet high, according to contemporary accounts, made of Italian marble, on a marble pedestal, with base of granite, erected at a cost of three hundred dollars. The monument was moved from Piedmont Hill to Longwood Cemetery and was rededicated on May 30, 1921. Most of the Confederate soldiers were moved as well. Harry Carder, a local mortician, reinterred the dead and sealed them in a concrete vault.

Sources differ on how many soldiers are buried here. The obelisk now stands over the resting place of 192 Southern soldiers, according to historian James I. Robertson Jr., although the bronze plaque addition, recently affixed, states that there are five hundred soldiers. A total of 707 Southern soldiers are said to be interred in Longwood and Oakwood cemeteries, including Mary Oney Fizer, a Confederate nurse and one of the few female members of the Confederate Army. It was she who met the troop trains that brought the wounded soldiers to Bedford.

Powhatan County

337. Powhatan, Courthouse Shaft

Monument is a granite shaft and cap surmounting a plinth, base, and dado.
LOCATION: 3880-D Old Buckingham Road, 23139
DATE: August 20, 1896
MEDIUM: Granite
Front

[RELIEF OF C.S.A. BATTLE FLAG]
ERECTED TO KEEP IN TENDER
REMEMBRANCE
THE POWHATAN TROOP
COMPANY E FOURTH VIRGINIA CAVALRY
SECOND BRIGADE FIRST DIVISION

STUART'S CAVALRY CORPS
A. N. V.
—
1865
APPOMATTOX
—
[C.S.A. BATTLE FLAG, UNSHEATHED
SWORD IN HIGH RELIEF]
TO HONOR VALOR IS
MANKIND'S DELIGHT.
—
1861
MANASSAS

Most county seat monuments are broader and more inclusive than the Powhatan County obelisk. This is the only county courthouse monument to focus on one company: it is a stout, imposing granite edifice standing outside the 1849 Greek revival courthouse. It excludes the Powhatan Artillery, for example, which served from Yorktown to Appomattox, as well as any other units that Powhatan County Confederates served in. In fact, there were no other monuments in the county to Confederate soldiers at the time it was erected. Still, as the county history notes, the "Powhatan plinth became a rally point of the old Confederate veterans until the last one of them passed from the scene." Whether the sponsors assumed that other monuments were forthcoming at this site is unclear, but a 1973 shaft was erected by "Powhatan Citizens . . . To Commemorate the Service and Sacrifice of Powhatan Servicemen of All Wars."

Like many Virginia militia units, the Powhatan Troop was formed after John Brown's raid at Harpers Ferry in 1859. The unit was activated in 1861 and fought at First Manassas before being incorporated into the 4th Virginia Cavalry. At Appomattox, only fifty-five men surrendered; the rest slipped through Union lines and disbanded in Lynchburg.

Confederate Veteran notes describe the monument:

It is of Virginia granite, twelve feet high, standing on a grassy mound five high, ornamented on all sides with symbols in bas-relief: an empty scabbard crossed with a naked saber, a lotus typifying eternal sleep, the star of destiny, and drooping Confederate flag, not furled, signifying defeated, not conquered. . . . Unveiled with appropriate ceremonies on August 20, 1896, by Miss Amy McRae Werth. . . . The monument cost about $1,500. It is in the care of the ladies of Powhatan County.

- Other 4th Virginia Cavalry tributes are at Little Fork (1904) and Appomattox (2000). Other units from Powhatan: the Powhatan Reserves and Powhatan Rifles (Co. D, 20th Virginia Infantry).

338. Huguenot Springs Obelisk

Monument is an obelisk surmounting a plinth, base, and dado.
LOCATION: Four miles north of U.S. 60, off C.R. 607 (Huguenot Springs Road)
DATE: September 15, 1915
MEDIUM: Granite

[C.S.A. BATTLE FLAG]
1861–1865
IN THIS LOT REST IN SLEEP

TWO HUNDRED AND FIFTY
CONFEDERATE DEAD.
WE KNOW NOT WHO THEY WERE,
BUT THE WHOLE WORLD KNOWS
WHAT THEY WERE. THEY DIED
FAR FROM THEIR HOMES, BUT FILL
HEROES GRAVES, AND GLORY KEEPS
CEASELESS WATCH ABOUT THEIR TOMB.
ERECTED BY
POWHATAN CHAPTER U.D.C.
SEPT. 15, 1915.
OUR
CONFEDERATE DEAD

Bronze plaque placed in sidewalk:

TO THE GLORY OF GOD
AND
IN MEMORY OF
THESE BRAVE SOUTHERNERS WHO HERE
HAVE FOUND THEIR FINAL REST. THAT THEIR
BRAVE DEEDS BE NEVER FORGOTTEN
NOR THEIR SACRIFICE HAVE BEEN IN VAIN
DEDICATED BY
J. E. B. STUART CAMP NO. 1343
SONS OF CONFEDERATE VETERANS
MAY 25, 1987

Huguenot Springs, founded as a resort in 1847, served as a convalescent hospital during the war. Local women served as nurses and attendants. The facility became a resort again after the war, but it burned down in the 1880s. In its time it was an elegant health spa, with a three-story hotel, a complex of cottages, and two mineral springs. Remnants of the spring-house were discernible in the 1980s, but at this writing the monument and cemetery are the most prominent vestiges of the resort. About half of the graves are identified and marked.

An elegant semicentennial pathos is presented: That "We Know Not Who They Were" may be a reference to the fact that burial records for this site have never been located. Visitors may also gain the impression that this is an isolated, even forlorn site. Suburban Richmond continues to advance west, but this area had yet to be developed at this writing. Although it strains credulity to declare that "The Whole World Knows What They Were," the claim that

"Glory Keeps Ceaseless Watch" is the more affecting for its pretense and poetic license.

The 1987 bronze plaque tribute is similar to other tributes in Virginia, but, like the 1982 Sutherland shaft, it bears a close and ironic similarity to the diction of the Gettysburg Address. The phrase "That Their Brave Deeds Be Never Forgotten Nor Their Sacrifice Have Been In Vain" bears a provocative similarity to Lincoln's assertion "that we here highly resolve that these dead shall not have died in vain."

Cumberland County

339. Cumberland, Courthouse Obelisk
Monument is a granite obelisk surmounting a base, plinth, and dado.
LOCATION: U.S. 60 and V.R. 45
DATE: November 28, 1901
MEDIUM: Granite
Front

TO THE

CUMBERLAND TROOP

1861–1865.

—

TO THE OTHER

CUMBERLAND SOLDIERS

1861–1865.

—

TO THE

BLACK EAGLE CO.

1861–1865.

—

TO THE

CUMBERLAND GRAYS

1861–1865.

This simple monument has no apologetics or sponsorships, just four successive tributes. The obelisk is modest in size, although its height is boosted by its placement atop a base of granite blocks. It stands adjacent to the Palladian-style courthouse erected in 1821.

The Cumberland Grays served as Company D, 21st Virginia Infantry; the Black Eagle Rifles served as Company E, 18th Virginia Infantry; the Cumberland Light Dragoons served as Company G, 3rd Virginia Cavalry.

340. Confederate Cemetery Tablet

Monument is a granite plinth, base, and obelisk.
LOCATION: V.R. 45, to Early Street, left on Jackson Street, 23040
DATE: May 30, 1903
MEDIUM: Granite

FAITHFUL

UNTO DEATH

CONFEDERATE

HEROES
1861–1865

This quiet hillside location is just north
of Farmville and inters the dead from local
wartime hospitals. Farmville was one of many
hospital sites strung out along the Southside
Railroad from Petersburg to Lynchburg and
Bedford, as well as at Danville, along the Richmond and Danville Railroad. Farmville General Hospital operated May 1862 to April 1865;
Wayside Hospital from 1863 to 1865.

The graves here are unmarked, but a plaque
at the entrance reads:

CONFEDERATE CEMETERY 1862–1865
600 CONFEDERATE SOLDIERS BURIED HERE
"LOVE MAKES MEMORY ETERNAL."

Buckingham County

341. Buckingham, Courthouse Obelisk

Monument is a granite obelisk surmounting a
plinth, pedestal, and dado.
LOCATION: U.S. 60, 23921
DATE: June 30, 1908
MEDIUM: Granite
Front

TO COMMEMORATE THE
DEVOTION AND HEROISM
OF THE
CONFEDERATE SOLDIERS

OF
BUCKINGHAM COUNTY.
WHO VALUED PRINCIPLE
MORE THAN LIFE,
AND FOUGHT FOR A CAUSE
THEY KNEW TO BE JUST.
1861 [C.S.A. BATTLE FLAG RELIEF] 1865

The Buckingham obelisk has the regional
simplicity common to central Virginia courthouse memorials at Cumberland, Powhatan,
and Amherst. The inscription commends the
"Devotion and Heroism" of the county's Confederate Soldiers. The soldiers are sanctified:
theirs was "A Cause They Knew to be Just."

The dedication included a double ceremony:
first the cornerstone was dedicated, and then
the "beautiful monument" was unveiled. The
occasion brought the largest crowd ever assembled in Buckingham. The cornerstone, with
a vault for relics, and was laid with Masonic
ceremonies. The dedication speeches included
a reading of Lee's farewell speech at Appomattox. The shaft was unveiled by an ex-soldier
described by *Confederate Veteran* as "Comrade Megginson, who, being an invalid, was
wheeled in front of the monument in his chair."

342. Lee Wayside Tablet

Monument is a slate tablet set atop a concrete
pillar.
LOCATION: U.S. 60: 1.1 miles east of Buckingham, 23921
DATE: circa 1920

MEDIA: Concrete, slate

> THIS STONE MARKS
> THE SPOT WEHRE
> GEN. R. E. LEE
> HELD HIS LAST CAMP
> ON THE RETURN FROM
> APPOMATTOX,
> APRIL 12, 1865

Robert E. Lee and a small entourage departed Appomattox for Richmond shortly after the surrender of the Army of Northern Virginia. They arrived here at nightfall and were offered accommodations at a local inn here, operated by William Shepherd. Lee declined the offer, as was his custom, so as not to inconvenience his hosts. Instead he camped here. (James Longstreet and his entourage are said to have bivouacked in the same woods.)

In 1920, the site of Lee's "last bivouac" was donated to the county. It was at about this time that this monument was erected. In 1932, the Buckingham Chapter of the United Daughters of the Confederacy helped buy fifty acres on which the inn, known as Rose Cottage, was situated. (Rose Cottage was struck by lightning and burned in the 1980s. It has not been rebuilt, and the ruins remain.)

The county history calls this site the last camp of the Army of Northern Virginia. Today it is known as the Lee Wayside, with the Historic Village at Lee Wayside, an outdoor museum, nearby.

- Of Lee's departure from Appomattox, historian Douglas Southall Freeman writes: "There was no theatrical review, no speech-making, no pledge to keep the cause alive in loyal hearts. All that was behind Lee. Quietly and unceremoniously he left his last headquarters on the 12th and started home."

Amherst County

343. Amherst, Courthouse Obelisk
Monument is a bronze plaque set on a granite obelisk surmounting a base.
LOCATION: Main and Court streets, 24521
DATE: July 19, 1922

MEDIA: Bronze, granite

> [CROSSED C.S.A. BATTLE AND
> NATIONAL FLAGS]
> TO THE MEMORY OF
> THE SONS OF AMHERST COUNTY
> WHO FROM 1861 TO 1865
> UPHELD IN ARMS THE CAUSE
> OF VIRGINIA AND THE SOUTH,
> WHO FELL IN BATTLE
> OR DIED FROM WOUNDS,
> AND SURVIVORS OF THE WAR
> WHO AS LONG AS THEY LIVED
> WERE EVER PROUD THAT THEY
> HAD DONE THEIR PART
> IN THE NOBLE CAUSE.
> THIS MONUMENT IS ERECTED
> BY THE LADIES OF
> THE DR. JOHN THOMPSON CHAPTER
> OF THE
> UNITED DAUGHTERS OF THE CONFEDERACY.
> 1922
> 1861 CONFEDERATE SOLDIERS 1865
> JOHN HARSCH CM
> CLEVELAND, O.

Contemporary newspaper accounts about this monument are not known to be extant. The United Daughters of the Confederacy chapter disbanded years ago, and no U.D.C. records are known to exist.

In some ways, this monument standing in front of the courthouse (colonial revival, com-

pleted in 1872) is more of a commentary on the twentieth century than a commemoration of the Civil War. The obelisk was dedicated in 1922, less than four years after the end of the World War I. The inscription is perplexing: it seems premature or discordant to give tribute to the memory of the "Sons of Amherst," and to assume or imply that they are dead—"As Long as They Lived." Surely at least some of the county's Confederate veterans were still living in 1922, and it is likewise possible that some were present at the dedication. It is tempting to conclude that the immediacy of World War I made the Civil War seem more distant than it was.

- A rare mention of the "Cause" is inscribed, the only mention in Virginia of it as being "Noble."

Nelson County

344. Lovingston, Courthouse Common Soldier

Monument is a private soldier standing at parade rest surmounting a plinth, base, and dado.
LOCATION: 84 Courthouse Square, 22949
DATE: April 1965
MEDIUM: Granite

> ERECTED APRIL 1965
> IN MEMORY OF THE HEROIC
> CONFEDERATE SOLDIERS OF
> NELSON COUNTY WHO SERVED
> IN THE WAR BETWEEN

> THE STATES
> 1861–1865
> "LOVE MAKES MEMORY ETERNAL"
> —
> [BLANK]
> —
> [RELIEF OF CROSSED SWORDS]
> —
> [BLANK]

This centennial monument standing by the 1809 courthouse is the most recent county seat Confederate soldier sculpture erected in Virginia. The monument stands only about eleven feet high and was erected at a cost of $5,600. The soldier was sculpted by Richard Cecchini of Georgia granite and is nearly at eye level, unlike some of its lofty counterparts at Appomattox, Charlotte, Chester, Richmond, or Norfolk, for example. The inscription continues the traditions of earlier monuments, however: the use of the term "War Between the States," for example, rather than Civil War, and the traditional evocation: "In Memory of . . ."

Lunenburg County

345. Lunenburg, Courthouse Common Soldier

Monument is a private soldier standing at parade rest surmounting a plinth, base, dado, and pedestal.

LOCATION: Intersection of V.R. 40, V.R. 49, and C.R. 675, 23952

DATE: August 12, 1916

MEDIA: Granite, marble

Front

CSA

1861

[C.S.A. BATTLE FLAG]

1865

IN MEMORY OF THE

CONFEDERATE SOLDIERS

OF LUNENBURG COUNTY,

AND THE CAUSE FOR WHICH

THEY FOUGHT FROM

1861 TO 1865

CONFEDERATE SOLDIERS

—

THE FAME AND DEEDS

OF HEROES WILL LIVE

—

WE FOUGHT FOR

THE SOVEREIGNTY

OF THE STATES

—

OUR PATRIOTIC

WOMANHOOD WAS AN INSPIRATION

A call-and-response of voices, representing several generations, holds forth in this semicentennial monument standing beside the courthouse, a Roman revivalist structure that dominates the village and was erected in 1827. The point-of-view shifts from a third-person tribute on side one—"They . . ."—to a first-person testimony and response—"We . . ." and "Our . . ."—on sides three and four. The relief of an unfurled Confederate battle flag on the dado adds bravado; the appeal of "the Cause" is unusually direct. The tenants of the Cause are specified as the "Sovereignty of the States," and the costs are vigorously acclaimed: sovereignty was "Fought For."

- The monument formerly stood at an elementary school in Victoria but was moved here in 1972 after a vandalism incident. The soldier's weapon was stolen but has been replaced.

Charlotte County

346. Charlotte, Courthouse Common Soldier

Monument is a private soldier, in marble, standing at parade rest surmounting a granite plinth, base, dado, and shaft.

LOCATION: Near intersection of V.R. 40, 47 and C.R. 604, 23923

DATE: August 27, 1901

MEDIA: Granite, marble

Front

1861–1865

GLORIA VICTIS

[SEAL OF VIRGINIA]

CONFEDERATE SOLDIERS

CHARLOTTE COUNTY

CHERISHES THE MEMORY

OF HER HEROES.

—

NOBLE DEEDS

ARE A PEOPLE'S INSPIRATION

—

ERECTED UNDER AUSPICES OF

H. A. CARRINGTON CAMP C. V. NO. 34.

AUGUST 27, 1901.

—

NON SIBI. SED PATRIAE.

The monument—sculptor unknown—stands about twenty-five feet above the courthouse grounds. Originally it stood in front of the courthouse. It was then moved to the middle of the intersection of highways 40 and 47, but its prominent place there proved to be a problem when a textile mill opened in the nearby town of Drakes Branch and truck traffic could not navigate around it. The monument was moved again and stands now beside the courthouse and away from the road.

Like many Southside monuments, there are no units or names inscribed. The inscription, though spare, is florid by comparison to the 1906 Appomattox monument in the adjacent county.

- "Gloria Victis" is translated from the Latin as "Glory to the Defeated." "Non Sibi Sed Patriae" is translated as "Not for himself but for country."

Pittsylvania County

347. Chatham, Courthouse Common Soldier

Monument is a private soldier, in marble, standing at parade rest surmounting a granite plinth, base, dado, and pedestal.
LOCATION: 21 North Main Street, 24531
DATE: June 8, 1899
MEDIA: Granite, marble

Front

1861 VIRGINIA 1865
[SEAL OF VIRGINIA]
CONFEDERATE DEAD
—
WE CROWN THE HEROES OF THE PAST
WITH A LAUREL WREATH OF MEMORY
—
IN MEMORY OF
CO. "I" 53RD VA. REGIMENT
ARMISTEAD'S BRIGADE
PICKETT'S DIVISION
AND THEIR
COMRADES IN ARMS OF
PITTSYLVANIA
—
GO TELL THE LISTENING WORLDS AFAR
OF THOSE WHO DIED FOR TRUTH AND RIGHT

Chatham's monument is well documented. The base and column are of Virginia granite, but the figure is of Italian marble. The monument is twenty-five feet in height and cost fifteen hundred dollars. A Memorial Association of Company I was formed in 1879 for the project and promptly initiated the fundraising process but did not complete it until 1899.

The dedication:

Owing to the illness of the President of the Rawley Martin Chapter, U.D.C., the unveiling of the monument was postponed from April 21 to June 8, 1899. It was a beautiful and ideal June day, and the population of Chatham, a little town of about a thousand inhabitants, was more than doubled.

Upon arrival at the platform by the courthouse, near where the monument is erected on the Public Square, prayer was offered by Rev. Chiswell Dabney, after which Dr. Martin introduced Maj. [John Warwick] Daniel, "Virginia's silver-tongued" orator," was at his best, and delivered one of his ablest orations. At its conclusion the veil was lifted by Misses Nellie Martin, Rebecca Tredway, Parke Whitehead, and Ada Carter—all daughters of gallant Confederate soldiers. [Afterwards,] the ladies served refreshments in a building near by. The tables were placed in the form of the Southern cross, while the same idea was followed in the decorations of the building. Here the sponsors were in charge, and the lunch was served elegantly by their fair hands.

Unit designations in the Confederate Army —brigades, divisions, and corps—often went by the unit's commander. "Armistead" is Brig. Gen. Lewis A. Armistead, killed in action at the Battle of Gettysburg. Pickett is Maj. Gen. George E. Pickett. Pickett's notoriety is largely negative and is based in part on his role in "Pickett's Charge" at Gettysburg, July 3, 1863, and his arguable dereliction at Five Forks, April 1, 1865, but no disrepute is implied here.

Franklin County

348. Rocky Mount, Courthouse Common Soldier

Monument is a private soldier, in marble, standing at parade rest surmounting a granite plinth, base, shaft, and pedestal.

LOCATION: 275 South Main Street, 24151
DATE: December 1, 1910
MEDIA: Granite, marble
Front

CSA
TO THE MEMORY OF
THE
CONFEDERATE DEAD
OF FRANKLIN COUNTY
ERECTED JOINTLY
BY
JUBAL EARLY CHAPTER
U.D.C.
AND
R. H. FISHBURNE
1861–1865
—

Co. D 2nd, Va. Cav.
Co. A 10th, Va. Cav.
Co. K 10th, Va. Cav.
Co. A 37th, Va. Cav.
Co. G 37th, Va. Cav.
Co. B 24th, Va. Inf.
Co. K 42nd, Va. Inf.
Co. D 24th, Va. Inf.

—

CSA
[crossed C.S.A. battle flags]

—

Co. G 57th, Va. Inf.
Co. B 57th, Va. Inf.
Co. D 58th, Va. Inf.
Co. E 58th, Va. Inf.
RESERVES
Co. B 3rd, Va. Inf.
Co. G 3rd, Va. Inf.
Co. D 3rd, Va. Inf.

This is a typical Confederate monument in several ways: it stands in a prominent place at the corner of Court and Main streets and was erected in the reconciliation era—when elegists were so apt to celebrate Confederate soldiers as heroes and to issue affectionate paeans to them.

The soldier is relatively aged, grandfatherly. The figure was sculpted in Italy by an unknown artisan of Italian marble. The base is North Carolina granite.

A pickup truck smashed into the monument on June 9, 2007, and toppled it. Fundraising to replace the statue was in progress at this writing. The Jubal Early Chapter of the United Daughters of the Confederacy remains active. The chapter formed in 1902 with the express purpose of erecting this monument. They received little public support, but private donors, including Dr. Booker T. Washington, contributed. R. H. Fishburne, a local merchant and veteran whose name appears on the monument, was another donor. Fishburne, according to the U.D.C. records, specifically "requested that the monument honor Confederate casualties rather than Jubal Early or another officer, noting that the War was fought by everyone, with the highest toll on the common soldier."

- Also on the courthouse grounds: a 1913 bronze plaque and granite base tribute to Jubal A. Early.

[CROSSED CONFEDERATE FLAGS]
THIS TABLET IS ERECTED IN MEMORY OF
JUBAL ANDERSON EARLY
WHO WAS BORN IN FRANKLIN
COUNTY, VIRGINIA,
NOVEMBER 3, 1816,
WAS APPOINTED TO WEST POINT 1833,
COMMISSIONED 2ND LIEUT.
3RD ARTILLERY 1837
AND SERVED IN SEMINOLE
WAR, RESIGNED 1838.
STUDIED AND PRACTICED LAW IN
ROCKY MOUNT, VIRGINIA,
REPRESENTED FRANKLIN COUNTY
IN VIRGINIA LEGISLATURE 1840–1,
APPOINTED MAJOR MEXICAN WAR 1847
WHERE HE RENDERED
DISTINGUISHED SERVICE.
MUSTERERED [SIC] OUT 1848
AND RESUMED PRACTICE OF
LAW AT ROCKY MOUNT
MEMBER OF SECESSION CONVENTION 1861,
APPOINTED COLONEL C.S.A. AT
OUTBREAK OF CIVIL WAR
PROMOTED TO BRIGADIER

GENERAL JULY 1861,
MAJOR GENERAL 1863, LIEUT.
GENERAL MAY 1864.
AFTER THE WAR HE DEVOTED HIS LIFE
TO THE PRESERVATION OF ITS' [SIC] HISTORY.
LIVED IN LYNCHBURG, VIRGINIA,
FROM 1870 TILL HIS DEATH MARCH 2, 1864.
VIRGINIA HAD NO MORE LOYAL
AND DEVOTED SON.

Brunswick County

349. Lawrenceville, Courthouse Common Soldier

Monument is a private soldier standing at parade rest surmounting a plinth, base, dado, and shaft.

LOCATION: 202 North Main Street, 23868
DATE: November 9, 1911
MEDIUM: Granite

C.S.A.
IN MEMORY OF
CONFEDERATE HEROES
OF BRUNSWICK COUNTY
1861.–1865.
LOVE MAKES MEMORY ETERNAL
VIRGINIA

The monument of Dinwiddie granite was dedicated on a rainy Thursday, November 9,

1911. The elegy is similar in appearance, inscription, style, materials, and design to the Emporia monument of 1910, just twenty miles to the southeast. The Lawrenceville text, however, strikes a different tone. Although the very act of erecting a monument to the Confederacy has an element of defiance invested in it, there is nothing of the sardonic tone of the Emporia monument.

Local library archives reveal that the monument cost twenty-one hundred dollars. The Brunswick Chapter of the United Daughters of the Confederacy raised eighteen hundred dollars, and the Board of Supervisors allocated a sum as well. Ella Hicks, president of the Brunswick U.D.C., sent letters requesting donations of one dollar or more to cover the balance.

- Excerpt from a fundraising speech to a gathering of veterans in 1905:

Here we are gathered to write in stone not only the names of those who fought and died, but also the names of the tattered, torn and bullet-scarred veterans who are gathered with us and still live, an honor to their country and exemplars of courage and fidelity to mankind.

Mecklenburg County

350. Boydton, Courthouse Common Soldier

Monument is a private soldier, in bronze, surmounting a granite plinth, base, dado, and shaft.

LOCATION: Madison and Washington streets, 23917
DATE: August 7, 1908
MEDIA: Bronze, granite
Front

[BLANK]

—

1861–1865

—

TO THE
CONFEDERATE SOLDIERS
OF MECKLENBURG

—

FROM BETHEL
TO APPOMATTOX

The terse inscription on this Southside monument arguably reflects the disquietude of the reconciliation era. The war years are dutifully inscribed, and the battles that opened and closed it, "From Bethel to Appomattox," give the appearance of closure. The soldier surmounting the base is holding a rifle and is poised for action, however, as if the war had not ended but only paused.

The monument is similar or identical in stance, appearance, and materials to the Charlottesville and Farmville courthouse monuments, but the sculptor is unknown. It was erected at a cost of two thousand dollars: the county contributed five hundred dollars, the rest came by private subscription. *Confederate Veteran* describes "a massive granite base ten feet high surmounted by a bronze figure of an infantryman with his gun at 'Ready.'" The bronze figure is over six feet tall and weighs approximately sixteen hundred pounds. The overall height of the monument is twenty feet. The size and scale are not extraordinary by Southside standards, and Boydton is a small town, but it stands in front of the county courthouse (1838–42), which is similar to Jefferson's state capitol design for Richmond. The combined visual impact of the courthouse and monument standing on a rise is dramatic.

- Two cannon flanking the monument were scrapped for their iron during World War

II, a not uncommon practice during the early years of the war.

- A restoration and rededication of the monument took place in 2002.

Halifax County

351. Halifax, Courthouse Common Soldier

Monument is a private soldier, in marble, standing at parade rest surmounting a granite plinth, base, dado, and pedestal.
LOCATION: 8 South Main Street, 24558
DATE: April 17, 1911
MEDIUM: Granite
Front

> THIS MONUMENT IS ERECTED
> BY AN APPRECIATIVE PEOPLE
> IN LOVING REMEMBRANCE OF
> THE CONFEDERATE SOLDIERS
> OF HALIFAX COUNTY, WHO
> FOUGHT FOR CONSTITUTIONAL
> LIBERTY IN THE WAR OF
> 1861–1865
> —
>
> THESE PATRIOTS LAID
> THEIR ALL UPON THE
> ALTAR OF THEIR COUNTRY
> THEIR VAI OR WILL EVER
> REMAIN PART OF
> HER STORY

The monument in front of the Halifax courthouse (1839) was dedicated on the semi-centennial of the Virginia legislature's vote to secede from the Union. The act of secession is a prelude to what the elegists modestly call "The War of 1861–1865." The Confederate soldiers are cited as "Patriots Who Fought for Constitutional Liberty." The past tense consigns the "Confederate Soldiers" to history—"Her Story." The elderly soldier is similar to the Rocky Mount figure: he may be in uniform and carry a weapon, but his service days, in a practical sense, are over. The monument confers a nostalgic "Loving Remembrance" upon the Confederate soldiers.

South Boston

352. Oak Ridge Cemetery Tablet

Monument is a bronze tablet set in a marble shaft on a granite base.
LOCATION: North Main Street and Cavalier Boulevard, 24592
DATE: May 31, 1952
MEDIA: Bronze, granite, marble

> [TWO C.S.A. BATTLE FLAGS]
> TO THE GLORY OF GOD
> AND TO THE HONOR OF THE
> CONFEDERATE VETERANS OF
> 1861–1865
> THE FOLLOWING CONFEDERATE VETERANS
> ARE BURIED IN THIS CEMETERY
> [81 NAMES]

ERECTED BY

HALIFAX CO. CHAPTER

U.D.C.   1952

The Oak Ridge monument is distinctive for placing the Confederate soldier in a mainstream of twentieth-century war veterans. It has more in common with World War I and World War II commemorations of its time than with Confederate monuments of earlier eras. The men are called "Confederate Veterans"—the phrase occurs twice—even though the 1952 Memorial Day dedication took place eighty-seven years after Appomattox, and nearly all of the veterans were dead. There are no apologetics, no rosters of soldiers or battlefields, and no reference to the war's outcome, although the religious flourish—"To the Glory of God"—has arguable parallels to the motto of the Confederacy, "Deo Vindice."

353. Staunton River Battlefield Cannon and Tablet

Monument is a cannon barrel on a fieldstone base.

LOCATION: American Legion Building, 1710 Jeffress Boulevard, off Broad Street (northbound B.R. 501), 24592

DATE: April 11, 1940

MEDIA: Bronze, fieldstone, iron

THIS CANNON USED IN THE BATTLE OF
STAUNTON RIVER BRIDGE, JUNE 25TH, 1864.
CAPT. BENJ. L. FARINHOLT 53RD VA. INFANTRY

WITH 296 MEN REINFORCED BY 642 CITIZENS
AND SOLDIERS FROM HALIFAX, CHARLOTTE
AND MECKLENBURG COUNTIES VA. DEFEATED
COL. R. M. WEST 5TH PENN CAVALRY
SUPPORTED BY THE 3RD NEW YORK.
THIS TABLET PLACED BY THE HALIFAX
COUNTY CHAPTER U.D.C.
AND HALIFAX COUNTY POST NO. 8,
THE AMERICAN LEGION.

The American Legion sponsorship is unique for a Virginia monument. Other artillery pieces from other wars are on this lawn, however, and this cannon barrel adds to a collective narrative linking nineteenth century local citizens who fought nearby to those in the twentieth century who served overseas, especially the World War I veterans who had a role in placing this marker.

The narrative summarizes the largest battle fought in this area during the Civil War. It does not describe an action in a war between national governments—Union troops opposing Confederate soldiers—but a war between states: Virginia infantry—296 men—and citizens opposing Pennsylvania and New York cavalry.

354. Staunton River Battlefield State Park, Battlefield Tablet

Monument is a granite shaft.
LOCATION: U.S. 360 to V.R. 92 west to C.R.
600 (Black Walnut Road) to C.R. 855, park
entrance to C.R. 975, 23962
DATE: 1955
MEDIUM: Granite

THE BATTLE OF STAUNTON RIVER BRIDGE
WAS FOUGHT HERE JUNE 25, 1864
CAPT. BENJ. L. FARINHOLT 53RD VA. INF. WITH
296 MEN REINFORCED BY 642 CITIZENS
AND SOLDIERS FROM HALIFAX, CHARLOTTE
AND MECKLENBURG COUNTIES VIRGINIA
DEFEATED
COL. R. M. WEST 5TH PENN CAVALRY
SUPPORTED BY THE 3RD NEW YORK.
THIS MONUMENT PLACED BY HALIFAX
COUNTY CHAPTER U.D.C. AND THE
STATE OF VIRGINIA

Union cavalry under brigadier generals
James H. Wilson and August V. Kautz sought
the destruction of the railroad bridge at this site
but were daunted by a combined force of Confederate infantry and Home Guards. Estimated
casualties were 150 from among four thousand
men engaged. Field officers are mentioned, not
the overall commanders, not even Confederate
Maj. Gen. William H. F. "Rooney" Lee, whose
cavalry had a role at the close of the action. The
inscription is drawn from the South Boston
monument, which in turn is consistent with
other monuments of this type—e.g., the Sons
of Confederate Veterans markers at Petersburg
or Clarke County—where citizens are lauded
for taking the initiative in defeating invading or
marauding forces, in this case, as with others,
without mentioning that the opposing forces
are in federal service.

City of Danville

355. Green Hill Cemetery Obelisk
Monument is a granite obelisk with aluminum
reliefs set on a plinth, base, and dado.
LOCATION: Off Main Street to Jefferson and
Lee Avenue, 24541
DATE: September 3, 1878
MEDIA: Aluminum, granite

Front

[RELIEF OF LEE]
GEN. ROBERT E. LEE.
CONFEDERATE DEAD
MEMORIAL TRIBUTE
OF VIRGINIA'S DAUGHTERS
TO THE FALLEN BRAVE.
DANVILLE VIRGINIA
1878
M. HAYES
RICHMOND, VA
—

PATRIOTS!
KNOW THAT THESE FELL
IN THE EFFORT
TO ESTABLISH JUST GOVERNMENT
AND
PERPETUATE CONSTITUTIONAL LIBERTY.
WHO THUS DIE,
WILL LIVE IN LOFTY EXAMPLE.
—

[RELIEF OF JACKSON]
GEN. THOMAS J. JACKSON.

THEY DIED
AS MEN WHO NOBLY CONTEND
FOR THE CAUSE OF
TRUTH AND RIGHT.
"THEY SOFTLY LIE AND SWEETLY SLEEP."

—

"QUIDQUID EX HIS AMAVIMUS
QUIDQUID MIRATI SUMUS,
MANET MANSURUMQUE EST IN
ANIMIS HOMINUM, IN
AETERNITATE TEMPORUM FAMA
RERUM."

This centennial-era monument is relatively large, even lavish, and is in keeping with Danville's status as a former national capital. The Virginia granite obelisk and base weighs sixteen tons and stands thirty-two feet high over a six-foot artificial mound. The monument was erected at a cost of two thousand dollars, raised by the local Ladies Memorial Association, founded June 5, 1872.

The contract for the obelisk was originally given to Maurice J. Soner of New York. Soner furnished the bronze medallions of generals Robert E. Lee and Thomas J. Jackson and transferred the contract for the granite work to a "Mr. M. Hayes, of Richmond, Virginia." The monument was placed so as to be in full view of passing trains on the Southern Railway.

Businesses in Danville were closed for the unveiling, according to contemporary accounts, and the "principal streets were handsomely decorated with flags, mottoes and festoons." The ceremonies were "probably the grandest pageant ever witnessed in Danville and was highly gratifying to the Ladies Memorial Association."

- The original bronze reliefs of Jackson and Lee were stolen in the 1980s. They were recovered and are now displayed inside the Sutherlin Mansion. The replacements are of aluminum.
- The Latin expression "Quid Ex His Amavimus . . ." is translated as "Whatever from these deeds we have loved, whatever we admire, remains and will remain in the souls of men in the eternity of times and the renown of things."

- The adjacent Danville National Cemetery was established for Union soldiers who died in local Confederate prisons.

Sutherlin Mansion: Danville Museum of Fine Arts and History

356. Last Capitol Shaft

Monument is a granite shaft supporting C.S.A. national flag, set on a base.
LOCATION: 975 Main Street, 24541
DATE: April 1995
MEDIUM: Granite

LAST CAPITOL
OF THE
CONFEDERACY
"THE LAST PROCLAMATION"
THE MEMORIES OF THE HEROIC
DEAD WHO HAVE FREELY GIVEN THEIR
LIVES TO ITS DEFENSE MUST EVER
REMAIN ENSHRINED IN OUR HEARTS . . .
PRESIDENT JEFFERSON DAVIS
C.S.A.
APRIL 4, 1865

—

"GUARDING OUR FUTURE

BY PRESERVING OUR PAST"
ERECTED
MARCH 26, 1995
THROUGH THE EFFORTS OF THE
HERITAGE PRESERVATION ASSOCIATION

Danville was the capital of the Confederacy, April 3–10, 1865. When Richmond was abandoned, what was left of the Confederate government moved south by train to here, and William T. Sutherlin offered the use of his home to Jefferson Davis. Davis remained here for eight days. Upon the surrender of the Army of Northern Virginia by Gen. Robert E. Lee on April 9, Davis and his entourage left Danville on April 10 and headed south. They were taken prisoner May 10, 1865, near Irwinville, Georgia. With their capture, the Confederacy effectively ceased to exist.

The monument was erected at a cost of six thousand dollars. It was given to the city of Danville by a local organization, the Danville chapter of the Heritage Preservation Association. About 150 people attended the dedication ceremonies, which included the raising of the Confederate Third National Flag. The six speakers included two African American professors. The issue of race was addressed. "People give you a hard time about this flag because they say it represents slavery," were the words of Edward Smith, assistant professor of American studies at American University in Washington, D.C. "That's pure nonsense."

"The War Between the States wasn't fought to free slaves," said Southern University professor Lenord Haynes, observing that "Fighting white people has been the destruction of black people."

- Davis's proclamation from Danville, excerpted here, defied the disintegration or surrender of the Confederacy's armies and government. The larger context reads, in part:

It would be unwise, even if it were possible, to conceal the great moral, as well as material injury to our cause that must result from the occupation of Richmond by the enemy. It is equally unwise and unworthy of us, as patriots engaged in a most sacred cause, to allow our energies to falter, our spirits to grow faint, or our efforts to become relaxed, under reverses however calamitous.

- The house stayed in the Sutherlin family until 1911. Interest in razing the mansion thereafter was resisted, and today it is owned by the city and serves as a museum and cultural center.

357. Women of the Southern Confederacy Tablet

Monument is a bronze plaque set in a granite shaft.
DATE: 1927
MEDIA: Bronze, granite

ERECTED TO THE MEMORY
OF THE WOMEN OF THE
SOUTHERN CONFEDERACY
1861   1865
BY
THEIR DESCENDANTS
DANVILLE VIRGINIA
1927
—
ANNE ELIZA JOHNS
16 JUL. 1831–22 OCT. 1889
ANNE ELIZA JOHNS, VOLUNTEER NURSE,
TEACHER, AND AUTHOR OF
COOLEEMEE: A TALE OF SOUTHERN LIFE,
WAS BORN IN PITTSYLVANIA CO., VA
SHE MINISTERED TO CONFEDERATE

SOLDIERS AND UNION PRISONERS
IN THE HOSPITALS IN DANVILLE, VA
DURING THE WAR BETWEEN THE STATES.
SHE RETURNED TO LEAKSVILLE,
NC AFTER THE WAR.

A statue of a woman holding her departed son's haversack originally surmounted this United Daughters of the Confederacy monument. The statue was judged to be too grim—"ugly" was one interviewee's assessment—and was removed. The tribute to women is similar to those at Winchester's Stonewall Cemetery and Richmond's Hollywood and Oakwood cemeteries. Danville's tribute is the broadest and befits Danville's former capital status by including all women of the Confederacy.

358. Last Capitol Plaque

Monument is a plaque on the capitol building.
LOCATION: Sutherlin Mansion
DATE: circa 1920s
MEDIUM: Bronze

CORONA POST IMPERUM
THE
LAST CAPITOL
OF THE
CONFEDERACY
APRIL 3RD–10TH 1865
"IF I FORGET THEE, O JERUSALEM"

The plaque is undated but was probably installed after the house became a city library in 1924. The Latin phrase "Corona Post Imperum" is translated as "Crown behind the empire." The lamentation "If I Forget Thee, O Jerusalem" is taken from Psalm 137 and arguably draws a parallel between Jerusalem, the chosen people of Israel, and the Confederacy. This may be the truest version of the phrase "Lest We Forget," so often invoked elsewhere in Virginia. "If I forget thee, O Jerusalem," is provocative enough. The psalm goes further, and is worth noting: "If I do not remember thee, let my tongue cleave to the roof of my mouth; if I prefer not Jerusalem above my chief joy." Ultimately the psalmist prophesies the destruction of Jerusalem's enemies:

> O daughter of Babylon, who art to be destroyed; happy shall he be, that rewardeth thee as thou hast served us. Happy shall he be, that taketh and dasheth thy little ones against the stones.

Henry County

359. Martinsville, Courthouse Common Soldier

Monument is a private soldier, in marble, standing at parade rest surmounting a granite plinth, base, dado, and shaft.

LOCATION: 1 East Main Street, 24112
DATE: June 3, 1901
MEDIA: Bronze, granite, marble

Front

GLORIA VICTIS
[SEAL OF VIRGINIA]
—

1861–1865.
HENRY HONORS HEROES.

—

[CROSSED SWORDS]
DEFEATED, YET WITHOUT STAIN.

—

ERECTED BY
MILDRED LEE CHAPTER,
NO. 74, U.D.C.,
TO THE TRUE
CONFEDERATE SOLDIERS
OF HENRY
[PLAQUE]
ERECTED
JUNE 3, 1901

A new courthouse replaced the edifice at Main and Franklin Street, but at this writing the courthouse monuments remain here. The monument's design is consonant with the Southside pattern: granite base and shaft with sculpted marble soldier, a tribute or apologetic, and no roster. *Historic Southern Monuments* describes it as a "graceful shaft of Virginia granite, surmounted by a Confederate soldier exquisitely carved from Italian marble."

The monument was built at a cost of $1,165 and was dedicated June 3, 1901—Jefferson Davis's birthday. June 3 was also the anniversary of the departure for the war of the first company of soldiers from Henry County.

- "Gloria Victus" is translated from the Latin as "Glory to the defeated."
- An adjacent 1985 monument to county veterans includes a roster of soldiers killed in the "Civil War"—not the War Between the States. The inscription reads, in part:

HONOR ROLL
CIVIL WAR 1861–1865

SOLDIERS KILLED IN ACTION
[45 NAMES]
SOLDIERS WHO DIED WHILE
PRISONERS OF WAR
[58 NAMES]

Patrick County

360. Stuart, Courthouse Common Soldier

Monument is a private soldier, in bronze, standing at parade rest surmounting a granite plinth, base, and shaft.

LOCATION: Intersection of B.R. 58 and V.R. 8, Main and West Blue Ridge streets, 24171
DATE: November 20, 1936
MEDIA: Bronze, granite

Front

[SEAL OF THE CONFEDERACY]
[RELIEF OF STUART]
[RELIEF OF CONFEDERATE NATIONAL FLAGS]
OUR HEROES
IN MEMORY OF
MAJ. GEN. J. E. B.
STUART, C.S.A.

BORN NEAR STUART,
PATRICK COUNTY, VIRGINIA
ON FEBRUARY 6, 1833
MORTALLY WOUNDED
IN BATTLE OF
YELLOW TAVERN
DIED MAY 12, 1864
—
ERECTED TO THE
MEMORY OF
MAJ. GEN. J. E. B. STUART
AND THE
CONFEDERATE SOLDIERS
OF PATRICK COUNTY
SPONSORED BY
JUNIOR STUART
BOOK CLUB
1936

This late commemorative monument is unusual for its focus on one person, albeit one of the Confederacy's best cavalryman. Stuart was born at "Laurel Hill" near present-day Ararat. The county seat, called Taylorsville until 1884, was renamed in his honor.

Passivism was not unpopular in the 1930s; nostalgia for a time when life seemed simpler was common as well. Those sentiments seem to be reflected in this monument: the head and shoulders relief of Stuart is comparatively unmilitary—he wears no hat and bears no weapon. Still, there are nationalist and military flourishes: the seal of the Confederacy, for example, and the relief of Confederate national flags. In addition, Confederate soldiers are remembered as "Our Heroes," and a county tribute is inscribed on the reverse side.

This was the last Virginia courthouse monument erected before World War II. Twenty-eight years would elapse before the next courthouse monument, at Lovingston in Nelson County, would be erected. There was no parade and no local United Daughters of the Confederacy at the dedication; Lieutenant Governor James H. Price spoke at the ceremonies. The Junior Stuart Book Club, a successor to the Stuart Book Club, had seventeen members on the rolls in 1936. Neither the junior nor senior book club is extant, although some members were still living at this writing.

Appendix
Index

Appendix: Common Mottos

Deo Vindice. The Great Seal of the Confederacy, with the monition "Deo Vindice" ("God Will Vindicate"), is inscribed on the courthouse monuments at Warm Springs, Eastville, Gate City, Culpeper, Louisa, Amelia, Bedford, and Stuart; and the cemetery monuments at Arlington National Cemetery, Marshall, Suffolk, and the Unknown at Stonewall Cemetery, Winchester.

The origin of the seal, in particular the motto Deo Vindice, is described in the *Southern Historical Society Papers* as follows:

> "In the latter part of April, 1864, quite an interesting debate was had on the adoption of the motto. The House resolutions fixing the motto as 'Deo Duce Vincemus' being considered, Mr. Semmes moved to substitute ' Deo vindice majores aemulamur.' The motto had been suggested by Professor Alexander Dimitry. Mr. Semmes thought 'Deo vindice' sufficient and preferred it. He was finally triumphant.

> . . . .

> No word appeared more grand, more expressive or significant than this. Under God as the asserter of our rights, the defender of our liberties, our protector against danger, our mediator, our ruler and guardian, and, as the avenger of our wrongs and the punisher of our crimes, we endeavor to equal or even excel our ancestors. What word can be suggested of more power, and so replete with sentiments and thoughts consonant with our idea of the omnipotence and justice of God?

> At this point the committee hesitated whether it were necessary to add anything further to the motto 'Deo Vindice.' These words alone were sufficient and impressive, and, in the spirit of the lapidary style of composition, were elliptical and left much to the play of the imagination. . . .

Mr. Semmes moved to amend by substituting "vindice" for "duce," and it was agreed to.

Dulce et Decorum Est Pro Patria Mori. The Latin proverb is translated as "It Is Sweet and Fitting to Die for One's Country." It is inscribed on the Virginia monument at Stonewall Cemetery, Winchester; the Groveton Cemetery monument on the Manassas battlefield; the Mosby monument at Prospect Hill Cemetery, Front Royal; and at the Chesterfield courthouse.

The proverb is attributed to Horace (Quintus Horatius Flaccus), Latin poet. His work, taught in English schools in the seventeenth and eighteenth century, served as "an essential element in the pattern of English culture."

Lest We Forget. The phrase is taken from Rudyard Kipling's poem "Recessional" and is invoked at Stonewall Cemetery, Winchester; Spotsylvania Confederate Cemetery; Oakwood Cemetery, Richmond; Elmwood Cemetery, Norfolk; Thornrose Cemetery, Staunton; and the courthouse monuments at Warm Springs, Marion, Pearisburg, Charlottesville, Goochland, New Kent, and Williamsburg.

The larger measure, first published in 1897, reads:

> GOD OF OUR FATHERS, KNOWN OF OLD,
> LORD OF OUR FAR-FLUNG BATTLE-LINE,
> BENEATH WHOSE AWFUL HAND WE HOLD
> DOMINION OVER PALM AND PINE—LORD GOD
> OF HOSTS, BE WITH US YET,
> LEST WE FORGET—LEST WE FORGET!

> THE TUMULT AND THE SHOUTING DIES;
> THE CAPTAINS AND THE KINGS DEPART:
> STILL STANDS THINE ANCIENT SACRIFICE,
> AN HUMBLE AND A CONTRITE HEART.
> LORD GOD OF HOSTS, BE WITH US YET,
> LEST WE FORGET—LEST WE FORGET!

> FAR-CALLED, OUR NAVIES MELT AWAY;
> ON DUNE AND HEADLAND SINKS THE FIRE:
> LO, ALL OUR POMP OF YESTERDAY
> IS ONE WITH NINEVEH AND JUDGE OF THE

NATIONS, SPARE US YET,
LEST WE FORGET—LEST WE FORGET!

Popular use seems to have subverted the author's intentions. The phrase is consistently invoked as a reminder that the dead should not be forgotten, but the poem, first given at the celebration of the sixtieth anniversary of the reign of Queen Victoria, is a cautionary note about the corruption and fall of great empires. To take Kipling's interpretation of the phrase would be to join the Confederacy with the Assyrian empire and Ninevah with Richmond, a powerful, corrupt, militaristic empire of pagan convictions. The fall of Ninevah in 612 B.C. was celebrated in the Old Testament book of Nahum. That association is not intended in popular use.

The Dinwiddie County monument (1909) offers a paraphrase: "That Their Heroic Deeds Sublime, Self-Sacrifice and Undying Devotion to Duty and Country May Never be Forgotten." Another paraphrase is inscribed at the Sutherlin House in Danville. The lamentation "If I Forget Thee, O Jerusalem," taken from Psalm 137, may be the truest version of the phrase as popularly intended.

Love Makes Memory Eternal. The sentiment is used on monuments at Spotsylvania and Lawrenceville and is common in southwest Virginia monuments, including the New Castle and Pearisburg courthouse sites, Taze-well's Jeffersonville Cemetery, and Roanoke's Fair View Cemetery.

The origin of this expression is obscure. It may derive from Luke 23: 42–43, the scene at the cross when the thief asks Jesus to remember him in eternity: "And he said unto Jesus, Lord, remember me when thou comest into thy kingdom. And Jesus said unto him, Verily I say unto thee, To day shalt thou be with me in paradise."

Go Tell . . . is invoked on the Georgia monument at Winchester, the courthouse monument at Chatham, and the central cemetery monument at Warrenton. The expression is similar not only to the Thermopolae epitaph to the Spartans, but also to the "Great Commission" of Matthew 28:19 ("Go ye therefore, and teach all nations. . ."). Simonides of Ceos (556–468 B.C.) is credited with the epitaph on the monument marking the Battle of Thermopylae (480 B.C.). Translated, it reads:

GO AND TELL THE SPARTANS, STRANGER
PASSING BY,
THAT HERE, OBEDIENT TO THEIR LAWS, DEAD
WE LIE.

Sic Semper Tyrannis. The Latin phrase on the seal of Virginia is translated as "Thus Ever to Tyrants." The seal appears on numerous Virginia monuments, at courthouses, cemeteries and battlefields.

INDEX

Raised in Pittsburgh, Pennsylvania, TIMOTHY S. SEDORE is a professor of English at Bronx Community College of the City University of New York, where he teaches composition, literature, and religious rhetoric. His work has appeared in *Southern Quarterly*; *AGS Quarterly: Bulletin of the Association for Gravestone Studies*; and *Journal X: The Literary Journal of the University of Mississippi*.